W9-BMG-885

The Complete Guide to

SUPERVISORY TRAINING and DEVELOPMENT

The Complete Guide to

SUPERVISORY TRAINING and DEVELOPMENT

Lester R. Bittel
Center for Supervisory Research
James Madison University

ADDISON-WESLEY PUBLISHING COMPANY, INC.
Reading, Massachusetts • Menlo Park, California
Don Mills, Ontario • Wokingham, England • Amsterdam • Bonn
Sydney • Singapore • Tokyo • Madrid • Bogotá
Santiago • San Juan

Acknowledgement is made to the following for permission to adapt or reprint copyrighted material:

To the American Management Association, for material adapted from "Supervisory Development," by J.E. Ramsey, in *Human Resources Management & Development Handbook*, ed. by William R. Tracey, pp. 979–980, © 1985 AMACOM, a division of the American Management Association, New York; and from *Quality Circles: A Team Approach to Problem Solving*, by F.M. Gryna, Jr., p. 57 © 1981 AMACOM, a division of the American Management Association, New York. All rights reserved.

To The Conference Board, for material adapted from *Supervisory Training* by Walter S. Wikstrom, copyright 1973.

To Human Resource Development Press, for material adapted from *Performance Based Supervisory Development* by Charles M. Macdonald, copyright 1982, HRD Press, 22 Amherst Road, Amherst, MA, 01022. All rights reserved. Reprinted with permission of the publisher.

To McGraw-Hill Book Company, for material adapted from *Instructional Techniques* by Ivor K. Davies, copyright 1981; from *Putting Quality Circles To Work: A Practical Strategy for Boosting Productivity and Profits* by Ralph Barra, copyright 1983; and from *What Every Supervisor Should Know* by Lester R. Bittel, copyright 1980, 1984.

To Scientific Methods, Inc., for permission to reprint the Supervisory Grid, from *The New Grid for Supervisory Effectiveness* by Robert R. Blake and Jane Syrgley Mouton, copyright © 1975, 1979.

To the American Society for Training and Development, for tables and figures adapted from *Training and Development Journal*, copyright 1986. Reprinted with Permission. All rights reserved.

Library of Congress Cataloging-in-Publication Data

Bittel, Lester R.
The complete guide to supervisory training and development.

Bibliography: p.
Includes index.
1. Supervisors—Training of. 2. Managers—Training of.
I. Title.
HF5549.5.T7B535 1987 658.4'071245 86-22267
ISBN 0-201-12220-0

Cover design by Virginia Mason
Text design by Carson Design
Set in 10 point Meridian by Compset, Inc., Beverly, MA

ISBN 0-201-12220-0

ABCDEFGHIJ-AL-8987

ACKNOWLEDGEMENTS

The idea for this book came from Robert L. Craig, the editor of the *Training and Development Handbook* (3rd edition, McGraw-Hill Book Company, 1988), with whom I was co-editor of its first edition in 1967. Bob, and his publisher, the McGraw-Hill Book Company, have graciously allowed me to include material in this book that appears in my chapter on "Supervisory Development" in the latest edition of his handbook. I am also indebted to Jackson E. Ramsey, who, as co-director of the Center for Supervisory Research and executive director of the Institute of Certified Professional managers at James Madison University, has made so much information available to me for inclusion here. In addition, I acknowledge the help offered me by Ross H. Johnson, D. Kent Zimmerman, and Jackson E. Ramsey in the preparation of the Model Course Outlines that appear in Appendix III. I must also mention the invaluable assistance received from my typist, Kathy Lawson, who was able to direct this book through the treacherous shoals of word processing. Finally, I owe a great deal to the hundreds of human resources development professionals who have shared their ideas with me over the years and, of course, to the thousands of supervisors who have made their mark on this book.

CONTENTS

Part I

SUPERVISORY ROLES AND COMPETENCIES

Chapter 1

The Challenge of Supervisory Development

INTRODUCTION

There is some truth to the old saying that "All development is self-development." When it comes to supervisory training, however, there is a greater truth: All development needs the genuine support of top management and the active involvement of a human resources professional. Why are these factors so important? First, because supervisors provide a critical link between high-level policies and workplace realities. The supervisory position is almost unspeakably demanding; yet at the same time it is characterized by ambiguous or uncertain authority. It is the rank-and-file employees—production and clerical staff, retail salespeople and service operatives, and an increasing array of highly-trained, specialized knowledge workers—who actually carry out the work of all organizations. Without supervisors to prepare, instruct, direct, translate, and otherwise communicate top management's concepts and operational strategies to the work force, most of these grand ideas would never be implemented. Thus, top management support of supervisory development—moral as well as financial—is essential. Second, human resources professionals must be involved in the supervisory development process because of the nature of supervisory work itself and those who traditionally are selected to perform it. Make no doubt about it: an organization's policies and procedures stand or fall on the competency of its supervision. This competency, in turn, depends in large measure on the quality of training and development its supervisors receive. Few supervisors have the inclination, knowledge, or resources to provide for their own development. Thus, supervisors are dependent upon the guidance, instruction, and structured support that only a human resources professional can give.

Supervisors as Key Factors in the Productivity Race

The supervisory-training target is very large. Supervisors, as an occupational classification, represent a major segment of the overall labor force. In the United States alone, there is a supervisory management force 2 million strong. It holds the power to turn on—or turn off—the productivity of most organizations. These supervisors are the men and women who maintain the tenuous interface between the management hierarchy and the vast body of employees who put their hands on, or apply their minds to, the real work of enterprise, both public and private. In most instances, they are technically, as well as legally, members of management. But their loyalties are strongly divided. Three out of four have risen from the ranks of labor—either blue-collar or white-collar. They rarely establish the goals of the organization they serve. Their upward mobility is severely limited. Yet it is ultimately their efforts that ignite or defuse the productive spirit of the more than 70 million people who generate the nation's output of goods and services.

Historical Background of Supervisory Development

Supervisory training began—conceptually, at least—during World War II, with the development of the Training Within Industry Programs. These programs, fathered by Channing Dooley of the Standard Oil Company of New Jersey and Glen Gardiner of the Forstman Woolen Company, targeted three supervisory skills: job instruction training (JIT), job methods training (JMT), and job relations training (JRT). Only the JIT program remains today in anything like its original form. The other two programs have largely been forgotten. Nevertheless, it is possible that JMT was the predecessor of today's courses in job design, although its emphasis was upon the technical rather than the self-determinant aspects of an employee's work. It also seems certain that JRT was the forerunner of modern human relations skills training. In any event, it is safe to say that supervisory training is rooted deeply in contemporary organizational culture. Almost certainly, supervisory training is the foundation from which management development has emerged.

Supervisory training is also big business. Nearly one out of every six organizations offers some form of program for first-line supervisors and/or foremen/forewomen, providing an average of thirty-two hours per trainee.[1] Supervisors in public administration receive the most training, almost five times as much as those in educational services. Of all training provided in industry and in the public sector, supervisory skills training ranks second only to management skills development. Furthermore, a 1985 study by the American Society for Training and Development showed that participation rates for supervisors in company-sponsored formal training programs was increasing faster than for any other occupation.[2] In terms of out-of-pocket spending, a good estimate places the annual budget for supervisory training at more than $5 billion.

A DISTINCTIVE SEGMENT OF MANAGEMENT

Despite its linkage to management development, supervisory training remains in most instances clearly differentiated from it. The reason stems from the unique character of the supervisor's role in the organizational structure. Of all managers in the hierarchy, supervisors are the only ones who must function at a dual interface, relating on the one hand to the rank-and-file operatives below them and on the other hand to the policy-oriented managers above them. Supervisors' employment origins are significantly different from those of other managers, too. As noted earlier, nearly three-quarters of all supervisors rise from the lower ranks rather than entering managerial positions directly from college or a high-level professional occupation. The unique nature of the supervisory job creates a supervisory segment of managers that is distinct from other managers. This may be inferred from table 1-1, which creates a statistical profile of the demographic characteristics of supervisors based upon a nationwide survey of a very large sample.[3]

TABLE 1-1
STATISTICAL PROFILE OF TODAY'S SUPERVISORS:
Characteristics of Respondents to a Survey of 8,500 Supervisors*

	Survey Average (%)	Kinds of Employees Supervised (%)		Level of Supervision (%)		Extent of Education (%)	
		Blue-collar	White-collar	1st Level	2nd Level	Max. 12 yrs.	16–20 yrs.
Kinds of employees supervised:							
Blue-collar	46			63	38	53	19
White-collar	45			58	42	21	55
Evenly divided	9						
Totals	100						
Level of supervision:							
1st (supervise only non-management employees)	59	62	58			40	33
2nd (supervise other supervisors in addition to non-management employees)	41	38	42			32	42
Totals	100	100	100				
Number normally supervised:							
Fewer than 5	28	14	43	34	19	20	38
6 to 10	26	21	32	28	25	25	29
11–20	22	27	15	23	20	25	18
21–40	14	23	6	12	18	20	8
41 or more	9	15	3	4	17	11	7
Totals	99	100	99	101	99	101	100
Function supervised:							
Production-oriented	39	65	13	38	41	56	24
Accounting/clerical-oriented	22	8	38	24	19	18	24
Sales/marketing-oriented	12	8	16	10	14	9	13
Engineering/technical-oriented	6	3	12	9	6	2	13
Other, including shipping	21	16	21	20	20	15	26
Totals	100	100	100	101	100	100	100
Industry:							
Manufacturing, mining, & construction	44	55	33	49	37	54	35
Banking & insurance	7	2	14	8	6	7	7
Communications, public utilities, & transportation	7	8	7	7	6	8	8
Hospitals, institutions, & education	11	9	11	9	14	8	13
Government & military	6	3	9	6	5	3	10
Retailing & wholesaling	7	7	7	6	9	8	6
Services	5	3	6	4	5	3	6
Other	13	13	13	11	18	9	15
Totals	100	100	100	100	100	100	100
Sex:							
Male	75	84	68	70	85	36	38
Female	25	15	32	30	15	42	34
Totals	100	99	100	100	100		
Race:							
White	92	92	95	92	94	37	37
Black, Hispanic, American Indian, & others	8	8	5	8	6	39	33
Totals	100	100	100	100	100		

Continued on next page

TABLE 1-1 *Continued*

	Survey Average (%)	Kinds of Employees Supervised (%)		Level of Supervision (%)		Extent of Education (%)	
		Blue-collar	White-collar	1st Level	2nd Level	Max. 12 yrs.	16–20 yrs.
Age:							
30 yrs. or younger	20	21	18	23	15	33	40
31 to 50 yrs.	58	56	63	58	61		
51 yrs. or older	22	23	20	20	24	52	27
Totals	100	100	101	101	100		
Number of yrs. with present employer:							
Fewer than 5 yrs.	33	31	34	33	31	19	46
5 to 15 yrs.	37	35	40	39	36	37	37
More than 15 yrs.	30	34	26	28	33	44	17
Totals	100	100	100	100	100	100	100
Number of yrs. a supervisor:							
Fewer than 5 yrs.	53	50	51	61	39	44	59
5 to 15 yrs.	33	36	33	29	40	37	30
More than 15 yrs.	14	15	15	10	21	19	11
Totals	100	101	99	100	100	100	100
Method of obtaining first supervisory job:							
Promoted from ranks	74	74	74	79	66	88	58
Hired directly from technical school or college	7	6	8	6	8	0	17
Enrolled in company training program for new management employees	6	10	3	4	9	5	6
Hired into this position from another company	13	11	15	12	16	7	20
Totals	100	101	100	101	99	100	101
Trade union relationships:							
Supervise employees represented by a trade union	29	42	14	30	27	38	21
Was once a member of a trade union	38	48	28	40	35	47	27
Maximum education attained:							
12 yrs. (graduated high school)	38	52	21	40	32		
13 to 15 yrs. (attended college)	25	28	24	26	26		
16 to 20 yrs. (college degree or beyond)	37	20	55	33	42		
Totals	100	100	100	99	100		
Annual salary without overtime:							
$10,000 to $15,000	16	18	13	21	8	14	9
$15,001 to $17,500	13	16	10	15	9	15	9
$17,501 to $20,000	14	17	11	16	11	16	11
$20,001 to $22,500	12	14	10	13	12	13	11
$22,501 to $25,000	13	15	12	13	14	15	13
More than $25,000	31	20	44	23	45	27	48
Totals	99	100	100	101	99	100	101

*Totals occasionally do not add up to 100 because of rounding.

Basic Characteristics

The data show that supervisors are not particularly young: 58 percent are between thirty and fifty years old; 22 percent are over fifty. They are long-service employees: two-thirds of them have been with their present employer longer than five years. The great majority of them (74 percent) came up from the ranks. (Not much change from a decade ago.) There are far more men than women, and a large proportion are white. Today's supervisors are surprisingly well educated: 25 percent have been to college; another 37 percent have graduated (compared with only 9 percent reported by Opinion Research Corporation in a survey conducted in 1970[4]). Many are very well paid: more than a third of them now make $25,000 or more a year. (See p. 10.)

Perceptions and Attitudes

Generally, supervisors believe that:

- Physical facilities are good, and the work environment favors productive employee efforts.
- Work force size is adequate, and labor relations at the supervisory level are harmonious.
- With the exception of the paperwork load and cost-control requirements, job pressures are moderate.
- Their relationships with superiors are good.

Supervisors' attitudes reflect a puzzling mixture of traditional common sense, prevailing concepts of employee motivation, and independent thought. For example, supervisors:

- Vacillate between seeing employees as (1) responsible and self-motivated and (2) dependent and disinterested.
- Approve of traditional seniority practices.
- Believe that employee performance-appraisal systems are effective.
- Would compensate employee performance in direct proportion to its merits but would be soft on poor performers.
- Place the blame for poor quality on their employees but believe that suggestion systems would be effective.
- Except in public administration, feel that minorities and women get little special treatment.

Supervisors are tentative about their alignment with management as a whole. Only 40 percent, for example, consider themselves a real part of the management team. In other areas, however, supervisors:

- Seem genuinely satisfied with their work.
- Do not rate pay as the job's most important ingredient, although they are slightly dissatisfied with their salary scales.
- Possess relatively low-level career goals.
- Do not recall undue difficulty in crossing over to the managerial ranks.

On the other hand, a disturbingly large proportion of supervisors (21 percent) appear to be unhappy in their work and reflect this dissatisfaction in their opinions and perceptions.

Supervisors project a perilously high degree of confidence in their managerial knowledge and skills. Their self-assessments of capability over a long list of vital job requirements are suspect. Data in this area appear to be useful in determining training needs only as a measure of self-confidence.

Certainly, this odd, often contradictory, assortment of characteristics poses an extremely difficult challenge to those in an organization who are responsible for supervisory training and development.

Environmental Pressures

The supervisor's job has also been shaped by the changing and ever-intensifying pressures placed upon it by the environment. Once, a supervisor could concentrate on the job and its requirements. Now, factors external to the immediate job make the supervisor's role much more complex and demanding,[5] as illustrated in figure 1-1. One need look no further than top management's many abortive attempts to impose participative-management techniques (especially those associated with quality circles) upon supervisors to confirm the changing expectations of supervisory performance. The implications for supervisory training are extensive and are reflected in the contemporary development programs discussed later in this book.

FIGURE 1-1 EVOLVING SOURCES OF ENVIRONMENTAL PRESSURE ON SUPERVISORS

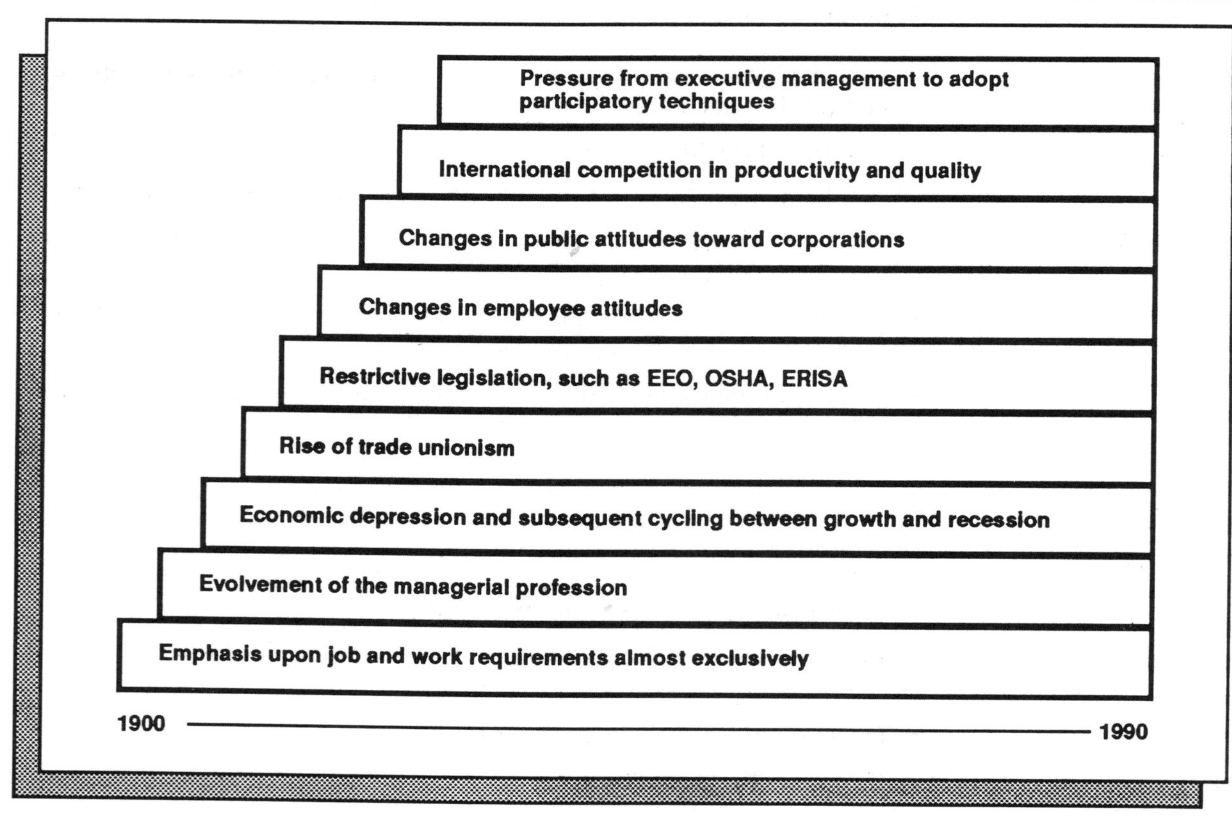

CRITICAL FACTORS IN SUPERVISORY DEVELOPMENT

Successful training and development of supervisors will be achieved only through a systematic analysis of conditions in each organization and the rigorous design of practical programs for improvement. This entails consideration and integration of the following topics, each of which will be examined in the chapter indicated:

- *The supervisor's specific role within the organization.* Roles vary widely within the same organization according to the kind of employee supervised (blue-collar or white-collar, for instance) and the functions each employee performs, differing significantly from production, say, to purchasing or marketing. (Chapter 2.)
- *The competencies expected of supervisors by their organization.* Generalizations about supervisory responsibilities are helpful for broad planning purposes, but specific requirements at the operating level vary widely, depending on the nature and mission of each organization. (Chapter 3.)
- *The quality and effectiveness of the supervisory selection process.* Traditional selection procedures tend to be haphazard and unsystematic. The result is often a far from homogeneous, and potentially incompetent, supervisory population. (Chapter 4.)
- *Initial orientation and assignment.* Proper preparation for and introduction to a new role in the organization has a long-lasting effect upon the morale and proficiency of the supervisor appointed to that position. (Chapter 5.)
- *Training-needs assessment.* In light of the high cost of supervisory training, every effort should first be made to identify the specific zones of skills deficiency before investing in program development and implementation. (Chapter 6.)
- *Training objectives.* Nuances of style and approach make supervisory training different from other forms of training, but good programs are built on a foundation of sound learning principles and carefully delineated objectives. (Chapter 7.)
- *Course content and subject matter.* Selecting subjects to be included and determining breadth and depth of course content form the building blocks (or modules) of ongoing and/or specially targeted programs. (Chapter 8.)
- *Methods and techniques.* A great variety of opportunities can be considered. Choices of methods and techniques should be based upon designing the optimum training delivery system for your organization and its supervisors. (Chapter 9.)
- *Program planning.* It is at this critical point that program designs are finalized. Successful implementation requires careful planning. (Chapter 10.)
- *Program management.* Initiating supervisory programs and sustaining their momentum and effectiveness requires systematic monitoring and control of their progress. (Chapter 11.)

- *Program models and examples.* Supervisory development programs vary widely in content, length, and format, but there are several good models. (Chapter 12.)
- *Areas of special pressure.* The world's renewed concern for improved productivity and quality of output from its organizations places special demands on supervisors. While skills in both productivity and quality improvement should probably be addressed in most training courses, organizations will benefit from supervisory-training programs that give special attention to these critical matters. (Chapter 13.)
- *Organization development concerns.* It is becoming increasingly clear that supervisory training and development are inseparable from the way in which organizations themselves develop. The changing nature of supervisory responsibilities and relationships requires regular consideration from those who design and administer their training programs. (Chapter 14.)
- *Program evaluation.* The bottom line for all training and development is an objective determination of the extent to which performance and behavior have changed in the desired direction. Although difficult and costly, evaluation is the ingredient that provides essential closure for the training process. (Chapter 15.)

Data gathered in 1986 shows relatively little change since the original survey, except in annual salaries. Current averages are:

under $15,000	2%
$15,001–17,500	3
17,501–20,000	4
20,001–22,500	5
22,501–25,000	11
25,001–30,000	11
30,001–35,000	19
35,001–40,000	21
over 40,000	24
	100%

Chapter 2

The Role of Supervisors in Organizations

INTRODUCTION

The design and conduct of supervisory-training programs derive from an analysis of (1) the traditional concepts of the supervisor's role in the organization, (2) the competencies needed to fulfill that role, and (3) the knowledge, skills, and attitudes that supervisors bring to their assignments. First, consider the influence of the supervisor's role.

Fifty years ago, the production-line supervisor on the shop floor of a manufacturing plant was probably accepted as a good model for the typical supervisor. Fifteen years ago, the role model was more nearly a clerical supervisor in a service organization—a bank, an insurance company, or in public administration. Today, the concept of a laid-back, participative supervisor of knowledge workers is a popular, if not entirely realistic, model. The fact of the matter is that none of these stereotypes has ever been realistic. And the concept of a clearly defined, universal model is even less likely today.

What roles do supervisors play in an organization? The behaviorists tell us that "a *role* concerns a social relationship between occupants of positions, with mutually understood expectations about behavior that should characterize this relationship." Thus, the supervisor must view his or her role in relation to superiors, subordinates, and peers in line or staff departments. This role, however, is inevitably constrained by the norms of the particular organization. Again, the behaviorists advise that "*norms* are patterns of shared understanding concerning the behavior appropriate to a member of an organization . . . and include work activities, beliefs, and attitudes."[1] Hence, a supervisor's role is defined, not only by his or her relationships with other members of the organization, but also by what the organization expects from that supervisor in the way of performance and attitudes.

Given the limitless number of combinations of positions, functional specialties, corporate missions, and organizational structures, it should not surprise human resources professionals that there are significant and practical differences among supervisory roles. Accordingly, trainers should be wary of generalizations and foregone conclusions in this area. A good grasp of possible role models, together with an insight into some major contributing variables, should precede the search for specific skill competencies required of supervisors in the target organization.

TRADITIONAL ROLE CONCEPTS

In the early years of this century, supervisors became known as the "people in the middle"—literally, in the hard place between genuine managers on the one hand and rank-and-file employees on the other. More recently, Keith Davis characterized supervision as "the keystone in the organizational arch," the supporting structural member between management and the work force.[2] (See figure 2-1.) In his book *New Patterns of Management,* Rensis Likert described supervisors more pragmatically as the "link-pins" between the upper and lower planes of an organizational structure.[3] (See figure 2-2.) Viewed in Likert's way, supervisors act as a series of flexible couplings, transmitting orders and instructions from above while absorbing shocks and disturbances from below. Likert's conceptual model still applies, even though the Taft-Hartley Act of 1947 declared supervisors to be legally part of management. The act specifically prohibits supervisors from joining unions of production or clerical workers, although they may form a union composed exclusively of supervisors. In the main, however, supervisors have not formed unions and have cast their lot, often with varying degrees of enthusiasm, with the management hierarchy, where they remain the lowest figures on the totem pole.

In the last two decades, the viewpoint of M. Scott Myers has become popular. Myers conceives of a supervisor's role as one of "facilitating"—making resources and information available to subordinates while allowing them to plan and implement their own work. Such "goal-oriented" supervisors (see figure 2-3) intervene to exercise control only when necessary.[4]

FIGURE 2-1 SUPERVISORS AS THE KEYSTONE IN THE ORGANIZATIONAL ARCH

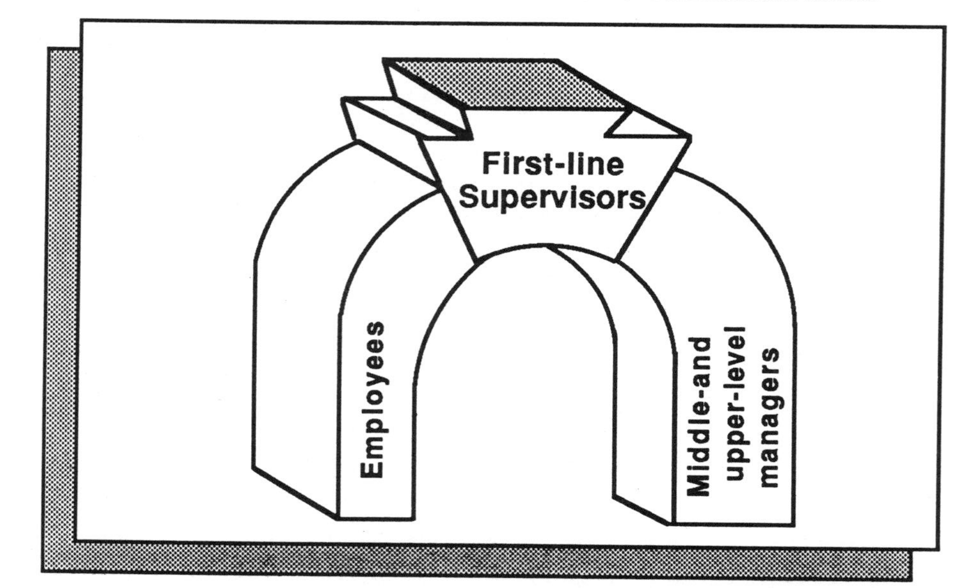

FIGURE 2-2 SUPERVISORS AS LINK PINS

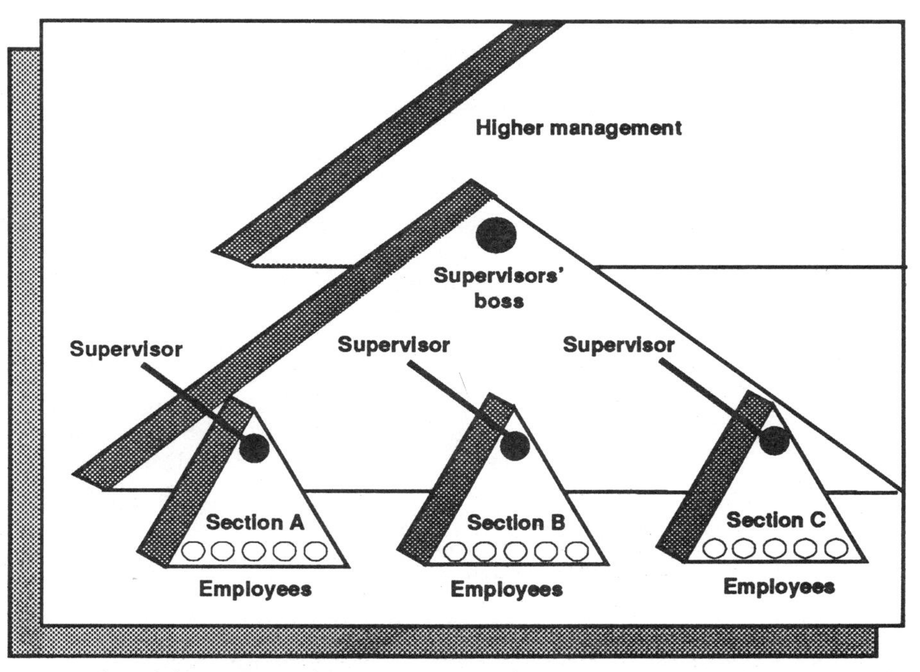

Source: Adapted from Rensis Likert, *New Patterns of Management* (New York: McGraw-Hill Book Company, 1961).

FIGURE 2-3 SUPERVISOR AS FACILITATOR

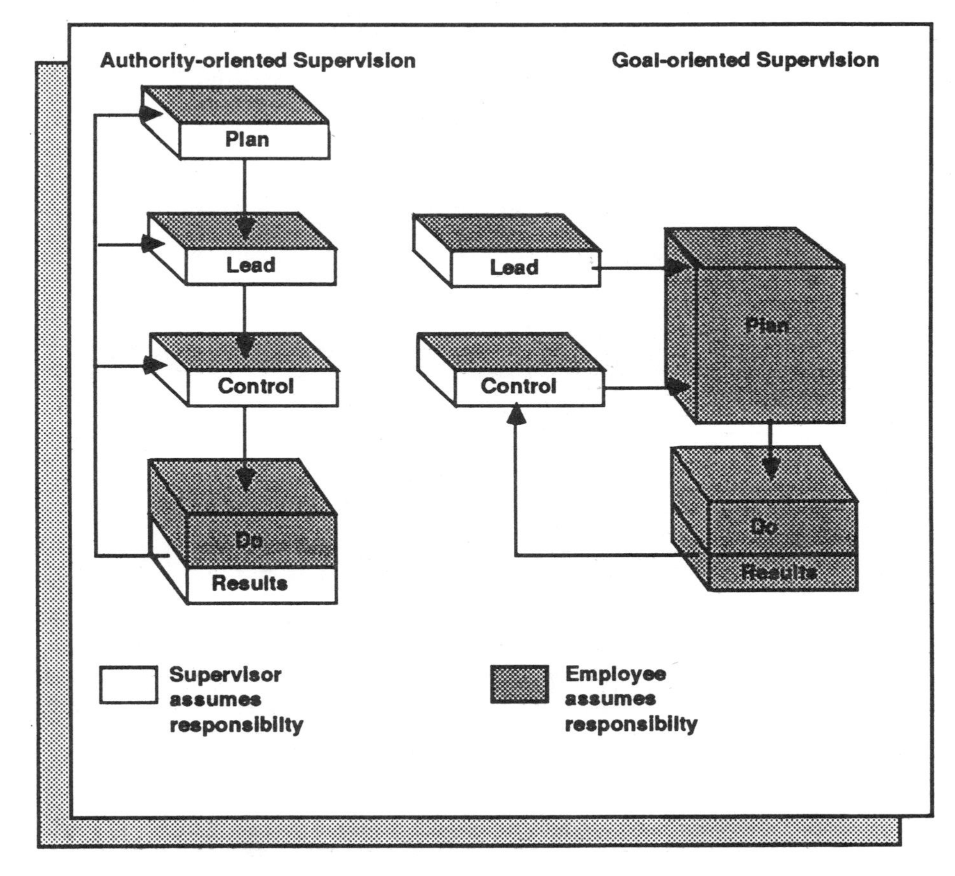

DEFINITION OF THE SUPERVISOR'S ROLE

Supervisors carry many titles: "supervisor," "department head," "section chief," "assistant department head," "office manager," even "foreman" or "forewoman." The federal government, in one of its publications, provides a simple, understandable definition of a supervisor's role:

> A first-line supervisor is the member of the management team who is in actual and constant contact with the non-supervisory workforce, who is responsible for their production output and who plans, assigns, and evaluates their work in accordance with directions given by the supervisor's superiors. To the overwhelming majority of workers, the first-line supervisor is their primary, if not their only, link with management. It follows, then, that the way supervisors manage their people, the department's materials and machinery—but especially the people—will determine whether or not that segment of the whole organization will be productive and effective, and will contribute to the desirable growth of the organization. An ineffective supervisor may well vitiate the plans and efforts of top management.[5]

While there are many other popularly accepted definitions of the widely used title of "supervisor," a simple one seems to serve best. It was developed by the International Labour Office after considerable study of the literature:

> Supervisors are usually first-line managers whose major function is working with and through non-management employees to meet the objectives of the organization and needs of the employees.[6]

A modification of this definition is proposed by the Opinion Research Corporation, which suggests that within the limits of the definition, another distinction can be made: there are *first-level supervisors,* who manage only nonmanagerial employees; and there are also *second-level supervisors,* who manage other supervisors in addition to nonmanagerial employees.[7]

CHANGING SCOPE OF SUPERVISORY RESPONSIBILITIES

In earlier years, supervisors were chosen for their technical skills or craftsmanship. The superior mechanic or typist was rewarded by being promoted to foreman/forewoman or chief clerk. In many uncomplicated situations, this method worked quite well. The journeyman/journeywoman or highly capable office employee, proud of his or her skills and knowledge, was naturally looked up to and respected as the most expert in the department. As time progressed, however, business and institutional activities have become more complicated. Divisions of organizations have become more specialized. Machines and computers have increasingly taken over the work formerly done by people. In this milieu, the supervisor's job requires, in general, less comprehensive technical knowledge. Instead, it calls for supervisors to possess a wider variety of skills, particularly those for dealing with people effectively and for planning, organizing, and directing operations. *Breadth* of skills, not necessarily depth in a specific craft, has begun to take precedence in the supervisory world. And skills in motivating and leading people increasingly constitute the "make-or-break" area of supervisory responsibility.

In fact, many observers believe the most important role a supervisor plays is that of a leader. This viewpoint is probably an exaggeration, since there are so many areas requiring immediate supervisory attention, such as productivity, quality, and cost control. Nevertheless, leadership is clearly a vital characteristic. Modern supervisors are responsible for the achievement of some sort of end product. This end product may be on paper, in the form of accounts, written material, diagrams, pictures, and so on; it may consist of certain types of services rendered; or it may consist of concrete items of manufacture. Whatever it is, supervisors must see that their workers produce it in the number and quality, and utilizing the method, required by organizational specifications, at the place and time stipulated. If supervisors do not get the production out, they are not doing their jobs: this is the be-all and end-all. In order to get out the production, they must see that their workers produce. Since supervisors can no longer be martinets—and force subordinates to produce—they must instead motivate and stimulate people to produce. This is accomplished by ingenuity and leadership. We can therefore conclude that supervisors' production is a function of their leadership abilities.

Leadership is the activity of influencing people to cooperate toward some common goal. It is a process that satisfies the needs and purposes of the organization it serves and at the same time allows for creativity and satisfies the fundamental human needs of the people in that organization. Most authorities agree that the qualities and skills of leadership can be learned. Identification and improvement of these leadership skills (communicating, motivating, personal problem solving, counseling, and so forth), are now necessary considerations in the design of supervisory development programs.

Robert R. Blake and Jane S. Mouton have repeatedly asserted that the manager's role has two important dimensions—a concern for people (the leadership aspects) and a concern for production. Based on their own research, Blake and Mouton identified two attitudinal dimensions, to be distinguished from the behavioral dimensions identified in the research originating at Ohio State University. They visualize these roles as being complementary and illustrate this relationship on a grid, or matrix. More recently, they have prepared a special version of their widely accepted Managerial Grid for supervisory roles. This is illustrated in figure 2-4. If nothing else, the grid concept helps to establish the potential dichotomy in the roles that supervisors must perform.

THE SUPERVISORS' OWN DEFINITION OF THEIR ROLE

Granting the flaws inherent in self-appraisal, the National Survey of Supervisory Management Practices, involving over eighty-five hundred supervisors, found them drawing these conclusions about their role:

1. They see themselves as the boss, often operating independently on their own best instincts and judgment rather than according to policy. Their

FIGURE 2-4 THE SUPERVISORY GRID

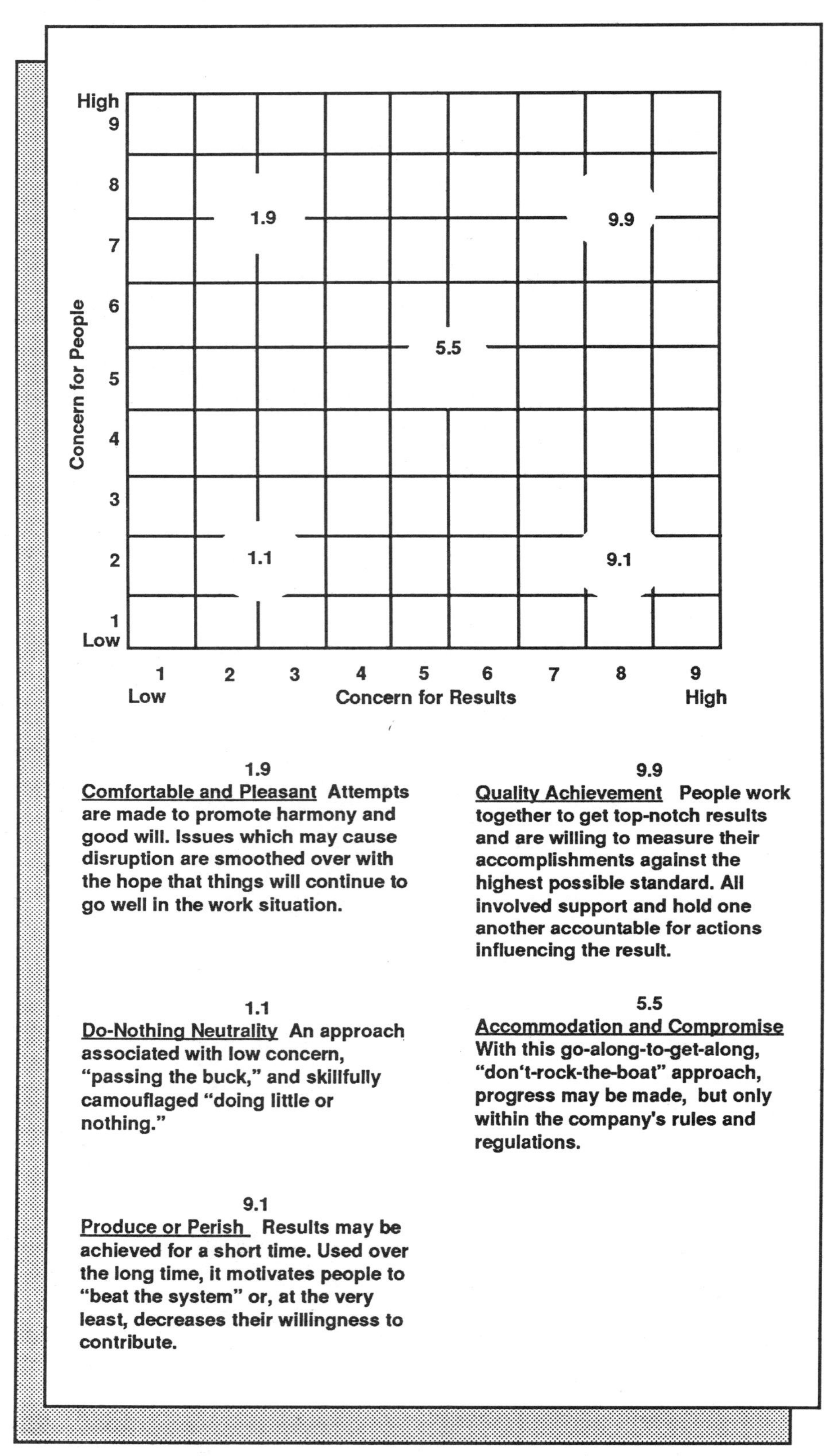

Source: Reprinted with permission from Robert R. Blake and Jane Srygley Mouton, *The New Grid for Supervisory Effectiveness*

alignment with management is tentative at best. Only 40 percent say they "feel a part of company management"; 19 percent say they "feel closer to my employees than to company management." Another 17 percent "feel closer to other supervisors," and still another 18 percent say, "I feel that I am on my own as a manager most of the time." Some 6 percent say, "I feel that my boss and I are the company management."

2. Their thinking is in line with the traditional values of hard work and experience leading to achievement. The seniority principle, according to which service is rewarded by promotion and security, appears to be "a good idea" to more than three-quarters of them. Performance appraisals as "effective guides to motivation and discipline" get the same degree of approval.

3. They are ambivalent about employee motivation. On the one hand, 93 percent of all supervisors say that "most employees want to do a good job," and 83 percent say that "most employees willingly accept responsibility for their own work." On the other hand, 66 percent say that "the main interest of most employees is to get enough money to do the things they want to do," while 61 percent say that "employees require close supervision," and 41 percent say that "most employees have to be pushed to produce."

4. All in all, however, supervisors are a vital, rather happy group. They are almost unanimous (95 percent) in saying that "what happens in my company or organization is really important to me." Only 24 percent say that "money is what's most important about my work." Eight out of ten (82 percent) say, "Generally speaking I am satisfied with my job."[8]

Many of these conclusions were repeated in the survey results published in 1984 by Opinion Research Corporation. In one area, however, the ORC study revealed a basic softness in supervisors' view of their roles:

> Many supervisors and middle managers feel abandoned by senior management. They believe that they have been left to "run the shop" while management decides what it wants to do, how it wants to do it, and when all this will happen, with little input from those closest to the operation. This perceived lack of involvement is particularly insidious where communications are poor and managers are not trained effectively. Furthermore, our profiles of middle and lower managers' attitudes indicate that their thinking, understanding, and commitment in such an environment mirrors that of their subordinates rather than that of their superiors.[9]

SEGMENTING SUPERVISORY RESPONSIBILITIES, FOR TRAINING ANALYSIS

Generalizations about supervisors—and the training they will need—become more meaningful when their responsibilities are segmented into certain basic classifications. A major research study,[10] for example, shows significant differences in demographic dimensions, problems, and attitudes when supervi-

Three Major Ways of Categorizing Supervisors

COLUMN A	COLUMN B
Job Function and Setting	
Blue-collar employees	White-collar employees
Unionized employees	Nonunionized employees
Production-oriented functions	Clerical-oriented functions
Manufacturing, construction, and/or mining industries	Banking, insurance, service, institutional, and/or government/military establishments
Level of Supervision	
First-level: supervise only rank-and-file hourly or salaried employees	Second-level: supervise other supervisors as well as rank-and-file employees
Educational Level Attained	
No higher than high school diploma	College degree or higher

sors are classified according to (1) the jobs they are asked to perform, (2) the extent to which they supervise other supervisors as well as rank-and-file employees, and (3) their educational level, as illustrated in the accompanying box. Supervisors who fit into column A, for example, tend to be alike in many ways. They differ significantly in many ways, however, from those who fall into column B, although those in column B exhibit similar characteristics among themselves. When supervisors are grouped by demographic factors in this manner, it becomes clear that they are different kinds of people doing different kinds of work.

Not only do supervisors differ categorically in their personal dimensions and in the jobs they perform; they also differ—as a result of variations in their demographic traits—in the way they look at their jobs and in the way they feel about important aspects of their work. This is dramatically illustrated by data showing categorical variations in the attention paid by supervisors to a number of key job activities. For example:

1. *Job function and setting.* The key distinguishing factor in this category is whether the employees supervised are blue-collar or white-collar. White-collar supervisors, for example, devote considerably more time and attention than do blue-collar supervisors to interviewing and placing employees, consulting with staff people, attending departmental meetings, and improving methods and procedures. Blue-collar supervisors spend significantly more time than do white-collar ones in planning production schedules, making job assignments, and coping with safety, production, and quality-control problems. Other related factors—such as whether or not the supervised employees are union members, the degree of production-oriented responsibilities, and whether the establishment provides a product or a service—reinforce even more the blue-collar/white-collar distinctions.

2. *Level of supervision.* Nearly half of all those surveyed said they supervise other supervisors in addition to nonexempt personnel. These are second-level supervisors, and there is clearly a difference between their job requirements and those of first-level supervisors, who manage only nonexempt employees. Many serious surveys, including Opinion Research Corporation's in 1970,[11] have recognized this distinction between levels, but their reports have failed to show how this affects the nature of supervisory problems and attitudes. The National Survey of Supervisory Management Practices, however, reveals significant differences all along the line. For example, second-level supervisors are far more concerned than first-level supervisors with production planning and control, discussing employee personal and performance problems, devising improved methods and procedures, and solving cost-related problems.

3. *Educational attainment.* Among supervisors in this study, differences in educational attainment are associated with dramatic variances in demographic dimensions, such as pay and age. This might be expected. Not expected was the fact that supervisors' assessment of problem intensity and attitudes was, in some cases, even more dramatically affected by educational achievement. More highly educated supervisors, for example, are far more jaundiced in their estimates of the effectiveness of cost-reduction and appraisal programs. They are also distinctly negative about the seniority principle. And somewhat surprisingly, they are much more likely to perceive minorities as being singled out for favoritism. Some 20 percent of the most highly educated supervisors thought blacks were given special treatment, 13 percent for Hispanics, and 14 percent for women. These figures compare with 12 percent, 6 percent, and 8 percent respectively among the least-educated supervisory group.

Analysis with a Four-Cell Matrix

Differences observed according to the three categories outlined above are, of course, more a matter of degree than absolute. There is a good deal of blurring of the lines between classifications. Nevertheless, before drawing any conclusions about supervisors, it is extremely helpful to first try classifying them according to the four-cell matrix illustrated in figure 2-5. Survey data support the matrix's presumption that there are—at the very least—four significantly different groups of supervisors: (1) blue-collar/first-level, (2) white-collar/first-level, (3) blue-collar/second-level, and (4) white-collar/second-level. Using survey data, it was possible to develop characterizing profiles of each segment, as shown in the figure. These differences and others will impinge heavily on the design of supervisory training and development programs. For example, further analysis of the National Survey of Supervisory Management Practices data showed significant differences according to the operating areas in which supervisors were employed:

Purchasing supervisors placed greater-than-average job emphasis on meetings with their bosses about work-related problems, solving scheduling problems, and dealing with customer-related problems. Purchasing supervisors, however, appeared to be much more confident than other supervisors regarding computer-related matters.[12]

Marketing supervisors said they experience greater pressures than do other supervisors with respect to discussing employee performance, keeping costs in line, and obtaining the required output of work. They were less concerned with work inaccuracies and labor and material shortages. They did, though, report an alarmingly high concern with the extent to which they

FIGURE 2-5 DESCRIPTIVE COMPARISON OF FOUR MAJOR CATEGORIES OF SUPERVISORS

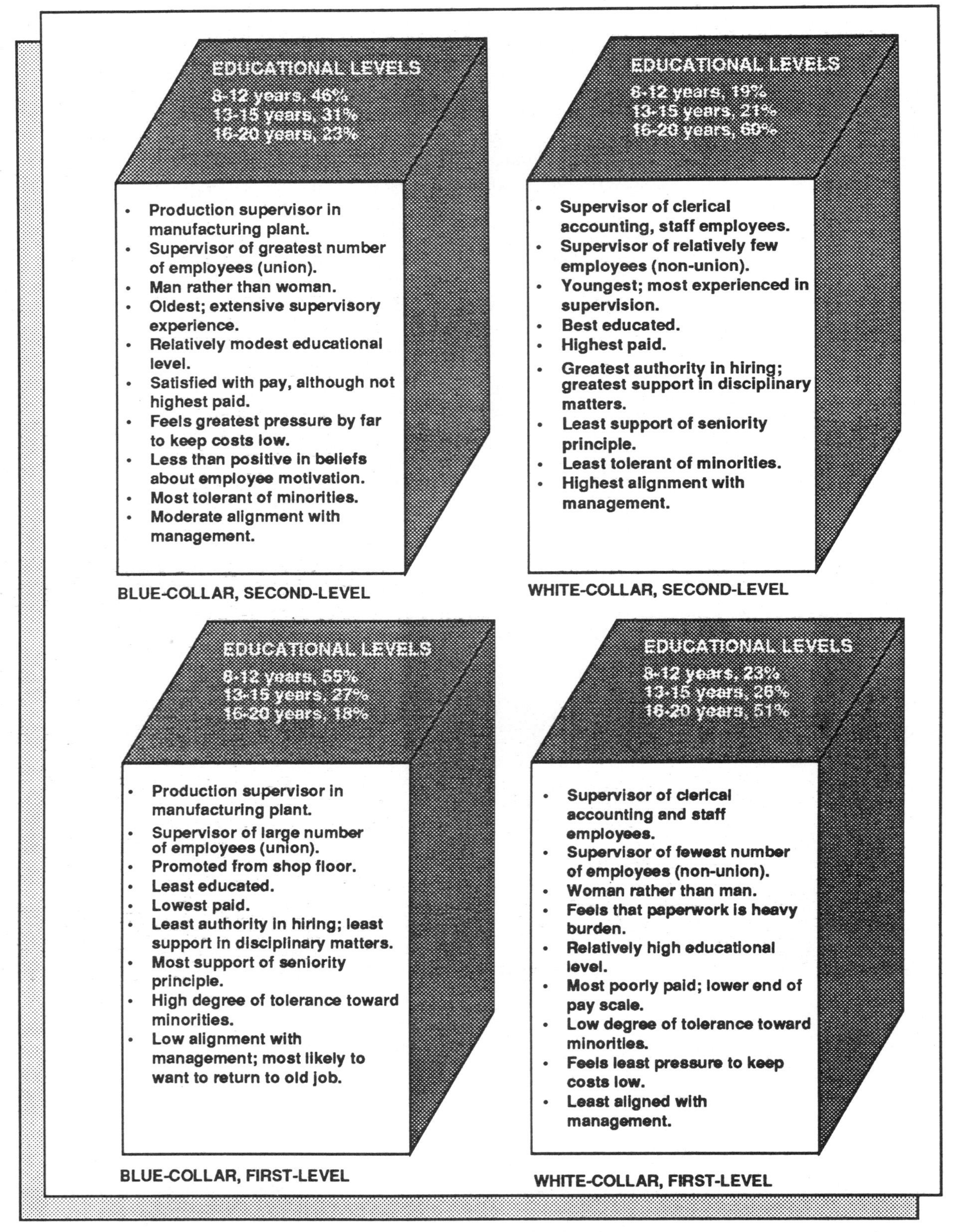

Source: Adapted from Lester R. Bittel and Jackson E. Ramsey, "New Dimensions for Supervisory Development," *Training and Development Journal* (March 1983), p. 15.

were asked to do things that are contrary to their moral beliefs regarding what is right and wrong.[13]

Engineering supervisors appeared to be unusually uncomfortable with the interpersonal aspects of their responsibilities, although they claim to engage more broadly in participative-management styles. They tend to expect more in the way of a support structure from their parent organizations, and they are not especially persuaded of the effectiveness of performance appraisals, suggestion systems, or cost-reduction programs. They rely more heavily than do other supervisors on the grapevine for vital information. And they, more than other supervisors, view their organization's treatment of minorities as preferential.[14]

It is not unlikely that such in-depth surveys and analyses of supervisors in most organizations would reveal similar, significant differences among supervisory role perceptions according to industry and/or function.

Chapter 3

Dimensions of Supervisory Competencies

INTRODUCTION

Probably the most significant philosophical advance in training made in the last twenty-five years has been the concept of competency-based training. Stated simply, competency-based training attempts to provide the skills needed to perform a particular task and only those skills. In some ways, it is a complete turnabout from the traditional craft, or journeyman, training, where it was expected that the apprenticeship would eventually enable the individual to perform a complete range of skills, whether or not these were ever required of the worker on a particular job.

Competency-based training got its impetus after World War II when Dutch consultants were brought into the Arabian oil fields to train relatively unskilled, unlettered employees. The consultants concluded that it would save time and money if the workers were trained only in a narrow, or selective, spectrum of skills required for the particular work involved. The workers trained according to this philosophy were deemed to be more than satisfactory by their employers. Their range of skills, however, was limited and often not transferable to other employers. The Dutch consultants called this selective approach to skills training "accelerated training."

This focused approach to specialized training, with its emphasis on company-specific rather than craft-specific skills, was slow to be accepted in the United States. Trade unions, understandably, were opposed to it. So, too, however, were trainers, who viewed it as a step backward in human resources development. Nevertheless, the basic idea was grudgingly acknowledged to be in tune with parallel advances in specialized technology. In fact, a closer study of supervisory-training programs in particular led many authorities to wonder whether or not many of the skills being taught might be off target. And many were. Supervisory skills training could be faulted, on the one hand, for offering developmental courses in skills that were not relevant and would never be used and, on the other hand, for failing to offer improvement in the vital supervisory skills needed to perform effectively on the job. The latter shortcoming is, of course, the most damaging.

It should be noted that competency-based training is related to, but different from, training-needs analysis (which will be treated separately in chapter 6). Needs analysis can take place only after the required competencies of a position have been determined. Competency-based training examines the position; needs analysis looks at the individuals filling this position.

Supervisory-training programs, then, should spring from a clear knowledge of the competencies employers require of their supervisors. Generalizations about competency are not nearly so good as specific definitions gathered by each organization through observation and research. Nevertheless, authorities have formulated many helpful hypotheses about necessary supervisory competencies.

FIVE ESSENTIAL RESPONSIBILITIES

Carroll and Anthony, for example, asked the question, "What do supervisors do?" and concluded that the supervisor's job involved five responsibilities:

1. *Responsibility to higher management.* The supervisor must:

- Plan the work of the department
- Coordinate the department's work with that of other departments
- Select and train employees when needed
- Make work assignments
- Interpret and implement management policies
- Understand and communicate to employees all aspects of company operations
- Make production decisions (for example, start jobs, stop jobs, authorize changes, take unsafe tools out of production)
- Maintain both morale and discipline
- Keep control of costs
- Send recommendations for change upward
- Motivate department members

2. *Responsibility to employees.* The supervisor must:

- Develop good morale
- Stand up for employees when they are being treated arbitrarily from above
- Establish a warm and trusting working climate within the department
- Handle employee problems promptly
- Be fair in all departmental matters
- Explain to employees all matters connected with their jobs
- Train employees when needed

- Assume the role of counselor, on occasion
- Distribute all departmental amenities fairly
- Discuss proposed changes before change takes place
- Maintain a safe and clean work area
- Provide sound policies for employee personnel problems (when not provided by higher management)
- Explain fringe-benefit plans and pay systems
- Orient new workers
- Coordinate and plan work so that work loads are as stable and predictable as possible

3. *Responsibilities to coworkers.* The supervisor must:

- Coordinate whatever work flows or paperwork needs to be exchanged among supervisors
- Communicate with other departments about mutual needs and problems
- Give them support as members of the same management team
- Coordinate policy interpretations with other departments to assure consistency and uniformity

4. *Responsibilities to staff departments.* The supervisor must:

- Comply with reasonable requests for information from staff managers
- Utilize whatever standardized reporting forms are necessary per the judgment of staff managers
- Listen to the counsel of staff managers pertaining to matters that fall into their areas of expertise
- Consult with appropriate staff managers to utilize their special expertise on problems
- Coordinate with staff managers where task requirements necessitate it

5. *Responsibility in labor matters.* If the company is unionized, then the supervisor must also:

- Become knowledgeable about every aspect of the labor agreement
- Attempt to maintain a conciliatory atmosphere in the relationship with the union
- Respect the terms of the agreement, even though the supervisor may personally disagree with it
- Effectively administer the grievance machinery of the labor contract
- Treat all employees fairly, including union members
- Represent management, for that is where a supervisor's first loyalty lies[1]

CRITICAL DIMENSIONS OF COMPETENCY

A number of authorities and concerned enterprises have compiled comprehensive lists of supervisory attributes, or dimensions. The lists are often long, and many include personal qualities as well as actual proficiencies related to specific job performance. There is, however, a useful consensus among most competency lists.

ASSESSMENT-CENTER DIMENSIONS

Byham states that the dimensions of supervisory competence most often measured in assessment centers include: impact, creativity, stress tolerance, leadership, sales ability, sensitivity, initiative, independence, problem analysis, planning and organization, judgment, decisiveness of delegation, flexibility, tenacity, management control, and risk taking. He adds that research findings have validated the use of these criteria (under professionally supervised assessment-center conditions) to be in compliance with the Equal Employment Opportunity Act as a means of identifying management potential.[2]

AMA COMPETENCIES MODEL

James L. Hayes, when president of the American Management Associations, advocated a somewhat similar but expanded list of desirable attributes for managers and, by implication, for supervisors.[3] (See the accompanying box.)

Model of Competencies of a Successful Manager—Developed by the American Management Association

Knowledge Competencies

1. *This is a threshold requirement.* All successful managers must have a certain amount, but a lot more knowledge alone will not make a superior manager.

Entrepreneurial Competencies

2. *Efficiency orientation:* a continuing interest in doing things better and finding the best combination of resources.
3. *Proactivity:* the urge to initiate action, write a report, call on a customer, start something going.

Intellectual Competencies

4. *Logical thought:* a dedication to placing events in a causal sequence.
5. *Conceptualization:* the ability to assemble information and seemingly unrelated ideas and events into a pattern.
6. *Diagnostic skills:* the ability to apply concepts and theories to real-life situations.

Continued on next page

Model of Competencies of a Successful Manager—Developed by the American Management Association—*Continued*

Socioemotional Competencies

7. *Self-control:* the ability to place organizational needs above personal reactions.
8. *Spontaneity:* the ability to express ideas freely and easily, even if not effectively.
9. *Perceptual objectivity:* the ability to understand and/or present contrasting points of view skillfully, especially in conflict situations.
10. *Accurate self-assessment:* an awareness of own strengths and weaknesses.
11. *Stamina and adaptability:* high energy levels and the ability to function effectively under pressure.

Interpersonal Competencies

12. *Self-confidence:* a compelling faith in own ability to attain goals.
13. *Developing others:* a conviction about his or her responsibility to help others, to seek and develop disciples, to coach and counsel.
14. *Concern about impact:* awareness of the way in which what he or she does and says will affect the organization and subordinates.
15. *Unilateral power:* the personal ability to get others to go along with prescribed directions, commands, policies, and procedures.
16. *Socialized power:* the ability to build a network of alliances and support within and outside the organization.
17. *Oral communications:* the ability to speak so that others can understand; the successful manager uses parables, develops anecdotes, and provides illustrations that people can grasp quickly.
18. *Positive regard:* a deeply rooted belief in the ability of others in the organization to perform effectively when given a reasonable chance.
19. *Managing group processes:* the ability to inspire teamwork; the successful manager praises cooperation and direct coordination in a way that promotes identity and morale in a work group.

Source: Adapted from "Management Measurement," a column written by James L. Hayes, president of the American Management Associations, in *Printing Impressions* (October 1980): 81; based on a study of over two-thousand managers by the AMA.

Company-Specific Dimensions

Honeywell has for years employed a validated testing program for the identification of supervisory potential. The criteria, or standards, are described as "performance standards statements for first-line supervisors." For each of the thirteen standards listed below, there are also a dozen or more "critical-incident" illustrations to support the identification of the particular competence:

1. *Ability to plan for the accomplishment of goals.* Includes determining subgoals to support company goals, anticipating possible problems, gathering relevant information, setting priorities, and implementing plans.

2. *Ability to administer rules and policies fairly and consistently.* Includes knowledge of company rules and policies, and ability to interpret and explain the purpose of policies.
3. *Interdepartmental relations.* Includes the ability to develop and maintain harmonious relations with other departments for the good of the company.
4. *Ability to train and develop subordinates.* Includes proper orientation of subordinates to company, department, and job; motivation of subordinates; performance counseling; and other developmental methods such as rotation of job assignments.
5. *Initiative.* Includes the ability to seek out solutions, make decisions, take action, and meet deadlines.
6. *Member of management.* Involves the ability to consider and express himself or herself as part of management and to work accordingly. Includes knowing what is expected and disseminating company policy despite personal feelings.
7. *Technical competence.* Includes familiarity with technology, principles, and processes of the area supervised and the ability to suggest and effect improvements in the quality and quantity of work supervised.
8. *Human relations skills.* Involves the ability to get along well with others, communicate facts clearly and completely in a tactful manner, and get work done without adverse feelings.
9. *Safety and housekeeping.* Involves knowing and enforcing safe practices and procedures.
10. *Communications.* Includes providing feedback to superiors on the status of projects, proper preparation, timely submission of required reports, and prompt and complete problem reporting.
11. *Willingness to accept responsibility.* Includes attending to assigned duties, following up on details, and meeting commitments.
12. *Integrity, trustworthiness, and honesty.*
13. *Department administration.* Includes forecasting, budgeting, cost control, cost improvement, record keeping, report preparation, inventory control, and justification of capital expenditures.[4]

At General Electric's facility in Columbia, Maryland, seven "dimensions" were singled out as essential competencies: technical knowledge, administrative skills, ability to develop a plan for achieving goals, ability to deal with the manager to whom one reports, communications ability, capacity for dealing with people outside the unit and outside the company, and ability to deal with employees reporting directly to the supervisor.[5]

Jones, Kaye, and Taylor[6] arrived at an important ranking of competencies using a scale developed by Pedler, Burgoyne, and Boydell.[7] (See table 3-1.) The supervisors/managers who made the rankings were individuals who had entered the organization (General Electric Nuclear Energy Business Group) as high-technology specialists and who had made the shift from a technology emphasis toward a "people/organizational problem-solving orientation." Interestingly, these supervisors looked at their competencies more as "corporate street smarts" or "political savvy" than as formally acquired

TABLE 3-1
COMPARATIVE IMPORTANCE RANKINGS OF COMPETENCIES

Competency	Importance for: Managers	Importance for: Technicians
1. Command of basic facts	Medium	High
2. Relevant professional knowledge	Medium	High
3. Continuing sensitivity to events	High	Medium
4. Problem-solving, analytical, and decision/judgment-making skills	High	High
5. Social skills and abilities	High	Low
6. Emotional resilience	High	Low
7. Proactivity and inclination to respond purposefully to events	High	High
8. Creativity	Medium	High
9. Mental agility	Medium	Medium
10. Balanced learning habits and skills	Medium	Medium
11. Self-knowledge	High	Low

Source: Adapted with permission from P. R. Jones, B. Kaye, and H. R. Taylor, "You Want Me to Do What?" *Training and Development Journal* (July 1981): 56–62.

proficiencies. For example, they said that part of their success was attributable to the fact that they:

- "Were able to recognize people with organizational power and clout and become associated with them."
- "Were able to recognize programs and efforts being carried on by the organization with the potential to gain recognition and become involved with them."
- "Were able to think on their feet, always looking for a chance to turn problems into opportunities."

Public-Employment Dimensions

Culbertson and Thompson surveyed 314 supervisors in public employment (Kentucky) and developed the following ranking of required supervisory competencies:

1. Motivating
2. Developing employees
3. Communications
4. Leadership
5. Planning/organizing
6. Human relations
7. Performance appraisal
8. Disciplining
9. Decision making
10. Handling complaints and grievances
11. Management methods such as MBO
12. Written reporting systems
13. Counseling
14. Functioning in the organization
15. Time management
16. Delegation
17. Affirmative action
18. Safety
19. Termination procedures
20. Interviewing
21. Hiring procedures
22. Budgeting[8]

Style or Substance?

Saul W. Gellerman has raised the question of whether many so-called competencies are more a matter of style than of substance.[9] He considers this bias to be a consequence of the Hawthorne studies, asserting that the assumption has been, and study after study bears it out, that workers are more collaborative—hence, more productive—under a supportive, or "employee-centered," style of supervision than they are under a style of distrust or low regard. Gellerman, however, observed that what a supervisor *does* is often equally important. If a supervisor stresses and keeps watch over output, quality, and cost, for example—which are usually paramount objectives of most productive organizations—then employees are likely to follow suit. Gellerman concludes that "the things to which the supervisor chooses to give his attention largely determine what his subordinates will channel their energies into."

A Return to Basics

Cover, too, takes issue with generalized managerial aspects of supervisory competencies and urges a "return to basics."[10] The emphasis would be on: production, quality control, sales support and customer relations, cost control, people, housekeeping and safety, administration, personal relationships, innovation, and attention to identifying and establishing performance and improvement objectives.

Other observers warn that statements of competencies often imply too much. For example, employee counseling is frequently included as a dimension of the supervisory job. Broadwell cautions that "The first-line supervisor is—or should be—a professional at recognizing work-performance problems, but to expect the supervisor to deal with an employee's personal problems is to court disaster."[11]

AT&T's Master Competencies

In probably the most exhaustive research ever conducted into the identification of competencies, AT&T isolated and ranked fourteen principal tasks of supervision, as illustrated in table 3-2. The research (described later in the

TABLE 3-2
AT&T'S COMPETENCIES FOR MASTER SUPERVISORS

Rank Order	Process	Percentage of Time Spent on the Process	Frequency of Performance
1	Controlling the work	17	Every day
2	Problem solving	13	Every day
3	Planning the work	12	Every day
4	Informal oral communication	12	Every day
5	Communication	12	Every day
6	Providing performance feedback	10	Every day
7	Coaching a subordinate	10	Every day
8	Written communication/documentation	7	Every day
9	Create/maintain motivative atmosphere	6	Every day
10	Time management	4	Every day
11	Meetings	4	Twice monthly
12	Self-development	2	Weekly
13	Career counseling a subordinate	2	Bi-monthly
14	Representing the company	1	Monthly

Source: Reprinted with permission from Charles R. Macdonald, *Performance Based Supervisory Development: Adapted from a Major AT&T Study* (Amherst, Mass.: Human Resources Development Press, 1982), 20.

FIGURE 3-1 HOW SUPERVISORS DISTRIBUTE THEIR TIME AMONG VARIOUS ROLES

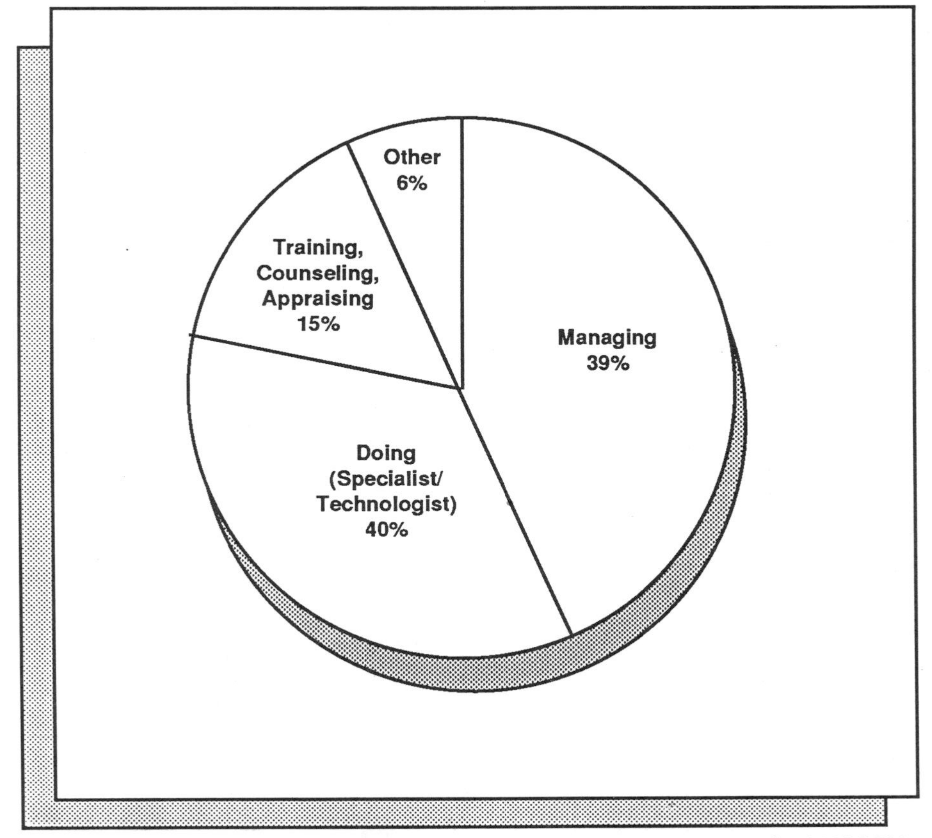

Source: Adapted from Philip Marvin, *Executive Time Management* (New York: AMACOM, 1980), 4.

chapter) began with the identification of a number of supervisors judged as "masters" in view of their outstanding performance and appraisals. Their competencies eventually became the basis for the list provided in table 3-2. AT&T's analysis identified not only the fourteen basic duties but also the major tasks, decision points, skills, and related knowledge areas associated with each.[12]

IMPORTANT COMPETENCY-RELATED VARIABLES

When the analyst's focus shifts to the activity of compiling lists, it is all too easy to lose sight of the main purpose of competency identification. Long lists of competencies often obscure important variables. There is the question of priorities and time demands, for example.

The AT&T list *is* prioritized, although each of the fourteen items is given almost the same weight, and provides an estimate of the relative time spent on each activity.

Baker and Holmberg analyzed data gathered by the American Management Association and derived the supervisory time distribution chart shown in figure 3-1. They also found that supervisory time devoted to managerial functions can be ranked from most to least in this order: implementing, planning, organizing, delegating, evaluating, innovating, and staffing.[13]

AN EYE ON THE BOTTOM LINE

It is well to keep in mind that supervisory performance will generally be judged by universal measures: (1) how well the supervisor manages the various resources made available to the department and (2) the value of the results accomplished. (See figure 3-2.)

MANAGING RESOURCES

It is expected that a supervisor will manage the following things effectively:

- *Facilities and equipment,* such as a certain amount of floor space, desks, benches, tools, production machinery, computer terminals, and microfiche

FIGURE 3-2 UNIVERSAL MEASURES OF SUPERVISORY PERFORMANCE

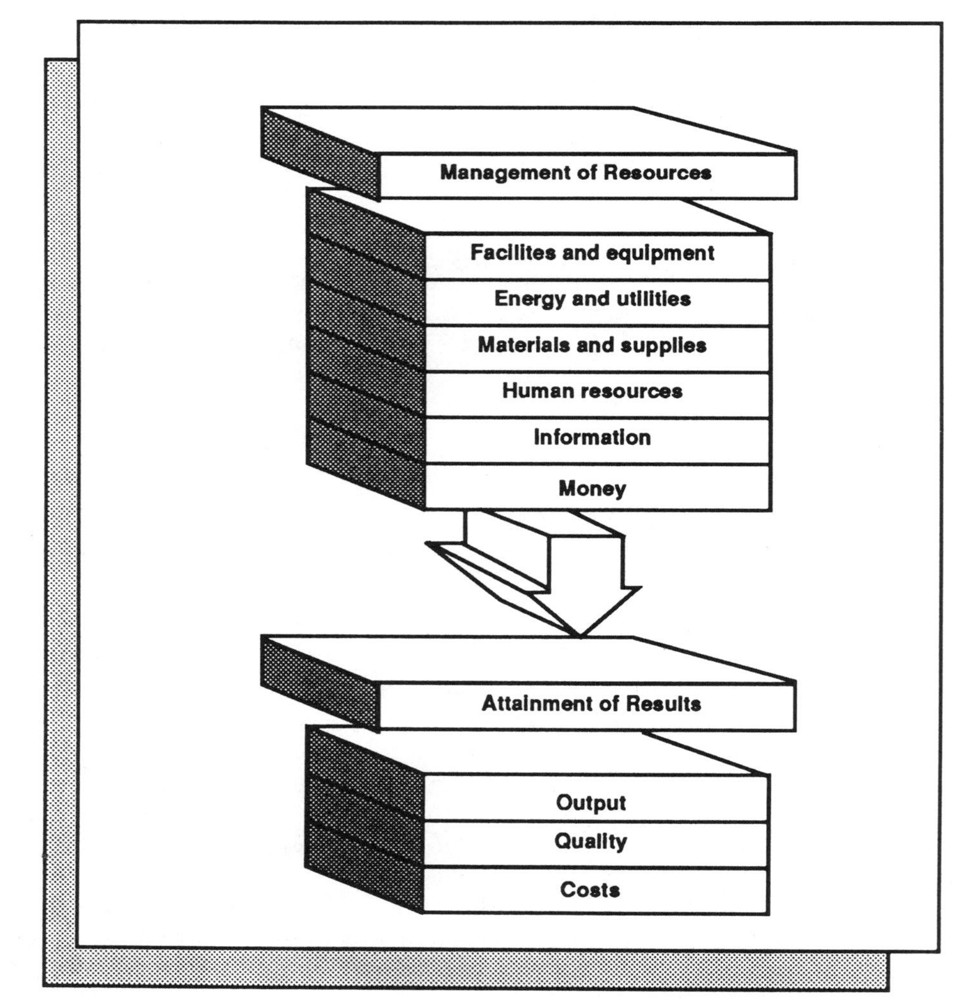

readers. The supervisor's job is to keep these operating productively and to prevent their abuse.

- *Energy, power, and utilities,* such as heat, light, air-conditioning, electricity, steam, water, and compressed air. Conservation is the principal measure of effectiveness here.
- *Materials and supplies,* such as raw materials, parts, and assemblies used to make a product as well as operating supplies, such as lubricants, stationery, cassette holders, paper clips, and masking tape. Getting the most from every scrap of material and holding waste to a minimum are prime measures here.
- *Human resources,* such as the work force in general and the supervisor's employees in particular. Since supervisors do little or nothing with their hands, their biggest job is to see that these people are productively engaged at all times.
- *Information,* such as that made available by staff departments or found in operating manuals, specification sheets, and blueprints. Supervisory success often depends on how well the supervisor can utilize the data and know-how made available to him or her through these sources.
- *Money.* All the above can be measured by how much they cost, although the actual cash will rarely flow through the supervisor's hands. Nevertheless, supervisors are expected to be prudent in decisions that affect expenditures and may have to justify these in terms of savings or other benefits.

Attaining Results

It follows (in managerial logic, at any rate) that when resources are managed properly, desirable, productive results will be forthcoming. In most organizations, the emphasis will be on the following:

- *Output, or production.* Specifically, the supervisor's department will be expected to turn out a certain amount of work per day, per week, and per month. It will be expected that this will be done on time and that the department will meet delivery schedules and project deadlines.
- *Quality and workmanship.* Output volume alone is not enough. Supervisors will also be judged by the quality of the work their employees perform, whether it be measured in terms of the number of product defects, service errors, or customer complaints.
- *Costs and budget control.* Departmental output and quality efforts will always be limited by the amount of money supervisors can spend to carry them out. Universally, supervisors attest to the difficulty of living up to cost and budget constraints.

METHODS FOR IDENTIFYING COMPETENCIES

If the human resources development professional wishes to go beyond the selection of logical competencies from one of the established lists, such as those provided above, there are three fundamental ways to proceed.

Traditional Job Analysis

Using the job-analysis approach, the analyst gathers data about the tasks and competencies required of supervisors in a particular organization by any of three methods:

1. Interviewing supervisors and their superiors to obtain a list of (a) tasks supervisors perform, (b) related responsibilities as well as performance standards and measures, and (c) opinions from these individuals and from staff specialists about the skills needed to perform the tasks and discharge the responsibilities indicated.
2. Surveying supervisors and their superiors (seeking similar information) using one of the established lists of competencies, with or without a request for some sort of ranking of importance (from 1 to 10, for example) and time allotments (in percentage of time spent, hours per day or week, or whatever).
3. Studying existing job descriptions and specifications to obtain such data.

Once the data have been gathered, they can be sifted, ranked, and consolidated by further interviews and/or surveys and/or group meetings of supervisors. Another approach is to assign the interviews and survey studies to a task force, with final refinement verified by consultation with incumbent supervisors.

Statistically Verified Research

Few organizations could afford to, or would wish to, pursue the kind of extensive supervisory competency research conducted by AT&T in the late 1970s and early 1980s before the breakup of the Bell System.[14] Nevertheless, the process that the AT&T study teams followed is worth keeping in mind while searching for your own organization's supervisory competencies. In *phase 1,* AT&T simply reviewed all the relevant data the corporation had accumulated in its years of research. The result was the identification of four generic duties: (1) organizing and planning; (2) directing, controlling, and delegating; (3) supervisor/subordinate relationships; and (4) communications and coordination.

Phase 2 involved the development of an interview checklist based on the four generic duties, along with five related tasks for each. Supervisors and their superiors were asked to (1) rank duties and assign frequencies to them and (2) rank tasks. Important open-ended questions asked during this phase included:

- "What about frequency? How is each performed?"
- "Look at each output separately. What does each look like? What form does it take? Who gets it? How?"
- "What does each contribute to achieving the company's purpose?"

A mastery model was developed from these interviews. (Refer back to table 3-2.) Next, survey participants were asked to rate the mastery model items according to their relative level of difficulty and the need for related training. Levels of difficulty were ranked as follows:

- *High-complexity processes:* planning the work, controlling the work.

FIGURE 3-3 PORTION OF THE FLOWCHART USED BY AT&T TO PREPARE ITS MASTERY MODEL FOR PLANNING TASKS AND DECISION POINTS

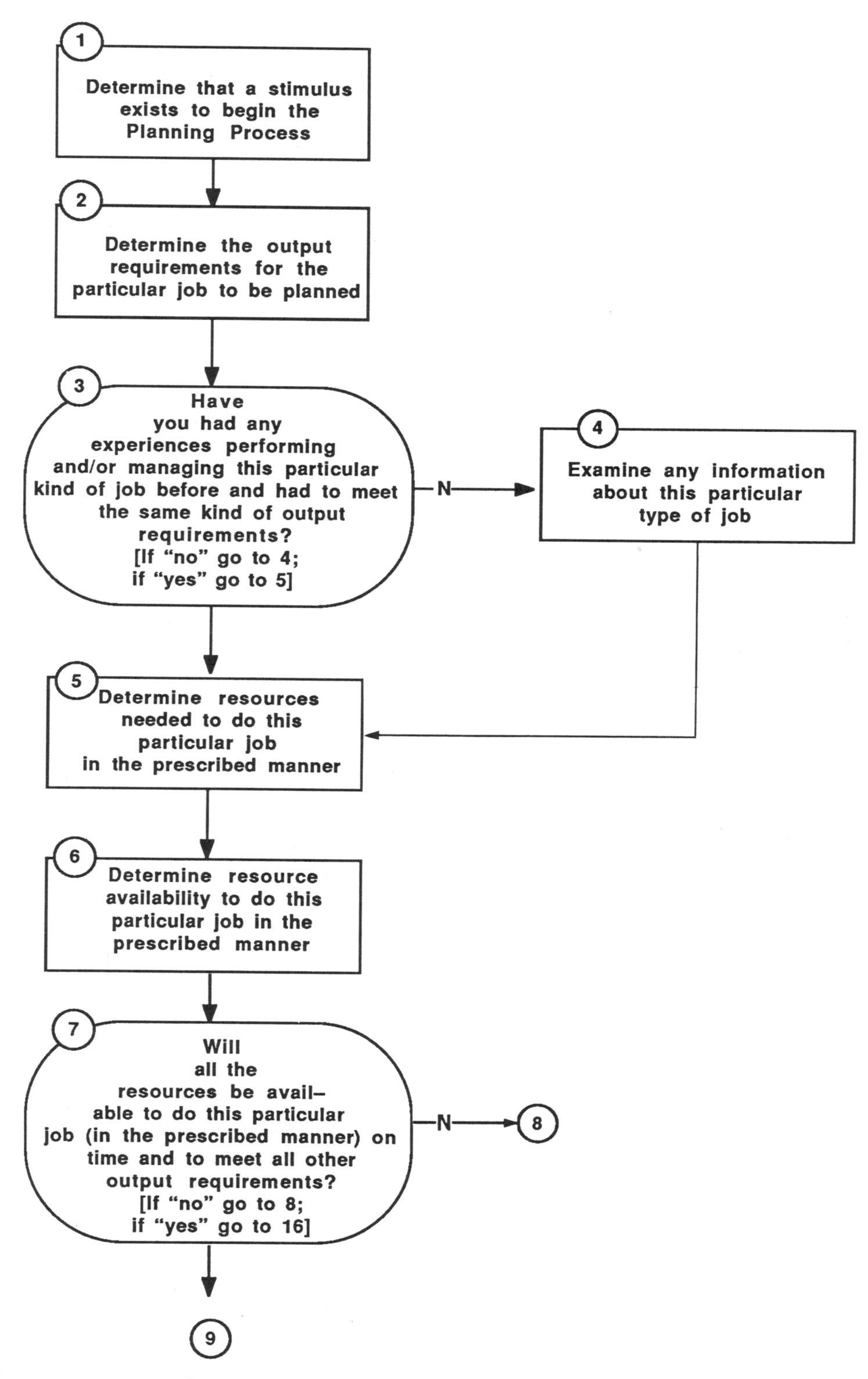

Source: Reprinted with permission from Charles R. Macdonald, *Performance Based Supervisory Development: Adapted from a Major AT&T Study* (Amherst, Mass.: Human Resources Development Press, 1982), 33.

- *Moderate-complexity processes:* problem solving, providing performance feedback, coaching a subordinate, creating/maintaining a motivating atmosphere, time management, communication, informal oral communication, career counseling.
- *Low-complexity processes:* self-development, representing the company, meetings.

The final element in the mastery model was the preparation of an analysis of the 14 principal duties, identifying for each:

- The *number of tasks* (from 5, representing the company, to 24, performance feedback).
- The *number of decision points* (from 1, coaching a subordinate, to 6, planning work and controlling work).
- The *specific skills* for each (from 1, communication, to 28, performance feedback) and the *knowledge areas* (from 3, representing the company, to 60, performance feedback).

In all, the complete model contains 187 major tasks, 42 decision (contingency) points, 196 skills, and 383 knowledge areas, for a total of 808 items.

Each of the 14 duties is represented in the mastery model report with: a *flowchart* (see figure 3-3); a set of *performance standards* indicating outputs expected and methods of measurement; *a step-by-step manual* indicating tasks, decision points, and skills and/or knowledge needed at each point; and a *diagnostic test* for determining the specific training needs for incumbent or candidate supervisors for that duty.

Psychological Testing

Honeywell, General Electric, AT&T, and others use standardized tests in validating their competency criteria and/or in selecting supervisory candidates according to these criteria. Legally acceptable validity testing must be checked against successful performance in the supervisory position. Many standardized tests are used, however, for selecting candidates. Examples include tests for general mental ability, personality and motivational inventories, and the Thematic Aperception Test, along with business games, simulations, and in-basket exercises.

Studies conducted over the years at AT&T have shown that middle-level "nonpromotable" managers are most likely to manifest deficiencies in the following competencies: leadership skills (82 percent), administrative skills (73 percent), achievement motivation (45 percent), managing interpersonal conflicts (45 percent), and intellectual ability (32 percent).[15]

Part II

SELECTION, ORIENTATION, AND ASSESSMENT

Chapter 4

Selection of Supervisors

INTRODUCTION

You can't make a silk purse from a sow's ear. It may be an unfortunate cliché, but it does make the point forcefully about the importance of initial selection to the ultimate development of supervisors. Accordingly, training professionals should try to do all within their power to influence the process their organizations follow for selecting supervisors.

AVOIDING MISFITS

Roughly one in five supervisors in the National Survey of Supervisory Management Practices volunteered that he or she would return to the ranks if it were possible to do so without loss of face or reduction in pay.[1] This group of supervisors ranked significantly lower in every aspect of satisfaction and confidence than the others in the survey.

Typical comments included the following:

- "The pressure to do my job well comes without support or understanding from my superiors."
- "I'm troubled by management's lack of confidence in me."
- "I'm unable to reward good work due to union and management policies."
- "You can't get definite answers from top management."
- "People higher up make promises about what we can do without first checking with us."
- "Upper management's goals are unreal."
- "There's more work to be done than manpower to do it."
- "There's too much paperwork and not enough time for personal contact."
- "It's impossible to work with the new generation of people."
- "The more I try to motivate employees, the less it works."
- "I don't have enough control."
- "I start to discipline an employee and the personnel department steps in. . . . My hands are tied on disciplinary problems."

These comments suggest that prudent human resources management of supervision should begin, not with training, but with a more careful and effective selection process.

Extensive studies reported by the University of Pennsylvania in 1978 conclude that employees with the greatest supervisory potential do not necessarily fill the key ranks.[2] To begin with, selection systems are poorly planned and implemented. Preference is traditionally given to friends and relatives. The seniority concept, too, carries over into supervisory selection. In effect, it says, give the longest-service employee a shot at the job first.

But the selection system is only part of the problem. Many good workers will not move into supervision if it means shift work. Pay differentials between hourly employees and their supervisors are narrow. Hourly jobs are seen as more secure, supervisory work as full of frustrations. This view is supported by Benson,[3] who contends that "superworkers" continue to be rewarded by promotions to supervision, a position that is often inappropriate for their skills or without any promise of advancement. "We may be building failure into the selection process," he warns.

Improving the Selection Process

Screening and selection of supervisors can be improved. A great many progressive companies have developed systematic methods, such as assessment centers, of choosing for supervisory positions those candidates most likely to succeed. Unfortunately, these methods are cumbersome and expensive, but they are effective. Companies that do not emulate them to some degree or another are overlooking one of the most proven ways to raise the level of effectiveness of their supervisory force. It is far better to start with the right people than to try making improvements if the potential isn't there. Statistically speaking, anything that would eliminate the 20 percent of the supervisory force who feel like a dead weight on the rest would be like releasing ballast from a balloon.

Good selection programs start with a study of the work to be performed. This is easier said than done. All too often such a study is the product of a facile job-description writer rather than a careful examination of the actual work, especially its make-or-break aspects. Progressive organizations develop historical data that help them to associate personal characteristics (measurable ones, preferably) of successful performers with each job requirement. Selection dimensions are derived from these studies. The selection process is then precisely prescribed and implemented. The better programs involve a combination of screening techniques—testing, multiple interviewing, in-basket exercises, and psychological evaluations.

TRADITIONAL APPROACHES TO SUPERVISORY SELECTION

Selection of candidates for supervisory positions from within a firm usually involves four steps or phases:

1. *Review of records.* Start with a systematic search and evaluation of personnel records, such as an employee's work history, record of promotion,

production output, attendance, and written tests. If candidates have been attracted from outside the organization by advertisements or referrals and/or are walk-ins, then make an attempt to gather similar information through application forms and reference checks.

2. *Observation and appraisal.* When firms have a performance-appraisal program, supervisors and executives are continuously observing and appraising their subordinates. All evidence of supervisory potential should be noted and explored, by:

- Assigning the potential candidates special jobs and opportunities that call for a display of leadership
- Detailing them to jobs requiring the exercise of supervisory responsibility, under adequate observation
- Using them as understudies to a regular supervisor
- Allowing them to perform in an acting supervisory capacity

3. *Personal interviews.* The purpose of these is to appraise the candidate's willingness to assume responsibility, depth of work experience, capacity to supervise others, and the like. A panel of interviewers who see a number of different candidates offers greater objectivity and is preferable to allowing only one or two persons to conduct the interviews.

4. *Testing.* A number of valid test instruments for supervisory work are available from such professional organizations as the American Psychological Corporation, Washington, D.C. (Also see the references in the subsection of chapter 6 on "Capability Assessments," pages 62–63.) When tests are used for appraisal purposes, it is important that only reliable, validated instruments be employed and that these be administered and evaluated by a person of proven competence in this field.

A MODEL SUPERVISORY SELECTION PROGRAM

William E. Fulmer, who participated in the University of Pennsylvania studies, suggests this "ideal" supervisory selection system:

1. The human resources development office periodically predicts the need for first-line supervisors.
2. When the apparent supply of trained candidates fails to meet the projected needs, notices should be posted, asking interested employees to submit applications on specially designed forms, which include information about previous supervisory experience or leadership positions, prior jobs that would be helpful as preparation, the candidate's reasons for wanting to become a supervisor, and the competencies the candidate feels are his or her most valuable qualities. (See figure 4-1, in the next section of the chapter, for an example of such a form.)

3. Applications are reviewed by the HRD department to verify accuracy and note any significant history, such as proficiency awards or disciplinary actions.
4. Applications receive a second review, by line management, and these appraisals should be put in writing.
5. Rejected applicants should be notified and the decision discussed with them by line and/or personnel management.
6. Recommended employees are then interviewed by a selection committee composed of several operating and human resources officials.
7. After each interview, committee members grade the applicants on some previously agreed upon set of criteria, preferably related to the dimensions and competencies established earlier.[4]

VOLUNTEERS

Voluntary candidates for supervisory positions or training can be either good or bad news for training professionals. Qualified individuals should be welcomed; few qualities can substitute for self-motivation. Unqualified or doubtful candidates present a problem, especially when the organization is responsive to pressures for affirmative action. Many public agencies maintain a sort of quasi-open enrollment policy for employees who believe they are qualified or wish to participate in presupervisory (or even supervisory) training courses. The unspoken hope is that unqualified individuals will be discouraged, either by exposure to the realities of supervisory requirements or by the rigors of course content.

One large midwestern manufacturing company (that prefers anonymity and is referred to as the ABC Company in figure 4-1), actively seeks volunteers, both because it believes that they represent a valuable source of supervisors and also to demonstrate affirmative action and good faith to its labor unions. The company's published documents, however, carefully spell out the program's requirements and commitments. For example, the invitation to partake in presupervisory training (which is intended to build a pool of candidates for promotion) reads in part:

> ***Policy.*** It is the policy of the company to provide reasonable training and development opportunities to full-time employees who demonstrate both interest in and capacity for supervisory responsibility.
>
> ***Objectives.*** The target of this program is to provide an environment in which personal growth can occur. This means allowing men and women the opportunity to gain insight into what is expected of supervisory personnel and obtain objective evaluations of their individual potential for supervisory responsibility. It means making available suitable classroom instruction and planned job assignments designed to build, then test, supervisory skills.
>
> This presupervisory training program is tailored to suit the needs of the individual. The program is designed specifically to bring to the supervisory ranks skilled bargaining-unit employees who are well grounded in the essentials of effective supervision.

Method. Applicants who are accepted into the program will participate in classroom training *outside* of regular working hours. Each session will cover a key unit of effective supervision. The sessions will be a mixture of theory and application of key concepts so that the new skills and knowledge gained can be applied to specific needs in real-life situations.

Participation is the thrust of the program: trainees will participate in individual and group exercises and complete homework assignments, all leading to becoming a successful supervisor.

How to Apply. Applications to the program will be accepted in writing only, on the form provided. [See figure 4-1.] Complete the form in detail and return it to the industrial relations department. After receiving the completed application, an industrial relations representative will contact you and set up a personal interview. During this interview, you will discuss your work history, background, the program, and selection requirements in more detail. In addition, the representative will set a date for the comprehensive testing and inventories.

Testing and Selection. The testing is designed to measure your reading comprehension in relation to the classroom material you will be studying. The purpose of the test is to help enable you to successfully master the material. Successful passage of the reading comprehension test is a minimum entrance requirement.

The inventories that will be administered will help us in designing future programs and following your success in the future. They will not be used as a minimum entrance requirement.

Total testing time is estimated at two to three hours. Applicants will be paid their regular hourly rate for time spent in testing.

Each applicant to the program will be notified individually of acceptance or rejection by a representative of the industrial relations department.

If an applicant is rejected, he or she will be told of the reason, and in some cases the industrial relations representative will counsel with the employee on opportunities to improve reading comprehension through local agencies or the company.

All applicants accepted for the program will attend a group orientation session prior to beginning the program. During this session, all textbooks and student material will be given to you, along with the schedule and first reading assignment.

INTERVIEWING SUPERVISORY CANDIDATES

William T. Wolz recommends that whoever interviews supervisory candidates, especially from internal sources, ask and carefully evaluate the responses to these twelve questions:

- Why do you want to be a supervisor?
- What are the functions and duties of a supervisor as you see them?
- What personal characteristics and other qualifications do you have that would help you to become a good supervisor?
- How do you feel about taking on the added responsibilities and demands that come with a supervisory position?

FIGURE 4-1 SAMPLE APPLICATION FORM FOR PRESUPERVISORY TRAINING

APPLICATION FOR ENROLLMENT
ABC COMPANY'S PRESUPERVISORY PROGRAM

Name ______________________ Supervisor's Name ______________________
Date of Birth ______________________ Service Date ______________________
Job Classification ______________________ Home Telephone No. ______________________
Shift ______________________

Formal Education

	Name of School	Dates Attended Mo/Yr - Mo/Yr	Graduated Yes	No
Grammar	______	______	___	___
High School	______	______	___	___
College	______	______	___	___

Other Education and Training (Military, Vocational, Company Programs, etc.)

Subject and Source (i.e. Military, Vocational, etc.)	Dates Attended Mo/Yr - Mo/Yr	Completed Yes	No
______	______	___	___
______	______	___	___
______	______	___	___

ABC Company Work History:

Dates From/To	Job Classifications Number/Title	Hourly Wage Rates Start/Finish
______	______	______
______	______	______
______	______	______

List Below Your Primary Reasons For Applying For This Program
____
____
____

PLEASE READ CAREFULLY BEFORE YOU SIGN THIS APPLICATION
I understand that I am enrolling in a pre-supervisory training program, sponsored by the company, to be conducted on a regularly scheduled basis, outside of my standard hours of work, and that I *will not* receive pay for time spent while attending classes or performing homework assignments.

I further understand that my progress and performance in the program will be rated against standards established by the company and my selection as a full time supervisor will be based upon satisfactory completion of both classroom and practical training as determined by the company, as well as on the availability of permanent supervisory openings within the plant after I complete the program.

Signature ______________________

Date of Application ______________________

Please return the completed application to ______________________ (name)
of the ______________________ Department, no later than ______________________ (date)

- Do you think you could be a supervisor in any department other than your own?
- If you were a supervisor, could you take disciplinary action against employees, including former coworkers, if it became necessary?
- You realize that as a supervisor you would no longer be in the bargaining unit. How do you feel about that?
- What type of supervisor was the best you ever worked for? What type do you think provided the least effective supervision?
- What kind of fellow workers do you get along with best on the job? What kind do you find it most difficult to work with?
- How would you react if you were a supervisor and your crew included workers of a sex or race different from your own?
- How far do you think you are capable of progressing as a management employee—to shift supervisor, general supervisor, superintendent, or beyond?
- What steps would you take to improve your performance as a supervisor after you were promoted?[5]

THE ASSESSMENT-CENTER METHOD

The assessment-center method is used by many businesses, government, and nonprofit organizations to improve the accuracy of supervisory selection and of development decisions.

An assessment center is a method, not a place. Assessment-center participants engage in a variety of job-related simulations designed to bring out behavior relevant to skills or dimensions determined by the organization to be critical to success in a target job or jobs. Managers who are familiar with the requirements of the supervisory jobs, and who have been trained in the assessment process, observe and evaluate this behavior.

By placing participants in situations similar to the ones in which they will be required to perform after promotion or assignment, the process is made relevant and fair to all participants. The odds for the accurate prediction of future job success are improved by (1) training the manager-assessors, (2) providing a structured method for observing and analyzing behavior, and (3) subjecting each participant to the same treatment.

Moreover, research findings indicate that the assessment-center method is valid for both minority and nonminority group members. Many companies use the method as a component of their program for achieving affirmative action goals. The landmark 1973 Equal Employment Opportunity Commission/AT&T compliance agreement established AT&T's assessment centers as the means for identifying management potential among previously overlooked employees.

Format and Methods

The number of exercises and the total time required vary greatly. First-line supervisory assessment centers typically last for a day or less. Generally, centers designed to generate developmental recommendations last longer than those designed primarily to yield selection or promotion recommendations.

Typically, six or twelve people are assessed simultaneously, although centers designed for initial selection often assess only one person at a time. Most centers involve one assessor to every two participants; some operate on a one-to-one ratio.

Many specially developed and tested assessment-center exercises are commercially available. They include such techniques as business games, in-baskets, leaderless group discussions (involving both nonassigned roles and assigned roles), analysis (in the form of a presentation and/or a group discussion), individual fact-finding and decision-making exercises, interview simulations, and written-presentation and oral-presentation exercises.

Exercises are selected according to the following criteria:

1. Level of sophistication and education of the assessees
2. Relative importance of the various dimensions
3. Actual job content of the target position(s)
4. Need to observe the participants in a variety of situations
5. Need to observe critical dimensions in several different exercises
6. Time available for assessment

Minimum training for assessors should include:

1. Discussion of the definitions of the dimensions
2. Practice in observing and recording behavior and in writing reports on at least one of each type of exercise used in the center
3. Practice in conducting interviews
4. Familiarization with the procedure for reaching final decisions

As an aid in assessor training, videotapes of exercises, sample exercises, and sample final reports are frequently used.

Operational Considerations

Assessment centers are usually initially designed by a trained psychologist familiar with the method but are generally administered by representatives of the organization's training or human resources department who are not psychologists. These representatives must administer the exercises, write a final report summarizing the consensus of the assessors regarding each participant, and usually, be responsible for feeding back assessment-center information to the participants. Administrators must go through assessor training and must have had additional training for their special responsibilities prior to serving in this function.

The percentage of candidates who do well in assessment centers varies markedly between and within organizations. In general, at the presupervisory level, approximately one-third of those individuals assessed are thought to have supervisory potential. The percentage goes up in higher-level centers, where there is more opportunity for preselection of the assessees.

Many small organizations have considered forming a consortium where they can pool resources to operate a cooperative assessment center. This rarely works out. The organizations tend to disagree on the dimensions to be sought and on the scheduling of centers.[6]

Chapter 5

An Orientation Framework for New Supervisors

INTRODUCTION

There are many formal programs for preparing fledgling supervisors to adjust to their new position, both presupervisory training and basic supervision courses intended for newly promoted supervisors. There are also programs that provide new supervisors with an orderly, structured introduction to their responsibilities and environment, as illustrated by the model program in Chapter 10 (see the section headed "Program Configuration by Levels of Experience"). Actually, much more should be done for the new supervisor. The transition stage from a nonsupervisory position to one with genuine managerial responsibilities can be damagingly traumatic. Special attention should be given to this transition, quite aside from the formally planned and conducted training program.

GUIDING THE TRANSITION

The sudden shift in relationships and environment brings about a culture shock for many new supervisors. For a major portion of their working lives, they have had a purely bottom-upward view of the organization. Their initiative has been limited, and the impetus and direction for action have come from above. The main job concern was to look out for one's self and to take charge of one's own work. Now, quite suddenly, the new supervisor must acquire a radically different viewpoint.

Dealing with Ambiguity

New supervisors are now in a position to push rather than be pushed, and they must concern themselves not only with their own work but also with that of several other people. On the other hand, confusingly enough, they must still maintain a bottom-upward view of the management organization that continues to tower above them. It is not surprising that individuals who are troubled by ambiguity have difficulty accommodating themselves to this new role. Accordingly, they will benefit greatly from the guidance that often only a trained professional human resources person can provide. And in turn, they will become avid supporters of the formal training that follows.

FIGURE 5-1 TRANSITION IN POINT OF VIEW AND ENVIRONMENT

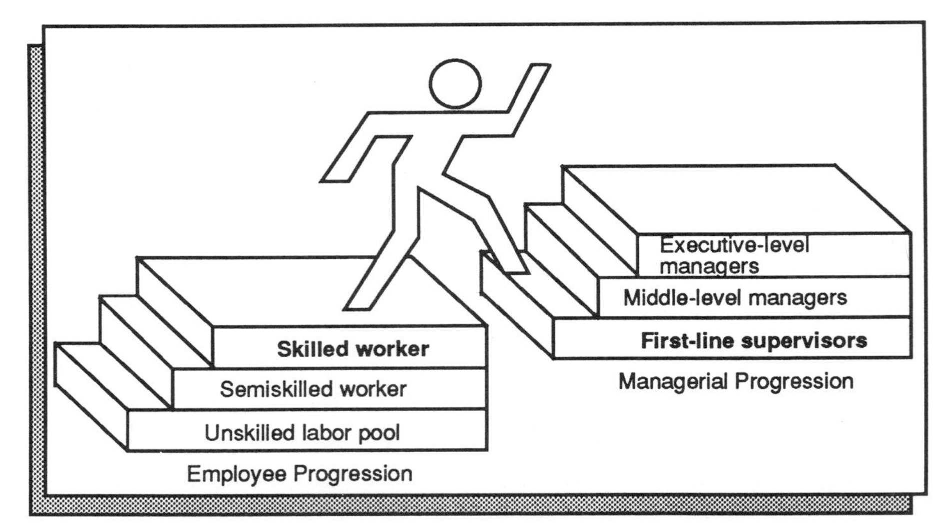

Source: Reprinted with permission from Lester R. Bittel, *What Every Supervisor Should Know*, 5th ed. (New York: McGraw-Hill Book Company, 1984), 6.

This crossover, or step-upward, dilemma can be portrayed in two ways. Figure 5-1 emphasizes the "step-upward" aspect, where one leaves behind his or her long-time associates and the easygoing ways of the rank and file. New supervisors then move into a stratum that is, at first, seemingly unfriendly and more formal. A second view of this critical stage of development is more complex. Here, the transition to supervisor implies an ambiguous change of function and technical role. The supervisor retains a portion of the operative role while attaining only a portion of the managerial role. Either way, new supervisors can be expected to flounder until they fully determine what their roles will be in their particular organization and adjust accordingly.

A Broader Environment

The work environment at the supervisory level is often significantly different from that at the operating level. The trappings and status of office may be slight, but they do have their effect—a shirt and tie rather than a T-shirt; a desk and telephone, or an office, rather than a group work area; lunch in the cafeteria rather than from a brown bag. The more dramatic environmental changes, however, will come from concepts, not objects—costs, budgets, variances, overhead, inventory levels, backorders, authority, motivation, conflict, and the like. Work that used to have a narrow, clear-cut focus on a particular machine, product, or service may now involve broad and complex new concerns.

There is also a shift in the degree of emphasis given technical, human, and administrative matters, as shown in figure 5-2. The reduced reliance on technical proficiency for power and influence makes itself felt.

During this brief, but critical, period of stress, training professionals can help newly appointed supervisors by:

1. *Reassuring them that the initial difficulties they are experiencing are not unusual.*

FIGURE 5-2 DIMINISHING RELIANCE ON TECHNICAL PROFICIENCY

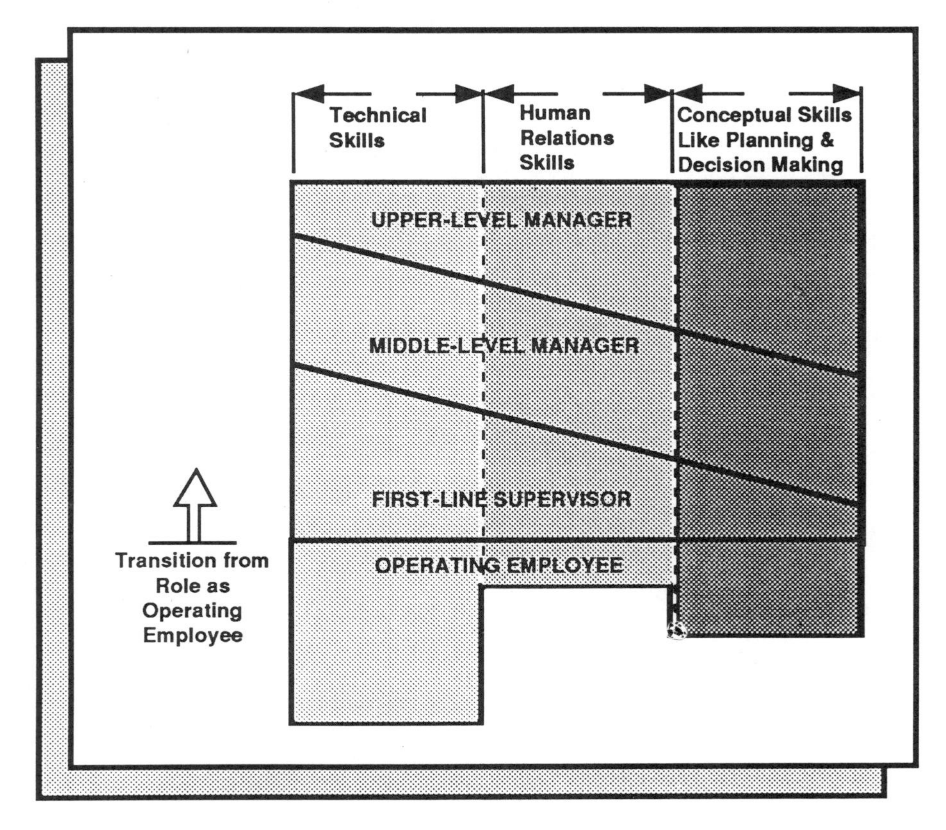

2. *Making informal counseling sessions readily available;* the need for this will diminish rapidly as adjustments are made.

3. *Directing them to specialized sources of information and support,* such as the information systems, industrial engineering, production and inventory control, and purchasing department staffs.

4. *Guiding them toward short-range goals that will build their confidence when mastered,* such as accomplishing a certain task or solving a particular problem "by the end of the month"—selecting only one or two targets at a time rather than trying to absorb and accomplish everything immediately.

5. *Helping to gain acceptance for them by the other members of the management group.* As with everyone else, supervisors' morale is lifted when they know that they are accepted and recognized as part of their new group—in this case, the real management group. The satisfaction that results from such relationships has a direct and dynamic effect on new supervisors. Higher-level managers can offer such personal incentives as a friendly manner, formal and informal commendations, or special assignments to build sound relationships with their subordinates. Inclusion of new supervisors in staff meetings with an opportunity to participate is a sound method for expanding their grasp of management problems and possible solutions. Many organizations write a carefully worded letter to new supervisors welcoming them into the management group. All such activities will stimulate personal growth and a sense of responsibility in new supervisors.

ASSISTING WITH STRUCTURED FRAMEWORKS

Stress is often most quickly relieved by hard physical work. New supervisors tend to be concerned at first with the mental and psychological aspects of their jobs rather than the physical ones. Yet mental and social accomplishments are hard to recognize and measure. The attainment of physical goals, however, is more readily observed and acknowledged. For example, it is easier to measure a supervisor's performance by counting the day's output of products made or client services rendered than by determining whether an interpersonal problem between two employees has been resolved. Accordingly, during the orientation period for new supervisors, a couple of straightforward pen-and-pencil devices can be offered that will enable them to assess the physical dimensions of their operations. After the first few weeks, these devices may diminish in usefulness and may not be necessary, but they can be invaluable in the beginning.

Planning the Long Day's Journey

The newcomer's first few days as a supervisor may be bewildering. An unspoken question in the supervisor's mind is often, "What do I do besides sharpen pencils and walk around looking important?" The philosophical answer is that the job will come to him or her. Problems will arise with alarming frequency. There will be little time for incidental chores or meaningless strutting. The "kitchen" will become quite hot, and if the supervisor stays in it for very long, he or she will soon learn how to get the meals out. Nevertheless, it does help for the new supervisor to prepare at the start a specific, procedural answer to the question "What do I do?" The box on the facing page provides a list of a number of typical steps to be performed each day. They are arranged roughly in sequence, with an estimate of the time to be allotted to each cluster of activities. The example given here is for a production supervisor. It can easily be modified to fit the tasks of a clerical, service, retailing, shipping, payroll, or any other kind of supervisor.

Mapping the Department's Territory

Another rather easy way to focus the attention of new supervisors on tangibles is to have them compile a data sheet like those in the box on page 55, listing the essential operating information about their new department. As the salesman in the show *The Music Man* advised the newcomer, "You've got to know the territory." When newly appointed supervisors map their operations, they've made measurable progress in understanding an important aspect of their work—its physical dimension and scope.

CLARIFYING CONCEPTUAL DIFFICULTIES

A clear grasp of the full responsibilities associated with a new job and a reliable knowledge of the limits of one's authority are usually slow in coming. So, too, is an awareness of relevant policies and practices, which affects the

Daily Sequence of Work Activities for a Production Supervisor

Do before the Shift Begins (15–30 Minutes)

1. Check production schedule and/or work orders for the day.
2. Check equipment to be used.
3. Check supply of materials for the day.
4. Check tools needed for the day.
5. Line up equipment, materials, and tools for the day.
6. Line up firm work schedule for the day.

Do at Beginning of the Shift (15–30 Minutes)

7. Check attendance and assign employees to work stations.
8. If necessary because of absences, balance the work force by rearranging assignments or by securing additional help from other departments.
9. Assign production and/or work orders.
10. Stress critical quality areas to watch.
11. Specify when the work should be completed.

Do during Each Day (6–7 Hours)

12. Check workmanship with each employee. Approve, correct, instruct, or train as needed.
13. Check work progress with each employee. Add help, allow more time, or assign additional work as appropriate.
14. Check on housekeeping. See that it is satisfactory at all times. Good work cannot be done in an untidy place.
15. Check back when production or quality appears unsatisfactory, especially with new employees.
16. Stay on the floor supervising and/or available for questions, assistance, and instruction most of the time.
17. Be on the floor immediately before and after breaks and for a full 15 minutes before quitting time.
18. Inspect critical quality areas as work progresses. Correct problems as soon as they are detected.
19. Perform final inspection of parts, subassemblies, and so on, before they move to next department.
20. Report recurring quality problems.
21. Check periodically to see that materials and supplies are on hand.
22. Check periodically to see that tools and equipment are in proper operating condition.

Continued on next page

Daily Sequence of Work Activities for a Production Supervisor—*Continued*

23. Report materials shortages or recurring defects.
24. Report and/or request maintenance, repair, or replacement of defective tools or equipment.
25. Check for accident hazards. Be sure employees are following safe practices and wearing proper protective clothing and equipment.
26. Prepare time cards, work-distribution sheets, work orders, material distributions, and other routine reports.

Do Once a Day (15–30 Minutes)

27. Observe one employee or work station continuously for 15 minutes. Look for time wasted, dull or improper tools, need for work-positioning jigs and fixtures, interferences, delays and bottlenecks, and expenditure of excessive time to get parts and materials. Try to find ways to cut costs or make improvements in any of these.

Do before Going Home (15 Minutes)

28. Make a list of unsolved problems that came up during the day. Consider ways to handle them.
29. Think about jobs that have to be done the following day: (a) check production and/or work orders; (b) check materials; (c) check tools.
30. Complete all paperwork. Avoid holding any paperwork for the following day.
31. Make a list of jobs that must be done the next day. Take it home with you and read it before coming to work.

supervisor's confidence in taking action, issuing directions, and responding to requests. Uncertainties about one's responsibility and authority, as well as about policy matters, add to stress and may cause tentative planning, directing, and decision making. When it comes to allotting a new supervisor's time, attention, and energies, the checklists presented in the next two subsections provide guidelines that may help to simplify and clarify these issues.

Tasks and Constraints

Just as a training professional may have difficulty in defining the tasks and competencies of the supervisors in a particular organization, so also will the new supervisor. The job's responsibilities may seem clear enough at first. Yet it will take only a very short time for the newcomer to learn of the constraints that limit his or her action. To provide a degree of relief from this initial uncertainty, it helps a new supervisor to complete a checklist like the one presented in the box on pages 56–58. It lists many of the specific tasks and responsibilities commonly associated with supervisory competencies. It also provides a set of columns for verifying the supervisor's authority, where appropriate. An uncompleted checklist can be given to the new supervisor as an open-ended guide to what to look for. Or it can be presented to the new

Sample Departmental Operations Data Sheets

EXAMPLE A

Clerical Processes Department

Overall department size ______ sq. ft.

No. of desks/work stations ________

No. of minicomputers ________

Make/model ________________

Capacity rating ________________

No. of personal computers ________

Make/model ________________

Capacity rating ________________

No. of modems ________

No. of word processors ________

Make/model ________________

Capacity rating ________________

No. of copy machines ________

Make/model ________________

Capacity rating ________________

No. of telephones ________

Names/extension numbers ______

____

____

Mainframe connection ___ yes ___ no

Access times ________________

Entry passwords ______________

____

No. of employees ________

Skill class _____; salary/wk. _____

Skill class _____; salary/wk. _____

Skill class _____; salary/wk. _____

EXAMPLE B

Production Processes Department

Overall department size ______ sq. ft.

Overhead height ________ ft.

Storage area ________ cu. ft.

No. of overhead cranes ________

Capacity ________ tons

No. of work stations ________

No. of type A machines ________

Make/model ________________

Capacity rating ________________

No. of type B machines ________

Make/model ________________

Capacity rating ________________

No. of type C machines ________

Make/model ________________

Capacity rating ________________

No. of computerized work stations

____

Process controlled ______________

____

No. of powered trucks ________

Make/model ________________

Capacity ________________

No. of work benches ________

Size ________________

Lighting levels ________ f.c.

No. of power outlets ________

110 volts ________

220 volts ________

240 volts ________

No. of employees ________

Skill class _____; wage/hr. _____

Skill class _____; wage/hr. _____

Skill class _____; wage/hr. _____

Responsibility/Authority Limits Checklist for Newly Appointed Supervisors

Class 1: Complete authority. Supervisors can take action without consulting their superior or staff departments.

Class 2: Limited authority. Supervisors can take action they feel is appropriate so long as their superior is advised of the action *afterward.*

Class 3: No immediate authority. Supervisors can take no action *until they have checked first* with their superior or appropriate staff department.

	Yes	No	Don't Know	Class of Authority (If Applicable)		
				1	2	3
Do you feel it is your responsibility to						
A. Select and train employees?						
1. Request that additional employees be hired as needed?						
2. Approve new employees assigned to you?						
3. Explain benefit plans to employees?						
4. Tell employees about upgrading and pay ranges?						
5. Make sure employees know rules of conduct and safety regulations?						
6. Train an understudy?						
7. Hold regular safety meetings?						
B. Make work assignments and maintain discipline?						
8. Prepare employee work schedules?						
9. Assign specific duties to workers?						
10. Assign responsibilities to assistants or group leaders?						
11. Delegate authority?						
12. Discipline employees?						
13. Discharge employees?						
14. Specify the kind and number of employees to do a job?						
15. Determine the amount of work to be done by each employee in your group?						

Continued on next page

Responsibility/Authority Limits Checklist—*Continued*

	Yes	No	Don't Know	Class of Authority (If Applicable) 1	2	3
16. Authorize overtime?						
17. Enforce safety rules?						
18. Transfer employees within your department?						
C. Handle employee problems involving provisions of the union contract?						
19. Interpret the union contract?						
20. Process grievances with shop stewards?						
21. Prepare vacation schedules?						
22. Recommend changes in the contract?						
23. Lay off employees for lack of work?						
24. Grant leaves of absence?						
D. Understand and administer pay and incentive systems?						
25. Explain to employees how their pay is calculated?						
26. Determine allowances for faulty material or interruptions?						
27. Approve piece rates or standards before they become effective?						
28. Answer employees' questions regarding time studies or allowances?						
E. Make these operating decisions?						
29. Start jobs in process?						
30. Stop jobs in process?						
31. Authorize setup changes?						
32. Approve material substitutions?						
33. Requisition supplies to keep your department running?						
34. Determine whether material should be scrapped or reworked?						
35. Replan schedules upset by breakdowns?						

Continued on next page

Responsibility/Authority Limits Checklist—*Continued*

	Yes	No	Don't Know	Class of Authority (If Applicable) 1	2	3
36. Take unsafe tools out of service?						
37. Correct unsafe working conditions?						
F. Tie in with other departments?						
38. Know how an order flows through the company from start to finish?						
39. Understand what the staff departments do? Understand your relationship to them?						
40. Authorize maintenance and repair jobs?						
41. Requsition tools?						
42. Investigate accidents?						
G. Be concerned with the way the job gets done?						
43. Make suggestions for improvements in operating procedures in your department?						
44. Recommend changes in department layout?						
45. Suggest material-handling methods to be used in your department?						
46. Discuss with staff members the operating problems caused by proposed design changes?						
H. Consider how much things cost?						
47. Cut down on waste of materials and supplies?						
48. Keep adequate production records for checking output per machine and per worker-hour?						
49. Participate in setting up your departmental budget?						
50. Investigate potentially unwarranted charges against your budget?						

Policy Source Checklist

Policy Areas	Written Policy			Established Procedures			Rules and Regulations			Individual or Department to Contact for Information
	Yes	No	Don't Know	Yes	No	Don't Know	Yes	No	Don't Know	
Schedules										
Changes										
Other										
Quality										
Specifications										
Overrules										
Other										
Purchases										
Services										
Supplies										
Shortages										
Repairs										
Budget Overrides										
Overtime Work										
Employee Discipline										
(etc.)										

supervisor with the blanks completed in advance, by the supervisor's immediate superior.

Policies and Practices

Knowledge of policies and practices is harder for the new supervisor to come by. Large, mature organizations typically have policy and procedure manuals to cover just about everything. It would be unrealistic, however, to assume that the supervisor will assimilate that information immediately or comprehend its implications overnight. In smaller, less formal organizations, policy may be more a matter of established practices than stated principles. Knowledge of policy in such organizations may reside mainly in the minds of experienced supervisors or in the know-how of various staff departments. The distinction between policies and procedures versus rules and regulations is also a difficult one for a new supervisor to make. For all these reasons, new supervisors in large or small, formal or informal companies will benefit from an early, systematic exploration of established practices. That is the purpose of the checklist provided in the box on page 59. It is left open-ended because it serves mainly as a guide to awareness rather than as a detailed reference.

Chapter 6

Assessing Supervisory-Training Needs

INTRODUCTION

Ideally, supervisory training needs should be determined by a comparison between (1) the required competencies of the position (AT&T calls these "mastery models") and (2) the measured knowledge, skills, and attitudes of the incumbent supervisors or supervisory candidates. In fact, many organizations begin with a generalized list of competencies such as those provided in chapter 3. They then use a number of techniques to establish the gaps between this list and the presumed capabilities of their supervisory participants. These gaps represent training needs.

Supervisory training and development are intended, of course, to narrow, or close, the gaps between required skills and current capabilities. Development extends a supervisor's skills beyond the minimum competency level and also broadens the individual's potential for assuming additional responsibilities. At this stage in which training needs are determined, a distinct word of caution is warranted. An objective, systematic process for the identification of needs, or gaps, will minimize the constant danger of either (1) jumping to generalized conclusions about needs or (2) following whatever training fad is currently popular. Not infrequently, organizational structure and morale problems are confused with a lack of supervisory skill or ability. As the chart in figure 6-1 shows, training and development needs may be greatly narrowed through organization development (OD) programs, more effective selection processes, and an improvement in the state of supervisory morale generally. Care should be taken to separate structural causes such as these from symptoms that may properly be attributed to training deficiencies. Supervisory training should concentrate on narrowing *real* gaps in knowledge, skills, and attitudes. Training that proceeds on that basis will be less costly, more effective, and more concise.

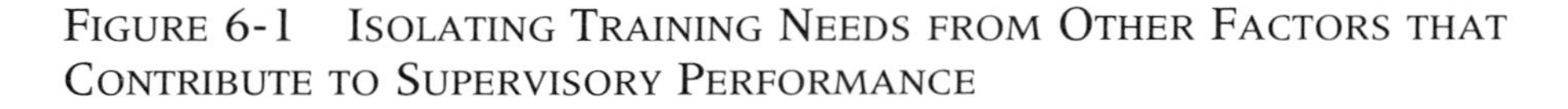
FIGURE 6-1 ISOLATING TRAINING NEEDS FROM OTHER FACTORS THAT CONTRIBUTE TO SUPERVISORY PERFORMANCE

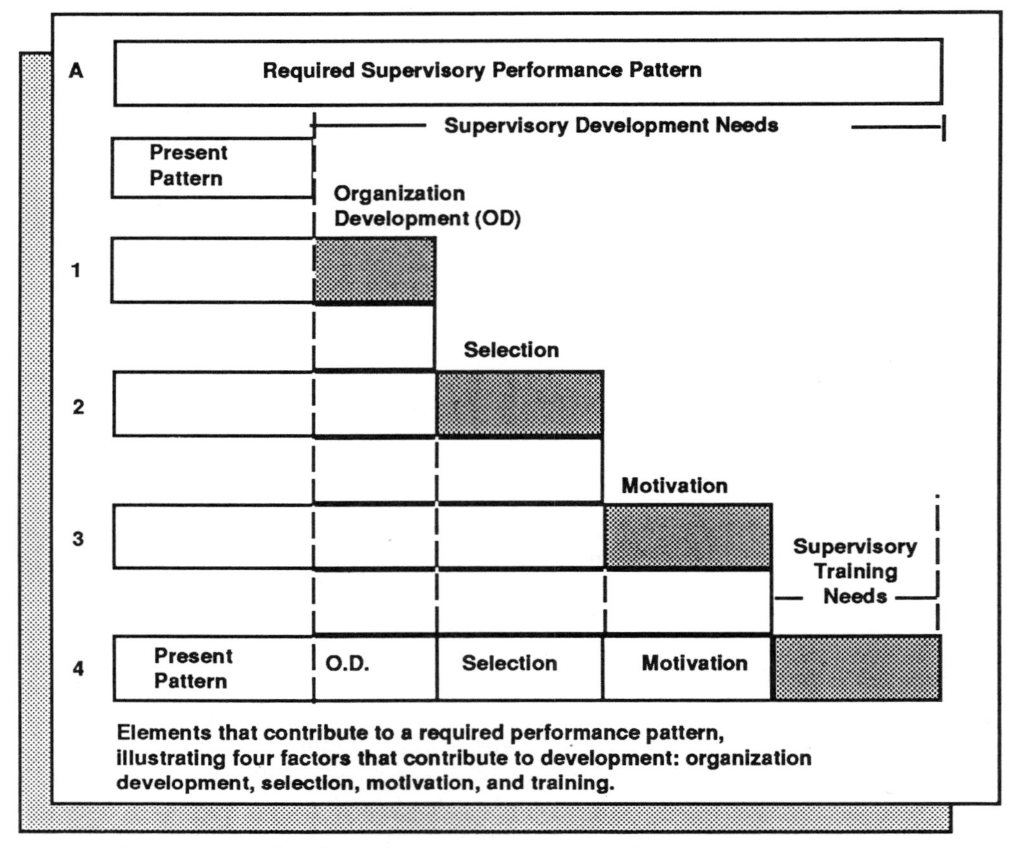

Source: Reprinted with permission from J. Prokopenko and Lester R. Bittel, "A Modular Course-Format for Supervisory Development," *Training and Development Journal* (February 1981): 19.

CAPABILITY ASSESSMENT

To establish the levels of capabilities already possessed or attained by an organization's supervisory population, human resources analysts commonly use as sources:

1. *Performance reviews,* from which specific and cumulative data identifying less-than-satisfactory performance against appraisal criteria are gathered
2. *Critical incidents,* complied from formal records or through interviews with supervisors, their peers in staff departments, and their superiors
3. *Attitude (or climate) surveys,* from which general indicators of unsatisfactory employee relationships are identified

In a relatively few instances, diagnostic instruments are also used. Popular among these are: *How Supervise?, Wexman Personnel Classification Test (PCT),*

General Clerical Test (GCT), Industrial Reading Test (IRT), and *Strong-Campbell Interest Inventory (SCII).* Inventory instruments developed especially for supervisors include Donald L. Kirkpatrick's *Supervisory Inventory on Communications* and Wyman and Kirkpatrick's *Supervisory Inventory on Grievances* (Brookfield, Wisconsin). Psychological tests are available commercially from such test developers and publishers as the Psychological Corporation (Harcourt Brace Jovanovich, Cleveland) and Management Research Systems (Ponte Vedra Beach, Florida) or by contacting the American Psychological Association (Washington, D.C.).

INTERNAL SOURCES OF DIAGNOSTIC INFORMATION

Many sources within an organization's information system will routinely accumulate for other purposes information that is also useful in diagnosing supervisory training needs. These data may be viewed as either indicators of general or more specific training needs.

General Training Needs

Sometimes, general conditions in an organization will indicate the need for supervisory training. Included in this category is (1) evidence that the general morale of employees is not up to a desirable standard, (2) wholesale expansion at a certain location, or (3) an increase in the responsibilities of a given group of supervisors. In particular, some factors clearly point to training needs. Among these are the following:

Safety. When accident hazards are increased through installation of new equipment or because of changes in procedures, some safety training will be required. Also, if the accident rate within a given unit is higher than normal and the physical hazards have been eliminated by safety engineering, it is reasonably certain that there is a need for supervisory safety training.

New programs or procedures. When new work programs are being initiated or when equipment of a type not previously used is installed, there is little doubt that there will be a need for supervisory training. This applies likewise to new forms and procedures in paperwork, especially with computerization and office automation.

Surveys. Reviews of operations are made from time to time for various purposes and by different persons. Analysis of reports of such surveys and oral comments of members of the survey teams frequently discloses the need for supervisory development.

Questionnaires. Although the use of employee questionnaires (attitude surveys) is fraught with certain dangers and difficulties (which will not be discussed here), analysis of results when they are used may well indicate the need for further training of supervisors.

Staff members. In many installations, members of specialized staffs are assigned to assist supervisors in better utilizing their work forces. These individuals may be able to point out specific ways in which training would be beneficial.

INDICATORS OF MORE SPECIFIC TRAINING NEEDS

In addition to the general sources, a number of indicators of supervisory training needs arise from studies and reports that may or may not be directly related to a needs assessment. Nearly all these indicators have to be considered in light of other factors involved and require judgment and experience to recognize the specific requirements for training. The methods used to find these indicators are varied. Among the most common are:

1. Examining any unusually low or high production records for both groups and individuals.
2. Studying existing problems and their causes, by organizing information on such matters as turnover, absences, grievances, and accidents.
3. Securing the views of supervisors themselves as to where they need assistance and additional skill, as in a needs inventory (described later in the chapter).
4. Discussing needs of supervisors with their superiors. In this connection, the review of performance appraisals by a personnel representative and the immediate superior is often helpful.
5. Surveying the views and attitudes of employees as to the kind of supervision they receive.
6. Continuously checking supervisory performance against established performance standards.
7. Comparing employee performance against established quantitative production standards.

The methods listed above may reveal useful information from which training needs may be determined, but possible needs revealed by the use of such methods must always be evaluated in light of other factors in the situation. For example, a study may show that production in a given unit is considerably below an adequate standard. Without further consideration, this might seem to indicate the need for supervisory training. Additional facts, however, may show that poor equipment, improper layout, or lack of adequate materials and supplies is at the root of the problem rather than poor supervision. Or a report may indicate an apparent training deficiency in a particular supervisor, only to have it turn out, upon more extensive analysis, that the need for improvement is in middle management.

ANALYSIS AND CLASSIFICATION OF SUPERVISORY-TRAINING NEEDS

Supervisory-training needs can be classified into several main categories:

1. One such classification differentiates between *qualitative* and *quantitative* training needs. In this approach, required supervisory characteristics are identified through analysis of job descriptions.

2. A second classification can be established in relation to *common* and *specific* training needs. This approach enables us to isolate professional universals in the supervisory job regardless of the kind of enterprise, sector, country conditions, and so on.

3. A third classification reflects not only common and specific features of a great number of supervisory jobs in different countries, industries, and organizations but also a division of these needs into three *application levels:*

   a. The *basic level* represents the training needs for any supervisor under any conditions. It involves information on very general, but valuable, knowledge and abilities required to qualify a supervisor as a professional in any sector and enterprise.

   b. The *sectoral level* adds to the basic training needs the knowledge and skills necessary for different sectors and industries. This information could be used for designing sets of supervisory-training modules for principal industries such as manufacturing, agriculture, construction, services, and transportation.

   c. The *enterprise (organization) level* reflects only those training needs that are relevant to a specific enterprise, with its own set of technological, cultural, and organizational conditions.

The point has repeatedly been stressed in this book that making generalizations about supervisors—and their training needs—is a misleading, and often costly, practice. Nevertheless, it is helpful to look at manifest differences in various segments of the supervisory population.

Surprisingly, the National Survey of Supervisory Management Practices (NSSMP) turned up few dramatic differences among the principal minorities—blacks and women. Its major lines of demarcation were, as noted earlier, between blue- and white-collar supervisors, between first- and second-level supervisors, and between those with maximum and minimum education. There was little differentiation, also, between "older" and "younger" supervisors strictly on an age basis. When age was related to *length of time as a supervisor,* however, especially duration of supervisory service with the same employer, there were significant differences in supervisors' perceptions of the job and its requirements, as well as in their attitudes toward it. Accordingly, it apparently does make sense to at least separate training needs into two experience classes: (1) needs of supervisors with under, say, five years of experience and (2) needs of those with more time on the job than that. In chapter 8, this distinction will be reflected by classifying supervisory training as either "basic" or "advanced" (often "introductory" or "refresher," although the latter term is frequently a euphemism for "back to basics").

Analysis of the NSSMP supervisory population according to their perceived needs for further training in eighteen designated skill areas showed significant (if not large) differences according to twenty-four paired classifications of supervisors: blue-collar/white-collar, first-level/second-level, least/most educated, male/female, white/nonwhite, under fifty/over fifty, union/nonunion employees, production/accounting/sales/engineering functions supervised, manufacturing/banking/institutional/government environments, and would/would not return to the ranks.[1] These data appear in table 6-1. The eighteen designated skill areas may be used as a basis for needs-inventory surveys, since the NSSMP data provide benchmark rankings for comparison purposes.

TABLE 6-1
A NEEDS INVENTORY USED NATIONALLY TO IDENTIFY AND RANK SUPERVISORY-TRAINING REQUIREMENTS

Supervisors' Confidence in Their Abilities to Handle Important Job Activities

	Average		For 24 Paired Categories of Supervisors Percent with High* Degree of Confidence													
			BC/WC		Level		Education		Sex		Race		Age		U/NU	
Important job activities	**Rating** Percent with high* degree of confidence	**Ranking** From most to least confidence	Blue-collar	White-collar	1st-level	2nd-level	Least educated 7–12 years	Most educated 16–20 years	Male	Female	White	Non-white	Under 50 years	Over 50 years	Non-union employees	Union employees
Talk to employees on a one-on-one basis	88	1	88	90	87	92	86	90	89	86	89	86	88	88	89	88
Maintain harmony within your department	80	2	79	80	78	82	79	79	80	77	80	80	79	78	78	80
Solve departmental problems as they arise	78	3	77	81	75	85	74	84	81	75	79	71	80	78	76	80
Conduct a group meeting in your department	76	4	72	83	71	85	65	86	77	74	74	72	76	74	70	79
Attain departmental goals set by the company	75	5	73	78	72	81	72	79	76	74	76	71	75	76	74	77
Plan and control use of personal time	72	6	66	75	71	75	70	76	73	73	73	69	72	75	72	74
Enforce disciplinary rules	72	7	76	69	67	79	74	68	69	68	73	70	72	72	74	72
Conduct an effective performance appraisal	72	8	71	74	70	76	70	74	73	70	73	72	73	71	69	73
Sell your ideas to your boss	69	9	67	72	68	75	66	74	70	68	70	65	71	65	69	71
Motivate employees	68	10	69	68	64	75	66	70	70	64	68	70	68	67	67	69
Write clear memos, letters and reports	68	11	61	76	66	72	54	82	67	70	68	65	69	67	64	70
Develop new ideas for improving productivity	67	12	66	67	62	74	61	71	68	61	66	67	67	66	66	67
Explain benefit program to employees	56	13	58	54	51	66	57	52	56	53	55	61	54	62	50	58
Use statistical techniques	51	14	53	51	49	57	49	54	54	44	52	58	52	52	51	51
Explain computer inputs and outputs for your department	47	15	39	54	45	51	38	54	47	47	47	48	49	40	39	51
Enforce OSHA rules and regulations	45	16	54	35	43	50	52	35	47	41	44	51	43	54	52	43
Counsel an employee who abuses alcohol or drugs	39	17	44	35	36	45	40	37	42	32	39	54	39	39	41	39
Counsel an employee who will retire next year	36	18	39	32	32	42	37	33	36	31	35	41	33	45	38	34

*"High" (4) + (5) percent rating, where scale is:
(1) not confident
(2)
(3) somewhat confident
(4)
(5) very confident

Source: Reprinted with permission from Lester R. Bittel and Jackson E. Ramsey, "New Dimensions for Supervisory Development," *Training and Development Journal* (March 1983): 16.

DIAGNOSTIC TESTS OF SUPERVISORY NEEDS

Aside from psychological tests, which are used infrequently for needs diagnosis, many organizations do employ objective tests (such as multiple choice and true-false), narrative exercises, and simulations for supervisory needs determination.

OBJECTIVE TESTS

In some programs, the training professional administers a general pretest of, say, from twenty to one hundred questions before launching the training program. If the questions are coded according to knowledge or skill areas, then analyzing summaries of correct and incorrect answers will reveal skill areas that are in good form or are deficient. Trainers typically utilize the standardized test banks that accompany a great many supervision texts. Obviously, if a parallel test is administered upon completion of the program or course, a comparison between pre- and posttest scores provides an indication of learning acquired.

The same concept is also used for specific skill areas. AT&T, to cite a good example, has a carefully designed quantitative test for each of its fourteen "duties," or competencies. One of these tests appears in the box on pages 68–69. Each question is keyed to a specific skill, knowledge, or process step associated with the duty under analysis (planning, in this case).

NARRATIVE EXERCISES

While narrative exercises are not often used and their interpretation is somewhat difficult to validate, some companies do explore supervisors' feelings of where their major problems and/or shortcomings lie by asking them to write a brief piece focusing on difficulty or proficiency areas. For example, in this "Good Times and Bad Times at Work" exercise, one company asks that the supervisor write a narrative according to the following set of instructions:

> Most people have had times in their working experience when they felt either very good or very bad about their work. Try to recall a couple of those times from your own experience.
>
> Please write a brief description of something that made you feel exceptionally *good* about your work. It may have made you feel good for just an hour or perhaps a day or maybe for much longer. What was the incident or the occurrence? That is, what was it that happened that made you feel very good about your work?
>
> Now, please write a brief description of something that made you feel very *bad* about your work.

SIMULATION EXERCISES

A few companies, notably AT&T, use variations of business games, simulations, in-basket exercises, and the like to diagnose and identify supervisory-training needs. In the AT&T simulation exercise for the planning duty, for example, there are sixteen assignments, each related to one or more knowledge, skill, or process steps associated with planning and controlling.

Sample Diagnostic Test of Supervisory-Training Needs in Planning

1. From the list below, what are the five activities that should always be performed to plan work successfully? (X-out the five activities on the answer sheet.)

   a. check with the boss

   b. document plan

   c. consult with other work groups

   d. determine alternative methods

   e. determine resources available

   f. determine what the work should accomplish

   g. determine resources needed

   h. identify checkpoints

2. Sequence your five choices from question 1 in the order in which they should be performed to plan work successfully. (Write the letter of each statement you selected from question 1 in the correct order on the answer sheet.)

3. How should you go about determining whether a task is your responsibility or not? (X-out the three best answers on the answer sheet.)

   a. check with your subordinates

   b. read Bell System Practices and/or local practices

   c. carefully consider the situation and make your own judgment

   d. consult your supervisor

   e. check with the methods group

   f. ask anyone who has previously held your position

4. Good planning is important because it guarantees (X-out the best choice to complete the statement on the answer sheet):

   a. meeting objectives for your work or office

   b. subordinate productivity

   c. the availability of information to monitor the progress of a job

   d. that jobs are completed early or on schedule

5. What is the best way to ensure that a job is completed efficiently? (X-out the best answer on the answer sheet.)

   a. weighing alternatives carefully

   b. discussing plans with your supervisor

   c. preparing a detailed budget

   d. performing the job as in the past

Continued on next page

Sample Diagnostic Test of Supervisory-Training Needs in Planning—*Continued*

e. predetermining a course of action

6. It is necessary to plan when (X-out the choice[s] to complete the statement on the answer sheet):

   a. work is generated by your boss

   b. work is generated by other departments

   c. unanticipated events interfere with current plans

   d. job objectives are received from the boss

   e. you want to achieve personal objectives

7. When you are planning work for which there are no standards (e.g., no quantity or quality measurements), you must develop your own standards. (X-out *T* for True or *F* for False on the answer sheet.)

8. No information exists for planning a particular job you have been assigned. What should you do next? (X-out the correct answer on the answer sheet.)

   a. document your reasons for stopping the job

   b. go ahead as best you can

   c. consider data on similar types of jobs

   d. give the job back to the person who assigned it

   e. put the job aside and come back to it later

9. You have no information or limited information about a particular task. What are seven sources from which you can obtain relevant information? (List seven sources on the answer sheet.)

10. You have been given an unfamiliar task. What are eight kinds of information needed to plan the task? (List the eight kinds of information on the answer sheet.)

11. Your boss assigns a job to you. You investigate all possible sources of information. You still do not have enough information to plan the job. What should you do next? (Write your answer on the answer sheet.)

Answer Key

1. a ~~b~~ c d ~~e~~ ~~f~~ ~~g~~ ~~h~~

2. 1st F 2nd G 3rd E
   4th H 5th B

3. a ~~b~~ c ~~d~~ e ~~f~~

4. a b ~~c~~ d

5. a b c d ~~e~~

6. ~~a~~ ~~b~~ ~~c~~ ~~d~~ ~~e~~

7. ~~T~~ F

8. a b ~~c~~ d e

Continued on next page

Sample Diagnostic Test of Supervisory-Training Needs in Planning—*Continued*

9. (1) BSP'S
   (2) SUBORDINATES
   (3) PRACTICES
   (4) HISTORICAL DATA
   (5) PEERS
   (6) S.M.E.
   (7) BOSS
   (8) PRIOR INCUMBENT
   (9) CUSTOMERS
   (10) METHODS/STAFF

10. (1) HOW LONG JOBS TOOK
    (2) WHAT RESOURCES WERE USED
    (3) TECH. COMPETENCY & TRAINING BACKGROUND OF SUBS.
    (4) UNUSUAL OBSTACLES
    (5) CONTINGENCIES TAKEN
    (6) OBJECTIVES—QUALITY, QUANTITY, TIME
    (7) TIME AVAILABLE
    (8) SOURCES OF INFORMATION ABOUT TASK

11. CONSULT YOUR BOSS ON HOW TO CONTINUE

Source: Reprinted with permission from Charles R. Macdonald, *Performance Based Supervisory Development: Adapted from a Major AT&T Study* (Amherst, Mass.: Human Resources Development Press, 1982), 42–43.

NEEDS INVENTORIES

The most common approach in designing supervisory-training programs, however, is to rely on an assessment of needs (made judgmentally) either by the managers to whom supervisors report, by human resources development (HRD) professionals, by the supervisors themselves, or by some combination of these three. Occasionally, employees will also be asked to contribute to this assessment. Such needs assessments, or inventories, may be made by direct interview, by written survey, or through nominal group techniques (NGT), in which training needs are itemized and ranked in group sessions conducted by HRD professionals. Burack[2] cautions that inventories consisting of self-assessments are liable to contain biases and should be subjected to "reality checks" from subordinates, peers, and superiors.

Traditional Needs Surveys

By far, the bulk of supervisory-training needs assessments are made using a standard needs-inventory survey form. Most of these question only the supervisory population, especially those who are candidates for a particular training program. Where the survey is also administered to the supervisors' superiors, results are likely to differ, sometimes significantly. Perspectives from above and below *are* different. Superiors' judgements are likely to be critical and harshly prescriptive, especially when their observations are assured of anonymity. On the other hand, supervisors' perceptions are bound to be subjective. One is rarely the best judge of oneself, as illustrated by the Johari window, which shows four possible concepts of the self. It makes the point that one's perception of oneself is often far removed from another person's view and still further from one's true self, and is always influenced by what kind of person one would like to be.

In any event, needs surveys will not yield entirely clear-cut, reliable results. Often, however, they produce the best information that the training professional can find. Needs surveys are relatively inexpensive and are fairly good at pointing to areas where needs are either very high or very low.

Format. A traditional, simplified needs-inventory format and content are shown in the box on page 73. This form, developed by Training House,[3] asks that items be rated as follows: 3, "extremely important"; 2, "fairly important"; and 1, "not too relevant." Other formats offer space for suggesting training needs involving topics or areas not listed. At the risk of making the survey form too complicated, other interrogative headings may be added. For example:

- *Degree of training required:* (1) an overview; (2) detailed, in-depth, or intensive; (3) none at all
- *Type of improvement desired:* (1) knowledge; (2) skills; (3) attitudes, feelings, or perceptions
- *Method of training preferred:* (1) seminars; (2) workshops; (3) lecture by qualified staff person; (4) on-the-job; (5) reference materials for reading; and so on

Expanded Descriptions. The AT&T study team also observed that single-word headings or short phrases were not descriptive enough of the subject areas queried. Hence, for its fourteen "duties," AT&T provided an expanded description (specific to the company's competencies) and also mixed up the order in the questionnaire so as not to imply a preferred ranking of importance. Here, for example, are the descriptions used by AT&T in its diagnostic surveys:

> *Career Counseling* is helping subordinates achieve realistic personal job goals. It includes the planning of activities to help place subordinates in appropriate jobs.
>
> *Coaching Subordinates* is the process which includes activities to help subordinates learn to do a job correctly.
>
> The *Communication* process includes such activities as face-to-face contact, writing letters or memos, formal meetings, and telephone conversations. Communication is the exchange of opinions, ideas, facts, and/or feelings.
>
> *Controlling the Work* is applying the results of Planning to the people who will be doing the work and to the materials they will use. This includes assigning the work, checking its progress, and measuring the work.
>
> *Creating/Maintaining a Motivative Atmosphere* includes activities which may help a supervisor and subordinate work together, and activities which may lead to an environment conducive to efficient work.
>
> *Providing Performance Feedback* is informing subordinates how their job performance compares with job requirements so that future job requirements can be met or exceeded.

Meetings (Formal Oral Communication) includes one-to-one encounters or meetings with more than one person. It requires some preparation beforehand and/or some structure during the communication.

Informal Oral Communication is the kind of communication that takes place in an unstructured situation and requires little or no preparation.

Knowledgeable Representative of (company name): As a manager within the ________________, you are perceived as a representative of the________ by customers, neighbors, civic groups, and your subordinates. This process involves representing and sharing knowledge of________________ when appropriate.

Planning the Work is the process performed by the supervisor individually before implementing a course of action. The end result of the Planning process provides all the information needed to begin to manage an area of responsibility.

Problem Solving is a process used by a supervisor to solve day-to-day problems while managing work.

Self-Development is identifying own requirements for producing better results on the current job and implementing plans to meet those requirements.

Time Management is the scheduling of administrative responsibilities. It includes handling telephone calls, office paper flow, and work activities most efficiently.

Written Communication/Documentation includes activities such as writing letters, reports, or memos, and completing forms, or maintaining local documentation.[4]

Most training professionals agree with the AT&T study team that the reliability of needs surveys can be improved by clearer, fuller subject definition. Consequently, the trend in needs inventories is to expand definitions of the items in order to more clearly specify the areas of deficiency, as shown in the box on pages 74–75, developed by Langdon. A similar "explosion" of a needs item is shown in the box at the bottom of page 75, this one an inventory developed by Thomas and Sireno.

Explicit Instructions. Oppenheimer advises that supervisors need precise directions for completing needs questionnaires if the results are to be reliable. The final box, on page 76, illustrates the type of participant instructions that Oppenheimer has found to be particularly useful in gathering information from supervisors.

Standardized Questionnaires. A number of standardized needs-survey questionnaires are available from publishers. Their value is that findings may be compared with the results from other organizations that have used the same questionnaire. Their drawback is that they may not bear a good relationship to company-specific competencies.

Another way for an organization to obtain needs-assessment data is to use a standardized inventory instrument and compare the results with standards established for a national, industry, or functional data base. The survey instrument used by the Center for Supervisory Research at James Madison University (Harrisonburg, Virginia 22807), for example, is especially appropriate not only for determining current training needs but also for monitoring trends in supervisory attitude development.

Needs-Inventory Format

Respondents rate each item according to a scale of 3 "extremely important," 2 "fairly important," and 1 "not too relevant."

_______ Ability to set realistic goals and standards, define performance requirements, and develop action plans for achieving and for controlling (tracking) performance.

_______ Skill in communicating effectively in face-to-face situations—with subordinates, peers, superiors, customers, etc.

_______ Ability to conduct selection interviews in a way that produces the information needed to make sound hiring decisions consistent with company policy and the law.

_______ Skill in balancing daily activities between the demands of the task (production-oriented side) and of the employees (people-oriented side).

_______ Ability to challenge and motivate subordinates, thereby increasing their job satisfaction and developing a team of "turned on" employees.

_______ Skill in giving on-the-job training and counseling relating to behavior at work.

_______ Ability to appraise performance objectively and to conduct regular, constructive performance reviews that are two-way dialogs.

_______ Skill in writing letters, memos, and reports that are clear, concise, complete, and compelling . . . writing that gets action.

_______ Ability to manage time (of self and others) effectively by prioritizing, controlling interruptions, measuring cost-effectiveness, investing rather than spending time, etc.

_______ Skill in cutting costs through methods improvement, work simplification or reallocation, flow charting, analysis of procedures, etc.

_______ Ability to hold meetings, briefings, conferences that are well-organized, crisp, and results-oriented.

_______ Skill in negotiating and resolving conflict as it arises in interpersonal relations.

_______ Facility in interviewing in depth, drawing out what is and isn't said, summarizing and clarifying, and organizing the speaker's message so that it can be acted upon.

_______ Ability to identify problems, to separate causes from symptoms, to evaluate evidence, to weigh alternatives, and to select and implement appropriate solutions.

_______ Ability to make effective presentations and to sell ideas in a persuasive, well-documented manner—to management, to subordinates, to users.

Source: Adapted from Scott B. Parry and Edward J. Robinson, "Management Development: Training or Education?" *Training and Development Journal* (July 1979): 9–10.

Detailed Items for a Needs Inventory

1. Analyzing problems and making decisions:
   - ☐ a. Identify the problem and describe it clearly.
   - ☐ b. Determine whether or not the problem is worth spending time on.
   - ☐ c. Use a systematic approach to collect information.
   - ☐ d. Identify the most important characteristics that a solution should have.
   - ☐ e. Generate a series of possible solutions and select the one which best meets the needs. Consider the characteristics of each possible solution.
   - ☐ f. Prepare an effective action plan for the solution you select.
2. Conducting fact-finding discussions:
   - ☐ a. State the need or the information in such a way that the employee will be encouraged to provide what you need.
   - ☐ b. Indicate clearly the kind of information you want.
   - ☐ c. Probe for relevant information (both positive and negative) even though the employee may be reluctant to speak.
   - ☐ d. Uncover all the relevant data without creating hostility or distrust.
   - ☐ e. Record the facts you collect.
   - ☐ f. End the discussion so that the employee feels he or she has made a significant contribution.
3. Motivating:
   - ☐ a. Identify situations that result from motivational problems rather than from lack of skill or organizational support.
   - ☐ b. Identify causes of motivational problems.
   - ☐ c. Indicate clearly the behaviors that you want to motivate.
   - ☐ d. Develop a plan for removing de-motivating elements from the work environment.
   - ☐ e. Identify incentives in the work environment which can be used to motivate the employee.
   - ☐ f. Demonstrate how to give effective motivational feedback.
4. Dealing with emotional situations:
   - ☐ a. Face up to, rather than avoid or be intimidated by, emotional situations.
   - ☐ b. Recognize and avoid using "emotional blackmail" as a way of controlling others.

Continued on next page

Detailed Items for a Needs Inventory—*Continued*

- ☐ c. Demonstrate respect for the feelings of others.
- ☐ d. Handle emotional situations by calming.
- ☐ e. "Defuse" the emotions of others so that the real cause of problems can be uncovered.
- ☐ f. Avoid responses that escalate emotional behavior.

Source: Reprinted from Danny G. Langdon, "The Individual Management Development Program," *Training and Development Journal* (March 1982): 79.

"Exploded" Items Categorized for a Major Segment of a Needs Inventory

Ranking of Control Competency Items from a Needs Survey

Competency Statement	Rank
1. Tactfully identify mistakes employees have made and help them constructively correct them.	8
2. Effectively handle the complaints of subordinates.	9
3. Follow proper channels of authority in the business organization.	10.5
4. Clearly define the duties of each individual and the standards of performance against which these are measured.	12
5. Develop and maintain effective control so that an orderly group effort results.	14
6. Identify any deviation from plans and take appropriate steps to correct the deviation.	15

Source: Adapted from Joe Thomas and Peter J. Sireno, "Assessing Management Competency Needs," *Training and Development Journal* (September 1980): 50.

Instructions for Participants Completing a Needs-Assessment Survey

The purpose of this form is to help identify what type of general training and/or development activities would be beneficial for our supervisory personnel to help them perform their jobs better. Since an overall evaluation of our training needs is sought and since we are anxious to ensure that the information provided is as complete and accurate as possible, you are not required to sign this form.

You are welcome to discuss your development needs with your immediate supervisor, as well as to retain a photocopy, should you wish to use this as part of your personal development plan in the future.

Specifically, what is requested is that for each of the skill and/or knowledge areas identified on the following pages, you answer the following four questions.

1. To what extent would training, designed to increase your skill or knowledge (for each particular area), help you to do your present job better and/or prepare you for other job responsibilities? Please use the following scale when answering in Column A of the attached form.

   1—Not at all helpful

   2—Somewhat helpful

   3—Reasonably helpful

   4—Considerably helpful

   5—Extremely helpful

2. In which of these major skill and knowledge areas would additional training or development be most helpful to you? Select only the five major areas (not sub-topics) that would be most desirable areas and rank them from 1 (most desired) to 5 (least desired). Please answer in Column B on the attached form.
3. What additional aspects would you like to see included in a training program and/or what other topics would you find helpful, if any? Please add your suggestions directly to the attached form.
4. Within each of the major skill and knowledge areas, please circle those sub-topics which are of particular interest or importance to you.

Source: Reprinted from Robert J. Oppenheimer, "An Alternative Approach to Assessing Management Development Needs," *Training and Development Journal* (March 1982): 74–76.

Part III

CREATING THE LEARNING ENVIRONMENT

Chapter 7

Laying the Groundwork for Learning

INTRODUCTION

From Aristotle and Euclid to the American philosopher John Dewey, educators have been advised to stick to the fundamentals. Pioneers of training and development like Skipper Allen and Glen Gardiner—as well as contemporary authorities like Donald L. Kirkpatrick, Brad Boyd, Clark Lambert, Martin Broadwell, Malcolm Knowles, Dugan Laird, and Gordon Lippitt—have advised trainers to respect the basic precepts of education and learning. Regardless of the subject matter or target population, anyone responsible for the design and implementation of supervisory training must keep those precepts in mind.

Before we look at theoretical principles, however, a hardheaded, practical overview may provide the clearest introduction to supervisory training. Stan Carnarius states flatly that those who train supervisors must first of all "be tough minded. . . . Try to turn your attention to what is going on in the minds of the learners. . . . After all, the purpose of the exercise is to benefit supervisors in a planned, effective way . . . so forget about yourself and get busy."[1] Carnarius puts his principles (paraphrased here) in simple language:

1. *Keep the inputs short.* Try not to lecture on one point for longer than twenty minutes or make more than six points in the same length of time. The attention of listeners wanders when you go beyond these limits.
2. *When an idea is new, allow for disorientation.* People defend themselves against new ideas, so when you get one to register, don't be surprised if they want to argue or get further clarification. Plan on it, welcome it, and help them "chew on it" so the idea digests better and more quickly.
3. *Practice reading the signs (getting feedback).* Watch for any indicators of what is going on inside the trainees' minds. Listen to what they say and try to understand what motivates their comments. Make yourself stop and listen. Slow down your tendency to defend yourself or your precious training program. Watch the nonverbal signs, too—heads leaning heavily on forearms, overly relaxed posture, avoiding your eyes, angry or defeated looks, and so on.
4. *When an idea has registered, try to apply it soon.* The best test of comprehension is use. Let supervisors see if they can actually use the concept. They often find there are a couple of points that need more explanation. Pro-

grammed instruction has conclusively proved the value of short steps of input, followed by application and feedback.

5. *When they have what they need, let them struggle.* After enough input to make the point clear, let supervisors try to put it into their own words or to get it to fit their own problems. Allow some frustration. Don't rush in right away with another explanation (in order to relieve your own uneasiness). Usually, supervisors come out of such frustration with a sense of discovery and accomplishment as they begin to get your material translated into their own types of situations.

6. *Don't be afraid to repeat yourself.* People become "ready" to learn at different rates. One person may get the point quickly; another may not hear it until the fourth or fifth repetition. Of course, as a courtesy to the quick learners, try to find slightly different ways to make your point each time so the repetition is not all that apparent.

The single biggest idea behind these admonitions is that all preparation and delivery of the training program should focus on the learning process and how it involves, or fails to involve and motivate, the supervisory participants. A preoccupation with course content will obscure the fact that learning is a very human activity and must proceed along psychologically—and sociologically—sound lines.

A CONCEPTUAL FRAMEWORK FOR SUPERVISORY DEVELOPMENT

The late Gordon L. Lippitt, who almost always advocated that supervisory training be viewed in an organizational behavior context, once cited the value of the training insights provided by the "path-goal" theories of development.[2] Robert J. House, the leading figure in this field, suggests a taxonomy, or systematic classification, of the "path-goal" variables affecting supervisory development. These are illustrated, first in a matrix of relationships in figure 7-1, then in a time-related dimension in figure 7-2. The core of House's taxonomy is the proposition that: "*For any given communication of information during the supervisor's learning process, a change in knowledge will be positively related to (1) the motivation to learn, (2) the ability to learn, (3) the amount of developmental effort the supervisor puts into the learning process, and (4) the supervisor's expectation that the skill or knowledge gained will be useful and rewarding to him or her.*" Thus, plans for supervisory training should take into account these four variables in particular. House adds many corollaries to his core principle. Most of them, however, focus on the need for proper preparation and motivation to learn, the inherent capability of the supervisor to assimilate the knowledge or skills inherent in the training being offered, the amount of real time and effort a supervisor is willing to devote to the training program, and what he or she expects to get from the training in the way of promotions, salary increases, job confidence, and other benefits from improved performance. The trainer's role, as House sees it, is that of (1) making certain that supervisors understand the path they must follow to their reward goals and

FIGURE 7-1 VARIABLES IN MANAGEMENT AND SUPERVISORY DEVELOPMENT PROGRAMS

	OUTPUTS I	II	III	IV	V
INPUTS	Desired change in knowledge	Desired change in attitude	Desired change in skill	Desired change in job performance	Unintended conflict, anxiety, or frustration
Participant and group characteristics	Motivation to learn Sufficient IQ	Col. I Plus	Col. II Plus	Col. III Plus	Insufficient IQ to attain knowledge objective or inability to develop skills to desired level
		Low ego involvement in subject matter being taught	Nonconflicting habits or personality traits		
Development effort	Direct method of instruction (programmed learning, lectures, films, readings, and so on) Competent instruction	Discussion of on-the-job applications and personal benefits	Practice of desired abilities Corrective training to extinguish undesirable habits and behavioral patterns	Opportunity for on-the-job practice of newly acquired abilities and for feedback of results	
Exercise of authority by superior		Neutral or positive attitude of superior toward development	Superior's attitude and example consistent with desired change.	Coaching, counseling and periodic performance review by superior consistent with desired performance	Negative attitude or behavior of superior
Formal authority system		Goals, top management philosophy, and policies consistent with learning phase		Philosophy, practices, and precedents of the policy-making executives consistent with desired manager performance	Conflicting elements of formal authority system. e.g., punishment for achieving desired change, constraining policies and procedures.
Primary work group		Cultural conditions and social beliefs consistent with desired attitudes		Primary group norms consistent with desired change	Conflicting primary group norms

Source: As reported in Gordon L. Lippitt, *A Handbook for Visual Problem Solving* (Bethesda, MD: Development Publications, 1973), 107.

then (2) easing or "facilitating" their progress up the path, providing the supervisors are willing to do their part.[3]

House also cautions about attitudinal changes organizations often hope will result from supervisory training. He observes that the supervisors' boss will have an important influence, depending upon the superior's own attitude and example. This is one reason it is wise to expose supervisors' bosses to training (in so-called appreciation sessions) before presenting the program to the supervisors. House also concludes that the extent of attitude change on the supervisors' part will be inversely proportional to their initial ego involvement in the changes proposed. Said in a simpler way, the more deeply en-

FIGURE 7-2 A MODEL OF THE DEVELOPMENT PROCESS

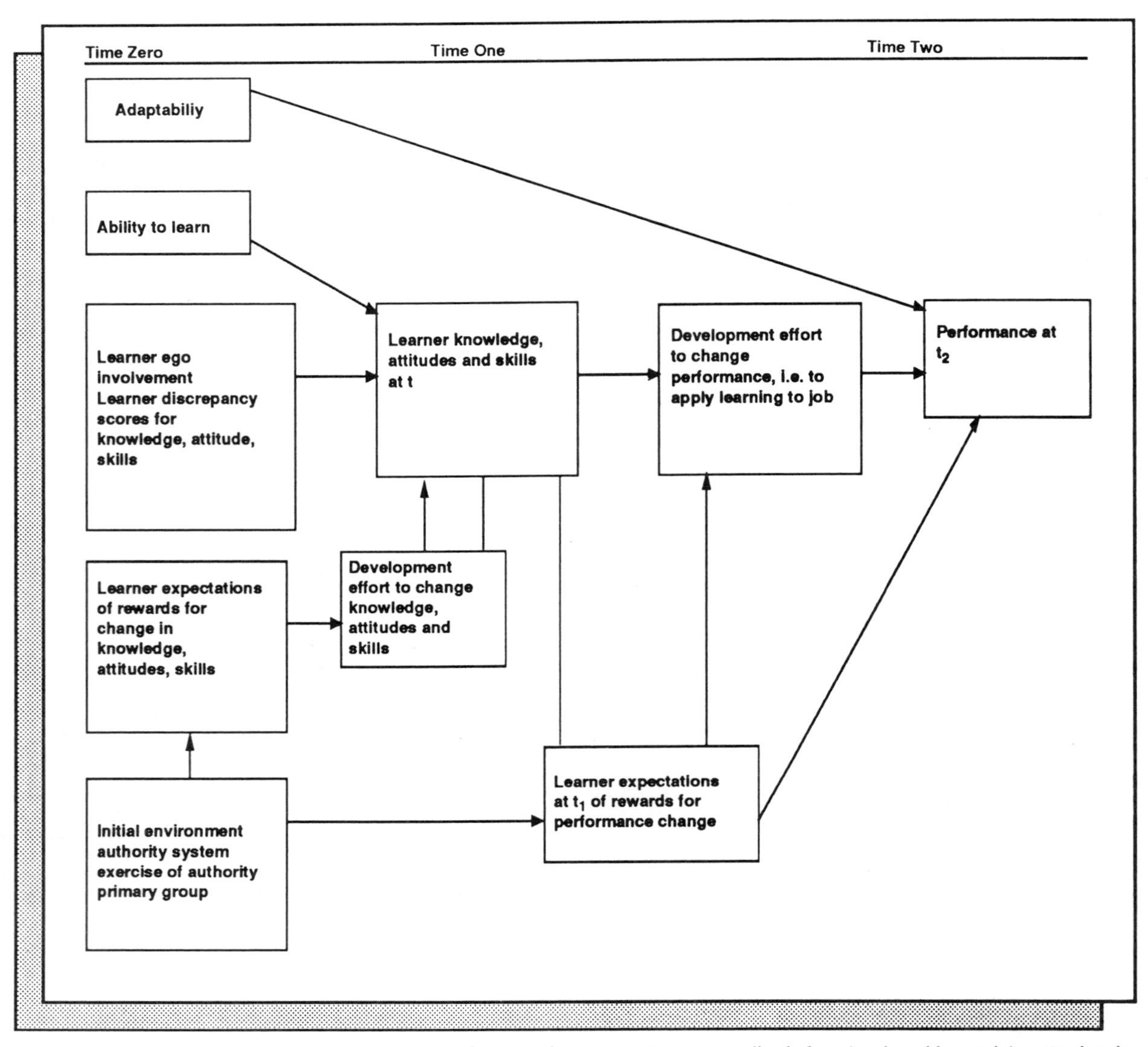

Source: As reported in Gordon L. Lippitt, *A Handbook for Visual Problem Solving* (Bethesda, MD: Development Publications, 1973), 108.

trenched the attitude, the more difficult it will be for the trainer to effect a change, especially if no face-saving mechanism is provided for the supervisor.

Figure 7-1 shows how several variables, or "inputs"—the supervisors' exercise of authority, the way in which formal authority is handled in the organization, and the norms or "culture" of the supervisors' work group—will produce specific "outputs" in the form of different training results. Figure 7-2 arranges these developmental variables according to time. It shows how the supervisors' adaptability, ability to learn, ego involvement, extent of learning gaps, and expectation of rewards, as well as the organization's environmental conditions, are all important *starting variables;* while the supervisors' development effort and expectations become critical *during the middle part* of the learning process. This model implies that supervisors must (1) persist in their efforts to apply what they have learned after the formal training period is over and (2) continue to believe in the ultimate rewards if they are to actually improve their job performance.

Distinguishing Learning from Performance

The goal of training and development is improved supervisory performance, and most organizations view training as merely a means to this end. Learning provides an individual with the potential to perform better; performance is the evidence that the potential has been realized. This distinction is significant, and it will affect the effectiveness of supervisory-training programs and those who participate in them. To differentiate:

- *Learning* involves the acquisition of knowledge, skills, and attitudes associated with a particular job competency.
- *Performance* involves application of the knowledge, skills, and attitudes and demonstrates mastery of the particular supervisory competency.

Important Aspects of the Training Process

Each characteristic of the learning process takes on a unique significance in planning supervisory training. The following precepts hold true:

- *The training must be purposeful and serve to further the supervisors' and the organization's goals.*
- *The training must include opportunities for gaining experience.* This experience may be simulated or "live," but all material included in the program should be as realistic as possible, meaningful in terms of the supervisors' experience, and appropriate to the job.
- *The training methods must be varied and must touch as many of the senses as possible.* To this end, psychologists sometimes classify learning according to types: verbal, conceptual, motor, problem-solving, and emotional.
- *The training must be an active process.* Remember the old adage that "training is caught, not taught." Learning involves reciprocal communication in which both trainees and instructor participate.

KNOWLEDGE, SKILLS, AND ATTITUDES

As illustrated in figure 7-3, people acquire knowledge, skills, and attitudes from the learning process. For each of a supervisor's competencies, it is possible, although not always easy, to define the necessary *skills* as well as the *knowledge* required to apply those skills. It is usually even more difficult to define the appropriate attitudes or the training methods needed to gain acceptance and internalization of those attitudes. Many supervisory-training programs provide instruction and learning experiences in knowledge and skills but stop short of stimulating the required attitudinal changes.

FIGURE 7-3 THE THREE ZONES OF THE SUPERVISORY LEARNING EXPERIENCE

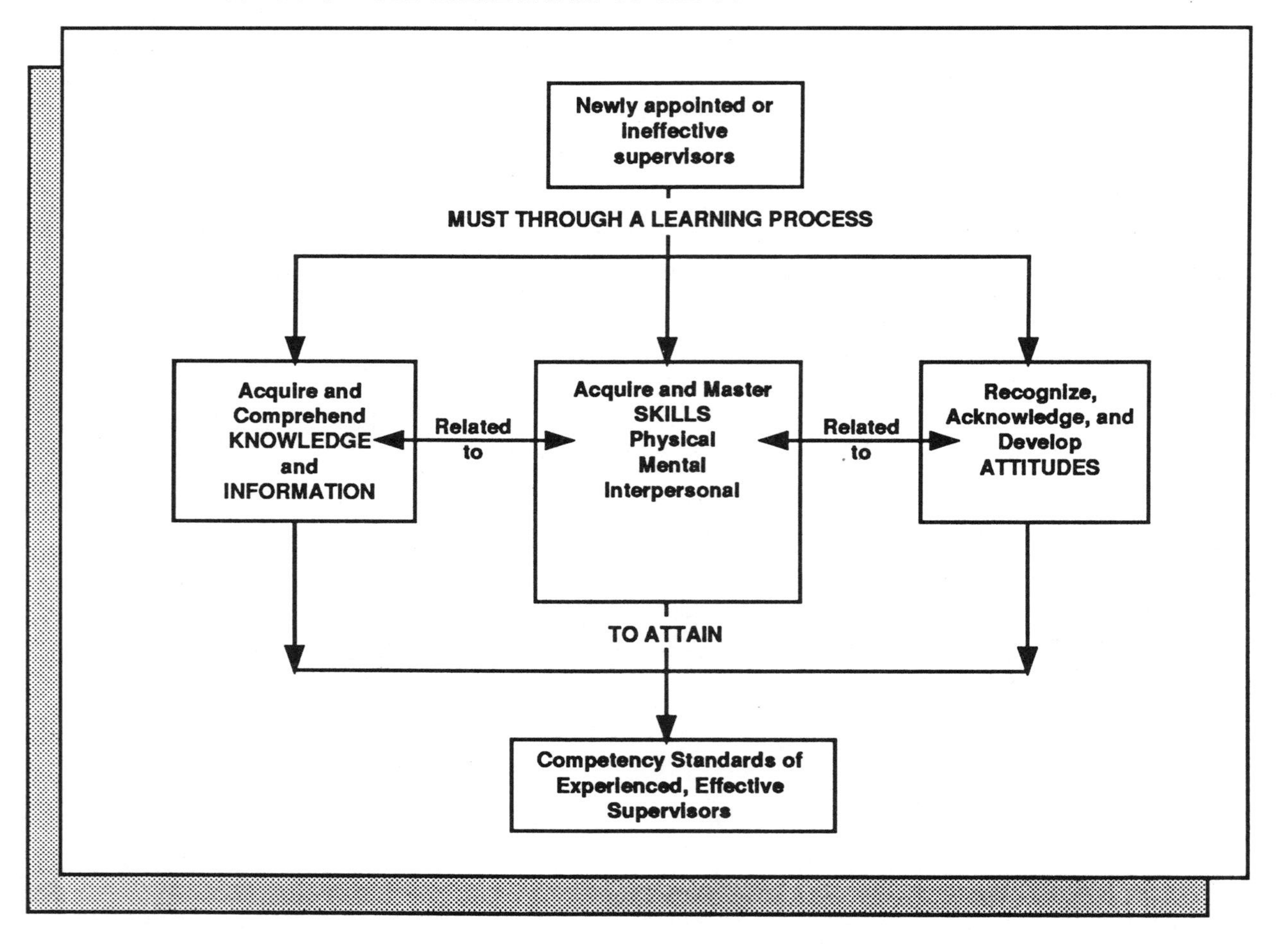

How Supervisors Acquire Knowledge

The teaching of knowledge is so commonly practiced in elementary and secondary schools that many of us have come to take the process for granted. Knowledge acquisition requires from the trainee (1) an attentive and receptive perception or mind-set, (2) a brain with the capability of absorbing and comprehending the knowledge content (a capability related to those abstract and conceptual abilities measured by IQ tests), (3) a retentive memory, along with (4) the ability to scan that memory and retrieve pertinent data from it.

Obviously, each of these factors varies somewhat within an individual supervisor and widely among all supervisors. We all know of people with good minds who are inattentive or who reject sound information because of rigid mind-sets. We know of others who have keen minds but whose memories are poor or retrieval systems are sluggish. Most supervisory selection procedures tend to screen out individuals with inadequate ability to assimilate knowledge. Many supervisors, however, do have a limited capacity to handle abstractions and are more comfortable with concrete specifics. This is often a restraining factor in development that emphasizes knowledge and comprehension.

Training programs can do much to encourage an attentive mind-set. It helps to schedule programs at the beginning, rather than the end, of the day. Fresh air and coffee breaks help to relieve boredom. Most important of all, perhaps, the supervisors must understand the program's relevance to their job and career. In House's vernacular, the expectation of rewards should outweigh the anticipated effort that the learning requires.

How Supervisors Acquire Skills

Most supervisors find it relatively easy to acquire skills, whether physical, mental, or interpersonal—although gaining the latter is by far the most difficult. They also usually require a context of knowledge and understanding of why and where they should apply these mental skills. Researchers in skills training have concluded that the acquisition of skills occurs in three phases:

1. *The knowledge phase,* wherein the trainees learn what to know, what to expect, how to do it, how well it must be done, and most of all, where things might go wrong and how to avoid having them go wrong. In other words, the negative instruction—what not to do—is almost as important as the more obvious, positive instruction. Good performance should be reinforced, of course, but supervisors should also be alerted to the pitfalls involved in practicing the skills.
2. *The acquisition phase,* wherein the trainees learn the correct patterns of behavior, mainly through demonstration of the skill and through imitating and practicing it until it is "fixed" in the mind and reflexes. The success of behavioral modeling of interpersonal skills for supervisors is based on such demonstration and imitation rather than on knowledge and comprehension.
3. *The automatic phase,* wherein the trainees gradually pick up speed and accuracy and then, through practice, develop a consistency and rhythm. Feedback about performance is especially important at this phase. Otherwise, trainees may get a mistaken idea about how good they really are. They need correction and help in identifying where their skills are weak and in developing ways to strengthen these areas—through practice on or off the job. Unfortunately, the automatic phase of supervisory training is more often than not outside the realm of the professional trainer's control. It is more likely to be the supervisors' bosses who must make certain the practice takes place and be on hand to coach and counsel.[4]

In general, training programs for developing supervisory skills should always:

- *Provide a clear-cut pattern to follow.* Step-by-step procedures are just as helpful for supervisory skills learning as they are for manual skills.
- *Provide opportunities to practice the skill without penalty for mistakes.* Classroom or workshop exercises, such as case analysis and role-play, enable supervisors to discover points of misunderstanding or shortcomings and to remedy them before attempting to apply the learning back on the job.
- *Provide prompt information about results.* In learning complex skills like those associated with supervisory development, the communications and feedback process is subtle. Cause-and-effect relationships are often not apparent or directly linked. Here again, the greater the degree of feedback during the course of the training program, the greater the chance that supervisors will experiment and apply the skills back on the job, where feedback may be less systematic.

FIGURE 7-4 THE CLASSIC LEARNING (OR EXPERIENCE) CURVE

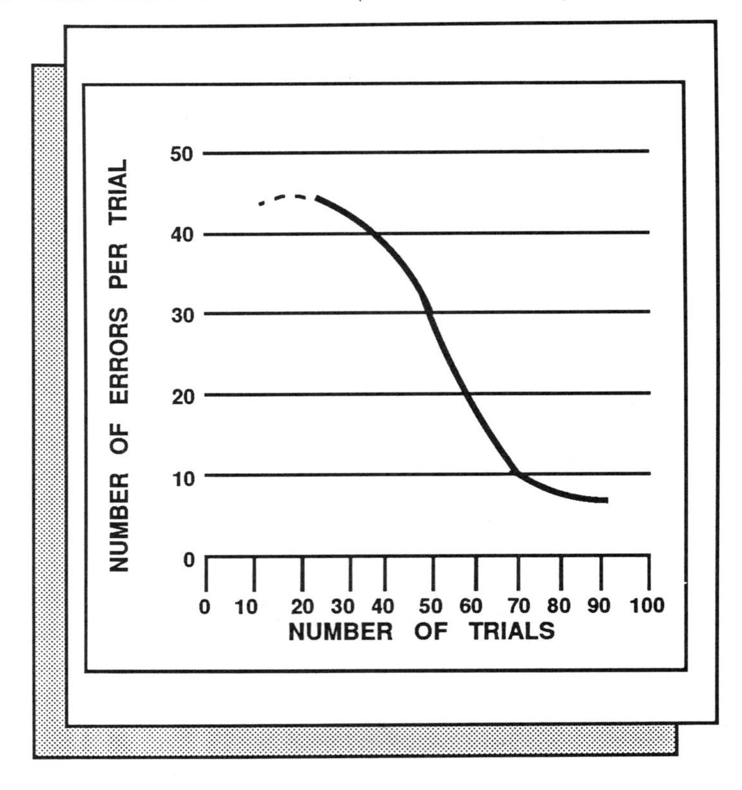

- *Recognize that progress follows a pattern.* The so-called experience curve or learning curve in figure 7-4 illustrates the typical learning pattern. There is rapid improvement in the early trials, but the curve then levels off and may stay level for a long time. Further improvement may seem unlikely to both trainer and trainees. Such a *learning plateau* may signify one or more of several conditions: the trainees may have reached the limits of their capability, be consolidating their level of skill, be losing interest, or need a more efficient training method for further progress. Keep in mind that the apparent lack of increase in proficiency does not necessarily mean that learning has ceased. The point is that a leveling-off process in learning skills is normal and should be expected after an initial period of rapid gains. You can prepare the trainees for this situation so as to ward off frustration and keep them trying to master the skill. Such preparation is vital in persuading supervisors to persist in applying interpersonal skills, where results are often discouraging.

- *Focus on applications.* Many supervisors will take a sort of academic pride in having acquired a new skill. Yet they may then fail to apply this skill where it matters most—on the shop or office floor. Trainers can therefore help to minimize this failure to transfer skills to the cutting edge of the supervisors' job by (1) pressing for a mastery that becomes so habitual and internalized that the skill becomes part of the natural behavior pattern and (2) building into the training program the kind of knowledge and understanding that enables supervisors to recognize the situations that are appropriate to the use of the particular skill.

How Supervisors Acquire Attitudes

Experts agree that attitudes are learned. Unfortunately for supervisory training, many have been learned and become deeply ingrained before supervisors enter development programs. Accordingly, the challenge for professional trainers is to find ways to change already existing attitudes. While this is not the place to digress too far on the subject of values and attitudes, a few generalizations may serve to identify the problem and to suggest some productive approaches for inducing attitudinal change.

Attitudes are a system of beliefs. They cause a person to feel "warm" or "cold" toward a person, an idea, or a situation. Attitudes are commonly expressed in terms of likes and dislikes.

Values are similar to attitudes, but these beliefs are deeply held and central. Values usually represent an ideal, such as a standard of conduct. They are hard to observe and usually do not involve tangible things like an automobile or people. Attitudes stem from values; thus, a supervisor's materialistic *value* might produce an *attitude* of disdain for people who put off buying a new automobile "because the old one will do."

The underlying principle for trainers to recognize and integrate into supervisory training is that *values serve as motivators, which induce attitudes, which in turn determine behavior.* A change in behavior, then, requires a change in attitude toward that behavior. If the attitude impinges upon a strongly held value, it will require a change in the supervisor's value system. That's a tall order for any training director. Nevertheless, being aware of these complexities may at least help us avoid promising too many changes from training.

Attitudinal Change. Attitudes are said to have three components: *knowledge* (what a person knows and believes about a particular subject), *emotion* (how a person feels about the subject, often in terms of like and dislike), and *action* (how a person behaves as a result—how the person expresses or displays his or her feelings).

Attitudes can be changed in either of two basic ways:

1. *Coercion*—such as through a reward and punishment system or through imposition of norms by the peer group. Coercion may be effective in the short run; in the long run, it is likely to fail and even to be counterproductive.
2. *Participation*—such as through supervisory involvement (especially in planning procedural change and suggesting ways to implement it) and through obtaining a commitment to something new. Participation-induced change is more likely to be evolutionary than dramatic, and time is the important ingredient.

Strategies for Change. Whatever strategy for attitudinal change is chosen, Davies advises, the approach must be systematic, because "People find ways of ignoring or reinterpreting what is happening." Instead of frontal attacks on a supervisor's values, Davies recommends these three more gradual approaches:

- *Imitation or modeling.* The role models, of course, must be respected and their behavior credible. And the models should project the belief that their "good" behavior has been rewarded.
- *Association or contiguity.* This approach involves creating an environment wherein exposure to the required attitude can be associated with a pleasant

situation or experience. If the training session is conducted under comfortable, cheerful, pleasant, nonthreatening conditions, the new attitudes are more likely to be accepted as rewarding.

- *Reinforcement or feedback.* Let the trainees know that their changed attitude (as reflected in improved behavior and performance) has been observed and is appreciated. Generally speaking, positive feedback is more effective than negative feedback, which tends to place pressure on the supervisors to defend their value system.[5]

Organization Development Techniques. Attitude changes can also be stimulated by following the basic organization development process used to induce change:

- *Unfreezing attitudes* by (1) inducing a feeling of uncertainty (or anxiety) about the appropriateness of the present behavior (a supervisor blowing his or her top, for example), (2) demonstrating that the present behavior is nonproductive through a focus on its outcome (such as a demotivated employee), and (3) removing procedural and psychological barriers to change (such as suggesting that the company is about to modify the policies that precipitated a particular incident).
- *Introducing change* through instruction, imitation, association, and reinforcement. At this stage, attitudes are notably unstable; consequently, the final phase becomes very important.
- *Freezing the desired attitude* in the supervisors' behavior pattern by (1) reinforcement and feedback, (2) helping the supervisors to see the benefits generated through the changed attitude and resultant behavior, and (3) encouraging the supervisors to persist in the behavior (which reinforces the attitude) until the attitude has become internalized and the behavior reflexive.

LAWS OF LEARNING: A REFRESHER

Professor Edward L. Thorndike of Teachers College, Columbia University, New York, was one of the pioneers in educational psychology. Early in this century, Thorndike postulated several "laws" of learning. In the years since, other psychologists have found that learning is a more complex process than some of these "laws" suggest. But while Thorndike's laws have some exceptions, they still provide valuable insight into the learning process.

The "laws" that follow are not necessarily as Thorndike stated them. During the years, they have been restated and supplemented, but in essence, they may still be attributed to him.

1. *Law of readiness.* People learn best when they are ready to learn. They do not learn much if they see no reason for learning. Supervisors with a strong purpose, clear objectives, and valid reasons for learning something make more progress than if they lack motivation. Readiness implies a degree

of single-mindedness and eagerness. When supervisors are ready to learn, they meet the trainer halfway, and this simplifies the trainer's job.

Under certain circumstances, the instructor can do little, if anything, to inspire a supervisor's readiness to learn. If outside responsibilities, interests, or worries weigh too heavily on the supervisor, if the schedule is overcrowded, if personal problems seem insoluble, a supervisor may have little interest in learning. Health, finances, or family affairs can also overshadow a person's desire to learn.

2. *Law of exercise.* Those things most often repeated are best remembered. It is the basis of practice and drill. The human memory is subject to error. The mind can rarely retain, evaluate, and apply new concepts or practices after a single exposure. Supervisors do not learn a new budgeting procedure at one sitting. They learn by applying what has been told, and every time they practice, their learning continues. Instructors must provide opportunities for supervisors to practice or repeat new skills and must see that this process is directed at a goal. Repetition can be of many types, including recall, review, restatement, manual drill, and physical application.

3. *Law of effect.* Learning is strengthened when accompanied by a pleasant or satisfying feeling, and learning is weakened when associated with an unpleasant feeling. An experience that produces feelings of defeat, frustration, anger, confusion, or hopelessness in the learner is unpleasant. If an instructor attempts to teach intricate procedures to a supervisor who does not know the basic procedures, the trainee is likely to feel inferior and be dissatisfied. As a demonstration that shows the trainee his or her ultimate goal, the intricate procedures might help motivate. But as material to be learned immediately, they might frustrate. In terms of the learning objective, this latter experience would be unpleasant.

4. *Law of primacy.* Primacy, the state of being first, often creates a strong, almost unshakable impression. For the instructor, this means that what is taught must be correct the first time. Correcting erroneous learning is more difficult than teaching it right the first time. Especially in teaching interpersonal skills, where ambiguity and contingencies abound, it is better to go slowly and carefully than to plunge ahead so as to cover more ground. First experiences should be positive and functional so they lay the foundation for all that is to follow.

5. *Law of intensity.* A vivid, dramatic, or exciting learning experience teaches more than a routine or boring experience. Supervisors will often learn more about fire fighting from watching a fire demonstration than from listening to a lecture on the subject, for example. The law of intensity implies that trainees will learn more from the real thing than from a substitute. Mock-ups, movies, charts, posters, photographs, and other audiovisual aids, as well as interactive computer exercises, add vividness to instruction. Demonstrations also intensify the learning experience of trainees.

6. *Law of recency.* Other things being equal, the things most recently learned are the things best remembered. Conversely, the further in time a trainee is removed from a new fact or procedure, the more difficulty he or she will have in remembering it. It is easy, for example, to recall a telephone number dialed a few minutes previously, but it is usually impossible to recall an unfamiliar number dialed a week earlier. Instructors recognize the law of recency when they carefully summarize the main points of a demonstration.

They repeat, restate, or reemphasize important points to make sure the supervisors remember them.

All the laws of learning are not apparent in every situation. These laws manifest themselves both singly and in clusters. When instructors understand the laws of learning, they can deal intelligently with motivation, participation, and individual differences, three major factors affecting learning.

Many of Thorndike's laws have been split apart or placed in different contexts. The box on page 91 restates the traditional laws of learning in the form of ten contemporary guidelines, or "commandments."

Dealing with Side Effects

The laws of learning, helpful as guiding principles, don't always allow for commonly encountered side effects of training, especially when training supervisors. These are, among others: (1) the problem of accommodating individual differences, (2) the difficulty some supervisors have in moving from the general to the specific or the reverse, (3) learning fatigue, (4) retention problems encountered by some individuals, and (5) the unfortunate fact that company and job procedures don't always flow in a sequence that is appropriate for training purposes (from easy to difficult and from simple to complex).

Accommodating Individual Differences. New instructors may be discouraged when they discover that a well-planned training session does not communicate to all supervisors with equal effectiveness. This is a natural and predictable state of affairs. Students of any class or culture or job function seldom learn at the same rate. Differences in rates of learning are based on differences in native intelligence, background, experience, interests, desire to learn, and countless other psychological, emotional, and physical factors.

Since supervisors do not learn at the same rate, it follows that their levels of understanding are not the same at any given moment. Supervisors do not all learn the same thing to the same degree.

An instructor can measure a supervisor's understanding or mastery of a lesson in several ways. Group discussions and question-and-answer sessions are generally reliable. Formal and informal tests or quizzes sometimes provide objective assessments. Informal talks or actual performance of the task also indicates a supervisor's progress.

After determining individual differences, good instructors attempt to compensate for them. They try to equalize the different levels of understanding—ideally, by raising the levels of some trainees without retarding the progress of others. This challenge can be met in a number of ways:

- The instructor can plan semi-independent activities in which the supervisor works alone or as part of a small group. The instructor is available to give help, but only when requested or needed. The trainee works on his or her own, aware that help is available if needed.
- The instructor can provide for supervised study, which requires his or her presence and guidance. The instructor gives personal and individual instruction where needed. This often reaches supervisors who hesitate to speak out before their coworkers but feel free to talk with their instructor.
- The instructor can also compensate for individual differences through flexible assignments in which the workload is adjusted to the capabilities of the individual.

Guidelines for Effective Training and Learning

1. *Learning involves attitudes* as well as knowledge and skills. People who want to learn will learn much faster than those who don't believe that the job is important or that learning will be of value to them.
2. *Learning is more effective when it touches all the senses.* It is important to use sight, hearing, touch—even smell and taste.
3. *Trainees who know in advance what is to be accomplished do better* than those who do not know what the expected outcome is to be. The trainer should set and explain the goal for each session.
4. *Training should proceed from the less difficult to the more difficult.*
5. *Learning takes place in "fits and starts" rather than smoothly.* It is normal for most people to learn a little bit quickly, then to go through a stage (or plateau) when no learning takes place. Trainers allow for this (absorption or rest) period before moving to the next higher level or speed.
6. *Learning goes better when there is timely "feedback" on how well trainees are doing.* The faster the correction or approval, the more certain it is that poor performance will be changed or good performance continued.
7. *Practice (repetition) does make perfect.* Trainees should be given enough time to form the "habit" of the operation so that they can do it without thinking.
8. *Learning sticks longer when trainees become involved*—with planning their training, making suggestions, asking questions, answering questions—and spend the training time doing rather than just listening or observing.
9. *Training is best when it provides a real challenge* to learners and yet is reasonably within their grasp. The goal should bring out the individuals' self-respect and sense of competition. It should not, however, be set so high that there is little real chance of attaining it.
10. *Each person is different from another. Each person learns at his or her own pace.* Each person finds some things easier—or more difficult—than others do. Training should therefore be personalized as much as possible to meet the needs of each individual.

Linking Generalizations to Specifics. Teaching for intellectual learning offers a challenge because this type of learning can only be inferred, not observed. A vast amount of literature on experimental psychology deals with the way people learn concepts and generalizations—the ideas to be known, understood, or applied. Briefly, a concept is a mental picture of a group of things with common characteristics. A generalization is a person's idea of the relationship between two or more concepts.

In preparing to train supervisors, it helps to examine the differences between concepts and generalizations—and their relationship to specifics—more closely:

- A *concept* is an abstract idea about a class of things. Concepts are formed by generalizing from one's experiences with one or more examples of a particular thing. Concepts represent concrete objects (computer, maintenance manual, employee) or abstract ideas (motivation, leadership, participation).

- A *generalization* is a statement of relationship (ordinarily, a statement about the relationship), usually of wide application. It is in most cases a statement about the relationship between two or more concepts. For example, a person may have formed the concepts of a grinding machine and of loudness. Through experience, he forms the generalization that grinding machines are loud. Not all generalizations are verbalized. A person may develop the generalization that a certain type of situation brings her satisfaction. She may seek out that situation but not know exactly why. It should be pointed out, of course, that the generalizations people form are not always true. Supervisors, like everyone else, sometimes have wrong ideas about the world in which they live and work.
- *Specifics* are concrete examples of concepts. They are usually visible, detailed, often quantified, frequently things that can be touched or manipulated. It is far easier to conceive of and deal with concepts and their related specifics than to understand and apply generalizations.

In supervisory training, a major obstacle occurs at the stage in which the supervisors must move from learning general principles to the specific behaviors that stem from those principles. For this reason, effective training relies heavily on the use of examples and illustrations. A generalization or principle must be illustrated by such examples as, "This is what happened to Marlene when she attempted to discipline one of her employees"; or, "Take the case of Peter, a supervisor in a grocery warehouse, who discovered that computer records of tonnage shipped did not match the tallies recorded by the shipping clerks."

A few other admonitions and suggestions should also be considered:

1. Guard against your trainees' accepting ready-made concepts or accepting the description of a concept from another person.
2. Reduce the concepts and generalizations taught so that the supervisors can thoroughly master what they do learn. There is little point in requiring them to memorize dozens of principles if they can realistically use only five. Teach those five principles so well that supervisors will always remember and use them.
3. Identify and organize typical experiences and examples that provide the basis for forming the concepts the trainees need. You can help supervisors organize their knowledge and identify the critical features of the desired concepts. As they develop greater experiential resources to draw on, they then reach the point where they can profit from vicarious experience: by listening to well-organized training presentations and by comparing experiences with other supervisors. The key word is *experience*. Provide practical and varied learning experiences so that supervisors can build a solid basis for their concepts. Provide sufficiently wide and significant experiences for them to develop clear and useful generalizations.

Minimizing Fatigue. As illustrated earlier, in figure 7-4, learning progress is also affected by boredom and fatigue. Especially among adult learners, fatigue manifests itself in the form of reduced concentration, a tendency to initiate off-subject or private conversations, horseplay, physical discomfort, and outright sleepiness. In planning the training session, follow these guidelines for minimizing boredom and fatigue:

- *Allocate the most exacting mental work for sessions early in the day.* (Or if the training session must take place late in the day or in the evening, schedule such work for early in the session.)
- *Plan to have the more interesting, entertaining exercises occur later in the day.* This tends to offer a form of relief and relevant, manageable diversion.
- *Structure instructional plans to incorporate a change of pace.* After an intensive hour of instruction, a less demanding subject can be introduced and allowed to proceed at a more leisurely pace.
- *Use a variety of training methods and activities.* Supervisory-training programs ought to combine small amounts of many techniques, such as lecture, discussion, role-play, buzz groups, report-back sessions, and outside speakers.
- *Provide periodic breaks.* Recognize human nature and allow participants free time to stretch, walk around, get some fresh air if possible, use the rest rooms, and enjoy a cup of coffee or a soft drink.

Improving Memory—Retention and Retrieval. Supervisors, like most people, remember meaningful information better than ideas and data that seem remote to their interests. Information that is presented so that it falls into an orderly pattern is easier to recall, too. Repetition, drill, and practice—although regarded as tiresome or childish by many supervisors—assures that information and skills are truly implanted in the mind. Mnemonic devices, acronyms, alliterations, rhymes, and association techniques are just as applicable for supervisory training as for an elementary-school class. The box on page 94 summarizes several widely used and effective techniques for aiding memory and recall.

Unscrambling Job Sequences to Facilitate Learning. The most logical way to provide instruction, especially in procedural skills, is to start with the simplest, least difficult concept and progress toward the most complex, most difficult concept. Unfortunately, few jobs and organizational procedures are structured that way. The task therefore falls upon the trainer to study and reorganize the job sequence before planning the training sequence. Typically, the presentation should reveal the total concept first so that supervisors get the big picture. That way, they can place each of the itemized skill-steps in context. A training progression that follows logical learning patterns is illustrated in figure 7-5.

JIT REVISITED

Few oversimplified concepts have ever had the impact of job instruction training (JIT). Conceived during a weekend at the summer home of Glenn Gardiner of the Forstman Knitting Mills and Channing Dooley of Standard Oil Company of New Jersey (now Exxon), the simple, four-step method for train-

How to Improve Supervisory Memory

Remembering improves when instructors emphasize:

- *Order, sequence, or place*
  Procedures, principles, components, and classifications depend upon order, sequence, or place. Memory devices like rhymes, mnemonics, catchy sentences, and stories help people remember.
- *Key points*
  Only a limited number of items can be transferred from one person's memory to another's at any given time. Material should therefore be reduced to "must knows." Distinguish the essential from the trivial.
- *Pattern or organization*
  Material that is organized into patterns is helpful. Diagrams, charts, tables, or other graphics aid people's memory.
- *Meaning*
  Material that is meaningful is better remembered than material that has little meaning. Try to make topics worthwhile and relevant to the learners. Stress importance.
- *Relationships in time and space*
  Material presented so that relationships are obvious is better remembered. Try to "key" material in to what the learners already know. Stress how one thing is related to another.

Source: Adapted with permission from Ivor K. Davies, *Instructional Techniques* (New York: McGraw-Hill Book Company, 1981), 256.

ing trainers was eventually used to train thousands of supervisors and hundreds of thousands of rank-and-file employees during World War II. The four steps are actually an amalgam of Thorndikes' laws of learning and educational precepts established by John Dewey, along with a philosophical underpinning from Aristotle's normal thought process (generally used elsewhere for problem-solving and decision-making models). The four steps (originally written on a reminder slip the size of a playing card) are: (1) prepare the worker, (2) demonstrate the job, (3) try the worker out, and (4) follow up.

MOTIVATION

The JIT program placed great emphasis on the first step: preparing the worker. Today, we know that motivation is the *sine qua non* ("without which, nothing") of adult (especially supervisory) training. The Department of the Army has spoken clearly on this subject, particularly in regard to supervisory training for its civilian employees:

> The factor that has perhaps the greatest influence on learning is motivation, the force that causes a person to move toward a goal. This force can be rooted in any or all of the personal-social needs of the supervisor; for example, the need for security, for new experience, for recognition, for self-esteem, for conformity,

FIGURE 7-5 REARRANGING THE JOB SEQUENCE FOR TRAINING PURPOSES

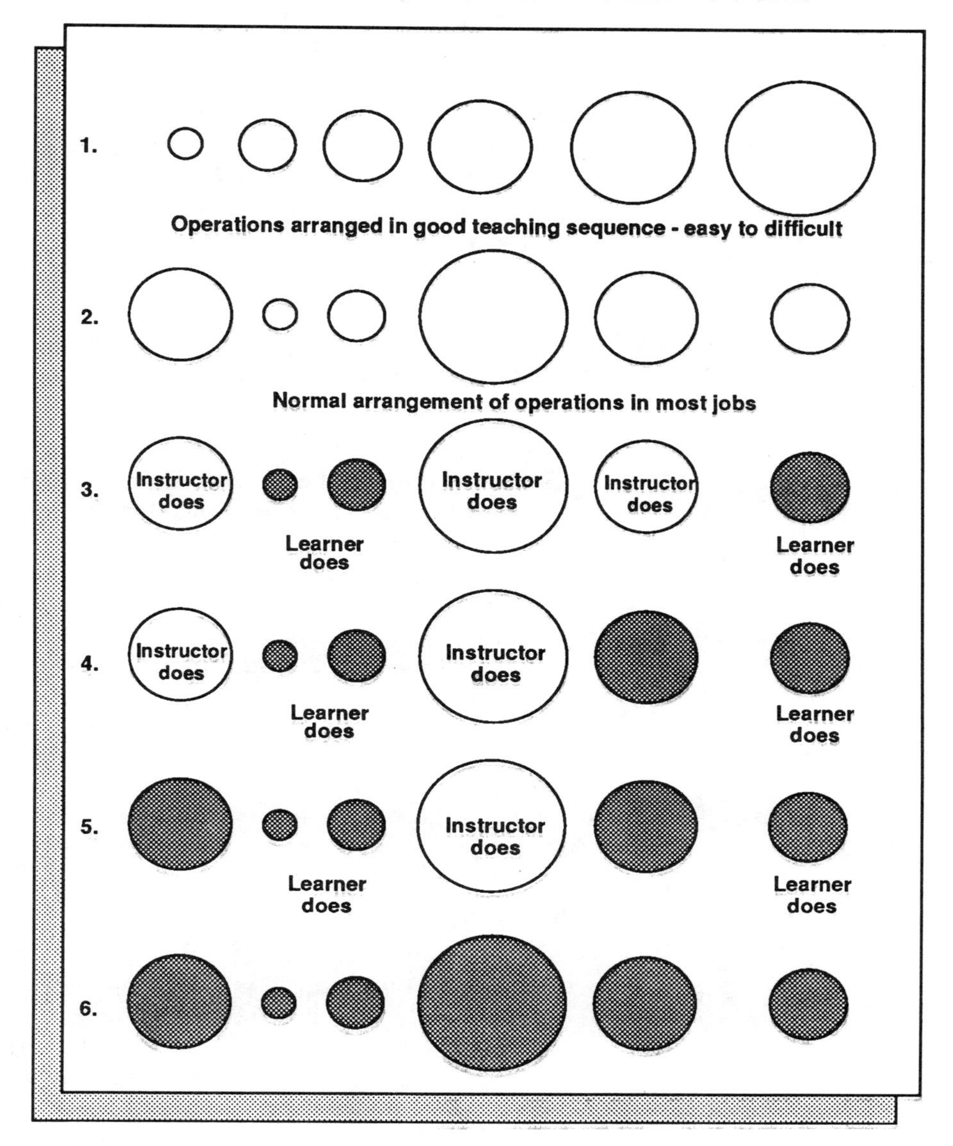

or the need to help others. Such needs compel people to act, to move, to start working toward an objective, or to achieve a goal. An instructor has a responsibility to recognize and identify these needs to the extent possible and then to seek ways to satisfy them through his instruction.

To be successful, the trainee must have a need to know, understand, believe, act, or acquire a knowledge or skill. The wise instructor realizes that these needs are not separate and distinct from the personal-social needs of the learner. The instructor must create the conditions that make supervisors want to learn, and if necessary, must remove obstacles that they sometimes place in the paths of their own learning. Trainees must have a reason for learning and if they cannot find it out for themselves, the instructor must help them find it.[6]

PREPARATION

JIT also acknowledged that there is more to preparation than pure motivation. A lot of groundwork has to be done before effective training can be launched. I have found that the procedure illustrated in the accompanying box is especially useful in communicating the value of preparation to supervisors. With a little reorientation, its preparatory steps apply just as well to trainers preparing to train supervisors. Also, a checklist for identifying the key points of any job is provided in the box on the facing page.

Steps in Preparing to Train

1. *Prepare a job breakdown in writing.*

   Think through the job from start to finish.

   Make a list of the operations that must be done. This is where you break the job down into pieces (operations or *steps*). Don't make the pieces either too big or too small. Think of having to do only one thing at a time. In general, you are more likely to make the pieces too big than too small.

   Arrange the steps in the best possible *sequence.* You may discover that supervisors don't always do a particular job the same way. Now is the time to decide exactly how it should be done.

   For each step, prepare a *key point.* A key point is some information, knack, or know-how that can make or break the job; failure to apply knowledge of the key point may result in injury to the worker, spoilage of a floppy disk, or damage to the computer, for instance. Key points are often what the experienced supervisor takes for granted but the beginner misses.

2. *Make sure everything needed is ready.*

   Materials or parts. Are they the right size and in good condition? Are there enough on hand?

   Tools and machinery. Are they sharpened and in good working order? Can you and the trainee use them without interruption?

   Workplace. Is it clear and uncluttered? Will there be enough room for both of you? Enough light?

   Process information. Do you know enough about the process itself so that you can explain what is taking place? How it fits into the big picture in the plant or office? Are any instruction sheets, blueprints, or manuals needed? Have you prepared a job-breakdown sheet? Can you post it at the workplace for the trainee to use as a reference?

3. *Set aside enough time.*

   Training is best done in little bits. Chances are, you may not have enough time at one session. Set a *goal* for the number of steps that should be covered at each session. Allow enough time to cover them thoroughly and for the trainee to try them out.

   Prepare a *timetable* for each supervisor. How much must he or she learn at each session? How many sessions will there be? What is the target date for the trainee to demonstrate accurate performance of the entire job?

Key-Point Checklist

Key points are those things that should happen, or could happen, at each step of a job that make it go either right or wrong. Key points include any of the following:

1. *Feel.* Is there a special smoothness or roughness? Absence of vibration?
2. *Alignment.* Should the form be up or down? Which face forward? Label in which position?
3. *Fit.* Should it be loose or tight? How loose? How tight? Can you show the trainee? How can a person tell when a part is jammed?
4. *Safety.* What can happen to injure a person? How are the safety guards operated? What special glasses, gloves, switches, or shoes are needed? What safety procedures are critical? When must an accident be reported?
5. *Speed.* How fast must the operation proceed? Is speed critical? How can a person tell if it's going too fast or too slow?
6. *Timing.* What must be synchronized with something else? How long must an operation remain idle—as with waiting for an adhesive to set?
7. *Smell.* Is there a right or wrong smell about anything—the material, the cooking or curing during the process, the overheating of a machine?
8. *Temperature.* Is temperature critical? How can a person tell whether it is too hot or too cold? What can be done to change the temperature, if necessary?
9. *Sequence.* Is the specified order critical? Must one operation be performed before another, or doesn't it make any difference? How can a person tell if he or she has gotten something out of order?
10. *Appearance.* Should surfaces be glossy or dull? Does it make any difference? Should the part be straight or bent? How can an unsatisfactory condition be corrected?
11. *Heft.* Is weight important? Can you demonstrate how heavy or light a part or package should be?
12. *Noise.* Are certain noises expected? Unacceptable?
13. *Materials.* What is critical about their condition? How can a person recognize that? When should the material be rejected?
14. *Tools.* What is critical about their condition? Sharpness? Absence of nicks or burrs? Positioning? Handling?
15. *Machinery.* What is critical about its operation? How is it shut down in emergencies? What will damage it? How can this be avoided?
16. *Trouble.* What should be done in the event of injury to persons or damage to materials, parts, product, tools, or machinery? How can damage be recognized?

Implementation

A contemporary approach to the original four steps of JIT follows. It, too, has been effective in communicating the principles to supervisors and is readily applicable to the face-to-face phase of supervisory training.

Step 1: Get the supervisors ready to learn.

- Get to know the supervisors first. What do they already know about the materials, tools, process, people, or situation?
- Put the trainees at ease. Take the pressure off. They can make mistakes now. For a while, they can be allowed to work at their own pace.
- Let them know why the job is important. Try to give an overview of how it fits into their performance.
- Give them a target to shoot at in terms of (1) how much and how good now and (2) how much and how good when they have attained mastery.

Step 2: Demonstrate how the job should be done.

- Do this two ways: by telling *and* by example. Neither telling alone nor demonstration alone will get results.
- Demonstrate the complete procedure or concept first. Repeat it several times if you can.
- Stress the key points at each procedural step. Show what happens if the key points are not followed. Help the trainees to observe or sense anger, frustration, or satisfaction.
- Ask the trainees to explain to you what has been demonstrated at each step. Encourage them to ask questions and to tell you when they can't follow what is being discussed.

Step 3: Try supervisors out by letting them perform.

- Start by having the trainees do only the easiest parts. You do the harder ones. Have them repeat these parts several times.
- Don't move on to more difficult procedures until each supervisor has shown that he or she can perform the easier steps accurately. Speed is not essential now. Accuracy, quality, and care are.
- Gradually let the trainees perform the more difficult steps. Have them repeat these until they can do them satisfactorily.
- Finally, let the trainees perform a complete sequence from start to finish. Expect mistakes and disagreements at this stage. Be patient. Have them repeat the complete sequence until they can do it without making a mistake. This often takes longer than you may have planned for. But don't rush it.

Step 4: Put the supervisors on their own—gradually.

- You won't be able to stand over their shoulders, but remain available. Be ready to answer questions or help out. For a long time, supervisors will need your assistance.

- Follow up until supervisors feel a mastery of the skill and their ability to apply it.

Closure

The follow-up phase of supervisory training is often the most frustrating for the training professional, since the supervisors are likely to leave the training scene so quickly. Back on the job, the supervisors themselves, or their bosses, must provide the follow-up, with only an occasional assist from the trainer. Closure can be approached, however, if supervisor, trainer, and the supervisor's superior—together—proceed as follows:

Check back regularly.

- For the first day, this may be a dozen times. For the first week, it may be two or three times a shift.
- Correct mistakes. Encourage questions. Demonstrate the complete operation again. Have the trainee repeat troublesome steps.
- Verify quality of workmanship. Don't settle for less than standard.
- Raise speed or output targets daily until the trainee meets standard performance requirements.
- Think of yourself as a coach or counselor, not a scold or taskmaster. Your job is to help the trainee learn. If he or she hasn't learned, chances are you haven't taught.

Introduce variations.

- Most jobs have an occasional unique problem. It may be a particular order, unique tooling, tighter or looser specifications, different situations than were covered during the training sessions.
- Demonstrate how to handle these variations as they come up. Or pick one a week to teach.
- Share your more in-depth know-how. Your original key points may not have included some of the knacks that you have acquired. It may be a way of checking the sharpness of a tool, verifying the fit of a fixture, handling an oddball situation. The sooner the supervisor has mastered the variations, the sooner you will be free to move on to the next phase of the program.

Double-check Your Approach

Just as it is important to respect the laws of learning and to build JIT principles into your approach, it is vital to be aware of, and avoid, common mistakes in supervisory training. Here are ten pitfalls to steer clear of:

1. *Don't try to cover too much at one time.* The mind can absorb only so much before it gets tired or bored.
2. *Don't move faster than the supervisors can follow you.* The trainer should adjust his or her speed to that of the learners. Otherwise, the learners won't see or hear what is going on.

3. *Don't set initial expectations too high.* Be satisfied with a goal of having the supervisors do the job (or a part of it) correctly. Later on, you can press for greater accomplishment.

4. *Don't stress the need for greater coverage to the detriment of quality.* It is important that the job be done well.

5. *Don't forget to give and get feedback.* Give the learners plenty of opportunity to ask questions. Don't wait too long before you correct or praise their performance.

6. *Don't threaten learners.* It is hard enough to learn a new job without someone making you worry about failure. It is important that the learning atmosphere be friendly, supportive, and positive. Attitudes are as vital as knowledge and skill at the learning stage.

7. *Don't let bad habits get started.* The time to correct mistakes is while supervisors are in training. People learn bad habits as quickly and easily as good ones.

8. *Don't expect that a beginning supervisor will learn just by observing or working along with an experienced one.* Effective training requires a systematic and complete approach.

9. *Don't continue training after supervisors show signs of boredom or fatigue or if distractions occur.* It is better to stop and begin again at a time when the supervisors are fresh and the distractions have been removed.

10. *Don't assume that good pay is a strong motivator.* The desire to do a job well, to be an effective member of the work team, to gain praise and acceptance are the strongest incentives to learning. Self-development is a powerful and positive persuader. *And that is what supervisory training should emphasize—an opportunity to learn how to be a more effective and productive manager.*

PARTICIPATION AND GROUPS IN TRAINING

Supervisory training can be viewed as a shared activity, with both individual and common goals for its participants. Supervisors wish to attain their own learning and performance goals. The training professional aims at transferring a prescribed amount of knowledge and skills. The organization that employs both the supervisors and the trainer expects that the training will yield improved organizational performance. In light of training as a shared activity, the introduction of participatory (or involvement) techniques helps gain commitment to the training plan from the supervisors and facilitates the transfer of learning to them.

Participation in Supervisory Training

Supervisors, like most trainees, learn best when they are active. Participation in a training workshop or seminar means action. This action profoundly influences learning. Because competent instructors realize that idleness, either mental or physical, is detrimental to learning, they plan a variety of activities in which supervisors can participate. Activity takes many forms: thinking, listening, observing, recalling, reasoning, generalizing, imagining, writing, discussing, answering, questioning, disagreeing, feeling, touching, moving, doing, and speaking. All help supervisors to learn.

Whatever the activity, effective instructors make sure that the trainees have something to do. There is a correlation between doing and learning. How much people learn is in direct proportion to how much they do or how much they become involved in what they do. Stated simply, the more of the five senses supervisors use to learn something, the more effective the learning will be.

Participation can make learning permanent. Supervisors who are required to think imaginatively and selectively learn more than those who merely absorb knowledge passively. Supervisors who receive information through the senses of touch, sight, sound, and smell learn better than if they receive information through one sense alone. If trainees hear something, then think about it, question it, discuss it, and listen to what others say about it, the learning is more effective than if they merely listen passively. Since participation improves learning so much, it is the instructor's responsibility to make participation possible.

Training professionals can encourage supervisors to take notes; pose problems and require solutions; assign practice exercises, readings, and research projects; form discussion groups and require supervisors to evaluate one another's handling of role-play in case-study analysis. Participation enhances the supervisors' chances of successfully learning the prescribed competencies.

Stimulating Supervisory Groups

Peer pressure within a supervisory-training group can enhance or endanger the effectiveness of a training program or session. Supervisors, exposed as they are to professional commentators and entertainers on television, have come to expect expert instruction. Jeanie Marshall, an unusually perceptive training consultant, advises that "silence is far from golden in a supervisory workshop." The participants may figuratively sit on their hands and wait for the trainer to amuse them. Or they may respond actively, regardless of how turgid the course content, to conditions and devices they find stimulating and interesting. Accordingly, she proposes these thirteen tips for extracting a maximum of participation from supervisory groups:

1. *Arrange your room for interaction.* Round tables take the emphasis off the trainer and promote participant interaction. Tables set up to form a square or chairs arranged in a circle establish equality between participants and trainer and promote group discussion. U shapes, too, promote interaction but establish the trainer as an authority.

2. *Use flipcharts.* On a flipchart, write questions to be answered or sentences to be completed. They can pertain to attitude, learning goals, content, or even trivia. As participants enter the training room, ask them to respond directly on the flipchart. This activity is an ideal icebreaker. It can also be used during the training to emphasize the importance of active involvement.

3. *Allow time for getting acquainted.* This helps build a climate of trust and makes it easier for participants to relax and respond.

4. *Prepare a program book or handouts.* Design your handouts in ways that promote note taking and distribute them before you begin speaking. Writing involves the learners. You do them no favors by saying, "You don't need to take notes; I'll give you handouts on everything later."

5. *Start with a self-scoring assessment.* Phrase the questions simply enough to involve all your participants. If possible, also design the assessment to give you useful information about the learners.

6. *Ask a question everyone can answer.* Early in the program, ask each participant to respond to a question or comment. It may be a get-acquainted question, such as, "What is the most important learning goal you have for this workshop?" or one related to the specific content area, such as "How do you expect your subordinates to react to this new procedure?"

7. *Ask questions that can be answered by a show of hands.* A simple, nonthreatening method for getting a response is to ask questions of the whole group. Each series of questions should enable everyone to answer at least once. Ask, for example, "How many of you have been managers or supervisors for fewer than six months? More than six months? More than two years?"

8. *Count to ten.* When posing a question to the group, count silently to ten before restating the question, answering it, asking a second question, or moving on. When you demand speedy responses, some learners will feel inadequate and discouraged about participating. By allowing more time, you show that you value all types of involvement—silent and thoughtful as well as vocal and immediate.

9. *Allow thinking time.* When stating a problem or posing a question, ask the participants to jot down a few notes before anyone responds. This gives those who are slower in responding an opportunity to go through the thinking process, even if they don't actually speak. It also allows deeper thinking, leading to less obvious responses.

10. *Ask what, not if.* The automatic "Any questions?" is best replaced with "What questions do you have?" Better still, state, "Please take a few moments to think about what I said and what questions you have."

11. *Use buzz groups.* Divide the participants into groups of four or five and ask a provocative question. While you personally will not hear from everyone, each participant will have a chance to speak. When you regroup, try to call on one member of each buzz group so that every participant feels represented.

12. *Listen.* Your body language, facial expressions, and words reveal how well you are listening. Show you are interested in every answer.

13. *Don't get stuck.* Stay too long on one activity and participants will lose enthusiasm. They'll do the same with a too-long lecture. Spice up and vary your training techniques; you will keep your group's attention, and you'll get a bigger, better response.[7]

Chapter 8

Course Design, Content, and Selection

INTRODUCTION

Typical course content for supervisory training can be inferred by examining established competencies and needs-analysis inventory lists. Beyond the nominal subject matter, however, it is important for the training coordinator to determine beforehand the exact focus and general context of each course or topic. Specifically, almost any subject or course may be approached with an objective of conveying *knowledge,* imparting or improving *skills,* or reinforcing or shaping *attitudes.* Many subjects, of course, lend themselves readily to these categories, but the larger context of learning should not be overlooked, since it will have a significant impact upon the effectiveness of course material and subsequent evaluation of the training by participants and their sponsors.

COURSE DESIGN

The more complete the rationale, objectives, content, and instructional plan, the greater the chances for successful course implementation and effective transfer of skills to the supervisory participants. Each course should have an underlying *educational rationale,* a demonstrable purpose of changing or improving supervisory performance—in terms of either a particular skill, such as computer procedures, or a broad functional area, such as human relations. There is a temptation to offer some courses simply because they are popular. This practice should be avoided unless there is a strong conviction that the course is needed to demonstrate the organization's awareness of current trends. In every case, however, the underlying rationale should be clearly spelled out, not necessarily for the participants but surely for those who sponsor and/or conduct the course.

It should go without saying that *course objectives*—clearly stated in terms of expected knowledge, skills, or performance improvement—are an absolute necessity. If a course is performance-oriented, then these objectives should be phrased in terms of what a supervisor will be able to *do* upon completion of the course. For example, if the course were on how to handle a performance review, one of its objectives might be stated like this: "Be able to conduct a face-to-face performance interview in such a manner that the discussion focuses on factual conditions of the employee's performance and on what the employee must do to bring performance up to standard."

The *instructional plan* should be as detailed as possible, specifying content, methods and sequence of instruction, time schedules, visual aids, handouts, procedures for follow-up, and so on. The box on the facing page shows an instructional plan for a course (job instruction training) to be presented in three units of two- to three-hour sessions with an expected enrollment of from fifteen to twenty.

Course-Design Components

While preparation of a truly thorough course design may seem like too large a task to attempt as a preliminary to instruction, the greater the number of elements the training professional can consider in the design, the smoother and more fault-free will be the ultimate implementation. A comprehensive design allows the course to be conducted by a greater variety of instructors, ranging from those on the corporate training staff, to line or staff people in the organization, to contract instructors from local colleges and universities or consulting firms. Consequently, it is strongly recommended that a comprehensive design be prepared in writing and that it contain as many of the elements listed below as possible:

1. *Synopsis.* A brief, narrative overview of the nature and scope of the course and its major objective.
2. *Target participants.* A description of the appropriate audience, in terms of the knowledge and experience they should bring with them; specifically:
   a. *Absolute prerequisites,* such as supervisory or management status; length of time in specified positions; and where essential, successful completion of a particular preparatory course.
   b. *Preferred prerequisites,* such as knowledge of algebra before enrolling in a statistics or quantitative methods course, or knowledge of grammar and spelling prior to taking a course in improving writing skills.
   c. *Precourse preparation,* such as identifying a relevant and specific problem area on the participant's job or gathering enough data about the work situation to enable working on a particular project during the seminar.
3. *Assumptions.* A description of the typical capabilities and aptitudes of the expected participants relevant to the course.
4. *Objectives.* The specific instructional objectives of the course should not be merely to impart knowledge but also to change behavior or improve performance. Phrase the objectives as active statements, describing what the participants will know or be able to do in a work situation following the course. For example, "After completing the course, participants will be able to discipline employees more constructively, reduce employee absences by more empathetic counseling, suggest effective ways for improving paperwork flow." Objectives should be developed along three basic lines:
   a. Cognition—knowledge or comprehension

Instructional Plan for a Course in Job Instruction Training

Unit 1: Preparation and Planning 120 minutes

1. Introduction to unit 1.
   a. Opening the unit; welcome address; getting acquainted; overview of course and objectives of first unit.
   b. Introduction of guest speaker.
2. Method of presentation.
   The first portion of this unit is presented as a lecture, preferably given by a top executive within the activity. Buzz groups are formed after the lecture to discuss key points presented by the speaker. Following group discussion of the subject, the group develops techniques to be used in planning to meet training needs by means of a training timetable and the task analysis. The main divisions of this unit are:
   a. The importance of training (lecture).
   b. Doctrine with regard to training in government in general and in the Department of the Army specifically (lecture).
   c. Objectives of skills training (lecture).
   d. The training cycle (lecture).
   e. Determining training needs (lecture).
   f. Reports by buzz groups.
   g. Planning to meet training needs (lecture and group discussion).
      (1) Training timetable.
      (2) The task analysis.
3. Summary by course leader.
4. Assignment for next unit.

Unit 2: Teaching 160 minutes

1. Discussion and critique of the task analysis (conference and demonstration).
2. The supervisor as an instructor—training methods. (Film: *Accent on Learning,* MF 21-8424—30 minutes for film viewing and discussion.)
   a. How people learn.
   b. Selecting a method.
3. The "four-step method" of skills instruction (discussion, demonstration, role-playing, and group critique). (Film: *Instructing the New Worker on the Job,* MF 61-7765—14 minutes.)
4. Summary by course leader. (Film: *The Follow Through,* MF 61-9045a—8 minutes.)
5. Assignment for next unit.

Continued on next page

Instructional Plan for a Course in Job Instruction Training—*Continued*

Unit 3: The Follow-up and Evaluation of Training **120 minutes**

1. The transference of training to the job (conference).
2. Evaluating and reporting training (lecture).
3. Summary and closing remarks.
4. Presentation of certificates.
5. Course critique.

Source: Adapted from "Guide to Supervisor Development," *Supervisor Development Program: Basic Course* (Washington, D.C.: Department of the Army, August 1962), 5.

b. Performance, in terms of basic application

c. Performance, in terms of analysis and interpretation

5. *Key concepts.* Precise statements of major principles or practice guidelines that will be emphasized in the course. A maximum of six for a one-day course or ten for a two-day course is recommended.

6. *Key terms.* Precise definitions of terms that participants must understand and be able to use in order to fulfill performance objectives.

7. *Outline of subject matter and recommended time allotments,* including:

a. Introduction and overview that call attention to unique aspects of the course.

b. Preparation or selection of a precourse (or entry) instrument to assess participants' knowledge of the subject (for the instructor's guidance only).

c. Suggestions for timing in the use of visual aids, case studies, role-play, feedback sessions, and so on.

d. Suggestions for preparation of a "take-home-action plan" assignment for participants.

e. Preparation or selection of an instrument to assess participants' comprehension upon completion of the course (to be compared by the instructor with the precourse assessment).

8. *Preferred methods of instruction.* Recommendations regarding the selective and proportional use of lecture, discussion, buzz sessions, case study, role-play, behavioral-modeling sessions, problem solving, participant reports, feedback sessions, project exercises, interactive exercises, or other training techniques.

9. *Suggested visual aids and instructional materials.* Identification and sources, including:

a. Films and filmstrips

b. Case studies

c. Cassettes

d. Transparency masters

e. Charts, posters, displays, and so on

   f. Simulations and games
   g. Three-dimensional models, devices, and the like
10. *Facilities and equipment,* including:
   a. Preferred location (on- or off-site)
   b. Optimum room size
   c. Preferred seating facilities
   d. Equipment, such as VCRs, computer modems and video display terminals, and audiovisual recording and projection equipment
11. *Bibliography, references, and suggested readings.*

An example of a comprehensive course design and plan appears in the box below.

Model of a Certificate in Professional Development Course Outline

Course No. 101: The Nature of Supervisory Work 1 day

1. *Course synopsis*

   An introductory course for recently appointed supervisors and all other supervisors who wish to acquire a basic understanding of the nature and scope of the supervisory management position and its responsibilities so as to better prepare themselves for developing the specific knowledge, attitudes, and skills needed to make their efforts productive.

2. *Target participants*

   a. *Absolute requirements.* Individuals must be currently employed as supervisors in state or local government, with less than five year's experience at the management level.

   b. *Preferred requirements.* No other prerequisites, except that individuals *not* currently employed as supervisors must have attended a Human Relations in Business seminar.

   c. *Precourse preparation.* Participants are to prepare a table of the resources they manage, to include: (a) facilities, equipment, and machinery—and an estimate of their replacement costs; (b) utilities and/or energy expenses per year; (c) materials and supplies typically on hand, as well as their amount and cost; (d) total monthly or annual budget for their operations; (e) kinds of instruction or procedures manuals, directives, and so on they are guided by; and (f) number and titles of people working for them and total payroll cost.

3. *Assumptions about participants*

   Even experienced supervisors rarely think about the basic nature or purpose of their responsibilities and their work. Nor do they give systematic thought to the specific performance required of them. Moreover, they tend to believe that the power needed to attain departmental objectives is derived more from status and organizational authority than from their own empathy for others.

Continued on next page

Model of a Certificate in Professional Development Course Outline—*Continued*

4. *Course objectives*

   Overall, to comprehend the nature and scope of the supervisory management job and the demands it places upon those who hold that position, in order that course participants may better prepare themselves to accept their responsibilities more knowledgeably and discharge them more effectively.

   Specifically, participants who complete this course can be expected to:

   a. More fully comprehend and accept a managerial point of view that entails a responsibility for results that are accomplished mainly through the efforts of others.

   b. Be able to make an informed assessment of the specific performance expected of them in their current supervisory assignments.

   c. Sense the degree of personal empathy and interpersonal skills needed by their employees, peers, and others in order to attain productive results from a work situation.

   d. Make a judgment as to which knowledge, attitudes, and skills they must develop in the future in order to provide an effective balance between their various technical, human relations, and administrative roles.

5. *Key terms*

employee	work
supervisor	goals (personal and organizational)
manager	interpersonal relationships
management	empathy
results	productive and counterproductive

6. *Key concepts*

   a. Management requires the ability on the part of supervisors to accept responsibility for the attainment of organizational goals, which are reached largely through the efforts of the employees assigned to them. To be successful at their work, supervisors must be willing to subordinate their own interests and goals and learn to work harmoniously and effectively with individuals and groups.

   b. In order for supervisors' performance to be judged as proficient, they must know (a) what their superiors expect from them in the way of managing the basic resources assigned to them and (b) precisely what is expected in the way of measurable results from their operations, especially output or productivity, quality and craftsmanship, and cost or expense controls.

   c. Different people respond differently to the demands of the work situation because they have different capabilities, preparation, interests, and goals. As a consequence, supervisors must lay the groundwork for harmonious and productive interpersonal relationships by developing an empathy with (or sensitivity to) the unique feelings and behaviors of others.

   d. Supervisory work requires that an individual perform three kinds of managerial roles: technical, human relations, and administrative.

Continued on next page

Model of a Certificate in Professional Development Course Outline—*Continued*

Looking toward their futures, supervisors should, as early as possible, determine which specific kinds of knowledge, attitudes, and skills they must develop in order to carry on these roles productively.

7. *Course outline and timetable*

Introductions and overview ½ *hour*

Review objectives, emphasizing the importance of (a) grasping the concept of management-mindedness, (b) bearing up under the pressure to obtain results through the work of others, and (c) understanding the breadth of the supervisor's job functions and responsibilities as well as, (d) how essential empathy is for results and (e) the ever-present need to balance a number of managerial roles.

ADMINISTER THE PRECOURSE ASSESSMENT INSTRUMENT.

Objective 1: Crossing over to management 1½ *hours*

a. What management is in terms of general objectives and basic process, rather than discussing the various functions.
b. Supervisors' position in the management structure; various views, such as middle person, keystone, link-pin, and so on.
c. Legal aspects of the supervisory position.
d. Relationships and responsibilities toward others in the organization (higher-level managers, peers, and employees) as well as toward the general public.
e. Typical crossing-over problems.

CASE STUDY illustrating crossing-over difficulties; emphasis upon how to handle each situation.

FILM (optional) illustrating the nature and scope of supervisory management.

Objective 2: Performance requirements 1½ *hours*

a. Explanation of simplified management process, especially the responsibility for converting organizational resources into valuable results.
b. Resource management and care—facilities and equipment, energy and utilities, materials and supplies, finances, information, and people.
c. Attainment of results—output and productivity, quality of service and craftsmanship, expense and waste control.

TAKE-HOME PROJECT. Suggestion: Participants are to find out exactly what their performance requirements are in each of the resource-management and result areas, and how they will be judged by their superiors.

Objective 3: The need for empathy 1½ *hours*

a. What work is.
b. How people feel about and react to their work.
c. The nature of individual goals.
d. The nature of organizational goals.

Continued on next page

Model of a Certificate in Professional Development Course Outline—*Continued*

e. CASE STUDY illustrating conflict between individual and organizational goals and the supervisor's role in resolving such conflicts.

f. What empathy is; why is it important and how to develop it.

FILM (optional) illustrating supervisors' human relations responsibilities.

FEEDBACK SESSION *½ hour*

Suggestion: Break participants into buzz groups—one group to summarize five important problems of crossing over, a second group to list typical resources available to supervisors at their job sites, a third group to come up with six ways in which supervisors can turn resources into the three key results, and a fourth group to list ten ways in which employees might aid or block attainment of operational goals.

Objective 4: Balancing supervisory roles ¾ hour

a. The concept of responsibilities, duties, functions, and activities as managerial roles.

b. Technical roles.

c. Human relations roles.

d. Administrative roles.

Suggestion: Ask the group to furnish ideas for a listing of activities that occur in each role.

e. Need for balance and for acquiring proficiency in each role.

EXERCISE. Suggestion: Participants are to prepare a list of at least ten activities required of them in each role; then make a list of five knowledge, attitude, or skill areas they wish to acquire or develop in the future.

Course summary ¼ hour

Repeat objectives, related terminology, and key concepts, recalling for each concept at least one observation or conclusion that the group has developed. Remind participants of their commitment to the take-home action plan and the way in which they should fulfill that commitment to their best advantage.

ADMINISTER POSTCOURSE COMPREHENSION INSTRUMENT.

8. *Preferred methods of instruction*

Instructors should be prepared to make a major informational input into this course; thus, lecture and induced discussion will prevail, especially in objectives 1, 2, and 4. Objective 1, which requires self-examination, will profit from a behavioral-modeling approach, case study, and/or role-play. Objective 3, which requires perception about the nature of empathy, will benefit greatly from case study, role-play, or sensitivity experience.

9. *Visual and instructional aids and materials*

Obj. 1: Chart or Transparency Master (TM); fig. 1, *What Every Supervisor Should Know* (WESSK)/4, "Crossing Over."

Case study, p. 22, WESSK/4, "Complaining Keypunch Operator."

Film, *Good Morning, Mr. Roberts,* Sandy/Direct Marketing.

Continued on next page

Model of a Certificate in Professional Development Course Outline—*Continued*

Obj. 2: Chart or TM; list resources and results, fig. 1-4, WESSK/4, "Measuring Supervisory Performance."

Obj. 3: Chart or TM; fig. 2-1, WESSK/4, "Surveys of Personal Satisfaction."

Case study, p. 32, WESSK/4, "Mildred and the Mickey Mouse Job."

Film, *Eye of the Supervisor,* National Educational Media.

Obj. 4: Chart or TM; fig. 1-7, WESSK/4, "Skills Needed According to Managerial Levels."

Fig. 1-8, WESSK/4, "Balance of Supervisory Concerns."

10. *Facilities and equipment*

a. Either on- or off-site.

b. Quiet conference room with space for projection equipment, chart boards, and a coffee table.

c. Comfortable seating for from fifteen to twenty supervisors around a single table.

d. Movie screen and projector, two easels and chart boards, one overhead projector.

COMMONLY OFFERED COURSES

Typical supervisory-training courses mirror designated supervisory competencies and assessed training needs, as they should. Those courses that seem most fundamental to supervision are shown in the box on page 112. This list was compiled by the International Labor Office (ILO) and includes nearly all the perennial subjects. Most comprehensive supervisory-training courses are selected from lists like this and from whatever needs areas are currently highlighted in the field.

The ILO Modular Concept

ILO envisioned the thirty-five courses in its list as modules that could be put together in sequences or clusters according to the needs and objectives of a particular organization. Module design was premised upon allocating program time to the various training methods in the following proportions:

TRAINING METHODS	PERCENTAGE OF TIME
Lecturing	10–20
Films, group discussion, role-play	35–45
Case studies, projects, problems	25–35
Homework, self-development	10–20
Performance (course evaluation)	5

Comprehensive Listing of Basic Supervision Courses: A Basic Modular Program for Supervisory Training

Course Nos.	Course Titles
I. Supervision	
1	The Organization and the Supervisor
2	Principles of Supervision
II. Supervisory Techniques	
3	Planning and Scheduling
4	Work Study and Organization
5	Directing and Coordinating Work
6	Controlling Work
7	Quality Control
8	Finance and Cost Control
9	Decision Making and Problem Solving
10	Role Analysis
11	Introducing Changes
12	Communications and Records
III. The Main Supervisory Areas	
13	Utilization of Equipment and Facilities
14	Maintenance Supervision
15	Material Handling
16	Energy Utilities and Auxiliary Services
17	Management of Time
18	Office Supervision
19	Purchasing
20	Marketing
IV. Supervising People	
21	Leadership
22	Informal Organizations and Groups
23	Individual and Group Discussions
24	Staffing
25	Motivating Workers
26	Job Evaluation
27	Performance Appraisal
28	Salary Administration
29	Training and Development
30	Interpersonal Relations and Behavior in Supervision
31	Industrial Relations
32	Safety, Health, Security
33	Maintaining Discipline and Morale
34	Complaints and Grievances
35	Supervising Special Groups

Source: Adapted from J. Prokopenko and Lester R. Bittel, "A Modular Course-Format for Supervisory Development," *Training and Development Journal* (February 1981): 15.

Each ILO module consists of five essential parts:

1. Overall learning objectives and table of contents
2. Basic overview of the subject or function, including key definitions, its importance to supervisors, and the supervisors' role and duties
3. Methods and techniques used to implement, or master, the function
4. Action exercises and case-study application
5. Summary

Within each part of the module, there is always a set of learning objectives for that part and a variety of self-administered progress-review questions. These questions are mostly objective in nature, although some are open-ended and require discussion.

Module content emphasizes what to do and how to do it. Module design strives for the most effective balance between theory and practical application, depending on the nature of the subject matter.

Side-by-Side Format Design

A unique aspect of the ILO module design is that for each page of learner instruction, there is a corresponding page of guidance for the trainer. The right-hand page of the module is designed for the supervisor; the left-hand page provides guidance for the trainer. Comments and answers for problems, tests, and cases are presented in the same side-by-side fashion.

This format enables trainers to use the modules three ways:

1. Trainer provides supervisors with guided instruction, based on the left-hand pages; supervisors use the right-hand pages as a resource text and for class and homework assignments.
2. Supervisors use the right-hand pages as a self-study manual, pacing their own work, checking their own progress; the trainer's role is mainly that of a resource person.
3. Some combination of approach 1 and approach 2. The trainer might choose to follow approach 2 for more complex material so that each trainee may progress at his or her own best learning rate. Or the trainer might choose to do just the reverse: self-study for the simpler material and guided instruction for the more complex material. The choice would depend, of course, on the trainer, the supervisors, the subject matter, and organizational and environmental factors.

Detailed instructional modules are available from the International Labor Office in Washington, D.C.

The Conference Board once surveyed large corporations engaged in extensive supervisory training to identify commonly offered subjects. The results are illuminating (see below), even though the data are now somewhat outdated.

Number of Companies Offering a Particular Kind of Supervisory Training

128 Leadership, human relations, behavior, motivation

62 Management theory, process

47 Company policies

42 Labor relations

41 Company organization

41 Problem solving and decision making

28 Safety, OSHA

27 Company paperwork

25 EEO

10 Goal setting and MBO

10 Work simplification

6 Economics (how America's business system operates)[1]

CLASSIFICATION BY COURSE LEVEL

The most common classification of course material has been according to level of experience of the participants rather than according to course topic. Course content, emphasis, and technique may vary, but the great majority of supervisory topics might be taught at any level of experience, as suggested by the ILO list shown earlier.

Many in-service programs and a great many institutional supervisory-training programs are classified, in terms of their target audience, as (1) *pre-supervisory,* (2) for *entering* supervisors, with one to five years experience, or (3) for *experienced* supervisors, with more than five years experience. An integrated program designed along these lines for a large state to offer a Certificate of Professional Development (CPD) to its public-service supervisors is illustrated conceptually in figure 8-1. Its designations are: level 0: presupervisory—to accommodate open enrollment and to prescribe preparatory requirements; level I: for basic (or inexperienced) supervision; level II: for advanced (or experienced) supervision; and level III: for middle management. Details of course offerings in this program appear in chapter 12.

Basic Supervision Courses

A great many organizations—ranging from manufacturing companies to banks and hospitals, from professional management associations to community colleges and university management development centers, and from the military to state governments—choose to present certain courses only, or principally, to entering or relatively inexperienced supervisors. Typical course descriptions in this category include:

- *Nature of supervisory work.* Management-mindedness; people as implementers; responsibility for others; self-awareness; sensitivity assessment; balancing work and people concerns.
- *Managing the supervisory job.* Planning, goals, and schedules; organizing/distributing work and accountability; assignment and instruction; control,

Figure 8-1 Synopsis of CPD Curricula Structure

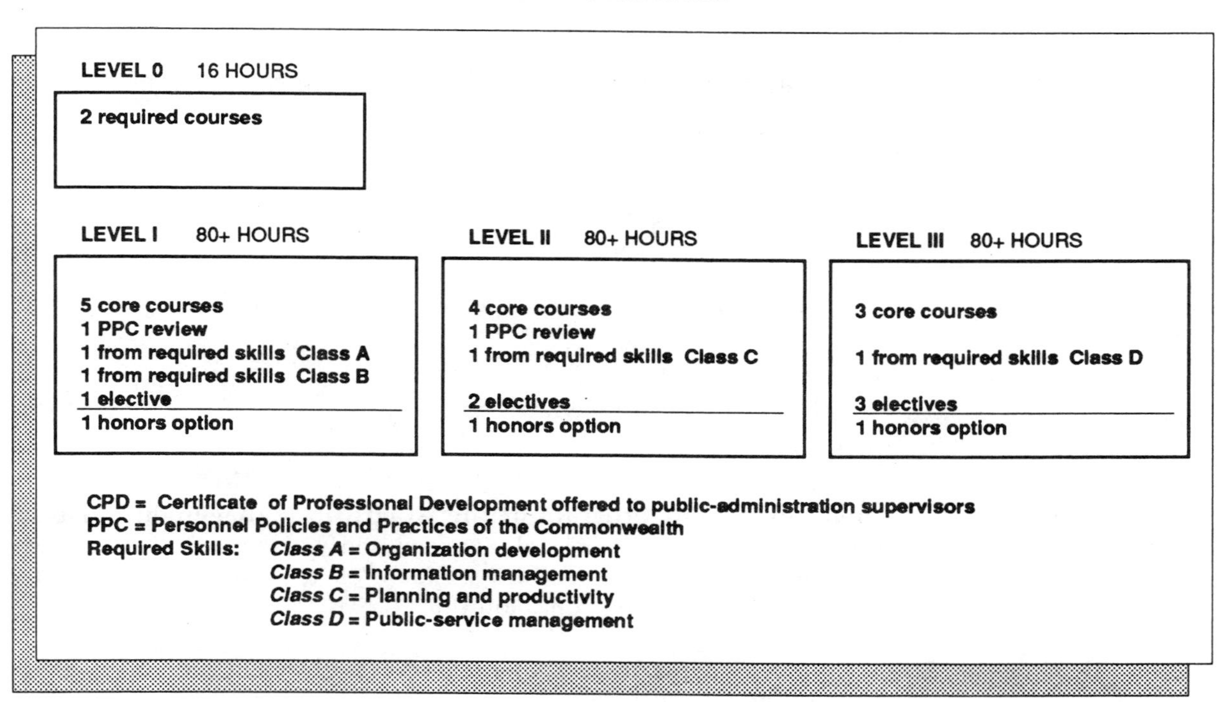

correction, and improvement; the need for problem solving and decision making.

- *Understanding human behavior at work.* Human behavior and motivation; interpersonal relations—with individuals and with groups; attitudes and morale; goal conflicts between individual and organization.
- *Helping employees to meet organization standards and goals.* Leadership; authority and responsibility; communications—organizational and interpersonal; induction, orientation, and training.
- *Preventing and resolving counterproductive situations.* Coping with change and conflict; grievances; performance deficiencies—absenteeism, alcoholism, and drug abuse; discipline and counseling.
- *Employee training.* Learning process; four-step method; job breakdowns; key points.

Selected Examples of Programs in Basic Supervision

The professional trainer can perhaps get a firmer grasp of course content by reviewing the courses offered in a number of successful, long-standing supervisory development programs, as illustrated by the following examples.

Civilian Personnel of the Department of the Army. Each course consists of three sessions of from two to three hours each:

1. Role of supervisor
2. Selection and utilization of personnel

3. Job instruction training
4. Position and pay management
5. Performance appraisal
6. Communications
7. Discipline
8. Health and sick leave
9. Safety
10. Career management
11. Grievances
12. Relationship with unions
13. EEO

Open-Enrollment Program of the American Management Association. This program is targeted "for men and women with less than two years' experience in a supervisory position." It runs for three days and is valued at 2.2 Continuing Education Units (CEUs). Topics include:

- How to establish yourself as a supervisor; the difference between the worker and the manager.
- How to get your ideas across clearly and forcefully.
- Planning, organizing, delegating, follow-through, control, goal setting, time management.
- How to develop the "results-oriented" employee: coaching, the job instruction training method, evaluating and improving the individual's performance, employee counseling.
- Decision making and problem solving.
- How to build team spirit and assure good employee relations: knowing your staff as individuals, dealing with grievances and discipline problems, supervising the union/nonunion employee, motivational techniques that work.
- Your legal responsibilities as a supervisor; how to protect yourself and your company: EEO and affirmative action; protected groups; attitudes and resistance—from the work force/from the organization.
- How to establish high productivity in your department: coordination of group efforts, technical versus managerial skills, differences between coordination and cooperation.
- How you can assure continued promotability for yourself: how to make your good ideas known to management—and be sure you get credit for them; ways to respond when you're asked for suggestions on solving management problems; how to adapt successful management strategies to your own needs.

On-Site Program for Manufacturing Supervisors. A major manufacturing corporation offers this program of "workshops" companywide.

Courses run two hours each and are spaced over a period of from six to ten weeks. The ten sessions are as follows:

1. Supervisor's job
2. Understanding the individual
3. Attitudes/morale/communications
4. Leadership
5. Motivation
6. Training
7. Labor relations
8. Accident prevention
9. Managing your job
10. Planning your career

Open Enrollment at a Midwestern University. The University of Kentucky calls this a "grass-roots" course for new and prospective supervisors. It is held at university locations and lasts only one day.

1. What supervisors do
   - The role of the supervisor
   - How supervisors spend their time
   - The difference between working and managing
   - Identifying with management's goals—the big picture
2. Leadership by example
   - Goal direction
   - Setting priorities
   - Consistency
3. A practical approach to motivation
   - The how and why of human behavior
   - Techniques for motivation
   - Setting up consequences for job behavior
4. Communicating for results
   - Saying what you mean
   - Listening with understanding
   - How to get the feedback you need
5. How to solve problems and make decisions
   - Identifying and defining problems
   - The problem-solving process
   - Relating your decision to your objectives

6. The typical qualities of an effective supervisor
   - Knowing what you want
   - Appropriate attitudes
   - Effective work habits
   - Interpersonal skills

Basic Program for Public Supervisors. This program is designed, in particular, for employees of the U.S. Department of Agriculture but is open to the public. It lasts forty hours and conforms to requirements of the U.S. Office of Personnel Management.

1. Motivation
2. Employee development
3. Self-confrontation
4. Team leadership
5. Problem solving
6. Decision making
7. Performance assessment
8. Analysis of efficiency
9. Consultation skills
10. Communications
11. Organization theory

Supervisory Management Course in a Rural Setting. James Madison University has presented this course for more than twelve years to supervisors and potential supervisors from a wide range of employers, both private and public—in such fields as banking, agriculture, manufacturing, retailing, and wholesaling. Courses take two hours each, and the program runs for twelve consecutive weeks.

1. The supervisor's job
2. Communicating
3. Leadership and authority
4. Motivating employees
5. Employee disciplining and counseling
6. Performance appraisal
7. Employee training and development
8. Cost control
9. Job improvement
10. Planning and scheduling

11. Self-development
12. Tying it all together

Subjects Required for Certification Program. The Institute of Certified Professional Managers requires that candidates demonstrate (through certification examinations) satisfactory knowledge in three broad subject areas, as shown below. Courses are guided through manuals provided by the institute or through standard textbooks and are conducted by private companies and public institutions at dozens of sites each year.

1. *Personal skills*
   a. Needs and roles of managers
   b. Self-knowledge and self-development
   c. Communications
   d. Creativity
   e. Time
   f. Ethics
   g. OSHA, EEO, and so on
2. *Administrative skills*
   a. Planning process
   b. Forecasts and budgets
   c. Problem analysis and decision making
   d. Organization and delegation
   e. Personnel planning
   f. Safety
   g. Control: production/financial/management
   h. Information systems/computers
3. *Human relations skills*
   a. Leadership
   b. Groups
   c. Labor-management relations
   d. Motivation: theory and approaches
   e. Change/facilitating

Advanced Supervision Courses

Those organizations that divide their courses according to their suitability for inexperienced or experienced supervisors often find it difficult to clearly distinguish (in course title, at least) between basic and advanced subjects. In many instances, course content differs mainly in depth of coverage and in sophistication of the situations presented. One organization tries to describe the difference between levels of coverage by publishing the following objectives that are particular to its advanced courses:

> To provide opportunities for experienced supervisors to refresh and/or refine their self-awareness and their knowledge of supervisory goals and responsibilities; to acquire or further develop techniques for improving the effectiveness of their leadership; to examine techniques for establishing and maintaining a departmental climate that encourages productive employee behavior; to acquire new techniques for planning, controlling, and improving the productivity of departmental operations.

Typical courses offered by a great many organizations in the advanced supervision category would include the following:

- *New perspectives in supervision.* The changing work environment; changing expectations of the work force; changing goals and standards in the system; impact upon supervisory responsibilities, approaches, relationships, and stress.
- *Techniques for making leadership more effective.* Participative, or shared, leadership; techniques for encouraging employee initiative and self-discipline; mutual goal setting and methods-determination in groups.
- *Techniques for improving interpersonal relationships.* Modifying and improving employee behavior; special behavior problems; counseling; active listening; positive approaches to discipline.
- *Techniques for improving employee performance and productivity.* Work-standards review with employees; performance counseling; mutual goal setting for improvement; job training for improved performance; coaching and reinforcement.
- *Techniques for improving departmental productivity.* Establishing performance standards for quantity and quality of work; work-flow analysis; work-distribution analysis; work-simplification techniques; employee suggestions and participation in work-improvement efforts.
- *Techniques for improving plans, schedules, and results.* Looking ahead, system limitations; anticipating work-load peaks and valleys; assessing and acquiring resources; planning for staffing and training needs; schedule design; establishing operating procedures; measuring and assuring results.
- *Problem solving and decision making.* Management as problem solving and decision making; interrelation of problem solving and decision making; problem and opportunity identification; problem solution, prevention, and improvement techniques; decision-making techniques; need for initiative, creativity, and decisiveness.

Selected Examples of Programs in Advanced Supervision

A comparison between programs offered for basic supervision and those offered by the same organizations for advanced supervision illustrates the repetition inherent in the classification and programming process. Such redundancy is not necessarily bad; in fact, many training professionals strongly believe that almost all subjects covered in the basic program benefit from a second exposure at the advanced level.

Advanced Program for Public Supervisors. This program, offered by the U.S. Department of Agriculture, takes only forty hours, as does the basic program, but many of the subjects are doubled up or integrated with related topics:

1. Supervision and management awareness
2. Behavior analysis
3. Interpersonal relations
4. Self-confrontation
5. Creativity
6. Employee development and performance appraisal
7. Performance standards
8. Incentives and recognition
9. Authority, strategies, and decision making
10. Managing time
11. Delegation
12. Equal employment
13. Labor-management relations
14. Adverse actions
15. Information sharing and communications
16. Conflict resolution
17. Planning an organization system
18. Synthesis of management concepts
19. Practical problem solving
20. Self-development

Middle-Manager Review in a Rural Setting. The James Madison University advanced course is designed mainly for second-level supervisors. Its twelve two-hour sessions are scheduled weekly. The principal differences from the basic program are an emphasis on the managerial functions and the addition of the budgeting, finance, and legal aspects of supervision.

1. Role of the manager
2. Planning
3. Organization and motivation
4. Leadership and authority
5. Communication
6. Budgeting and finance
7. Controlling
8. Decision making

9. Job appraisal and employee training
10. Current legal topics
11. Self-development
12. The manager as integrator

SPECIALTY COURSES AND WORKSHOPS

There are a number of courses that might be classified as either basic or advanced, or they might fall outside a particular organization's concept of what should be included in either. Typical of these "nonrequired" (or perhaps "nonessential") courses are the following:

- *Information management.* Principles of data processing; computer operations; insights into computer language; record keeping.
- *Budgeting and expense control.* How budgets are built; relationship to departmental operations and limitations.
- *Team building.* Developing morale and initiative in small groups; participative leadership.
- *Job and work design.* Developing morale by focusing on the work elements rather than on people.
- *Understanding statistics and quantitative methods.* An overview stressing concepts, applications, interpretation.
- *Scheduling techniques.* Straight-line; parallel; Gantt-type; overview of PERT (program evaluation and review technique) and CPM (critical-path method); short-interval scheduling.
- *Work-sampling workshop.*Methodology; applications; limitations; project experience.
- *Paperwork-simplification workshop.* Systems and procedures methodology; work simplification in the office; paper-flow analysis; project experience.
- *Counseling workshop.* Nondirective interviewing; active listening; special problems—family, physical, emotional, absences, lateness, bizarre behavior, alcohol, drugs, and so forth; referral procedures.
- *Organization development techniques.* An overview; intervention; group development (team building); performance-factor analysis; reward-system analysis; force-field analysis; conflict resolution.

FOCUS CLUSTERS

It is popular in the in-service field to offer short courses containing clusters of related topics focusing on a particular skill or knowledge area. Many such courses are designed around selected chapters in a particular text or reference book. For example, the following focus clusters are commonly used in conjunction with one popular book in the field:

- *Interpersonal relations.* Work-group behavior; conflict and cooperation; appraisal of employee performance; the art of leadership; effective oral and written communications; giving orders and instructions; counseling troubled employees; handling complaints and grievances; how and when to discipline.
- *Management process.* The supervisor's management job; supervision and the management process; making plans and carrying out policy; exercising control over people and processes; problem solving and decision making; organizing an effective department; staffing with human relations.
- *Productivity and quality improvement.* Supervision and the management process; training and development of employees; job design and enrichment; job assignments and work schedules; improving productivity and controlling costs; advancing toward a higher quality of workmanship.
- *Building personal skills.* Problem solving and decision making; taking charge of your career; managing time and handling stress; putting your best foot forward in the organization.

Special-Interest Courses

There are always a number of topic areas that enjoy a brief popularity and are relevant to current problems. Other courses hold high value periodically for any organization. Among both kinds of special-interest subject areas, these seem to retain perennial value: performance appraisal, equal employment opportunity, job instruction training, productivity improvement, time management, stress management, grievance handling, leadership, communications, transactional analysis, problem solving, and most recently, innovation and entrepreneurship.

Chapter 9

Selection and Use of Training Methods and Techniques

INTRODUCTION

Supervisory training draws from the same array of sources, methods, and techniques as other forms of training. Although documented evidence is sparse, some of these approaches seem more appropriate than others for training supervisors. Prime consideration must be given to the characteristics of the supervisory-training population. Today's supervisors are used to comfortable accommodations and have high expectations for any training activity they are directed to attend. Accordingly, careful thought must be given to the selection of a training site that does not demean the supervisors' role in or contribution to the organization. If, for example, middle managers meet in sumptuous surroundings and exotic places, supervisors should meet in at least proportional comfort. Also, today's supervisors are generally well-educated adults, with long and varied experience in their organizations. Your training methods should respect these qualities and treat supervisors like the mature, capable, often creative people that they are.

ON-THE-JOB VERSUS OFF-THE-JOB TRAINING

For convenience and economy, if for no other reason, the great majority of supervisory training takes place at formal conferences. Thus, trainers are regularly faced with choosing a location for the training program. Unfortunately, there is a scarcity of reliable data on the relative advantages of conducting training on-site or off-site, the use of internal versus external instructors, or even the particular methods of training utilized.

Bula in 1982 found that the primary source and locale for supervisory training were as follows:

Internal	57 percent
Outside	36
Vocational-technical, on-site	30
Vocational-technical, off-site	26
University, on-site	19
University, off-site	27
Other organizations, on-site	9
Other organizations, off-site	14[1]

This survey does not, however, tell us the relative advantages and disadvantages of training off the job or on the job.

An earlier study by the Conference Board found that 90 percent of all formal training for supervisors takes place off the job in a classroom, conference, seminar, or workshop format. Only about 10 percent of the companies surveyed conducted formal supervisory training *on the job* that met a three-part criterion: (1) stated, written objectives for each participant, (2) one or more designated individuals (line managers or human resources development [HRD] professionals) to guide the experience of the trainees, and (3) a specific schedule setting forth the types of experience to be obtained and a timetable of intended progress.[2]

Off-the-job classroom-type training is obviously more convenient for the trainer and easier to control. The Conference Board survey showed a distribution of methods used in off-job classroom supervisory training greatly favoring group discussion (95 percent) and formal presentation or lecture (90 percent), followed by case study (85 percent), role-play (60 percent), required reading (55 percent), and business games (40 percent). These figures do not tell the whole story, since other comments regarding this survey indicated that case studies and role-play were accorded less than 20 percent of the training time by those organizations using them. In a related study of off-site meetings attended by supervisors, McKeon provides some specific insights into the particular classroom methods that can make them effective. Participants observed that presentations and discussions accounted for about 60 percent of their training time and yielded 43 percent of the perceived learning value of the activity; working on problems in small groups took about 25 percent of the training time and accounted for about 27 percent of the perceived value. Interestingly, required reading and related outside work accounted for about 15 percent of the time and 16 percent of the value. The balance of perceived value was derived from incidental exchanges during meals and coffee breaks. The conclusion is that small-group assignments and self-paced learning for supervisors appear to be more effective, hour for hour, than formal presentations.[3]

The Conference Board survey also indicated that HRD professionals provided the faculty for 75 percent of in-house, off-the-job classroom training for supervisors. The balance of the faculty was provided by line managers and other functional specialists in the organization.

THE INFLUENCE OF TRAINING METHODS

As with other training, the methods used for supervisory training should be varied to achieve the established objectives with the greatest simplicity and economy. The generally agreed-upon advice regarding choice of methods is this:

- To increase *knowledge,* consider especially: assigned reading, lectures, guided discussions, observational tours, case studies, programmed learning, and self-tests.
- To improve *skill,* consider especially: modeling, role-playing, demonstrations, case studies, problem-solving conferences, job rotation, and supervised practice on or off the job.
- To influence *attitudes,* consider especially: role-playing, demonstrations, case studies, problem-centered conferences, job rotation, and films.

In general, supervisors tend to prefer and to learn more effectively from specific, concrete examples, experience and reality-oriented practice, and interactive exercises than from abstract, conceptual presentations or from reading assignments.

As an adult, a supervisor has moved out of the full-time passive student role into the role of "doer." With this change comes the need to be treated with respect, to be in charge of his or her own decision processes, and to be seen as a unique individual. The supervisor's experience may be the biggest asset—or in some cases, a monumental liability. While past experiences are useful as comparisons and benchmarks, they establish habits and patterns of thought difficult to alter. This may cause some learning problems. Nevertheless, to deny the learner's experience is to thwart the greatest potential available. Things begin to happen when the learner connects the educational experiences with "real life."

PARTICIPATIVE, CONFERENCE-BASED TRAINING METHODS

As a direct consequence of the supervisor's mature role in the organization, the instructor's role must shift from one of didactic authority to that of a facilitator of learning, a guide, and a resource. The instructor or conference leader must create a training environment and a set of experiences from which supervisors can learn and progress. The lecture method runs counter to this objective. It encourages passivity rather than active involvement on the part of the participants. The one-against-the-group presentation is, of course, necessary to impart certain information. However, it should be used sparingly and as often as possible be reinforced with discussion, small-group activities, and other involvement techniques.

In a conference situation, the individual supervisors have the opportunity to think through the topic or problem as it relates to their own experiences, to voice their opinions, to ask questions, and to clarify their thinking. This participation increases the probability that performance will actually be improved on the job after the training session is over.

SELECTION GUIDELINES

In general, as recommended earlier, in chapter 7, training methods should be varied. Each technique has its place and degree of appropriateness according to the variables in a particular training situation. In this section, useful guidelines for evaluating and selecting techniques usually associated with conference-based supervisory training are itemized.

Formal Presentations and Lectures. Because of the limited opportunity for participation, the lecture method should be used as sparingly as possible. Its primary value lies in providing uniform information in a short time to a supervisory group. It is not effective for imparting interpersonal skills. It should go without saying that, in every case, the lecturer should know the subject authoritatively and be fully prepared before taking the podium.

Group Discussions. While more time-consuming than lectures, the group-discussion approach has the advantage of drawing participants into the learning process and enabling supervisors to come to grips with practical aspects of the subject matter. Consider the following:

Structured discussions tend to provoke the kind of involved reflection that adds to participants' growth. The process of thinking about the questions and the willingness to engage in the discussion are often more important than right or wrong answers.

In order for supervisors to exchange ideas and determine how new ideas apply to them, the facilitator must stimulate the process by asking open-ended questions, by paraphrasing, and by directing the discussion toward the goals set for the session. The line of questioning can follow a kind of continuum, progressing from observable facts (without opinion), to ideas and opinions, then to more general conclusions.

In preparing to lead a discussion, instructors should:

1. Set a goal or goals for the discussion. Be certain of exactly what you intend to accomplish.
2. Have in mind questions that will lead toward the goal or goals. But try to develop questions that do not imply a specific answer.

During the discussion, ask open-ended questions—questions for which no specific answer is implied and that cannot be answered by a simple "yes" or "no." Essentially, open-ended questions ask for opinions or for the development of substantive information. These are the questions that begin with "What," "Where," "Why," "How much," "When," "In what way," "How," and so on. The purpose of this kind of questioning is to draw out opinions, disagreements, and confusions so that they can be either reinforced or cleared up. Since so much of what a supervisor has to do with people is not rigidly programmed, even in well-structured organizations, participants must be helped to reach a basic rationale rather than directed to memorize "cookbook" formulas.

When leading a discussion:

1. Guide the thinking of the group according to the prepared questions. Amplify, clarify, and summarize the ideas generated, using a chart board to focus the group's attention.
2. Be aware of the participation or nonparticipation of each group member. Since you are searching for everyone's ideas, try to make certain everyone participates.
3. Don't approve or disapprove (for example, "I like what you're saying"). Listen, paraphrase when needed for further clarification, ask questions, and draw participants out. When summarizing, you can make the essential points, most of which hopefully will already have been made by the group.

Demonstration. Demonstration is a useful technique for imparting both process-related skills—such as how to use a piece of hardware—and interpersonal skills. It requires extensive preparation, but it is realistic and interesting and helps to clarify important and difficult points of procedure.

Discussion (Buzz or Interaction) Groups. If space permits, divide the supervisors into groups of six persons each (simply by turning chairs around). Assign a particular subject area (such as absenteeism). Ask each group to spend no more than ten minutes to develop what it thinks is the most critical supervisory problem regarding that area. Then have each group give its report. If done quickly enough, there will be time for the group to discuss the problems that seem most urgent and how they might be handled. Such discussion groups provide a large degree of participation, while ferreting out areas of confusion and misunderstandings.

Research Panels. On a rotating basis, assign five supervisors to a reading or on-site research project on a particular topic, such as quality circles. Have them report their findings to the group and field questions from the group about the subject.

Case Studies. While a very time-consuming approach, case studies are especially useful in enhancing problem-solving ability, developing an awareness of interpersonal situations, and providing supervisors with an opportunity to test the worth of their ideas by sharing them with other supervisors, as well as helping them learn to work productively with others.

Case studies stimulate participation in group discussions. It is important to engage supervisors in the process of thinking through each situation, not only from a supervisor's viewpoint but also from the viewpoint of all the other people involved in the case. Debate and disagreement among supervisors should be encouraged so that each can try out his or her feelings about the case. Cases sometimes frustrate participants, since there is rarely a single, infallible, "correct" solution. The learning process, especially as it helps to change attitudes, is aided by such uncertainty.

Since a case-study discussion can be so effective when properly conducted, it is helpful for the instructor to understand both its objectives and the dynamics of the analysis and discussion process.

Goals. The primary goal of a group discussion about human relations problems is understanding—an awareness of the interplay of human ambitions, aggressions, hostilities, withdrawals, motivations, and satisfactions that cause employees and supervisors to act the way they do, for better or for worse.

The case-study discussion approach to human relations understanding and improvement depends on simulated experience. The participants observe a realistic supervisory situation—one easily recognized, one in which they can perhaps identify their own roles, and one with which they can compare their own experiences. Within a single meeting and with a minimum of risk, participants may test their own conclusions, attitudes, and interpersonal skills. During the same period, supervisors can observe the conclusions, attitudes, and techniques of their peers. Repeated experience with the case-study discussion tends to develop in supervisors a self-awareness of their misconceptions about human behavior—their own behavior, that of their associates, and that of the people they supervise.

Process. Participants in a case-study discussion progress through four stages of mental development as they approach understanding.

First, as the participants view the case and its inherent problems, they "look for the villain." That is to say, supervisors with conceptions of human behavior as either good or bad try to find the single person who is at fault. They may brand as the culprit almost anyone in the case study. Or they sometimes blame people who don't appear—with such objections as "The company policy should have been spelled out," "The union must be behind this complaint somewhere," or "The supervisor just asked for trouble."

The second stage of development takes place shortly after the search for the culprit has been thwarted by the objections of the more sophisticated members of the group. Stage two is characterized by the desire of the participants to "play God." In other words, they see that the problem could have been avoided or resolved quickly had the employee done this, the supervisor that, or the superior still another thing.

In the third stage, the participants seek a simple solution and start to feel frustrated. They now begin to ask for more facts. "Surely," participants say, "We can't be expected to solve a problem from which so many facts are omitted." They want to know what went on between the supervisor and the employee before this problem came to the fore. How old is the employee? What has been the company policy in the past?

It is in this stage that true understanding starts to blossom. Supervisors begin to see that (in this kind of situation, at any rate) the reasons for a particular human behavior are not as simple as they once thought. They slowly become aware of the need for knowing the background and experience of individuals in order to interpret their current behavior. This is the critical stage of the case discussion. It is absolutely essential that the participants not be permitted to explain away their frustration on the simple grounds that the case study itself, or the instructor, has not supplied them with adequate information. They must see that this is the heart of the matter in human relationships—that for every act there is a reason, that this reason is often not obvious, and that only by finding and controlling the cause can employee behavior be anticipated and possibly improved.

Stage four is really the informed outgrowth of stage three. It is after the participants become enlightened, so to speak, that they begin to discuss the total picture of human behavior as presented in a particular case study. They see the whole web of circumstance in which the compromise, give-and-take, mutual understanding, and reasonable expectations develop.

Incident-Process Case Discussion. Using this technique, a printed description of an incident requiring a decision is presented, and the group must decide what action is required.

The discussion leader often retains additional background material, which he or she furnishes only as members of the group request specific items of information. If the information is not requested, the discussion leader does not provide it. Thus, supervisors may be required to decide a case on the basis of only partial information because they failed to elicit all available data. After obtaining the desired information, each participant presents a decision and the supporting reasons for it. The decisions offered by the supervisors are then discussed, with the objective of arriving at a common conclusion.

Role-Playing. As a natural outgrowth of a case-study or incident-process discussion, role-playing can be instructive—provided the participants are seriously inclined and intensely interested in the outcome of the case situation. Otherwise, role-play may invite horseplay and humor, negating any value it could have.

The role-play technique involves the instructor's calling on one or more of the participants to act out the part of the characters in the case. This may be done informally, or a carefully planned procedure may be followed. In any event, the objective is to provide the role-player with an opportunity to try out his or her ideas about human relations in a simulated situation—without risking the consequences of real-life reactions. If, in the session, participants can act out roles they are unfamiliar with, they may be helped to understand their own roles as perceived by a subordinate or an associate. For instance, if a supervisor were to act out the role of an employee in a role-playing skit, the supervisor might become better able to understand the employee's point of view in the future. In the long run, this deeper insight may encourage changes in the supervisor's own attitude.

Role-playing can do more than change attitudes. By providing simulated job experience, it may enable a student to actually learn by doing. For that reason, it has been called by some "reality practice."

In summary, role-playing requires very skilled leadership and extensive preparation, and may appear artificial or embarrassing to participants. On the other hand, it is a proven way for supervisors to acquire an awareness and understanding of interpersonal relationships and to gain "protected experience" without penalty for mistakes.[4]

Behavior Modeling. The behavior-modeling technique combines demonstration and practice in a particularly effective way. It calls for extensive preparation, however, and often expensive materials. It is especially appropriate for developing interpersonal skills in handling the basic, difficult employee-related problems that are common to supervisory management. The process itself (shown in figure 9-1) is complex, though, and requires unusually professional leadership.[5]

Because behavioral modeling has received so much attention and also because of the sophistication of its materials and application, a fuller discussion of it appears in appendix 1.

Simulations (Business Games). Simulation exercises are generally more appropriate for management development, although an increasing number of them are available for supervisory training.[6] Interactive, computer-based exercises, however, can accelerate group experience or provide an individual supervisor with the opportunity to gain group-related experience under self-study conditions.

FIGURE 9-1 BEHAVIOR-MODELING SYSTEM IN SUPERVISORY TRAINING

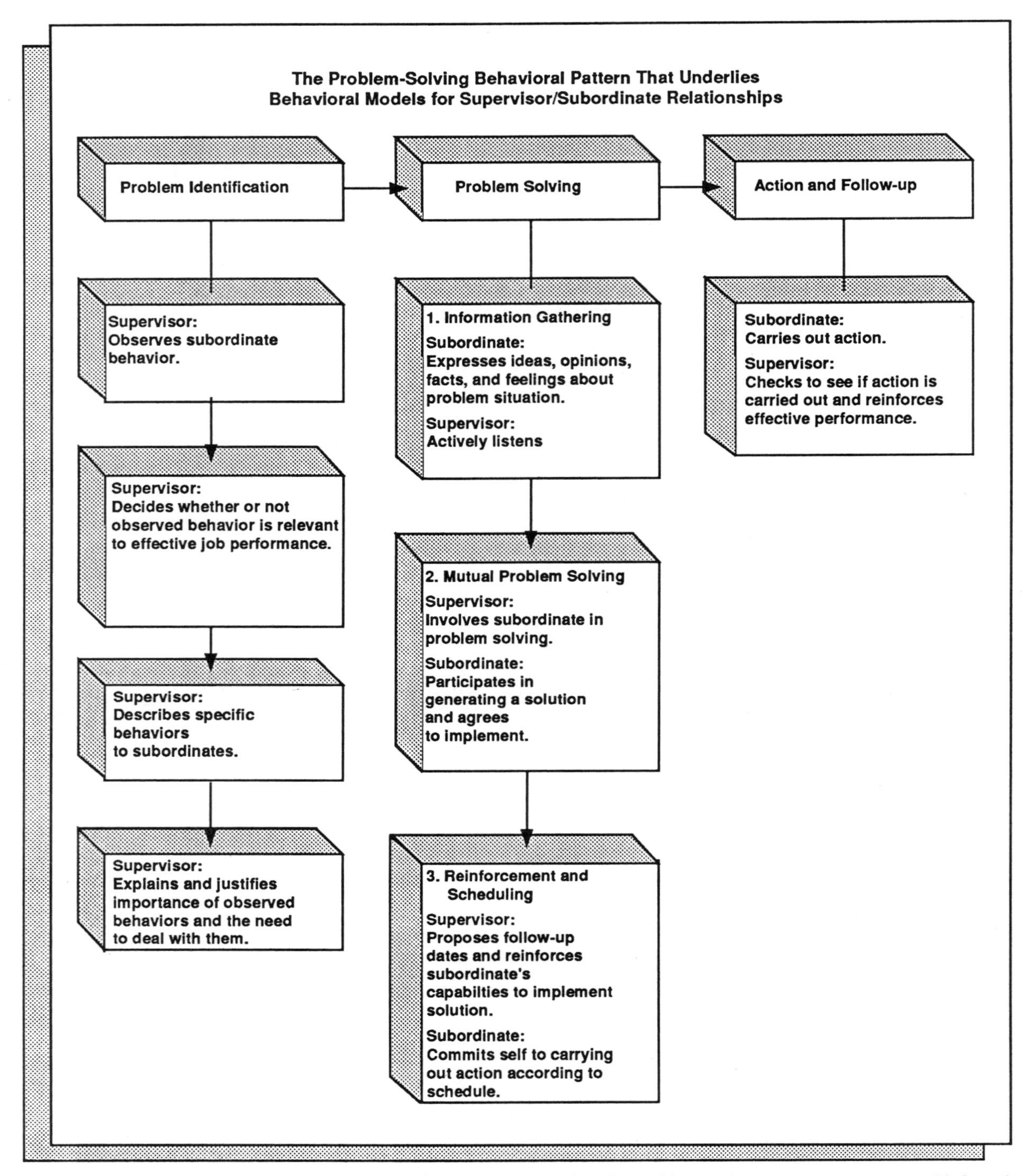

Source: Adapted from Lester R. Bittel and Ronald S. Burke, *Course Management Guide* for *What Every Supervisor Should Know,* 5th ed. (New York: McGraw-Hill Book Company, 1984), 7.

The management (or business) game is essentially a learning device that enables supervisors to learn by participation and involvement. The simulation, or game, is a contest among participants, either as individuals or as teams, who must follow a set of rules and who aim to win the contest. The game is successful when the participants have obtained a better understanding of that portion of reality simulated within the game model.

Learning involves three successive steps:

1. Acquiring the common language and the facts expressed in the game
2. Learning the process simulated within the game model, including restrictions
3. Understanding the relative trade-offs—the costs, the advantages, and the disadvantages—required of the different strategies and alternatives

Torgerson and Foley observe that games are usually conducted in three phases: (1) preplay description and briefing of the rules; (2) play itself—in sequential, discrete, and compressed periods of time; and (3) postgame critique of the decisions and consequences, possibly with participant suggestions for improving the realism of the game.[7] Because of the competitive nature of the game, participants are usually motivated to learn by their desire to win.

Games differ in their use of *interactive* or *noninteractive* relationships. Those that attempt to reproduce the competitive aspect of business and that include, in particular, a marketing component are likely to be interactive. Within this framework, the action taken by one supervisory team (or "firm") may affect the results of an action taken by one or more opponents, as well as the action of the team in question. An interactive game is analogous to tennis, where the tactics and success of an individual depend on the actions of the opponent.

Games may or may not employ a computer. The advantages of using a computer are much the same as the advantages of using one for any day-to-day processing task: speed, accuracy, and comprehensive reports. The computer-based game is likely to be more complex because more complex relationships can be modeled and mathematically manipulated. However, the noncomputer game has the flexibility of being carried into the classroom or on the road without concern for computer accessibility and compatibility.

Films, Videos, and Audiocassettes. Audiovisual aids continue to be used mainly to highlight or supplement other training methods for supervisors. However, they can provide excellent demonstrations of technical and behavioral procedures. They are, of course, very expensive. Audiocassettes have a solid niche in providing information and case studies to supervisors in off-the-job, self-study situations. There are a great number of traditional films (in reel or tape format) available that are especially appropriate for supervisory training. A list is provided in appendix 2.

Guest Speakers. Role models and a sense of reality may be provided by guest speakers who are presently employed either as (1) supervisors or middle-level managers or (2) executives to whom supervisors report. Both kinds of speakers can offer conference participants insights that will reinforce classroom discussions. Be sure to encourage informal presentations with give-and-take questioning rather than carefully prepared lectures.

SUPPLEMENTAL TRAINING METHODS FOR SUPERVISORS

There are a great many more methods that may be used for supervisory training, either (1) in the conference situation or as a supplement to it or (2) independently in connection with supervisory on-the-job training and self-development. These are discussed in this section with a view toward helping training professionals evaluate their suitability to particular needs and situations. The matters of transferring conference-based training back to the job and techniques for coaching will be discussed in chapter 11.

GROUP-ORIENTED ACTIVITIES

Some methods and techniques are more appropriate for unifying a particular supervisory-training course than for individual pursuit of training and development. The following methods are particularly suitable for supplementing training in group-oriented programs.

Plant and Office Visits. Especially for participants unfamiliar with an important aspect of business or industry, a trip to a nearby plant or office early in the program will provide a context for what they are learning. For such trips to be truly effective, participants should be prepped beforehand on what to look for: the working environment rather than details of the process (although attention to specifics should not be discouraged); work stations; computer terminals; conveyor belts; clock alleys; rest rooms; fire extinguishers; employees at work; and supervisors in action.

Attendance at Professional-Society Meetings. Many professional societies welcome visitors to their meetings (or will furnish speakers and arrange for company visits). Here again is an opportunity for participants to rub up against reality and to find role models. The clubs of the International Management Council (affiliated with the YMCA of Des Plaines, IL) and clubs sponsored by the National Management Association (Dayton, Ohio) are particularly appropriate, although there are literally hundreds of technical and management associations with suitable program content.

One can find a professional association or society connected with almost any kind of work. A few typical organizations are the Purchasing Management Association, American Marketing Association, American Society for Production and Inventory Control, Public Relations Society of America, Hospital Personnel Association, American Society for Quality Control, and National Association of Accountants.

Additionally, membership in the appropriate organization can enable supervisors to improve their technical expertise, thereby assisting in the training and development process, and to cultivate peer contacts useful in solving technical problems. Many organizations support the participation of supervisors in these organizations by paying their expenses and encouraging them to become actively involved through taking an office, serving on a committee, or working on a special project.

Trade-Show Visits. Another way to extend supervisors' awareness of subject matter is to encourage their visits to relevant trade shows and exhibits, such as those sponsored by the National Safety Council and various other professional trade associations featuring computer developments, office automation, maintenance equipment, and the like.

Exposure to Management and Trade Journals. A good way to ensure timeliness and relevance to the course is to make available to supervisors (or to encourage their reading in the library) copies of supervisor-oriented magazines such as *Supervisory Management* and *The Personnel Journal* as well as publications like *Venture, Inc.,* and *Working Woman.*

Certification Opportunities. A nationally recognized program for certification of proficiency in management exists under the sponsorship of the Institute of Certified Professional Managers (ICPM), James Madison University, Harrisonburg, Virginia 22807. ICPM prescribes a course of preparation and conducts certification examinations semiannually.

Individual-Oriented Activities

Some supervisory-training methods are more effective in situations where an individual wishes to pursue self-improvement independently or under the guidance of a training professional. As with the group-oriented methods listed in the preceding subsection, some of the individual-oriented methods are appropriate for either independent or group training situations.

Computer-Assisted Instruction. With the growing availability of affordable, reliable microcomputers, computer-assisted instruction (CAI)—teaching with the aid of a computer—is increasingly being applied in industry to meet educational and training goals. In CAI, the trainee interacts directly with the computer by typing responses on a typewriterlike keyboard. Messages inputted by the trainee are displayed on a TV-like monitor screen as they are transmitted to the computer. The computer then communicates with the trainee by displaying preprogrammed text on the monitor screen.

Computer-assisted instruction, when combined with computer-managed instruction, can improve training programs through its ability to provide (1) individualization of instruction through self-pacing, (2) diagnosis of a trainee's strengths and weaknesses in the development of desired skills and attitudes, and (3) prescription of appropriate instructional content.

Ramsey advises that the decision to implement computer-assisted instruction should be based on its potential for achieving specific training objectives.[8] The traditional forms of CAI most easily adapted to training programs are drill and practice, tutorial, simulation, and games. The first two are good for knowledge and skill training for supervisors, although they have drawbacks similar to those associated with programmed instruction. Simulations seem to have the most promise for supervisory training.

Under the *drill-and-practice mode,* the trainee is presented with exercises designed to provide practice in or to test knowledge gained from instruction received from a source other than the computer itself. Multiple-choice questions are a common format in this mode. Under the *tutorial mode,* instruction is presented directly by the computer. Highly individualized instruction is possible in this mode. *Simulations* are designed so that the trainee may study some real situation or environment, such as operation of an expensive or dangerous piece of equipment, in a risk-free manner.

Correspondence Courses. As is true of any self-paced, self-motivated learning, correspondence courses have exceedingly limited application with supervisors. Sufficient motivation is often lacking. There are, of course, some organizations that have found such courses the only way to provide supervisory training in small, remote locations.

Required-Reading Programs. Programs of required reading also have very limited application and should be employed quite selectively due to the difficulty and disinterest most supervisors have in acquiring information this way.

Programmed Instruction. As with the required-reading approach, programmed-instruction techniques have limited appeal to supervisors, not because the techniques are ineffective but because they do not match the learning preferences of the supervisory population.

Special Assignments. As a result of observation and appraisal, it is possible for executives to identify specific aspects of a supervisor's performance that can be improved. On the basis of this knowledge, special project assignments or task forces and committees can be arranged to encourage the use of the skills to be developed. The effects of such carefully planned assignments are cumulative: increased job interest, greater confidence, and effective work habits.

Job Rotation. Job rotation is a more formal approach than special assignments, in that a supervisor must be temporarily or permanently assigned to a full-time job, with all the responsibilities and authority associated with it. In principle, this is a very good method, but it often encounters organizational practicalities that make it difficult, if not impossible to implement. It is probably most feasible and effective under an organizationwide management development plan.

Phillips observes that there are a number of ways to overcome the structural difficulties in implementing job rotation:

> Two or more people may exchange places (temporarily) with each taking on new responsibilities. For example, in the inspection department of one manufacturing firm, several supervisors inspect employees' work at different stages in the process. These supervisors rotate systematically in order to wrestle with different types of inspection and quality control problems. In one hospital new department supervisors rotate through all major departments and stay for one month.[9]

A variation, *internal lateral replacement,* involves filling vacancies with transfers from within the department, eliminating the extensive orientation that would be required for someone brought in from outside.

A part-time or temporary job rotation allows two people to train each other in certain job duties. For example, one organization temporarily assigns district sales supervisors to headquarters when corporate staff supervisors are on vacation. This not only provides additional training for district supervisors but also improves the cooperation and working relationship between field and headquarters staff.

Phillips also advises that

> if budget and organizational setting permit, an extra employee can be allocated for a permanent training slot. One person may be kept in the work unit to learn as many jobs as possible. This extra employee is usually preparing for the next opening. The extra employee also can be cross-trained or used to relieve others involved in cross-training. One manufacturer keeps an extra production supervisor in each major department—usually a newly promoted supervisor who fills in when someone is on vacation, jury duty, or a short leave of absence.[10]

Self-Development. Many supervisors have a high level of interest in their jobs. Such persons respond favorably to reasonable suggestions as to how they can increase their competence. Reading relevant books or articles, attendance at appropriate meetings, evening courses at local colleges, or participation in professional management associations are but a few of the activities open to ambitious supervisors. Supervisors who are willing to use some of their own time to improve job performance identify themselves as potential middle- and upper-level managers. They do need guidance, however, if they are to use their time effectively. This subject will be examined more closely in chapter 14.

Part IV

PROGRAM DESIGN AND IMPLEMENTATION

Chapter 10

Program Planning and Design

INTRODUCTION

Once data on all the variables of competency, selection, needs assessment, course content, and method have been assembled and reviewed, the trainer faces the major task of determining and implementing the supervisory-training strategy. In the planning and design phase, the trainer must set program objectives and policies and consider a number of important factors, including, for example: the cost, format, participant selection, and basic configuration of the program. The trainer must also decide between traditional and modular approaches and between packaged and custom-designed programs; and he or she must then prepare the appropriate program and course manuals. Finally, the planning process itself warrants an audit to check it against common guidelines and proven models.

SETTING OBJECTIVES

It is essential that you clearly define and write down the program objectives. You must also secure agreement on those objectives beforehand—*in fact* from the principal line managers and *by inference* from the supervisors themselves. Express the objectives in terms of incremental improvements in knowledge, skills, or attitudes directly related to the acknowledged supervisory competencies and the assessment of developmental needs. The more quantitatively these goals can be defined, the better, although certain objectives must be expressed in qualitative terms. Some examples of program or course objectives are:

- *Basic objectives of supervisory training:*
    1. To give participants essential knowledge of their responsibilities so that they may make decisions that are compatible with company goals and policies.

2. To give participants knowledge vital to good management practices so that this knowledge may guide day-to-day management decisions.
3. To provide participants with the skills needed to direct the work of their departments and people in a positive and productive manner.

- *Introduction to supervision.* To provide inexperienced supervisors with a basic understanding of management functions and of their specific responsibilities in carrying them out in their organization.
- *Advanced supervision.* To provide experienced supervisors with a review of job-related, fundamental management practices and to introduce them to a selected variety of important new concepts and techniques directly applicable to their work.
- *Time management.* To instill in supervisors an awareness of the degree to which personal time may be controlled and, along with this, to provide them with a number of specific tools and techniques for increasing the productive use of their time on the job.

Whenever possible, objectives should also include a statement of how the acquired learning will be evaluated. These evaluation measures can include a number of methods, such as:

1. Before-and-after comprehension testing
2. Self-evaluation feedback from supervisors after returning to their jobs
3. Evaluation of critical incidents by superiors
4. Routine performance-appraisal criteria
5. Measurement of performance-related data from the supervisors' departments, such as absence and turnover rates, grievances lodged, productivity and quality measures
6. Identifiable achievements, such as reports prepared, problems solved, and conflicts resolved

Evaluation will be discussed in more detail in chapter 15.

ESTABLISHING POLICY

It is essential that policy guidelines be established in order to assure that program planning moves along a broad but focused channel toward the program's objectives. The difficulty at this stage from a professional trainer's point of view is which comes first—on the one hand, a review of the organization's constraints or, on the other hand, the establishment of policy to be modified later by a recognition of constraining factors affecting program design. Policy will be considered first, in order to provide a context for discussion in the next section of factors that may limit policy choice.

The major elements of supervisory-training policy usually cover such matters as:

1. Participant selection
2. The role of the professional training staff
3. The roles of line and staff managers whose supervisors are enrolled in the program
4. The roles and responsibilities of the supervisory participants
5. Hours of the day, and days of the week, that training sessions will be conducted
6. Participants' pay while attending training sessions, during or after working hours
7. Selection of instructors and their remuneration (if they are company personnel not employed as members of the training staff)
8. Use of tests
9. Choice of training sites
10. Use of outside consultants or proprietary programs
11. Extent of participant travel and reimbursement
12. Tuition reimbursement for voluntary attendance at outside seminars or courses related to, but not required in, the program
13. Attendance
14. Maintaining records of program completion, including the award of Continuing Education Units (CEUs), for the purpose of recognition
15. Conformance with legal requirements and established company policies

The box below illustrates a rather comprehensive policy statement for a program conducted by a state agency.

A simpler, but very straightforward policy statement is furnished in the box on page 146. It was prepared for supervisors attending the companywide basic-training session of a major eastern manufacturer.

Policy Guidelines for a Certificate Program

Participant Requirements and Preparation

1. An individual may enter any program level without first having completed successfully a lower-level program, although a progression from Levels 0 or I sequentially through Level II to Level III would be most productive in developing individual competencies.
2. There will be no aptitude, acceptance, or proficiency testing of participants or potential participants—neither to determine their preprogram or

Continued on next page

Policy Guidelines for a Certificate Program—*Continued*

course qualifications nor to judge their competency at the conclusion of a program or course. (See course outline format for evaluation instruments to be used by instructors to measure instructional effectiveness as a guide to course improvement.)

3. Course participants will typically represent a mixture of individuals from different agencies (state and local) and with differing functional responsibilities; thus, a certain degree of generality in course content will prevail.

4. Participants may be required to spend up to two hours of specified preparation at their job sites before a course begins.

Course Design and Structure

5. Program and course designs should, of necessity and practicality, target on improving supervisory problem areas rather than merely providing a broad spectrum of typical offerings on supervision subjects; thus, there will be a highly selective, albeit narrow, curriculum at each program level.

6. As a consequence of No. 5, each course will attempt to cover only a relatively few, but critical objectives, in order to assure maximum time for participants to acquire competency in each objective area.

7. The learning process in most courses will stress participant involvement ("active" versus "passive" learning) and will allow time for purposeful case analysis, role-play, and individual problem solving.

8. Courses will not be structured so as to qualify them for CEU registration, although they may be modified for that purpose at a later time.

9. Courses required in the certificate program will, in the main, be unique to the program and will not be assumed to be equivalent to other courses offered by the state under similar listings.

10. Certain courses within a program may require that participants first take and complete another course (prerequisite) within the program.

11. Courses may range from one-half day to three days in duration. A one-half day course will be the equivalent of four contact hours, a one-day course the equivalent of eight contact hours, and so forth.

12. Required courses will be offered with enough frequency to assure that a program participant can complete a particular program within any consecutive twelve-month period.

13. For each program level, a basic reference text for participants will be prescribed from a list of recommended texts.

14. A supplemental text or workbook may be prescribed for a particular course, dependent upon the degree of specialization and approval of an instructor's request for such a text or workbook.

15. Visual and instructional aids specified for a particular course will be limited to those already on hand or available at a participating institution, or as obtainable through the program's operating budget.

Continued on next page

Policy Guidelines for a Certificate Program—*Continued*

Course Conduct

16. In courses dealing with employee performance and/or interpersonal relationships, maximum usage will be made of behavior-modeling techniques. For example, such courses will be structured with:

    a. An emphasis on the behavior itself (what to do and what not to do, and how to do it effectively) rather than on personality or psychological analysis.

    b. Provision of examples (models) that illustrate ways of handling a particular situation (such as a reprimand) productively.

    c. Opportunities for participants to imitate the model (role-play) so as to get the feel of how to behave in an effective way themselves.

    d. Provision of social reinforcement by having the role-play take place under observation of their peers, who can help participants judge whether or not they will be effective in an actual job setting.

17. In all courses, the instructional process will utilize the principles of transfer training. That is, each course will provide:

    a. Specific, detailed instructions about how to proceed (in discussing off-standard performance, for example) as well as general (big-picture) rationales for cause-and-effect (stimulus-response) relationships.

    b. A high degree of overlearning—in effect, as much practice (such as role-play or problem solving) as possible.

    c. As much similarity as possible between seminar settings and actual job conditions. This will require a high degree of reality and believability in the selection of cases and examples presented for examination and experience.

    d. Feedback that reinforces and approves satisfactory participant performance (or corrects and coaches unsatisfactory performance) at the seminar (by peers and the instructor) and, very important, by superiors after participants return to the job setting.

Course Instructors

18. Course instructors will be expected to conform to all facets and conditions prescribed in the course outlines, but especially to course objectives, subject matter, pre- and postcourse comprehension evaluations, methodology guidelines, and take-home action-plan implementation.

19. Course instructors will be expected to select or develop case studies, examples, and problems that illustrate and offer experience in the public sector (rather than in private industry) and to feature office-type activities and situations rather than factory functions and settings.

20. Course instructors will not be permitted to substitute their own similar-sounding, "standard" courses for those specified in the program. This will require special preparation on the part of each instructor to conform to course outline guides.

Policy Regarding Requirements for Course Completion

Attendance

At least 80 percent attendance is required for course completion. Participants absent for more than 20 percent of the classes will not be awarded credit. However, to fulfill completion requirements, those missed sessions may be made up at the next scheduled offering of the program. Participants absent for job-related reasons are required to discuss this with the instructor so that material missed can be made up.

Instructor's Requirements

Each course has specific goals that the instructor is responsible for achieving. Participants are required to meet the standards that the instructor requires for satisfactory completion of the course. These standards may include participation in class, tests, reviews, readings, and projects.

Participants' Responsibility

Participants who fail to meet the requirements for course completion are responsible for making up what was missed. If there is any question about meeting either the attendance or instructor's requirements, participants should *discuss this with the instructor before the end of the course.* Participants will be expected to contact Personnel Training for dates of future programs in order to make up attendance.

PROGRAM-DESIGN FACTORS

Policy and program design will both be affected by a number of factors. The most important and controversial of these are discussed below.

Costs, Benefits, and Budgets

Program design is most limited by (1) its *cost* (participant time, training salaries, facilities, travel, materials, and so on), as balanced against (2) the *potential benefits* resulting from the training. Intangible, unmeasurable benefits are always harder to justify than measurable ones like improvements in productivity, reduction in errors or defects, or a decline in absences.

Few organizations actually charge the time lost by supervisors attending training sessions against the training budget. Nevertheless, it is helpful to make some sort of comparison between the cost of this time (in terms of participants' salary) and the total cost of the training. A common measure of training cost is participant-learning-hours, or PLH. If, for example, a program cost $2,800 and 14 supervisors attended for a total of 20 hours each, the PLH would be 280, and the cost per PLH would be $10. Weinstein and Kasl have shown that the ratio of the cost of supervisory time lost to the cost of all other PLH is 150 percent.[1] The inverse of this figure (about 0.66) indicates that the cost of training is relatively small when compared with the value of the supervisor's time to the organization.

In 1982, Weinstein and Kasl surveyed the cost of training and arrived at the following estimates in terms of average costs per PLH: instruction, $3.30; instructional materials, $1.00; facility usage, $2.60 (often not assessed when performed on-site); administration and overhead, $4.00; curriculum development, $7.40; travel and per diem, when training was off-site, $6.50 (although this came to less than $1.00 when training took place in the local community). In another study, McKeon suggests that in 1981 it cost $100 per supervisor to develop a training program and another $119 to deliver it off-site in a two-day meeting (or sixteen hours); when the participant's salary, travel, and per diem were added, this cost another $190. Thus, the basic cost per PLH came to $14, and the ratio of the cost of participant time, travel, and per diem to this cost was 0.86.[2]

It is a foregone conclusion that expense budgets allocated to supervisory training will be directly influenced by the extent to which the organization sanctions and encourages a particular course or program. A recent survey showed that, on average, first-line supervisors in organizations staffed by training professionals receive 32.5 hours of training a year.[3] This varies, of course, from industry to industry and from company to company. Public-administration supervisors, for example, were reported to receive an average of 37.5 hours. Nevertheless, it will be difficult to secure approval for supervisory-training programs that greatly exceed these averages.

Format Choices

Decisions must also be reached regarding to what extent programs should be conducted:

- On the job or off the job. The great proportion are held off the job in classroom settings.
- On-site or off-site. Most full-scale programs are conducted on the premises.
- During working hours or after. Most programs are held during working hours, although this varies widely.
- Continuously or on intermittent schedules, such as two hours a day for two weeks or one day a week for ten weeks. Schedules vary widely, but the intermittent approach prevails.
- Using internal human resources development faculty, line faculty, or outside organizations such as vocational-technical institutes, community colleges, university extensions, independent consultants, or professional societies. (See bottom of page 148.)

Participant Selection

There are two almost unrelated but important questions here. First, *should supervisors be chosen, or should they volunteer for the program?* Ideally, selection should proceed from an indication, on an individual's performance appraisal, of either (1) an immediate competency shortcoming or (2) potential that can be developed for the good of the individual or the organization. In practice, supervisors may be nominated by their superiors for the training for a variety of reasons. The choice may be viewed simply as a reward to recognize long service. It may also be made as a veiled but threatening expression of dissatisfaction with the supervisor. Or it may represent the superior's eagerness to go along with the current political climate in the organization and to indicate a willingness to conform. All of these reasons are likely to be bad ones. Few training professionals may hold the organizational power to challenge such selections directly. A better approach is to counsel the nominators on possible negative outcomes (at the least, boredom; at the worst, demotivation) and to mount an educational campaign stressing systematic and productive ways for making these selections.

Volunteers represent a special problem, as indicated earlier. Those with good potential who have somehow escaped the appraisal net should be welcomed and procedural obstacles to their enrollment cleared. The occasional insistence on participation by an obviously unqualified candidate requires sensitive handling in order to (1) verify such an assessment and (2) make certain that all legal considerations have been taken into account in reaching the decision.

The second question is, *should supervisors from one department be mixed with those from different departments and with middle- and upper-level managers?* Most authorities agree that much is to be gained by placing line supervisors from different departments and divisions in the same training classes and including equivalent-level staff supervisors. The classroom interaction is likely to be democratic and vigorous, with valuable exchanges of on-the-job and course-related information and perspectives. Some courses are particularly appropriate for this exchange of viewpoints. In general, however, there are risks involved in mixing participants from different levels of management. The learning experience can be threatening to lower-level supervisors and their degree of participation in discussions inhibited.

Some companies are also wary of sending their supervisors to outside seminars and courses (such as at a local community college). The fear is that their supervisors will be exposed to organizational policies and practices—especially those involving compensation—different from their own. Some organizations whose employees are not represented by labor unions also believe that mixing their supervisors with supervisors from unionized companies may present a problem.

Selection of Instructors and Session Leaders

Opinions regarding the choice of trainers vary widely according to the conditions of each particular training situation. Common practice seems to be to utilize training staffs for many of the basic managerial and human relations courses. Subject matter that has a significant technical or legal content is often delegated to line or staff specialists who have demonstrated an affinity for conference-type training. Chaddock, however, strongly recommends employing a company's managers to conduct as much of the supervisory training as possible. He says, "Putting training into the hands of line managers stems from my basic perception of the role of the manager as one who has a charter with his or her subordinates to improve their competence."[4] Many others agree with the philosophy but observe that the realities of an organization's situation often dictate the use of professional trainers or contract instructors. Still others challenge the managers-as-trainers concept, saying that the techniques required for conference-style, participative training—as opposed to lectures—is a capability that few line managers possess.

Program Configuration by Levels of Experience

Generally speaking, supervisory-training programs fall into three levels of general progression and may be supplemented by any number of single-focus or modular courses. The typical categorization of programs is:

- *Presupervisory, introductory, or orientation programs.* These are designed for newly appointed supervisors or those with relatively little experience. Such programs are sometimes identified as "crossover" training, because they help supervisors deal with the abrupt change from employee to managerial status.[5] Participants in the National Survey of Supervisory Management Practices, however, tended to minimize this trauma. Of the 75 percent of all supervisors who were promoted from the ranks, only 39 percent of them recalled that the crossover was difficult, and just 7 percent said it was *very* difficult.[6] Nevertheless, progressive organizations routinely provide such orientation. Wickstrom gives an example of one such program in the box below.
- *Basics, or fundamentals, of supervision.* Whether or not an organization engages in presupervisory training, this basic program becomes the fundamental, or core, program for supervisory training. Its content, with variations, was presented earlier, in chapter 8. Such a "basic program" may be the only program an organization offers to either inexperienced or experienced supervisors. It may be designed to provide a solid foundation within 40 hours; or it may be presented in intermittent fashion over 120 hours and a period of from one to three years. It may be offered as a continuous program or as an intermittent one.
- *Advanced, or refresher, supervision.* If an organization chooses to differentiate between the level of content offered in its supervisory-training programs, then the advanced course for more experienced supervisors will be more sophisticated both in subject content and in approach. Many organizations are sensitive to the way in which training is regarded by experi-

Sample Orientation Program for New Supervisors

Total time: 40 hours *Location:* classroom, off the job
Schedule: intermittent

Subject	Time Allotment
Orientation to supervisory management	½ day
Introduction to management principles	½ day
Corporate personnel policies and practices	½ day
Wage and salary administration	½ day
Attendance, discipline, and related matters	½ day
Productivity and quality goals	½ day
Behavior in organizations	½ day
Motivation and job satisfaction	½ day
Employee instruction and training	½ day
Leadership	½ day

Source: Adapted from Walter S. Wikstrom, *Supervisory Training,* Conference Board Report No. 612 (New York: The Conference Board, 1973).

FIGURE 10-1 RELATIONSHIP OF A CERTIFICATE OF PROFESSIONAL DEVELOPMENT PROGRAM FOR SUPERVISORS TO OTHER TRAINING AND DEVELOPMENT PROGRAMS IN A STATE SYSTEM

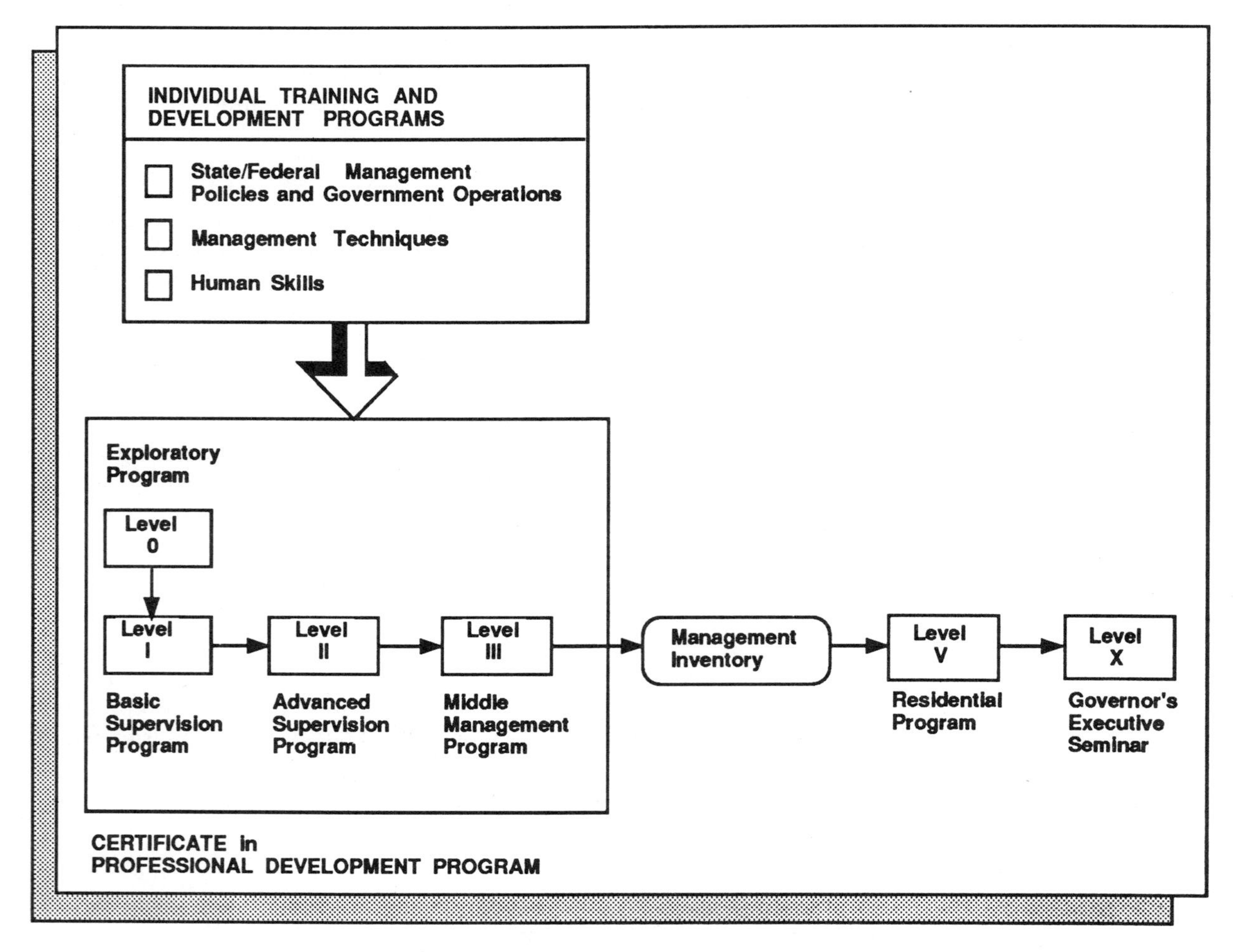

enced supervisors and are highly selective in what is directed toward them and the methods that the program incorporates.

Relationship of Training to a Management Development Program

It is also helpful for planning purposes to place the supervisory-training program into the greater context of management development, as illustrated by the model (see figure 10-1) originally designed for use by one eastern state in its Professional Development Certificate program for public supervisors and managers.

Traditional versus Modular Format

Because the number of subjects that might be judged as essential aspects of supervisory development is so large, some authorities advocate a departure from the traditional approach to program design. They believe that training is made more effective and less costly by targeting *selected* elements in modular fashion. Each module is thus integrated into a comprehensive, long-range program for supervisory development.[7] There is considerable justification for this approach, as illustrated by the example in table 10-1.

TABLE 10-1
TRADITIONAL VERSUS MODULAR APPROACHES TO SUPERVISORY TRAINING AND DEVELOPMENT

	Traditional Management Development	Modular Management Development
Scheduling	Meetings are scheduled at the convenience of the instructor, usually same time each week (e.g., Tuesday mornings for eight weeks). Or, if many participants are required to travel, course may be held at hotel/ conference center and run continuously (e.g., over one week).	Meetings are held as often as demand requires, at the convenience of participants. Thus, if 67 people sign up for "Time Management," it will be run four times (16–17 persons each time); a topic with 34 enrollees will be run twice. Offerings can be scattered throughout year.
Length of sessions	Each class meeting is same length as others. Some topics are "rushed" or "crammed" to cover all the content; others fit comfortably.	Length of meeting is determined by content and intent. Half day, full day, two days with two weeks between, and so on.
Participants	Same people go through course cycle together. They become a group and function as such after the first meeting.	Different faces at each meeting. Composition of group is based on need to know and availability to attend.
Enrollment	Selection is usually done by Personnel or Training Depts. Participants are drafted, with the approval of their immediate supervisor. Such programs usually try not to mix too wide a spectrum of grade levels in any one group: senior managers attend first, then middle, then first level.	Selection is done by department heads, who fill out a "selection matrix" at start of year. They then confer with their subordinate managers (the participants) and enroll. A boss and subordinate can attend the same offering without disrupting their work flow or the group composition.
Content	Over time, all members of the organization's management team get the same common core of concepts, skills, procedures, and policy. It becomes part of the "puberty rites" of passing into management in the organization. Once a manager has attended, there is often no further training within the organization.	Different managers take different selections, based on their needs (e.g., some supervise people, others manage projects; some do a lot of writing, or negotiating, or presenting, or running of meetings; others don't). Of course, some matrix offerings can be required of everyone (e.g., those dealing with policy and procedures, budgeting, etc.).
Instructor	The instructor carries the burden of responsibility for making the course a success. Usually the same person(s) teach all subjects and should speak with authority on all topics.	Different instructors can be used for different modules, so the most qualified person (from within or outside) can be made available for a given topic.
Follow-up	End-of-course activities are done on a group basis (e.g., graduation, post-course evaluation, joining of Supervisory Association, follow-up meeting to report on composite Action Plans). Usually there is little or no follow-up.	Follow-up is the responsibility of participant and immediate boss. There is more time to implement Action Plans after each module attended, and more commitment to do so. Better communication is possible between instructor and participant-and-boss, who can function more as a team.

Source: Reprinted from Scott B. Parry and Edward J. Robinson, "Management Development: Training or Education?" *Training and Development Journal* (July 1979): 9.

Packaged versus Custom-Designed

Almost all good packaged training programs are built on a framework of generally accepted, fundamental methodology. Usually, however, packaged programs add original features and proprietary learning aids that are sometimes hard for an in-house training organization to originate. Packaged programs suffer, of course, from their universality and the generalizations that result from it, although most of these programs do allow for some modification and customization.

Custom-designed programs, on the other hand, can be developed internally to provide a perfect fit to the organization's needs and culture. They can be as expensive to develop as those purchased from publishers or created by consultants, but their cost is often hidden in the ongoing salaries of the permanent training staff.

Program design is only one of the factors that contribute to effective supervisory training. The costs of a program's purchase or internal development should be totaled up realistically and weighed objectively against the benefits and learning it is expected to produce.

TRAINING MANUALS

It is a prudent practice to record supervisory-training policies and procedures in a training (or instruction) manual—sometimes called a leader's guide. Such a manual may serve many purposes: as a written reference, as an operational guide for in-house or contract instructors, or as a basis for preparation of trainee (or participant) manuals or workbooks. Training manuals may contain a wide variety of materials and take many forms.

For example, a major federal agency of the United States provides instructors with a detailed, procedural sequence to be followed. On the left-hand side of each page, the manual presents a background or philosophical overview. On the right-hand side, it presents a script that can be read or paraphrased. In the section of the manual covering the opening session of the agency's basic supervisory program, typical headings are:

Overview

Introductory Remarks

Course Content

Manner of Course Presentation

Clarifying Your Own Role

Clarifying Participant Roles

Distribution of Handouts

Administrative Details

- Hours of class sessions.
- Phone number for emergency messages while in class.
- Coffee breaks.
- Location of cafeteria and other lunch accommodations.
- Rest rooms.
- Fire escapes, health unit location, etc.
- Information on parking facilities.
- Advise participants that they may keep notebooks and other materials for future reference.

- "Please fill out the tent card. Use the markers provided and put your name on both sides of the card. Write first name or nickname in large letters."
- "Please complete the registration form provided."

Anticipating Participants' Expectations

Presentation Outline

Another common use of training manuals is for program planning at branch locations of large companies. A western computer-program developer, for example, expects each branch plant or office to plan and operate its own supervisory program. To assure consistency, it furnishes each location with the checklist shown in the box below, together with a set of instructions for each course, following a similar format.

Leader's Guide for Planning and Operating a Supervisor's Workshop Program

The Supervisor's Workshop will be as good as the leader's skill in planning, coordinating, evaluating, and follow-up. The checklist below should be used as a guide in presenting a complete program.

I. Planning the Program

A. Clarify objectives	Obtain management approval—relate to company goals.
B. Determine needs	Secure facilities, equipment, books, handouts.
C. Select leaders	Ensure competence—adequate preparation.
D. Establish schedule	Notify participants in advance.
E. Review lesson plans	Consider text, outline, handouts, other sources
F. Visual aids	Prepare charts, V-graphs, films, other media.
G. Physical arrangements	Establish location, seating, tables, lighting.
H. Orienting trainees	Review format, expectations, participation, evaluation.

II. Coordinating the Program

A. On-schedule	Set example.
B. Trainee-oriented	Focus on individual needs, interests.
C. Handling problems	Keep all participants informed.

Continued on next page

Leader's Guide for Planning and Operating a Supervisor's Workshop Program—*Continued*

III. Evaluating the Program

A. Reaction	Assess acceptance and adjust as necessary.
B. Learning	Trainees must be ready—see a need to know.
C. Behavior	Will follow enthusiasm of leader.
D. Results	Contingent upon leader skills and materials.

IV. Follow-Up

A. Session leaders	Assess total experience, alter materials as needed.
B. Job application	Evaluate trainees, use of materials.
C. Refresher session	Hold review sessions annually.

Some companies also include course outlines in their manual, and these are updated periodically. One southern company follows a convenient left-hand/right-hand format (see the next box), which indicates the presentation sequence in one column and the places where the various instructional aids are introduced in the other column.

An Ohio-based service company, which selects session leaders from within the company at its branch offices, provides this guideline in their manual:

> Workshops should be presented by qualified and experienced training staff or by carefully selected senior management personnel. Outlines have been prepared with this in mind. Staff members with in-depth knowledge in computer operations, office automation, personnel policy, planning, and scheduling make ideal conference leaders; they contribute local experience and thus give added value to sessions. Additionally, their personal growth is enhanced as discussion leaders. Each leader should, however, be selected *first* for knowledge and experience, *second* for his or her willingness and potential to play the role of session leader. Results of any workshop are dependent on the knowledge, experience, ability, self-confidence, enthusiasm, and image of the leader.

Leader's Guide for Course in Planning, Organizing, and Controlling

Basic Management Training
Planning, Organizing, and Controlling
Session II

AIDS	OUTLINE
MOVIE:	i. Review session I; ask what role of supervisor is
1. *I Told 'em Exactly How to Do It*	I. Introduce session A. Survey on organization

Continued on next page

Leader's Guide for Course in Planning, Organizing, and Controlling—*Continued*

Aids	Outline
	B. Definitions
HANDOUT: 1. "Management Wheel"	—Planning, organizing, and controlling; role of supervisor; refer to "five main management activities," session I
HANDOUT: 1. "Carla's Confusion"	II. Case study; discuss questions; "Carla's Confusion"
HANDOUT: 1. "Management Planning"	III. Overview A. Discuss handout—"Management Planning" B. Discuss overhead
OVERHEAD: 1. "Seven Steps in the Planning Process"	IV. Lecture—planning and the management-minded supervisor A. Time occupied in routine work; crisis jumping B. Takes time to let go of production activities C. Planning (definition) *Definition:* Determining what needs to be done, who will do it, and when 1. Substitution of thinking for worry 2. Making things happen D. Good planning builds respect for the supervisor—only if employees know the job doesn't run the manager E. "If you can't plan, you can't manage," many executives say F. Lack of planning skills is the reason why managers are not promoted G. Supervisor's plans must fit into those developed at higher levels; mark of management-mindedness is the degree to which supervisors are cooperative in the most efficient and effective way H. Importance of planning
OVERHEAD: 1. "Consequences of Poor Planning"	1. Consequences of poor planning a. Lower production b. Dissatisfaction among employees c. High cost d. Misunderstanding and confusion e. Poor-quality work f. Lessening of chance for promotion
OVERHEAD: 1. "Benefits of Good Planning" 2. "Barriers to Planning"	2. Benefits of good planning a. Better coordination b. Effective control of operation (goals, results, objectives defined) c. Easier delegation d. Economical and efficient use of resources e. Increased personal effectiveness—giving direction and controlling it f. Tendency toward improvement; increase in goal targets (100 → 1,000 units produced)

Continued on next page

Leader's Guide for Course in Planning, Organizing, and Controlling—*Continued*

Aids	Outline
OVERHEAD: 1. "Types of Plans"	I. Types of plans 1. Based on duration a. Short-range—lower levels b. Long-range—higher levels 2. Based on function a. Production b. Marketing c. Finance

PLANNING MODELS

The use of models, or flowcharts, illustrates the planning process schematically and helps to provide a unifying context. In principle, planning for supervisory training follows, with only slight modifications, the same process as for any other kind of sound training. A simple, fundamental planning model is illustrated in figure 10-2. A model that emphasizes a performance-based approach for supervisory program design is shown in figure 10-3. Still another model, linking supervisory training to career planning, is illustrated in figure 10-4.

PLANNING GUIDELINES

The trainer's use of analysis and models should not obscure the essentially human nature of the learning process. There is danger in too much abstraction. Broadwell, for example, cautions about a new generation of supervisors who are younger, better educated, and impatient with the ponderous, didactic methods used in traditional supervisory training. He also calls attention to the increasing number of white-collar, knowledge-oriented supervisors whose expectations and life-styles differ from before the "baby boom."[8] Fulmer advises that the focus of supervisory-training programs should not exclude the need to regularly familiarize supervisors with the internal workings of their own organizations.[9] And Short urges that program design allow supervisors to "unlearn" well-entrenched, ineffective habits. He observes that good design will entail discomfort or "disequilibrium," and its success will depend, in large measure, on the supervisor rather than exclusively on the trainer.[10]

Byham also emphasizes how important it is that training actually *change* a supervisor's behavior—and performance. Accordingly, he offers these negative precepts for program design:

- Practice does not make perfect.
- Tenure does not make a good supervisor.

FIGURE 10-2 SIMPLIFIED PLANNING MODEL

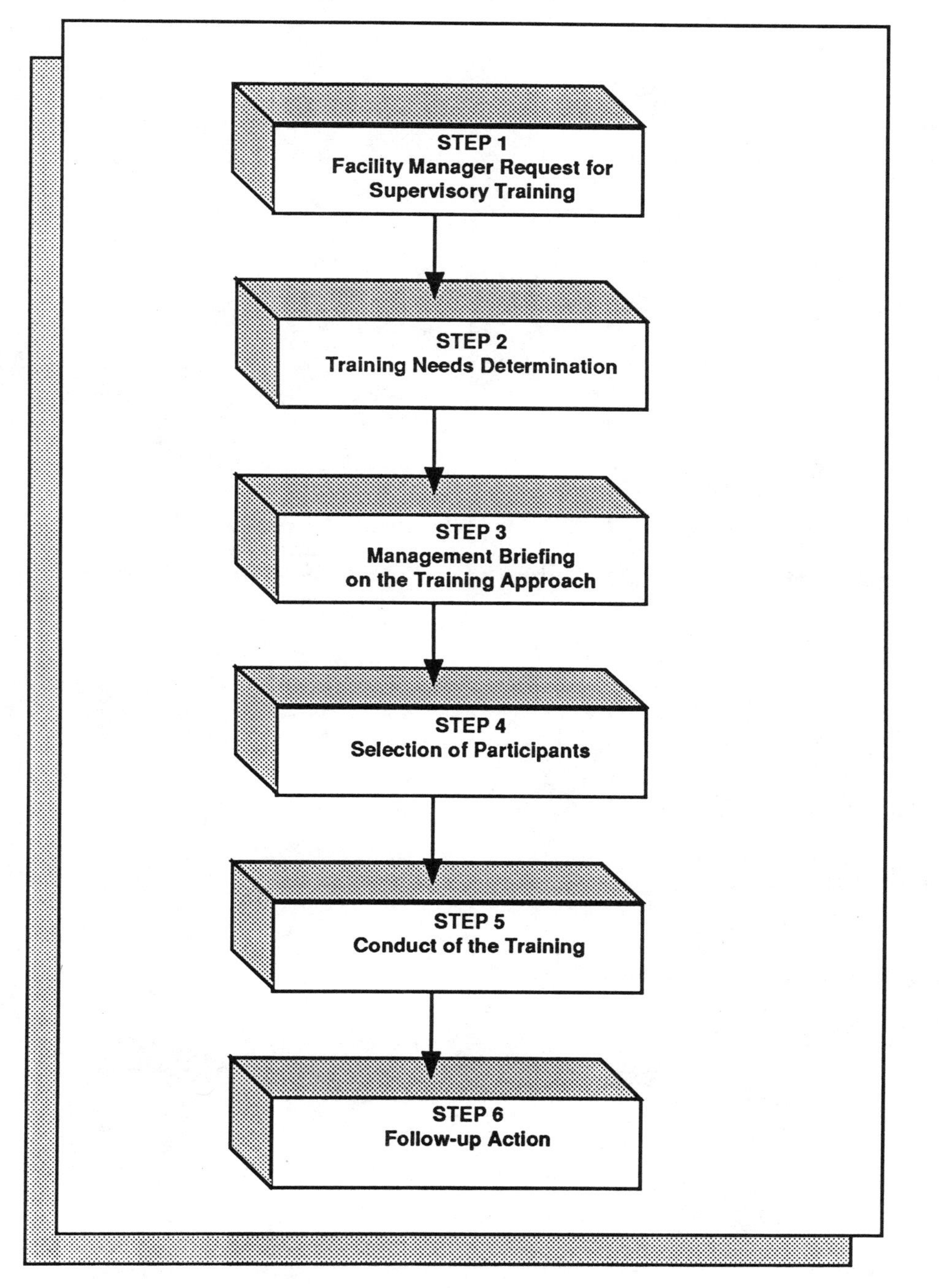

- Experience is a poor teacher.
- Learning by mistake is a waste of time.
- Systems can't change people.
- Self-study is not enough.
- Bosses are often poor models.

FIGURE 10-3 PERFORMANCE-BASED PLANNING MODEL

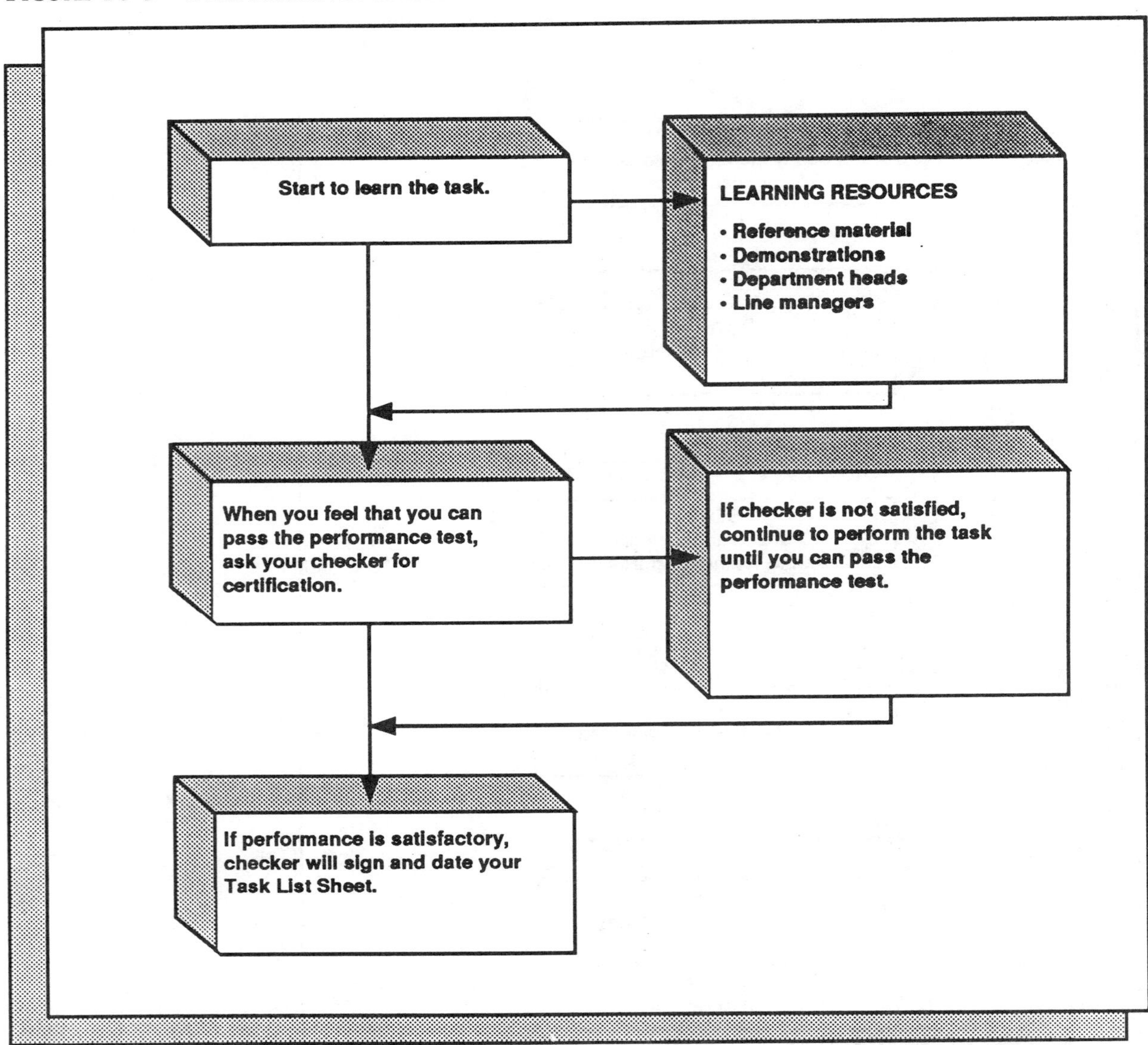

Source: Adapted from C. V. Crumb, "Performance-Based Line Supervisor Training," *Training and Development Journal* (September 1981): 44.

On the positive side of program design, Byham advises that:

- Adequate diagnosis of training and development needs is critical.
- The supervisor's immediate superior is vital in bringing about behavioral change.
- The individual's needs must be integrated into program design.
- Development plans must be put in writing.
- A follow-up procedure must be integrated into the program.[11]

Finally, in order that no important aspect be overlooked in program design, a checklist for trainers is provided in the accompanying box.

FIGURE 10-4 INTEGRATION OF SUPERVISORY TRAINING WITH CAREER DEVELOPMENT PLANNING

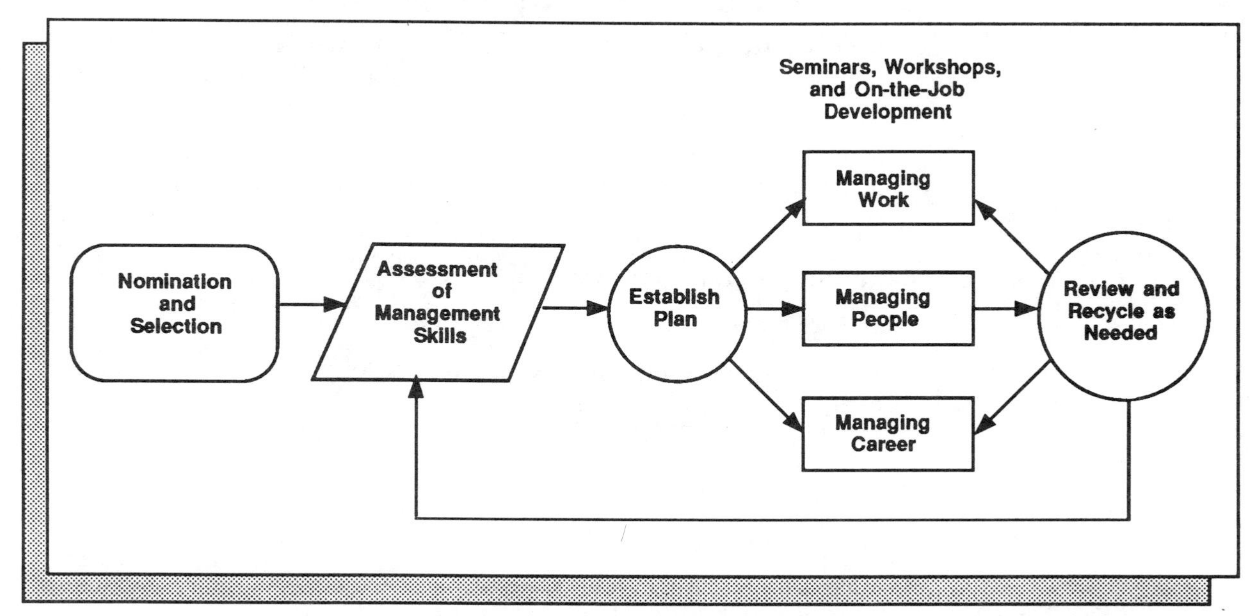

Source: Adapted from Marlys C. Hanson, "Training Employees and Managers for Their Roles in Career Development," in *Career Management: Implications for Organizations and Individuals* (Alexandria, Va.: Career Development Division, American Society for Training and Development, 1980), 10.

Program-Planning Checklist

Identify the Basis for Program Development

- ☐ Know the purpose of your organization, including present mission and future directions.
- ☐ Identify a personal philosophy of program development for adults, including your beliefs about training in general, adults as learners, and the role of the trainer.

Compile a List of Needs/Ideas for Training Programs

- ☐ Conduct a formal needs assessment of present employees using a variety of techniques (e.g., task and job analysis, written questionnaires, telephone surveys, focus groups, Delphi technique).
- ☐ Respond to specific overall organizational needs for training (e.g., installation of microcomputers for all secretarial personnel).
- ☐ Respond to legislative mandates (e.g., affirmative action).
- ☐ Use ideas generated from previous training programs.
- ☐ Use informal suggestions from colleagues and associates.
- ☐ Search appropriate professional literature.

Continued on next page

Program-Planning Checklist—*Continued*

Identify the Specific Objectives of the Program

- ☐ Screen the data gathered from above through these filters: (1) institutional purposes; (2) interests of potential program participants; and (3) feasibility.
- ☐ State the program objectives in such a way that they will be understood by all parties involved. These objectives should describe the intended results of the training activity and give focus and direction to the program.

Make the Program Arrangements

- ☐ Prepare budget plan.
- ☐ Choose the most appropriate instructional format (e.g., individual, media).
- ☐ Identify training staff and outline their roles.
- ☐ Obtain needed facilities.
- ☐ Promote program as needed.
- ☐ Make sure the program fits into the participants' work, home and family schedules and responsibilities.
- ☐ Develop a working calendar for all the activities in the program planning process.

Prepare the Specific Instructional Plan(s) in Cooperation with the Individual Instructor(s)/Facilitator(s)

- ☐ Define specific learning objectives for each training activity.
- ☐ Outline content.
- ☐ Select methods/techniques.
- ☐ Accumulate and/or design the instructional materials.
- ☐ Design the sequence of learning events.
- ☐ Consider the nature of each individual learner.

Formulate a Continuous Evaluation Component

- ☐ Define precisely the purpose of the evaluation and how the results will be used.
- ☐ Specify what will be judged.
- ☐ Determine the kind of evidence you will need (e.g., participants' self-evaluation, cost-benefit materials).
- ☐ Decide who will evaluate.
- ☐ Determine what method(s) you will use to conduct the evaluation.
- ☐ Specify what criterion you will use in making judgments about the program.

Continued on next page

Program-Planning Checklist—*Continued*

Carry Out the Program

- ☐ Provide access for monitoring the program and revise the activities as needed.
- ☐ Gather needed data for both formative and summative evaluation purposes.
- ☐ Make sure the program presented matches that promised to participants.

Measure and Appraise the Results of the Program

- ☐ Analyze and interpret the evaluation data.
- ☐ Use this data for new or improved training programs.

Communicate the Value of the Program to Appropriate Publics

- ☐ Develop a report on the program.
- ☐ Communicate this report to key individuals and groups.
- ☐ Follow up as needed with appropriate individuals and groups to clarify questions or concerns about the program.

Source: Reprinted from Rosemary S. Caffarella, "A Checklist for Planning Successful Training Programs," *Training and Development Journal* (March 1985): 84.

Chapter 11

Program Management and Control

INTRODUCTION

A well-planned supervisory-training program deserves sound, professional execution. This implementation phase requires meticulous handling of each operational element, such as announcements, registration, and scheduling. Careful attention to procedural details is important for the program as a whole and for each course in it. Program management, however, will demand much more from those in charge. It will also benefit from the development of support mechanisms throughout the organization, the injection of ideas that stimulate and reinforce participation, and rigorous monitoring of program progress.

OPERATIONAL LOGISTICS

Generally speaking, management of supervisory-training programs differs from the management of other training programs only to the degree that the supervisory population is more conforming than the middle and executive levels of management and less conforming than nonmanagerial trainees. Thus, the individual providing supervisory training can usually focus on the mechanics of program management rather than the typical problems of attendance and out-of-class preparation. Three areas, however, warrant special attention: (1) course announcements, registration, and scheduling; (2) conference preparation and conduct; and (3) maintenance of the relevant training records.

Schedule Announcements and Registration

It is essential that the carefully laid plans of the training department be communicated to the participants and their sponsors in an effective and timely fashion. Accordingly, a system must be established for providing the proper information well in advance of program kickoff dates and scheduled course times. To make certain that this takes place, a simple logbook or schedule checkoff sheet should be maintained. Format is not particularly important. The information in it will be.

Some organizations publish (internally) a *program calendar* based on the supervisory schedule. Such a calendar typically contains the following information:

1. A listing of existing and proposed courses
2. For each existing course, a description of:
   a. Eligibility requirements
   b. Course objectives
   c. Course structure (lecture, workshop, and so on)
3. Schedule information for the entire program and/or for each course, including:
   a. Frequency of course offering: yearly, semiannually, monthly, and so forth, or one time only
   b. Schedule dates
   c. Locations
   d. Instructor or coordinator
   e. Registration deadline(s)
   f. Maximum enrollment
   g. Cost (if any) to be charged to the sponsoring department

This kind of data can be transferred to (or from) a Gantt-type progress-control chart so that each course can be monitored both during schedule preparation and during program implementation.

Conference Preparation and Management

Many supervisory-training programs have a conference or workshop setting. Special care should be taken with the physical arrangements and procedures for this kind of program.

Physical Arrangements. It is almost always desirable for participants to sit facing each other, generally around a table. A round table is ideal, but it does not use space economically or lend itself to flexible arrangements.

U-, V-, and T-shaped tables are among the variations. At U- and V-shaped tables, do not seat members on the inside, because they will then have their backs to at least part of the group. In some training situations, the trainer may be tempted to walk into the "slot." This can provide an effective change of pace but must be done quickly (in and out) because obviously the trainer, too, will be facing only part of the group.

Programs often use a rectangular conference table or some combination of square or rectangular tables. The first problem here is to avoid having legs located so that they restrict the spacing and movement of group members. Pedestal tables are available, with legs near the center rather than around the perimeter.

Most people do not sit still in any meeting, nor do they sit neatly facing the center of the table. They tend to move and shift their bodies in keeping with the focus of discussion. Therefore, swivel chairs are preferred over straight chairs, and the kind used should be well padded, seat and back. Because people shift positions (seat directions) even in straight chairs, provision must be made for adequate space. Simply allowing the width of one chair for each person will result in intolerable cramping. Twice the width of a chair is a more reasonable allocation of space. By all means, make certain that there is room between occupied chairs and the walls so that members may enter and leave without inconveniencing others.

Certain housekeeping details must not be overlooked: place cards, if indicated (and markers for filling them out); ashtrays and matches; a pitcher of fresh water and glasses or paper cups; provision for emptying ashtrays and refilling water pitchers at major breaks; and note paper and pencils. See the box on page 166 for a useful checklist.

Procedures and Control. Malott advises the instructor to share the course's assumptions with the participants and adhere to a number of procedural conventions. For example:

1. Instructors should set a realistic schedule to ensure that time is distributed properly within the allotted time frame. The schedule should permit a degree of flexibility; no one can really tell in advance just how much time will be required, especially if group participation is required.
2. It is absolutely essential, however, that the meeting start on time and adjourn no later than the announced time. It is a matter of simple courtesy to the attendees, makes it possible for them to plan their time efficiently, and establishes credibility for the instructor. Attendees are then much more apt to be prompt (and enthusiastic) at future meetings. One way to preserve flexibility is to allow somewhat more time for breaks than will be necessary; another is to allocate discussion time, which can be abbreviated.
3. An agenda should be worked out in advance and circulated so that participants can prepare themselves effectively.
4. It is important for participating supervisors to know each other or to be able to identify each other. Where members are not already acquainted and the group is small, place cards (with names in large block letters) are helpful. An opening routine in which each member also states her or his name and organizational identification is a convenient icebreaker and helps others to match faces and voices with names.[1]

Encouraging Participation. In most small-group supervisory-training meetings, a degree of participation by the group members is desired, and this poses many problems for the group leader. A number of principles are fundamental. The leader must put aside the traditional assumptions that he or she knows more than anybody else or has all the answers. Instead, the leader performs given functions—or makes certain that they are performed by members of the group—such as gatekeeping (ensuring that each member has a fair chance to speak), pacing, stimulating, summarizing, and avoiding premature voting or polarization. The leader also protects the members, not only by assuring them "entry to the board" through gatekeeping but by decreasing any threat that might result from participation and by avoiding or deflecting "put-downs." In this role, the leader is very much an "officer of the court"—in favor of justice, but not for or against either side.[2]

Record Keeping. Records of those supervisors who have successfully completed training programs and courses should be maintained, by either the training department, the human resources department, or the sponsoring or-

Checklist for Instructor Planning and Preparation

Have you	Yes	No
1. Fixed in your mind the objectives to be attained through the training session?	____	____
2. Secured, prepared, or thoroughly familiarized yourself with the necessary training aids:	____	____
a. Charts ready?	____	____
b. Case studies prepared?	____	____
c. Checksheets to be distributed ready in sufficient quantities?	____	____
d. Demonstrations predetermined?	____	____
e. All special materials obtained?	____	____
f. Visual aids to be used previewed and a plan made for their use?	____	____
3. Prepared for your opening talk?	____	____
4. Carefully studied your agenda or outline?	____	____
a. Determined the important points to be emphasized?	____	____
b. Considered anticipated responses and group reactions?	____	____
c. Determined points at which quick summaries will be made?	____	____
d. Considered experiences and stories to be used for emphasis?	____	____
e. Determined ways and means of getting trainee participation, stimulating thinking, and creating interest?	____	____
f. Considered what the summary of the group's thinking might be?	____	____
5. Planned carefully to be sure adequate time has been allotted?	____	____
6. Notified everyone concerned of time and place of the session?	____	____
7. Checked physical requirements for conducting the session?	____	____
a. Blackboard or chart paper available?	____	____
b. Seating arrangement conforms to good training procedure?	____	____
c. Facilities for showing films ready?	____	____
d. Ashtrays provided if smoking is permitted?	____	____
e. Chalk, crayons, Scotch tape, thumbtacks, erasers, paper, pencils, and so forth on hand?	____	____
f. Ventilation, heat, light, trainee comfort adequate?	____	____

ganization. In fact, it's a good idea if all three keep records. This helps to prevent loss of records due to transfers and changes in the organization's information system. An individual's *training record sheet* should contain, at the minimum, the following data: (1) title of course; (2) date completed; (3) relationship to a larger program (such as a company's advanced supervision course); (4) credit toward a program of certification or other recognition; and (5) if appropriate, the number of continuing education units (CEUs) awarded.

ONGOING MANAGEMENT

Once the program is underway, a number of techniques and procedures can be employed for ensuring its effectiveness. These include:

1. Precourse conditioning of supervisors
2. Ideas for obtaining the continuing support of their sponsors
3. Internal publicity activities
4. Formation of in-company supervisory clubs to build cohesiveness and serve as ongoing forums for information and development
5. Introduction of formal recognition features, such as awarding CEUs and encouraging certification

Preconditioning Participants

In order to stimulate an active, rather than passive, stance toward a particular training program, some companies try to preview the course for participants and then secure a commitment from them in the way of written personal goals. The box on pages 168–169 illustrates the form one company uses to guide a supervisor in shaping his or her goals. The goals are developed progressively from stage I (one week before the course begins), to stage II (at the end of the course, where the individual evaluates the goals already set), and then to stage III (where goals are projected for six months after completion of the course). This approach builds in (1) a self-evaluation during the course and (2) a stimulus for the supervisor to apply what has been learned after the course is completed.

Other organizations take special pains to make sure that supervisors arrive at the course site fully prepared to relate what they are about to learn to their actual work. One statewide public agency makes this preparation a part of its program policy, as follows:

> Advance participant registration will be acknowledged by a letter from the training department to participants, with copies to their superior officer. The letter will specify the need for and extent of precourse preparation, such as:
>
> - Identifying a relevant problem area or project possibility for course analysis and discussion.
> - Gathering information about relevant departmental procedures or history—absences, lateness, turnover records, supplies inventories and usage, costs, etc.

Fundamentals of Supervision: Goal-Setting Worksheet

INSTRUCTIONS: To help establish some type of working agreement among ourselves for learning together this week, please indicate your feelings in item A of stage I. You will be expected to complete stage II and items A–D of stage III at the end of this week, and you will be asked to complete item E of stage III six months after the course is over.

I. Week Prior to the Course

A. Based on what I have evaluated as my effectiveness as a supervisor and what I know about this course at this point, my goals and objectives for learning during the week of the course are:

1. ______________________________

2. ______________________________

3. ______________________________

II. At the End of the Training Week

A. Based on the goals and objectives I set for myself last week, I find the following have been accomplished:

1. ______________________________

2. ______________________________

3. ______________________________

B. They were (met, not met, partially met) by:

1. ______________________________

2. ______________________________

3. ______________________________

C. My original goals were unrealistic and have been redefined as:

1. ______________________________

2. ______________________________

3. ______________________________

III. Six-Months Projection

A. At this point, based on analysis of my goals and what has been accomplished to date, I project that in the next six months, relating this training to my job, I will:

1. ______________________________

2. ______________________________

3. ______________________________

B. Obstacles and roadblocks—what stands between me and my goals:

1. ______________________________

Continued on next page

Fundaments of Supervision: Goal-Setting Worksheet—*Continued*

2. ____________________
3. ____________________

C. Solutions—I will overcome the obstacles by doing the following:

1. ____________________
2. ____________________
3. ____________________

D. Rewards—I see the following benefits to myself, to employees, and to the organization:

1. ____________________
2. ____________________
3. ____________________

E. Progress to date—feedback on my performance:

1. ____________________
2. ____________________
3. ____________________

- Conducting a minisurvey of departmental activities, attitudes, or problems related to the course subject area.

The copy sent to the superior will alert him or her to expect the participant to bring back an Action Plan . . . for discussion and follow-up.

Hoffman suggests that the supervisors' managers also be drawn into the program at an early stage. He observes that there are a number of things the managers can do before the supervisors actually attend the course. They can, for example, familiarize themselves with course content and, if possible, attend a managerial briefing session beforehand. A week or two before the course begins, managers and supervisors can also discuss:

- Why the trainee was selected and why the superior feels the course will be of value
- Mutual expectations of what the person should try to get from the course, in terms of learnings or skills
- How the supervisor can prepare herself or himself to get the most out of the training
- How strong points can be further strengthened, and weak points shored up, by the training
- The manager's plans for job coverage while the supervisor is in class (how the manager will make uninterrupted attendance possible)
- What kind of performance is expected from the trainee
- What the manager will do to give the supervisor an opportunity to apply the new knowledge or skills on the job

- Possible ways the newly acquired skills can be used on the job
- How selection, new skills, and postcourse assignments may relate to performance appraisals and career plans[3]

Maximizing the Learning Environment

Prudent trainers seek to manage the program so that results will be maximized. Rosenthal and Mezoff suggest that supervisory-training practitioners not only make certain that the supervisors' managers understand the benefits to be derived from the training but that they also follow a series of steps during the training process to assure that what happens during the training occurs in the most favorable organizational atmosphere. Rosenthal and Mezoff urge trainers to inform the supervisors' sponsors of the "ceremonial effects" of the development program (such as awards, certificates, completion banquets, and so forth) because: (1) it acts as a motivator and a builder of confidence and self-esteem, (2) it serves to remove stress and helps newly appointed supervisors make the crossover to management more effectively, and (3) it improves working relationships between participants and their coworkers and employees. These two authors also lay out the following ten-point program for assuring the optimum learning environment:

1. Inform participants about training well in advance of the training event.
2. Conduct a pretraining interview with participants.
3. Encourage sponsoring managers to discuss the program beforehand with their participating supervisors.
4. Design the training to address issues of the supervisors' organizational role.
5. Provide ample opportunities for participants to discuss work-related issues.
6. Structure the program to include free time for social interaction and individual reflection.
7. Conduct training off-site or at a location that minimizes distractions and interruptions.
8. Structure the training to make it significantly different from the normal work routine.
9. Publicize the training in the organization's newspaper or newsletter.
10. Provide certificates of completion.[4]

Enlivening the Program

There are a number of other activities that can add organizational significance to the program while at the same time providing variety and a form of social reward. Pelfrey, who conducted a large in-company program for eight hundred supervisors at a major shipyard, recommends the following:

- An opening welcome to participants from a highly placed manager. This demonstrates executive approval and support as the program gets underway.

- An occasional special luncheon for those supervisors who have completed the program. Upper-level management guests and selected speakers can use this opportunity to report on items of organizational interest and to reinforce learning themes. Some firms institute periodic lunches as a regular means of maintaining the morale of first-line supervisors.
- A management action log. In courses that have organizational problem-solving components, the instructor may collect supervisors' suggestions or queries and forward them to upper-level management for action and a personal response to the supervisors while they are meeting.
- An evaluation report, prepared in writing by supervisors at the program's conclusion and presented orally to a member of top management. This formal report helps underscore the meaningfulness of the training and commit supervisors to drawing firm, action-oriented conclusions from their learning experience.
- A closing ceremonial dinner with sponsoring managers in attendance. This is the time for presentation of certificates and for higher-level management to urge that supervisors transfer training skills to the workplace.[5]

Formation of In-House Supervisory/Management Clubs

As has often been said, the supervisor's job is a lonely one. Women and men who hold that position are commonly disturbed by its ambiguity. They must find a way to maintain sound relationships with rank-and-file employees while at the same time carrying out the ideas and will of management. When the Taft-Hartley Act was passed in 1947, the supervisors' position was legally established as being part of management. Supervisors may not join unions of the people they supervise, but they are specifically guaranteed the right to form a union of their own. For a brief period during the 1950s, there was fear in many corporate circles that this would happen. Formation of a supervisory union, however, has occurred only in the rarest of instances.

Instead, many firms have initiated the formation of internal supervisory clubs, sanctioned and supported financially by the company. Many firms have also affiliated their clubs directly with the National Management Association in Dayton, Ohio. Many other firms have encouraged their supervisors to join, or attend the developmental activities of, one of the hundred or more local clubs of the International Management Council, which is affiliated with local YMCAs and directed by an executive of the national board of the YMCA, with headquarters in Des Plaines, Illinois. A typical organizing charter for an independent supervisors' club is shown in the box on pages 172–173. The two main benefits a company expects to derive from such organizations are: (1) maintenance of supervisory *esprit* and encouragement of "management-mindedness" and (2) creation of a permanent forum for supervisory information exchange and personal development.

Awarding of CEUs

The Council on the Continuing Education Unit (Silver Spring, Maryland) is a nationally recognized organization that has established a formal way of awarding, and recording the award of, educational credits to individuals for courses completed by adults under conditions that meet the council's criteria. While these credits are not in any way related to those granted, or accepted, by institutions of higher learning, the continuing education unit (CEU) has acquired a great deal of use and credibility in management circles. The grant-

Organizing Charter for a Supervisors' Club

1. *Establishment.* An organization is established to be known by the name of "Supervisors' Group."
2. *Purpose.* The purpose of the Supervisors' Group is to create an atmosphere whereby a group of people with supervisory responsibilities can get together at regular intervals on an informal basis to exchange ideas that will help them to expand their horizons and experiences.
3. *Membership.* The group will have two types of membership:
   a. Regular membership—composed of supervisory personnel employed at the company.
   b. Honorary membership—presented to those who have given outstanding assistance to the group. This membership will be awarded on the recommendation of the executive committee of the group.
4. *Officers.* The group will have a president, vice president, and secretary. The president will hold the office for one year and will be succeeded automatically by the vice president.

   The secretary may hold office for one other period of time, depending on the wishes of the regular-membership personnel.
5. *Duties of the officers.* The president will conduct both the executive and the regular group meetings, whereas the business for the executive meeting may be instituted by any member of the committee. The president will assist the secretary in formulating the agenda for the group meetings and the topics discussed at the executive meetings. He or she will then see to its execution.

   The vice president will assist the president and will preside in his or her absence.

   The secretary records the minutes of the executive meeting in triplicate, one copy being given to the president, one copy kept by the secretary, and the third added to the cumulative file. He or she also sends notices to the group members concerning meetings and other items of immediate concern.

   The secretary also takes the minutes of the regular group meetings, which are then duplicated, a copy being sent to each group member. In this way, members unable to attend regular meetings will be kept informed of group activities.
6. *Executive committee.* The membership will have an executive committee consisting of __________ officers. The members will be appointed to the executive committee on a rotating basis of ________-year terms. The new members of the executive committee are appointed by the existing committee at the last meeting of the year.

   Upon completion of the current term of office, the president will become a member of the executive committee for one year.
7. *Operations.* These consist of the following:
   a. Allotting time to various activities.
   b. Appointing a chairperson for various functions throughout the year.
   c. Nominating new members of the executive committee.

Continued on next page

Organizing Charter for a Supervisors' Club—*Continued*

d. Members of the executive committee will meet ________ weeks in advance of every regular meeting of the group. They will discuss ways and means of executing ideas and suggestions that may have been proposed during previous meetings of the group. They will propose new business and determine the agenda of the regular meeting.

8. *Meetings.* Monthly meetings of the group will be arranged on a Monday-through-Friday rotating basis, so as to give those supervisors who work on a particular night or have other commitments an opportunity to attend a maximum number of meetings.

ing of CEUs represents a formal and impressive way of adding credibility to courses included in supervisory training. The council offers memberships and provides guidelines and criteria to organizations that wish to incorporate the CEU into their programs.

CERTIFICATION

One of the most attractive ways to emphasize the importance and lasting value of supervisory training is to integrate it with the certification opportunities provided by the Institute of Certified Professional Managers. This organization, jointly sponsored by the National Management Association and the International Management Council, is located on the campus of James Madison University in Harrisonburg, Virginia, where it operates independently. It conducts a full-scale, recognized certification program based on education, experience, and three certification examinations. The substance of the certification examinations parallels the range of subjects offered in a comprehensive supervisory-training program, and participant's and trainer's manuals are available for preparation purposes.

PROGRESS MONITORING AND FOLLOW-UP

Formally and informally a supervisory-training program needs continuing surveillance. If allowed to take its own course, the program will almost certainly lose momentum and direction. The training coordinator must tightly monitor progress during program operation and plan concretely for follow-up after the program concludes.

PROGRAM MONITORING

It is essential that training sessions begin and end at the stated time and that their conduct follow principles of good management. The human resources development professional becomes an important role model in this regard. Rigorous attendance records should be kept; absences should be followed up (in a sensitive manner, of course) to determine their cause and to let individuals know that their participation is missed. If the program calls for out-of-class assignments, these, too, should be logged in, to indicate their importance to the training experience and to the trainees' progress. If assignments are optional, make certain that this is clear to all participants (although it is better for assignments to be an integral and required part of the program if they are to be included at all).

Warning Signs

As a less formal aspect of program monitoring, the training professional should be alert to the signals of program deterioration, as it affects participants either collectively or individually. Absences and tardiness are the most obvious signs, of course, but other signals of a dysfunctional program can also be observed. These include: difficulty in keeping participants' attention focused on the main theme, sluggish participation in discussions, distracting personal conversations, outright expressions of disinterest, and complaints regarding the irrelevance of subject matter to the workplace. Many of these symptoms do not have serious causes and can be minimized or erased by a well-prepared, experienced trainer. Some symptoms, however, reveal genuine flaws in the program and call for immediate action to adjust either the content or the conduct of training sessions. It is often a good idea, too, to maintain contact with participants' superiors during the program in order to receive ongoing, current feedback and also to sustain motivation at the sponsoring end.

Follow-Up

The training job is not over when the course has ended or the award certificates have been presented. So much can be lost between program completion and the supervisor's job itself that it is essential for the training coordinator to build bridges between the learning experience and the workplace.

Postcourse Reinforcement. Hoffman warns that "Too often, the postcourse follow-up is just a perfunctory 'Welcome back.'" He observes that trainees need help in overcoming the "culture shock" between learning theory and the realities of the workaday world.[6] Their bosses can go a long way toward overcoming this reaction by helping them to focus on specific ways to apply their new skills and to internalize what they have learned. The supervisors' bosses themselves will often need coaching here from the training professional, who can encourage the superiors to take some of the following actions:

1. Hold an interview with the returning trainee. This interview should cover such matters as:
   a. What value the trainee thinks he or she got from the course
   b. What parts of the course the trainee thinks can be applied in the job
   c. Laying plans for how the trainee will use the training
   d. Securing the intention to follow through on application plans developed in this meeting
2. Show interest and stimulate trainees by talking to them regularly about how they are applying the training. Ask them about certain materials or concepts they should be using, to see if they are in fact using them.
3. Continue to request that, in staff meetings, supervisors present ideas they think have worked well. This should only take about ten minutes out of a meeting. Once the trainee is committed in front of others as believing in

certain practices, he or she will be more apt to use those practices back on the job. The rest of the group will benefit also.

4. When reviewing specific operating problems, question whether concepts taught in the course were used and were helpful.
5. Provide actual job duties designed to strengthen the supervisors' abilities to apply certain principles.
6. Ask trainees to turn in periodic reports on how they are using the training and what the results are.
7. Observe progress and judge it against performance before the training started. Compliment supervisors for their improvement.

Take-Home Action Plans. One good way to build in a degree of assurance that knowledge and skills learned during the program will be applied on the job is to institute some sort of commitment to an action plan. A standard format can be devised for each course or for the program as a whole, but an effective plan would include the following:

1. Identification of a specific job-related problem or project area.
2. Preparation by the participant during the program of a brief, but clearly stated, plan of action covering:
   a. *What will be done.* For example, "Counsel Bill X about the number of errors he makes in his daily log entries," "Prepare a work-distribution chart for improving job assignments," or "Delegate preparation of the weekly summary sheet to Mary J."
   b. *When it will be done and how long it will take.* For instance, "Complete by April 15. Estimate it will take six hours of my time to do."
   c. *How it will be done.* The specific plan or method to be employed, such as: "by analyzing departmental records for the last six months," "by speaking to Bill at least three times, preferably for fifteen minutes before the end of the workday," or "by conducting a work-sampling study."
   d. *Where it will be done.* For example, "at the mail-sorting racks," "in the departmental records office," "in the field," or "at home."
   e. *Who will be involved and who can assist.* For instance, "the employee, and me," "the employee, my boss, and me," or "with advice from the personnel office."
3. The action plan should be prepared in duplicate, with one copy to be delivered to the superior by the participant upon the latter's return from training, as a form of commitment.

Additional Reinforcement at the Job Site. One organization formally establishes the training professional's responsibility for triggering follow-up action by making it part of the program's policy statement, as shown below:

> Periodically, the headquarters training department will mail to program participants a *Progress Report* showing how many courses have been completed in a particular curriculum. The report will encourage participants to reconsider what they learned in their courses and to look anew for job areas where the principles

or techniques may be applied. It will also suggest that they discuss such opportunities with their superiors.

A copy of the report will also be sent to participants' superiors, urging them to take time (1) to discuss possible application opportunities with participants, (2) to offer praise for positive changes in behavior and improvements in performance, or (3) to offer constructive criticism and assistance in course areas where performance does not reflect applied learning.

Chapter 12

Examples of Effective Programs

INTRODUCTION

When it is time to put all the elements of a supervisory-training plan into a specific program, there is room for great creativity and ingenuity. In practice, however, most programs are quite similar, partly because competency requirements across different organizations are also similar. But the real reason most programs resemble each other is that organizations often fail to analyze their own particular competencies and training needs. In the absence of such in-depth analysis, training professionals may be willing to copy programs that were successful elsewhere or accept a proprietary or public program "off the shelf." This approach has the benefit of speed and economy; but in the long run, it may penalize the entire organization. The best way to maximize the effectiveness of supervisory training is to follow a planning model that leads, in stages, from the identification of competencies to an analysis of needs to a review of appropriate methods to a thorough evaluation of content and operational options.

Supervisory programs vary widely in content, length, and format, but most comprehensive programs contain some of the subjects and topics considered in chapter 5. The reader will find twenty-five outlines for model supervisory training courses in appendix 3. It will also be helpful at this point to look at how some of the different aspects of supervisory development have been treated and at a few programs with distinctive features and broad applications.

PROGRAM SPECIFICATIONS

At Morrison-Knudson (MK)—a large, diversified construction, design, and engineering firm with thirty-five thousand employees, based in Boise, Idaho—the supervisory program is constructed on explicitly stated policies and criteria.[1] These are especially useful when selecting vendor-supplied training components. The policies specify that all content must:

- Be needs-assessment-based.
- Employ performance/task objectives.
- Be how-to, or skill, oriented.
- Be highly interactive.

- Incorporate behavioral modeling.
- Utilize job aids—reminders that can be taken back to the workplace.
- Concentrate on team effort.
- Involve the supervisors' managers in the planning process.
- Fit into an ongoing employee-performance and career-development program.
- Be demonstrably cost-effective.

Danny G. Langdon, manager of corporate training at MK, explains that its program places an "umbrella" over three areas of common need: (1) management skills training; (2) professional, or job, training; and (3) project management. The management skills training focuses on individuals and is called the Individual Management Development Program (IMDP), while project management emphasizes team effort. In either case, much of the supervisory training is contracted to vendors at the various construction sites.

A Restructured Selection Process

Supervisory-training problems usually become apparent when something goes wrong. The symptoms of such training problems mainly include an ineffective supervisory team and generally poor morale and performance from the labor force. Few organizations, unfortunately, are willing to go back to what may be the root of the problem—poorly defined supervisory roles and a hit-or-miss supervisory selection process. Those that do remove the underlying causes of ineffective training results are likely to reap considerable benefits for their time and trouble. For example, at Tri/Valley Growers Plant 7 in Modesto, California, the success of its supervisory-training program was based on a complete redefinition of the supervisor's role in the organization and a more effective selection process. Key elements in this effort included: (1) differentiation between roles that were heavily weighted toward administration and those requiring technical know-how, (2) documentation of each position as to content and required skills, (3) redefinition and clarification of relationships between supervisors and staff departments, (4) screening of supervisory candidates through an assessment center conducted by an outside consultant, and (5) changes in supervisory responsibilities, authority, and method of selection made clear to the union.[2]

PROGRAMS IN THE INDUSTRIAL SECTOR

The pattern for most supervisory training was developed years ago in America's manufacturing plants. Programs that originated there have been copied and modified for almost every kind of organization in both the private and public sector. The great majority of programs for manufacturing supervisors consist of a simple, straightforward series of classroom/conference, lecture/

discussion sessions. Many companies also place great emphasis on long indoctrination periods for new supervisors (many of whom are recent college graduates). The latter kind of program typically stresses rotating, on-the-job experience under the hard-nosed tutoring of old (and hopefully) master supervisors. In almost all cases, the on-the-job component is supplemented by lectures from the training staff and from knowledgeable company specialists. Several representative manufacturing programs are discussed in the balance of this section.

A Human Relations–Oriented Program

A manufacturing company that has used a human relations–oriented program for years to train supervisors in its various plants calls this its Basic Management Training, or BMT, program. It also offers an advanced program for second-level supervisors and middle managers. The ten sessions of the BMT program are held twice a week so that the program can be completed in a little over a month. Sessions last three or four hours and are scheduled during working hours, except that shift supervisors attend during their time off. Participants include not only production supervisors but also those from the various support departments. Sessions are carefully prescribed by detailed manuals, and a variety of visual aids and handouts are provided. The company employs local contract instructors from community colleges, but the training coordinator opens and closes the program. The ten sessions are:

1. The Role of the Supervisor
2. Planning, Organizing, and Controlling
3. Time Management
4. Communications
5. Motivation
6. Employee Training and Development
7. Performance Appraisal
8. Counseling
9. Handling Problem Employees
10. Summary and Evaluation

An Eclectic Program

One large chemical company with many branch plants follows a wide-ranging program for its supervisors. Its ten sessions last only two hours each and are spread out over a ten-week period. Here again, the corporate training office provides a detailed manual for session leaders, a summary sheet from which appears in the box on pages 180–181. This program uses a popular text on supervision as a reference and as a source of case studies. Sessions are conducted, in the main, by independent contract consultants. The kickoff session is handled by the corporate training coordinator. Sessions on grievances are presented with a representative from the labor-relations staff on hand. The accident-prevention session is conducted by the company safety director.

Summary Sheet from a Training Manual Used for a Supervisors' Workshop Program by a Major Chemical Company

Session No.	Schedule Date	Reference Chapter	Subject/Content	Session Leader	Special Equipment
I	Mar. 4	1	*THE SUPERVISOR'S JOB* • Tomorrow's supervisors • Objectives, functions, and attitudes • Why do supervisors fail? Handout(s): 1 Exercise(s): ____	Jones	OP
II	Mar. 11	2–3	*UNDERSTANDING THE INDIVIDUAL* • Human relations and the individual • Survey: "What Employees Want Most" • Human relations and work groups Handout(s): 2, 3 Exercise(s): A	Smith	VCP
III	Mar. 18	4–5	*IMPROVING ATTITUDES/ MORALE AND COMMUNICATIONS* • Attitudes and morale • Emotions—positive versus negative • Principles for effective communications Handout(s): ____ Exercise(s): B	Smith	VCP
IV	Mar. 25	7–8	*THE ART OF LEADERSHIP* • Supervising people • Styles, characteristics, principles • Organization fundamentals Handout(s): 4 Exercise(s): C, D	Smith	VCP
V	Apr. 1	26–33* 47–51* 351–355*	*PRINCIPLES OF MOTIVATION* • Physiological and emotional needs • What people want from work	Smith	VCP

*Page nos.

Continued on next page

Summary Sheet from a Training Manual Used for a Supervisors' Workshop Program by a Major Chemical Company—*Continued*

Session No.	Schedule Date	Reference Chapter	Subject/Content	Session Leader	Special Equipment
			• Insight into motivation/ enrichment Handout(s): ____ Exercise(s): E		
VI	Apr. 8	13	*TRAINING EMPLOYEES TO WORK WELL* • Training the trainer • Systematic approach—six steps • Training programs for subordinates Handout(s): 4 Exercise(s): F	Vheca	OP
VII	Apr. 15	14–18	*GRIPES, GRIEVANCES, DISCIPLINE* • Influence of labor laws • Guidelines to discipline • How to handle gripes/ Avoid grievances Handout(s): 5, 6 Exercise(s): ____	Walton	VCP
VIII	Apr. 22	15	*ACCIDENT PREVENTION* • Three *E*s—engineer, educate, enforce • Supervisor's role—safety education • OSHA guidelines Handout(s): 7 Exercise(s): ____	Miti	OP
IX	Apr. 29	26–29	*MANAGING YOUR JOB* • Planning the work schedule • Controlling costs Handout(s): 8 Exercise(s): G	HRD	OP
X	May 6	35	*HELPING YOURSELF TO SUCCEED* • Continual self-development • Rating yourself for self-development Handout(s): 9, 10 Exercise(s): H	Jones	OP

An Orientation Program

The problem of indoctrinating a newly appointed supervisor is exacerbated when the operation for which he or she will be responsible is complex. This is especially true in many chemical and processing firms. The question arises as to whether the technical side or the interpersonal side of the job should get the most attention at the start. Some company programs, like the one illustrated in the box below, assume that the supervisor must be absolutely certain of the physical and technical dimensions of the job before he or she will be able to usefully assimilate training in human relations skills. This particular on-the-job orientation program is for production supervisors and lasts for over two months. Much of the learning is from observation, experience, coaching, and interviewing on a one-on-one basis. Classroom training in interpersonal and administrative skills will occur within the next six to twelve months.

A Combination On-Job, Off-Job Program

Perhaps the best programs are those that (1) are fully comprehensive in methods and techniques and (2) combine classroom instruction with related and practical experience on the job. That is the intent of the program illustrated in table 12-1 on page 184. It exposes the trainee to a wide variety of company functions and activities. It also employs counseling from line and staff managers and the training coordinator, self-study (using computer-aided instruction), and routine classroom training with other supervisors.

PROGRAMS IN THE SERVICES AND COMMERCIAL FIELDS

As our society moves from a production-oriented to a service-oriented economy, more and more supervisory-training programs are being developed for

On-the-Job Production-Supervisor Orientation Schedule

Training Schedule

Inclusive dates: ________________ to ________________

Subject	Days Allocated	Date
Familiarization	1 or 2	
Storage sheds	2	
Receiving and storage	3	
Casing and blending	3	
	Evaluation	________

Continued on next page

Subject	Days Allocated	Date
Cutting	5	
Drying	3	
	Evaluation	________
Union contracts	2	
VCT process no. 1 VCT process no. 2 VCT process no. 3	3	
Assistant floor supervisor—on *1st* shift, *4th* floor	5	
	Evaluation	________
Packing machinery	4	
Assistant floor supervisor—on *1st* shift, *3rd* floor	5	
	Evaluation	________
MIS	1	
Quality control	2	
Shipping	1	
Supply	1	
Stockroom, planning, and scheduling	2	
	Final evaluation	________

Total days: 45

During your assignment in VCT shop, you are expected to become familiar with the union contracts and AMA's *The Supervisor's Responsibility in Labor Relations.* After your final evaluation in VCT, ½ day is allotted to discuss these contracts and labor relations in general with Mr./Ms. ________________ ________________. Other areas with which you should become familiar are as follows:

Factory safety	Mr./Ms. ________________
Factory security	Mr./Ms. ________________
Waste control	Mr./Ms. ________________
Export operations	Mr./Ms. ________________
Production reports and payroll	Mr./Ms. ________________

Additionally, you should observe a closedown in VCT on Saturday morning and a cleanup in fabrication on Friday night.

Source: Adapted from Jackson E. Ramsey, "Supervisory Development," in *Human Resources Management and Development Handbook,* ed. William R. Tracey (New York: AMACOM, 1985), 979.

TABLE 12-1
COMBINED ON-JOB, OFF-JOB NEW-SUPERVISOR TRAINING PROGRAM

Assignment	Presented by (Contact)	Where (Location)	Schedule		Date Assigned (Exclude Sat., Sun., and Holidays)
			Minimum	Actual	
Orientation:					
Orientation (Introduction and Local Tour)			1 day		
Orientation (Carton and Mill Tour)			1 day		
Orientation (Filer Mill)			1 day		
Staff. Services			½ day		
Personnel and Indus. Relations			½ day		
Accounting			1 day		
Sales Function:					
ROI			½ day		
Sales Office			½ day		
Sales Visit			1 day		
Production Planning and Control:					
Factory Scheduling			10 days		
Other Scheduling			5 days		
Waste Control			1 day		
On-the-Job Training with Press Supervisor			18 wks (on trainee specialty)		
On-the-Job Training with Finishing Supervisor			7 wks (other departments)		
Parts Room Supervisor					
Concurrent Counseling and Review:					
1. Policies and Procedures			Continual		
2. Objectives, Plans, Profit Concepts			Continual		
3. Waste Control			Continual		
4. Community Relations			Continual		
5. Fundamentals of Supervision			Continual		
6. Cost Reduction			Continual		
7. Safety			Continual		
8. Labor Relations			Continual		
Self-Instruction:					
Supervisor's Self-Development course or Similar Formal Program			Concurrent		
Cost Reduction and Control—Prime I			Concurrent		
Safety and the Supervisor—Prime II			Concurrent		
Labor Relations and the Supervisor—Prime III			Concurrent		
Formal Seminar:					
1. Basic Economics					
2. Fundamentals of Supervision			5 days		
a. Human Relations					
b. Foreman's Roles as Mgr.					
c. Discipline					
d. Selection, Orientation, and Placement of Hourly Employees					
3. Methods of Instruction					
4. Communications					
5. Methods of Improvement and Creative Thinking					
6. Administering Provisions of the Union Contract Agreement					
7. Safety, Housekeeping, and Fire Prevention					
8. Container Division Policies and Objectives					
9. Company, Profit, and Marketing Concepts					

Source: Reprinted from Jackson E. Ramsey, "Supervisory Development," in *Human Resources Management and Development Handbook*, ed. William R. Tracey (New York: AMACOM, 1985), 980.

service industries. The basic concepts of such programs are the same as in regular supervisory training, but both the kind of participants enrolled and the specific content are different. The supervisory population is usually better educated and more adaptable to classroom situations. On-the-job training is often more difficult in service industries because the work is done at a desk, counter, or computer terminal, and the specific activities are not so clearly observable as on a production line. Much of the training emphasizes knowledge. Interpersonal skills may be a difficult subject for the trainer, since good manners, polite talk, and conventional courtesies are such an important part of the service environment. The training professional must be sure to accommodate these nuances in program plans.

Several companies have developed unusually effective programs in the services and commercial fields, some of which are presented in this section.

Retail Supervisor Training

Zale Corporation is a major operator of jewelry stores, with eleven hundred retail outlets. Its training director designed a comprehensive, trainee-paced, modular supervisory-training program that "must take place on the job and complement, rather than interrupt, regular duties."[3] The CDP (for Career Development Program) is divided into three phases: (I) learning experiences that are related directly to the company's products and processes, (II) management experiences that are oriented to aspiring or relatively inexperienced supervisors, and (III) management experiences for supervisory trainees and incumbent supervisors. Each of the latter two phases contains twelve management learning projects that direct the trainee through a series of step-by-step on-the-job experiences. The procedure for each project encompasses several steps and each may take as long as one year:

- A supervisory/manager trainee is assigned to a limited area of the store as a surrogate manager of that area. The trainee is encouraged to experience, observe, and participate in as many management activities related to that area as possible.
- A list of required skills and knowledge (learning objectives) and reference resources for self-study are furnished.
- The trainee performs management learning exercises that provide an information base for the follow-up analysis and develop basic proficiencies in the assigned area.
- A management analysis of the assigned area is performed by the trainee, who makes a list of all areas with potential for improvement in that department. This is an indicator of the trainee's conceptual and creative depth.
- All the possible improvement activities listed in the above step are compared with store policies, budgets, inventory constraints, and so on, and the list is modified to allow for realistic implementation within the restrictions of the store's environment and management climate.
- The trainee prepares a plan of action that documents how improvement activities can be identified, prioritized, and applied in the store to increase productivity, sales, and profits.
- The trainee implements those activities that will enhance, rather than interfere with, normal store operations.

- The store manager and/or district manager evaluate the trainee's action plan, activities attempted, sales/efficiency results, and management effectiveness.
- When the trainee has satisfactorily completed all requirements in a project, the store manager certifies the trainee's ability to effectively manage that particular area. The trainee can then proceed to the next project, as dictated by his or her job assignment in the store.
- If the trainee's results are not judged by the store manager as the best possible, the trainee is asked to repeat the learning project and action plan until he or she achieves acceptable results.
- Once an employee completes all three phases of the program and has gained some expertise in all areas of store management, he or she is given an opportunity to manage an entire store for up to two weeks, often while the manager is on vacation.
- Assuming the trainee has met an acceptable standard of achievement throughout the program, he or she attends a six-day Management Candidate Seminar in Dallas for intensive review and additional management training.[4]

Bank Operations Supervisor Training

Except for the specifics, supervisors in banks, insurance firms, and other financial-services institutions must build a foundation for the managerial side of their jobs by first assimilating the technical aspects of the processes involved, just as do industrial supervisors. Surveys indicate that, in many instances, a knowledge of operations must precede the more formal, conference-type supervisory-training program. A good example is provided by the schedule prepared for training operations supervisors in a southwestern bank, illustrated in the box on the facing page. This bank emphasizes the trainees' performing the work as a basis for being able to supervise it. Each major work area (eight in all) is scheduled in sequence, with the trainees spending from one to five weeks in each area, or a total of twenty-five or twenty-six weeks in the program. Training is coordinated by the human resources development department, but it is conducted on the job by the line departments. When the training is completed, each trainee is assigned as an assistant operations supervisor or an operations supervisor, according to (1) proficiency demonstrated and (2) the availability of openings.

Word-Processing Supervisor Training

With the explosion of office automation and the many changes in responsibilities it has brought about in the office, a closer look at the competencies associated with word-processing supervision is instructive. Davis and Balderson, in their excellent book *Word-Processing Supervision,* imply the following knowledge and skills components for the training of word-processing supervisors:

The supervisor's responsibility

Conducting a feasibility study

Training Schedule for Banking Operations Supervisors, by Order of Exposure

A. *Bookkeeping*—2 weeks

1. Holdovers—debits and credits.
2. Return items.
3. Familiarize with status reports.
4. Assist customers—emphasis on customer relations.
5. Perform related clerical duties.

B. *Commercial teller*—5 weeks

1. Paying and receiving operations.
2. Process mail deposits.
3. Balance "cash paid items" and "cash."
4. Vault teller operations:
   a. Maintain and control cash requirements (ordering and shipping).
   b. Prepare change orders and process night deposits.

C. *Collections*—3 weeks

1. Process incoming and outgoing collection items.
2. Receive and process payment on time deposits.
3. Calculate interest.
4. Maintain records.
5. Prepare reports.

D. *Note teller*—5 weeks

1. Receive and process commercial-loan payments.
2. Set up new loans and necessary documentation.
3. Calculate interest and prepare notices.
4. Maintain collateral records.
5. Maintain liability cards.
6. Prepare loan reports.
7. Prepare loan receipts.

E. *General ledger*—3 weeks

1. Balance cash.
2. Prepare general ledger tickets.
3. Verify all general ledger tickets against general ledger and cancellation.
4. File general ledger tickets and general ledger sheets.

Continued on next page

Training Schedule for Banking Operations Supervisors, by Order of Exposure—*Continued*

F. *Safe deposit*—1 week (this could be part of bookkeeping phase)

1. Admit authorized personnel to safe-deposit vault.
2. Receive and process rental payments.
3. Lease and surrender boxes.
4. Assist customers.
5. Perform related duties (issuing monthly call statements, preparing stop-payment orders, lost-key procedures, and so on).

G. *General operations*—4 weeks

1. Perform functions of operations supervisor.
2. Run monthly accruals and balance interest receivables (notes).
3. Run monthly accruals (collections).
4. Monthly certifications and month-end reports (general ledger).
5. Become familiar with budget procedure.

H. *Miscellaneous*—2 weeks

1. Open new accounts, at least one week.
2. Instructional visit to home offices (especially Bank-Americard).
3. Instructional visit to operations center.

Source: Adapted from Walter S. Wikstrom, *Supervisory Training,* Conference Board Report No. C12, (New York: The Conference Board, 1973), 28–29.

Configurations and types of equipment

Selecting word-processing equipment

Selecting dictating equipment

Preparing a budget and controlling costs

Designing a word-processing area

Selecting personnel

Developing operating procedures and procedures manuals

Conducting orientation and training classes

Working with people

Measuring productivity

Indexing, filing, and keeping records

Related functions, such as mail, reprographics, telecommunications, and data processing.[5]

PROGRAMS WITH SPECIAL FEATURES

A perusal of supervisory-training programs often shows that each program distinguishes itself by reliance on a feature that may not be unique in itself but that gets special attention from the program planners. Four such features are discussed briefly in the following subsections.

SUPPLEMENTARY REFERENCE MATERIAL

Take-home material—or in the vernacular, "handouts"—seem to be an especially popular ingredient of supervisory-training programs. Handouts typically include copies of magazine articles, inspirational clippings, checklists, and the like. Instructors feel comfortable knowing that they have placed in the trainees' hands either (1) material for reference or (2) information that reinforces or supplements what was covered during the training session. Surprisingly, since supervisors are not known as great readers of textual material, handouts are popular with trainees. They, too, are comfortable knowing that, if they were unable to grasp a particular idea in the training session, they have a ready reference to place in their files back in the shop. No published research verifies the value of the comfort both parties receive from the use of handouts, and trainers should not rely on them as a main feature of training transfer.

It is far better to set fewer and more realistic objectives for a program—and attain them—than to try to throw everything possible into the course and rely on outside, backup reading for learning. If outside materials are to be used, it is preferable to integrate the program or course with an appropriate commercial text. As the course progresses, trainees can be urged to earmark, underline, or otherwise note passages that can serve as references later on. That way, the reference material is integral, rather than supplementary, to the program.

Despite philosophical objections to the practice of relying on handouts, there are some instances (legal, safety, union matters) where an oral presentation at a training session should definitely be backed up by a written document. This helps to make certain that, when needed for application purposes, the information will be available in accurate form. In some organizations, especially public agencies, supervisors are expected to operate according to carefully defined legal procedures. These may have to be distributed during training courses. In a comprehensive supervisory development program periodically offered to the civilian personnel of the Department of the Army, for example, the following brochures are prepared in advance and distributed to supervisors as the training program progresses:

"Selection and Utilization of Personnel"

"Job Instruction Training"

"Position and Pay Management"

"Performance Appraisal"

"Discipline"

"Recognition Programs for Employees"

"Health and Sick Leave"

"Safety"

"Career Management"

"Grievances"

"Relationships with Employee Organizations"

"Equal Employment Opportunities"

Many organizations, of course, issue a supervisor's manual, which provides supervisors with operational information (especially regarding personnel administration) prescribing the policies, procedures, and regulations that must be followed.

Key Points for Supervisors

Some program planners are particularly adept at developing and distributing to trainees key points about operations in their organizations that are especially critical to the success or failure of the supervisor's performance. At each stage of course work or on-the-job training, the training coordinator obtains from a panel of master supervisors or operational specialists a list of key factors that make or break a particular situation or process.

Key factors for interpersonal matters, such as handling discipline, for example, would be:

1. Listen to the employee's complete story. He or she is entitled to a full hearing—if not from you, then later on up the line, where you may be embarrassed.
2. Check with other people to verify the facts. The employee may be in the right; it's better to know this sooner than later.
3. Discuss the situation with the proper authority (such as personnel, labor-relations manager, your boss). Don't assume that your own judgment is best.
4. Find out whether there is an established policy that applies. Precedent will carry more weight than your logic.
5. Try to be the person who hands down the ruling. Otherwise, you may be regarded by employees as just an intermediary, with no real authority in the disciplinary process.

Key factors for administrative and technical processes follow the same pattern. They attempt to provide the supervisor not only a set of guidelines but also a clear indication of what may go wrong if a critical point is not recognized or fails to get the attention it warrants. For example, trainees at the Brown and Williamson Tobacco Company are given a key-point reference sheet at each of the departments in which they will receive their on-the-job training. An excerpt from a checklist given to supervisors training in the packaging department appears below:

How to line up the shift.

Moving employees off the floor as affected by seniority and classification.

How to counsel an employee; the role of the shop steward.

How to build a case; use of "Suggestions for Improvement."

How to handle mix-ups; whom to inform.

How to handle machinery problems; whom to call.

Delineation of operator/fixer responsibilities.

Use of parts catalogue and requisitions.

Handling of time cards, reports, etc.

How to cope with case elevator problems.

Key points of safety and good housekeeping.

How to handle power failures, air, vacuum, etc.

How "units per man-hour" are computed.

How to recognize good from bad raw materials.

How to clean machinery.

How to inspect for cleanliness.

Importance of lubrication.

Proper handling of waste.

How to deal with tardiness and absentees.[6]

Incorporation of CEUs

The use of continuing education units (CEUs) was discussed in the previous chapter (see the subsection on "Awarding of CEUs"). For courses offered to the public especially, but also for internal programs, the CEU provides an added learning incentive to participants. Official criteria can be obtained from the Council on the Continuing Education Unit, but the two main essentials are (1) the number of contact hours provided (ten, sixty-minute contact hours are required to gain one CEU completion) and (2) evidence of satisfactory completion—such as some sort of proficiency test administered at the close of the course. Indiana State University, for example, has offered a Principles and Practices of Supervision program in two parts. The two parts contribute a total of fifty hours toward CEU credits. Those who complete each part receive a certificate from the university attesting to the CEUs awarded. The program content at Indiana State is as follows:

PART I

1. Organization and its structure
2. What is supervision; goal setting, decision making
3. Qualities of successful supervision; delegating, directing
4. Planning; scheduling
5. Human resources management; organizing
6. Understanding human behavior
7. Authority, cooperation, leadership

TABLE 12-2
A SIMPLIFIED SCHEMATIC MODEL FOR AN INTEGRATED SUPERVISORY AND MANAGEMENT DEVELOPMENT PROGRAM LEADING TO A CERTIFICATE OF PROFESSIONAL DEVELOPMENT

Level 0	Level I	Level II	Level III
001 Understanding Supervisory Work 002 Understanding Interpersonal Relations	101 Introduction to Supervision 102 Understanding People at Work 103 Supervisors, Activators, and Facilitators 104 Job/Work Design and Control 105 Building an Effective Team 000 Personnel Practices and Concepts *Skills Cluster A:* Organization Development (choose *one*) 111 Employee Training and Development MGT 100 Personnel Selection GOV 113 Making Lawful Employment Selections MGT 101 Personnel Evaluation *Skills Cluster B:* Information Management (choose *one*) 121 Information Management for Supervisors 122 Budgeting and Expense Control 123 Improving Quality of Office Work Output *Electives* (choose *one*) From A, B, GOV, MGT, or HUS *Proficiency Demonstration* 555 Project in Work Improvement	201 New Perspectives in Supervision 202 Techniques for Improving Interpersonal Relations 203 Techniques for Making Leadership Effective 204 Techniques for Improving Employee Performance 000 Personnel Practices and Concepts *Skills Cluster C:* Planning and Productivity (choose *one*) 211 Techniques for Improving Departmental Productivity 212 Techniques for Improving Plans, Schedules, and Results 111 Employee Training and Development 123 Improving Quality of Office Work Output *Skills Cluster D:* Skills Development (choose *one*) 221 Problem Solving and Decision Making MGT 140 Time Management HUS 160 Meetings for Results HUS 170 Managing Stress *Electives* (choose *two*) From A, B, C, D, GOV, MGT, or HUS *Proficiency Demonstration* 555 Project in Work Improvement	301 Managing the Management Process 302 Human Relations to Organizations 303 Managerial Leadership 304 Managing Other Managers 305 Managing Organizations 000 Personnel Practices and Concepts *Skills Cluster E:* Public Service Management (choose *one*) 311 Principles of Public Administration 312 Program Management 313 Organization Development GOV 100 Federal Grants: An Overview *Skills Cluster F:* Quantitative Management (choose *one*) 321 Understanding Statistics and Quantitative Methods MGT 003 Data Processing for Non-Data-Processing Managers MGT 005 Financial Management *Electives* (choose *two*) From A, B, C, D, E, F, GOV, MGT, or HUS *Proficiency Demonstration* 666 Project in Operations Improvement

8. Morale factors and productivity
9. Counseling

PART II

1. Communication/listening; interpersonal skills
2. Meetings/memos/reports
3. Employee training
4. Discipline/complaints/grievances
5. Problem cases
6. Performance rating
7. Civil rights
8. Unions
9. Health and safety

Comprehensive Certification Program

In very large organizations, it is possible to develop a comprehensive program, integrating supervisory training with management development and linking the two through the award of a formally recognized proficiency certificate. One such program set as its objectives that it should:

1. Meet (a) the career and personal development interests of individual supervisors and managers while (b) serving to make them more effective in the pursuit of operational goals established by state and local agencies, especially the objectives of improving work force productivity.
2. Prescribe a normative curriculum of study for each of three levels of managerial responsibility and competency.
3. Reward successful completion of a specified curriculum (a) with a certificate (or diploma) that officially recognizes the individual's pursuit of professional development and (b) that becomes a significant document of accomplishment in the individual's personal and career record.

Certificates (designated as Certificates of Professional Development, or CPDs) were awarded at appropriate ceremonies and became important documents in participants' personnel history files. Table 12-2 illustrates the courses offered at each level of the program and their relationship. Figure 8-1 (in chapter 8) and figure 10-1 (in chapter 10) provide conceptual views of the program levels and show how they fit within the states' overall management development program.

Part V

ENHANCEMENT AND EVALUATION

Chapter 13

Productivity, Quality, and Employee-Rights Training

INTRODUCTION

Three areas of supervision have, in recent years, received renewed, or special, emphasis. These are (1) the need for increased productivity and (2) improved quality of product or service outputs from the work force while (3) displaying a sensitivity to employee rights, especially those protected by Equal Employment Opportunity legislation. Almost all enterprises, institutions, and public agencies now give some consideration to productivity and quality problems and rather intense attention to employee-rights issues. A great many companies have mounted supervisory-training courses in productivity improvement, often associating these with an improvement in quality, too. Thousands of organizations, of course, have instituted some sort of quality-circles programs, with or without their direct association with supervisory training. Almost all organizations have also provided supervisors with training in the knowledge and skills related to EEO legislation, although this training is often integrated with such subjects as interviewing, performance appraisal, and discipline.

The purpose of this chapter is to provide a broad overview of the training that is appropriate for supervisors in each of these three areas, while acknowledging that much of the responsibility for improvement in productivity and quality—as well as for legal compliance with EEO—must be shared by the technical staff and middle and upper levels of management.

PRODUCTIVITY-IMPROVEMENT TRAINING FOR SUPERVISORS

The level of productivity in an organization can be affected by many factors besides the nature of the supervision provided to the work force. Productivity may be lowered by: inadequate tools and equipment; poorly conceived operational processes and procedures; substandard raw materials and supplies; hit-or-miss schedules; improperly delineated specifications; and of course, a poorly paid, inadequately trained, sloppily directed, and unmotivated employee work force.

In the past, there has been an unfair and unfortunate tendency on the part of upper-level management to place the blame on either supervisors or employees, or both. No amount of supervisory training will improve an organization's productivity unless other factors outside the supervisors' control are also brought into line. After—and only after—proper conditions have been established, *then* training supervisors in leading, communicating, and motivating skills will lay the groundwork for a significant improvement in productivity. The improvement may not occur, however, unless the training is carried one step further—namely, supervisory training in the specific technical and procedural methods that can lead to work improvement. The advances that qualify circles have wrought can largely be attributed to a similar combination of changes at the departmental level: (1) an improvement in motivation and (2) a rise in the level of technical knowledge needed to detect and suggest remedies for operational problems.

A Work-Improvement Program

Detailed in the box that follows is a model for designing and planning a productivity-improvement training program for supervisors in any industry, institution, or public agency. The program component presented here is a course outline with an action-project focus. Appendix 4 provides (1) a set of operational guidelines for instructors and for the supervisors who participate in the training, as well as (2) a portfolio of commonly used forms for the analysis of productivity-improvement projects.

The term *work* (or *operations*) *improvement* was chosen because, in many fields, where tangible products are not manipulated or manufactured, productivity is difficult for supervisors and employees to comprehend. Work improvement is a broader and less threatening concept.

Prototype Course Outline: Work/Operations Improvement-Training for Supervisors

Course Length: 2 days

A. Course Synopsis

Under professional guidance and with the assistance of the course instructor, participants will (1) select from among target opportunities at their job sites a project for the improvement of a particular condition (cost, waste, service, maintenance, workmanship, allocation of human resources, absences, turnover, procedures, contract fulfillment, and so on), (2) develop a comprehensive plan for improving that condition, (3) implement that plan, and (4) measure and report its results.

B. Target Audience

Individuals who have completed the core courses of the curriculum at their program level (new, inexperienced supervisors and experienced supervisors).

1. *Precourse preparation.* Participants are to accomplish the following before attending the seminar: (a) identify at least three potential improvement targets, (b) review with their immediate superiors their suitability for project work, and (c) gather in writing such basic data about the target areas

Continued on next page

Prototype Course Outline: Work/Operations Improvement-Training for Supervisors—*Continued*

as relevant time frames, period costs, materials consumption, number of personnel involved, related payroll expense, and any other pertinent data.

2. *Postcourse assignment.* Participants, after returning to their job sites, must (a) complete the comprehensive improvement plan for their project in writing according to specifications provided during the seminar; (b) submit the completed plan to the course instructor for review and comment within the next thirty days; (c) implement, with their immediate superior's consent, the approved plan as soon as possible, but within the next sixty days; and (d) measure the results and report these to the immediate superior.

C. Course Objectives

Overall. To provide participants with a set of skills for identifying and implementing improvement projects and to enable them to demonstrate this proficiency by successfully preparing and implementing a project of their choice from among suitable target areas at their job sites.

Specific Course Outcomes. Participants who complete this course and follow through with their assignments can be expected to:

1. Identify-short-range targets of opportunity for work and/or operations improvement.
2. Analyze an improvement project to estimate (a) potential savings (or other measurable benefits) and (b) the costs of obtaining these savings.
3. Select an improvement project that represents an optimum combination of savings potential and ease of attainment.
4. Establish a set of project objectives in specific, measurable terms.
5. Learn about, and learn how to apply, a number of basic approaches for improving work methods and conditions and for reducing cost or waste.
6. Anticipate and prepare for conditions, especially human factors, that may aid in or detract from project fulfillment.
7. Prepare a written, comprehensive, detailed plan for attaining project objectives.
8. Be able to implement an improvement project based on a comprehensive, detailed plan.

D. Course Outline

Day 1

1. *Improvement identification.* Typical project sources; recognition of conditions that are symptomatic of wasted effort, materials, equipment, people, and/or other resources.
2. *Input/output analysis.* Estimating current conditions and factors that contribute to input expenses and output values; estimating improved conditions and factors that would contribute to input expenses (plus initial cost of equipment, for example, to correct or improve conditions) and output values.

Continued on next page

Prototype Course Outline: Work/Operations Improvement-Training for Supervisors—*Continued*

3. *Project selection.* Optimizing input expenses and output values; ABC, or Pareto analysis (the separation of the vital few from the trivial many) as a basis for project selection; short- versus long-range projects; incremental versus radical improvements.
4. *Project objectives.* The need to be specific and to quantify; citing expected improvements and the cost of obtaining them; estimates of required resources; establishing time frames.

Day 2

5. *Survey of improvement methods.* Factors that contribute to waste or poor productivity; techniques for eliminating or minimizing wasteful conditions; basic methods-improvement concepts and reference sources; work simplification; work sampling; value analysis for purchased materials and for services required or provided; other sources and references.
6. *The improvement environment.* Examination of conditions that favor or discourage project implementation; handling the problems of change and employee motivation.
7. *Preparing the comprehensive plan.* Specifying target objectives; estimating and acquiring the necessary resources (equipment, materials, funds, human resources); planning sequential and parallel procedures; establishing a timetable; securing approvals; preparing employees for change; assigning responsibilities; measuring results.
8. *Implementation and follow-up.* Timetables for completing the written plan, review by course instructor, and approval by the immediate superior; picking a starting date; monitoring progress; measuring, verifying, and reporting results.

Note

The instructor must provide (1) a format for the comprehensive plan, (2) a set of summary or reference sheets for each improvement technique surveyed under No. 5 above, and (3) some sort of mechanism for reporting the results of his or her review of trainees' plans to the supervisors and to the training department, presuming that the plan must be completed in order to receive credit for the course.

Optional Approaches

- Participants might return for a one-day session during which they present their completed plans to the seminar group. This would obviate the need for the instructor to handle reviews by mail.
- Participants might be required to study course material beforehand. This would permit greater depth of discussion during the seminar. On the other hand, most of this material needs the presence of an instructor in order to assimilate it.
- The course might be extended to three days. This would permit greater depth in surveying the various improvement methods and would almost assure that participants could complete their plans during the course.

Productivity Training: Tying It in to the Bigger Picture

Three experienced management development directors were queried about the best approaches to productivity-improvement training. Generally, they cautioned about losing sight of the long-run objective for supervisory training, which is to build a broad base of competencies. All three, however, acknowledge the need for most management (and supervisory) development programs to pay closer attention to productivity improvement than in the recent past.[1] For example:

William S. Mitchell, of Metropolitan Life Insurance Company, recommends:

- Build heavy technical productivity-improvement skill building into supervisory training.
- Don't abandon the teaching of behavioral science–driven management skills, but place them in proper perspective and weight the curriculum toward the kind of management we need now.
- Return for guidance and inspiration to the supervisory training used before the behavioral sciences approach came into vogue. But reinterpret and remodel the old subjects in light of advances in instructional technology and, of course, in work systems themselves.[2]

Georgia Eckelman, of Anheuser-Busch, says:

- Narrow the breadth of the supervisory-development curriculum. Focus on fewer topics in more depth, and take a skill-building approach.
- Tie generic skill development to organization-specific productivity issues and situations.
- Place plenty of energy in customized development for branch offices or plants. Concentrating on the needs of managers and supervisors in their intact work teams can yield high productivity-improvement results.[3]

Mike Walsh, of Continental Grain Company, suggests:

- Avoid the arbitrary imposition of an outside "productivity consultant." It may yield quick results, but it doesn't contribute to management or supervisory development; in fact, it teaches managers not to manage.
- Use teams of supervisors, managers, and professionals to identify and develop recommendations. This gives them the "live" experience they need to develop and test critical management skills.
- Structure the teams so that they do not have intimate knowledge of the productivity problem they are assigned to solve. This lessens the potential for "vested interest" stances and assures cross-skill development.[4]

QUALITY-IMPROVEMENT TRAINING FOR SUPERVISORS

The well-deserved enthusiasm about the potential of quality circles has tended to obscure that there is, and always has been, a universal appreciation for the impact a supervisor can have, for better or worse, on quality. In the past, this awareness has been most evident in product-oriented industries, where defects are more likely to show up in a customer's usage. Increasingly, however, the results of poor quality control have become a major concern in such unlikely places as hospitals (wrong medication administered), motels (guests assigned to rooms that have not been cleaned), and offices (incorrect addressing of envelopes, misfiles of correspondence, and inaccurate posting of figures). In the National Survey of Supervisory Management Practices (NSSMP), for instance, 77 percent of blue-collar supervisors reported that "damaged or rejected work, inaccuracies, and work that needs to be done over cause a problem regularly or sometimes";[5] white-collar supervisors almost matched this assessment with a figure of 70 percent.[6]

As with productivity, responsibility for lapses in quality has traditionally been placed at the feet of either supervisors or employees, or both. In the NSSMP, for example, supervisors themselves seemed quick to place the blame on employees. The following data show their perception of who is at fault when errors are made:

RESPONSIBLE SOURCE	RANKING
Employee carelessness	1
Company pressures for greater or faster output	2
Wrong or incomplete specifications or blueprints	3
Ineffective inspection or quality-control procedures	4
Conflicting or imprecise operating procedures	5
Off-grade materials or supplies	6
Faulty or inadequate tools and equipment	7
Design deficiencies	8[7]

The Supervisor's Role in Quality

From general knowledge, it would appear that upper-level management "scapegoats" supervisors for quality problems and—from the survey data—that supervisors, in turn, "scapegoat" employees. In fact, the problem, rather than the blame, must be tracked to four general sources:

1. The extent of the technically oriented organizational support that quality assurance receives
2. The extent of the knowledge, information, and skills that supervisors have about quality assurance
3. The extent of the knowledge, information, and skills that employees have regarding quality performance
4. The degree to which supervisors and employees are motivated to assure the production of quality products, services, and workmanship

In this context, supervisors become the key sources for factors 3 and 4 above—training and motivating employees for better-quality performance. Supervisors themselves, however, urgently need training in the knowledge and skills areas that help to assure quality as well as in the skills areas of training and motivating employees.

Basic Training in Quality Assurance

There is a large body of technical knowledge and skills that supervisors must acquire if they are to be effective in assuring quality performance from their employees. Content of a basic course should include, as a minimum, the following:

- What quality really is: the level of product or service performance designated by an organization's management
- Terminology: standards, standardization, specifications, reliability, quality assurance, acceptable quality levels (AQL)
- Costs associated with quality: internal failure costs (rejects), external failure costs (those discovered by customers and clients), appraisal (inspection) costs, prevention costs
- Process or operational aspects of quality: process capability, tool and equipment capability, operator training
- Methods for detecting defects: critical, major, and minor defects; inspection and test methods
- Measurement and control of quality: 100 percent inspection versus sampling; statistical quality-control techniques; quality-control charts
- Quality reports: trouble-code lists, defects-control chart, departmental deviation (or errors) report, quality-performance report

Subjects contained in this list typically require a minimum of forty hours of training. Instruction must be provided by specialists, knowledgeable not only in the broad fundamentals of quality assurance but also in the company-specific aspects of quality.

Motivational Training for Quality Assurance

Relatively few companies target their motivational and interpersonal skills training courses for supervisors solely toward quality. This is not necessarily bad: a supervisor's motivational and interpersonal skills should apply broadly to many operational areas. Nevertheless, somewhere during the course of quality-assurance training, special attention must be given to such skills as leadership, communication, and employee training.

Quality-Circles Training for Supervisors

The move toward quality circles as the ultimate solution for problems of quality assurance (and for that matter, productivity) has superficially shifted the emphasis from technical concerns to team building and employee involvement. In the process, QCs often place supervisors in ambiguous, untenable positions.

Ambiguity in Roles as QC Leaders. Gryna observes that most QC programs, while encouraging the use of rank-and-file employees as circle leaders, end up with the department supervisor as a leader.[8] Rieker remarks that supervisors understandably fear a decline in their decision-making authority and display a resistance to QCs as a consequence.[9] Supervisors may voice approval for QCs simply because they have no other alternative except to go along with them and accept a leader assignment. It is interesting to note that, in the planning of most QC programs, supervisors are not apprised of the decision until after a steering committee has been formed and objectives set.

Ralph Barra, who directed the QC program for Westinghouse, comments that it is essential to establish an understanding of circle leadership, which differs significantly from "traditional" leadership.[10] Barra's view is made clear in the following comparison:

TRADITIONAL LEADERSHIP	CIRCLE LEADERSHIP
The leader directs, controls, polices, and leads the members to a solution. Basically, it is the leader's group, and the leader's authority and responsibility are acknowledged by members.	The circle is owned by the members, including the leader. All members, with the leader's assistance, contribute to its effectiveness.
The leader personally focuses attention on the problem to be solved, and performs many of the functions needed to arrive at the proper solution.	The circle is responsible (with occasional help from the leader) for reaching a solution that includes the participation of all and is the product of all. The leader is a servant and helper to the circle.
The leader sets limits and uses rules of order to keep the discussion within strict limits set by the agenda. The leader controls the time spent on each item, preventing the group from wandering fruitlessly.	Members of a circle are encouraged and helped by the leader to take responsibility for its task productivity, its method of working, and its plans for using the available time.
Because the need to arrive at a solution to a problem is all-important to the leader, the needs of individual members are considered less important.	With help and encouragement from the leader, the members come to realize that the needs, feelings, and purposes of all members should be met so that an awareness of being a group forms. The circle can then continue to grow.[11]

Most managements apparently accept the notion that they will create an authority problem if the QC leader is not the supervisor, although some managements are not troubled by the employee-as-leader approach.

The problem is aggravated, of course, when the QC leader (and department supervisor) becomes the principal trainer as well as the coordinator of employee involvement in the circles.

QC Leader Training. The box on the facing page provides insight into the special participative-management skills necessary for the supervisor serving as a leader of a quality circle. Leader training at Westinghouse, for example, focuses on human relations. Its five skills-training areas include: (1) small-group meetings, (2) instructor (employee) training, (3) communication, (4) supervisor assessment (identification of employees with potential for promotion to supervisor), and (5) motivation. While the company does not specify course length for these skills, the impression is that each area is given a full day's coverage.[12]

Training Program for Quality-Circle Leaders

Day 1

8:00 A.M.	Introduction—meet each other History Training materials (A/V introduction to quality circles) Why quality circles? Brainstorming—quality-circle objectives
9:30	Break
9:45	Group dynamics (Wilderness exercise)
10:45	Cause and effect I
11:30	Morning summary
11:45	Lunch
12:30 P.M.	Motivation
1:15	Pareto
2:00	Break
2:15	Starting, training, and operating your circle
3:15	Group discussion
3:45	Training assignments and summary

Day 2

12:30 P.M.	Review
1:00	Brainstorming (leader teach)
1:45	What circles are doing
2:15	Break
2:30	Cause and effect II (leader teach)
3:15	Histograms (leader teach)
4:00	Summary

Day 3

8:00 A.M.	Review
8:15	Communications and leadership
9:00	Graphs (leader teach)
9:30	Break
9:45	Check sheets (leader teach)
10:30	Case study (leader teach)
11:00	Management presentation (leader teach)
11:45	Lunch
12:00 P.M.	Management presentation (continued)
1:15	Group discussion
1:30	Simulation
4:00	Summary

Source: Reprinted with permission from Frank M. Gryna, Jr., *Quality Circles: A Team Approach to Problem Solving* (New York: AMACOM, 1981), 57.

Problem-Solving Training. The technical side of quality circles is, at its core, a problem-solving process, as shown in figure 13-1. Problem solving is a highly intellectual capability, and most training focuses on (1) understanding the process and (2) practice in applying it. As taught in the various QC programs, the process is enhanced by instruction in a number of procedural techniques (such as cause-and-effect analysis, histograms, and force-field analysis). These are not simple concepts to grasp, and effective training of supervisors (who—in theory, at least—are supposed to be able to pass these skills on to employees) is predictably time-consuming.

QC Member Training. Quality-circle leaders, in many organizations, are expected to take the knowledge and skills they have acquired during their own training and then transfer these to the circle members. At Harley Davidson Division of AMF, for example, ten problem-solving modules are presented by the leader at the first series of circle meetings:

Introduction to quality circles

Problem identification

Brainstorming

Cause-and-effect diagrams

Pareto diagrams

Histograms

Check sheets

Case study

Graphs

Presentations of recommendations[13]

Again, it is interesting to note that while the popular impression of quality circles is based on their impact on employee involvement, the hard core of employee training in QCs, like that for supervisors, consists of technical skills.

EQUAL EMPLOYMENT OPPORTUNITY TRAINING FOR SUPERVISORS

Almost all comprehensive training programs include course material on the supervisors' role in implementation of the various equal employment opportunity laws. Many programs devote at least one full session to the subject, often stressing specific policy areas in the supervisors' organization that require careful attention. A few programs also extend supervisory training to include the less central issues of employee rights as they pertain to privacy, sexual harassment, restraint of management prerogatives, due process, freedom of inquiry, and so forth. David Ewing, in writing on this subject, is sym-

FIGURE 13-1 PROBLEM-SOLVING CONCEPT IN QUALITY CIRCLES

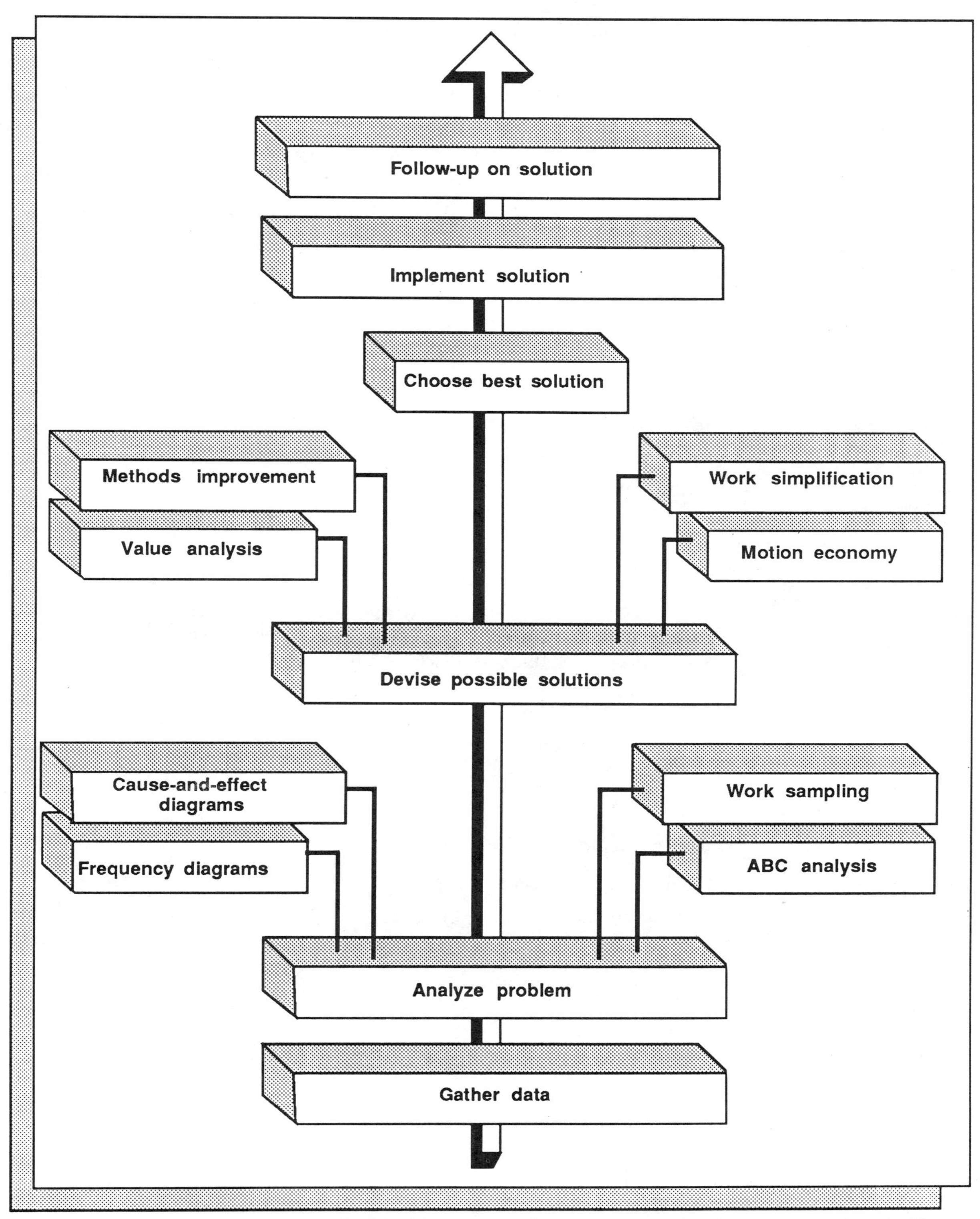

Source: Adapted with permission from Lester R. Bittel, *What Every Supervisor Should Know,* 5th ed. (New York: McGraw-Hill Book Company, 1984), 459.

pathetic toward supervisors and believes that "supervisors presumed to be at fault should be given some benefit of a doubt."[14] Agreed that, in the great majority of cases, supervisors are well intentioned,[15] or believe that they are carrying out management policy correctly, the chances for misinformation and lack of authoritative knowledge are great.

EEO Training

At a minimum, supervisory-training programs in equal employment opportunity and employee-rights areas ought to cover the following:

- Equal Employment Opportunity legislation
  - Title VII of the Civil Rights Act
  - Equal Pay Act of 1963
  - Age Discrimination in Employment Act
  - Executive Order 11246
  - Section 503, Rehabilitation Act of 1973
- Impact of legislation within the particular organization
- The supervisors' role in carrying out EEO policy[16]

Application or Relevance Training

In most instances, supervisors want to know *what* to do rather than to hear an in-depth recitation of the philosophy or legal implications behind compliance regulations. Hence, EEO sessions with an emphasis like the following may appear more useful and relevant to supervisory participants:

- How to release the full work potential of handicapped employees
- How to help hard-core unemployed workers and/or disadvantaged employees adapt to their jobs
- Working productively with minority employees
- Working productively with female employees
- Working with younger employees
- Working with older employees

Chapter 14

Organizational Change, Self-Development, and Career Paths

INTRODUCTION

In a great many organizations, supervisors feel as if they are buffeted by constant changes in the structure of relationships over which they have no control. These perceptions are often justified. Organization development (OD) tends to focus on the integration of middle- and upper-level functional structures. Such a top-down approach is probably warranted by the costs of time and disruption inherent in the OD process. Nevertheless, because they provide the productive interface between management and the work force, supervisors are vital in such changes.

On a broader scale, the general role of supervisors in organizations has also been changing. This has taken place both with and without a formally conceived OD program. To help supervisors become more effective in their new roles—whether the role changes are planned or not—supervisors must be drawn more actively into the change process. Their commitment to new responsibilities must not stop at that point. Supervisors should also be guided toward developmental activities that will extend their potential. There are many supervisors, too, who view the supervisory job mainly as an entry gate to a higher management position. These individuals will need professional assistance in planning their careers.

AN EVOLUTIONARY ROLE CHANGE

It is becoming increasingly difficult to generalize about the supervisors' role. Each organization places its supervisors in a slightly different context from other organizations. Generally, however, supervisors have moved from a position of one-on-one authority, as shown in figure 14-1, to a position requiring some form of team, or group, relationship. Bramlette illustrates in figure 14-2 the changing nature of supervisory leadership as it progresses from an autocratic, authoritative style to a more participative, consultative style in which the supervisor plays the role of resource person.

As mentioned earlier, nearly 20 percent of supervisors feel that they are miscast and ineffective in their current participative roles. Part of this dissatisfaction arises from the ambiguity of their position and the lack of strong organizational support systems.

FIGURE 14-1 THE CHANGING ROLE OF THE FIRST-LINE SUPERVISOR

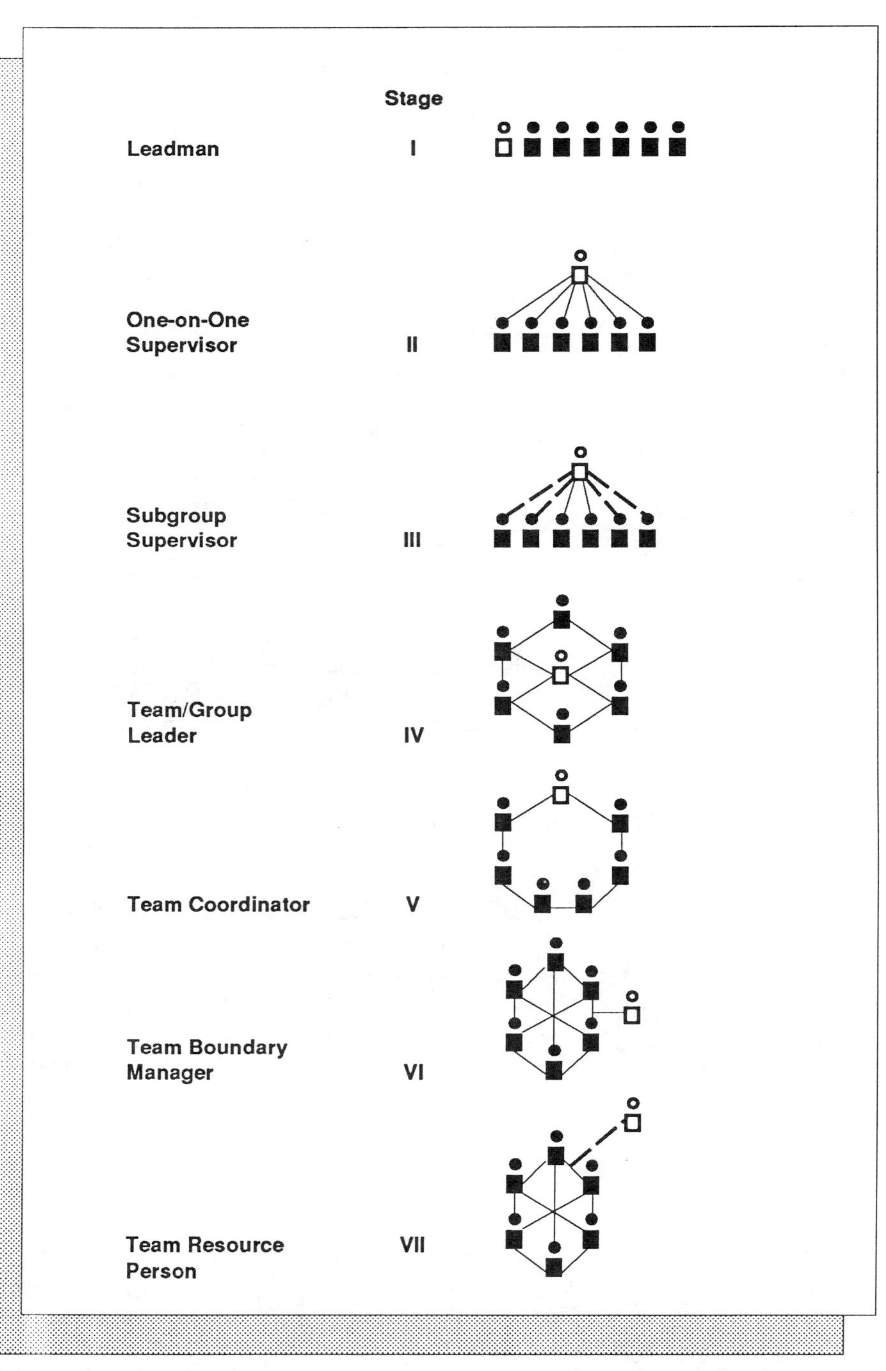

Source: Adapted with permission from Carl A. Bramlette, "Free to Change," *Training and Development Journal* (March 1984): 39.

FIGURE 14-2 HOW SUPERVISORY STYLES CHANGE AS ROLES CHANGE

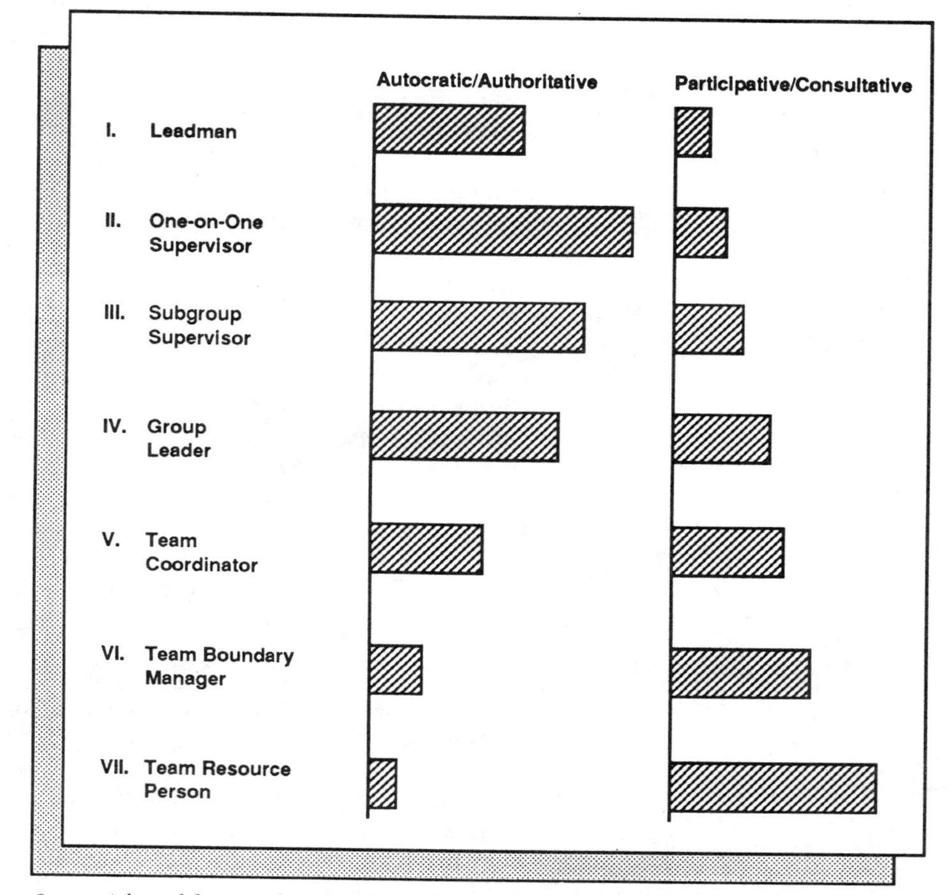

Source: Adapted from Carl A. Bramlette, "Free to Change," *Training and Development Journal* (March 1984): 41.

A REALISTIC ROLE DEFINITION

In view of these changes, some authorities prescribe a redefinition of the supervisor's role—one that is more in tune with organizational realities. Wolfe, for instance, observes that for supervisors to be effective, their roles must be established by a realistic organization strategy.[1] He faults the present concept of the supervisor's role in the following respects:

- Supervisors are expected to act as the linkage between management and nonmanagement, which requires balancing two divergent viewpoints.
- Supervisors are expected to be action takers when change is required, despite the fact that their authority for introducing change is often nonexistent.
- Supervisors are frequently at a dead end in terms of promotability, even though they may be fully committed to the management team. Cummings deplores this. He says: "To be promoted to a supervisory position early in one's career and never again be promoted can create a demotivating attitude. . . . Career development and human resources planning programs

can appear incoherent and paradoxical to these supervisors."[2] In fact, the National Survey of Supervisory Management Practices showed that a great many supervisors view themselves as "shelf sitters," with relatively low career expectations in terms of advancement.[3] To this situation is added the factor of supervisory pay scales that often differ only slightly from those of the people supervised. A survey conducted by the American Management Association in 1977 highlighted the extent to which the absence of overtime pay for supervisors was especially upsetting to them.[4] This disparity in compensation between supervisors and supervised persists today.

Wolfe also observes that "The supervisor's job has little real authority and, in a practical sense, is not viewed as a real management job." That is a harsh conclusion to draw, but it is one that should get greater attention from organization development people. Wolfe goes on to say that since supervisors have so little real leverage, they must learn to exercise influence and use available resources, especially through staff specialist groups. This influence, Wolfe says, should have two dimensions: (1) functional information, which requires that the supervisor know not only his or her own job but subordinates' jobs well enough to supervise them effectively, and (2) all the managerial-process and interpersonal skills needed to build an effective work group. As a consequence, Wolfe suggests a more functional definition of the supervisor's role:

> The role of the supervisor is to use influence and management work to maintain and measurably improve the return on the use of organizational resources at the point where physical work takes place.[5]

Such a definition would help to make supervisory-training objectives more concrete. It would depend, however, on (1) a specific articulation of how supervisors are to perform management work, (2) greater clarification of the kinds of relationships supervisors should have with management and nonmanagement personnel, and (3) improved reinforcement and support from middle- and upper-level management.

A Positive Program for Role Misfits

Supervisory role changes as dictated by changes in the philosophy of organizational structures have left a large number of supervisors either unqualified to fill the new role or disinterested in doing so. Management, with the guidance of human resources development professionals, should take positive action to correct this condition.

The following pragmatic program for dealing with this ambiguity of roles and high incidence of unmotivated, ineffective supervision involves remedial action to be taken over a long period of time, in seven distinct phases:

1. Make sure that the supervisors' organizational support system is in order.
2. Improve the supervisory selection process.
3. Take special pains to orient supervisors during the crossover, or transition, period.
4. Maintain a constant watch over progress and implement a more articulated training and development program in accordance with these observations.

TABLE 14-1
PERFORMANCE GOALS SET BY A SUPERVISOR

Performance Measure	This Year's Goals	This Year's Performance	Variance Better: + Worse: −	Next Year's Goals
1. Percent of budgeted hours utilized on spot welder	80%	75%	−5%	80%
2. Percent yield on copper wire supply	90%	88%	−2%	90%
3. Water usage in gal per 1,000 units of product	500 gal	550 gal	−50 gal	400 gal
4. Cumulative dollars over or short in petty cash fund	$5 short	$1 short	+$4	$5 short
5. Days lost due to absences (% of days worked)	120 days lost (4%)	150 days lost (5%)	−30 days (−1%)	120 days lost (4%)
6. No. of lost-time accidents	0 lost-time accidents	2 lost-time accidents	−2 lost-time accidents	0 lost-time accidents
7. Hours of employee overtime	30 hr	100 hr	−70 hr	60 hr
8. Percent of orders shipped on time	90%	92%	+2%	95%
9. No. of defects per 1,000 units of product	30 defects	50 defects	−20 defects	20 defects
10. Dollars of indirect labor costs per unit of product output	36¢	36¢	—	27¢

Source: Reprinted from Lester R. Bittel, *Improving Supervisory Performance* (New York: McGraw-Hill, 1976), 369.

5. Be prepared to retrain—or retread—veteran supervisors for their evolving roles.
6. If all else has failed, reexamine and redesign the job requirements of supervisors who cannot perform up to the needed competencies of the contemporary role.
7. Transfer, demote, or separate those supervisors whose performance remains unsatisfactory.[6]

MBO for Supervisors?

One approach toward integrating the supervisors' new role might be their more active participation in management by objectives (MBO) programs. Few organizations make serious moves in this direction, however. The most successful MBO programs seem to stop somewhere in the middle levels of management and go no further down the line. It is probably prudent for training professionals to preserve the status quo in this regard, but there is one related step that might be taken. Supervisors can be counseled to initiate and prepare performance objectives for themselves, hopefully with the encouragement and assistance of their bosses. Table 14-1 illustrates a realistic set of objectives that would help to shape an awareness on a supervisor's part of the new role he or she is expected to play in the organization.

SUPERVISORS AND THE OD PROCESS

Involving Supervisors in the Change Process

Alpander observes that "Traditional training programs that are intended to improve supervisors' abilities and skills are beneficial, but they cannot produce the synergistic effects of unified organizational development programs that combine managerial skills training and the improvement of organizational conditions."[7] He went on to study the impact of such an OD program on supervisory performance, as perceived by the supervisors' employees. The company's OD program targeted the departmental levels and brought together supervisors and their employees with a facilitator, or change agent. Problems were identified, and action plans were developed mutually as a result. Before-and-after "climate" surveys of employee viewpoints revealed a significant improvement in the perceptions of supervisory leadership behavior. Alpander concluded that supervisory-training programs alone were not enough to bring about needed changes in supervisors' performance. When supervisors participated in OD, however, the synergy between the two programs created the necessary changes.

The OD process engages three sets of individuals or groups: (1) the change sponsor—that is, the person or group that initiates the change; (2) the change agent—the person responsible for making the change take place; and (3) the change targets—those individuals whose responsibilities and behavior are expected to change as a result of the OD process. Supervisors are usually among the primary change targets. The change sponsors (higher-level management) ordinarily expect that the supervisors' roles, with their associated changed responsibilities and authorities, will accommodate the revised organizational design. For the training professional, this means the need to provide supervisors with new knowledge, skills, and attitudes.

Securing a Commitment to Change

Conner and Patterson have concluded that if a commitment is to be secured from supervisors to make the required changes and acquire the new knowledge and skills, supervisors can be expected to have to pass through three distinct stages:

- *Stage 1—preparation.* This requires moving the supervisor from (a) an unawareness of the need, resultant confusion, and a negative reaction to (b) an awareness of the imminent change.
- *Stage 2—acceptance.* This requires moving the supervisor from (a) a decision not to accommodate the change but rather to try to abort it to (b) an understanding of the need for the change and a positive perception of it.
- *Stage 3—commitment.* This requires moving the supervisor from (a) continued resistance and overt attempts to block the change to (b) a nominal

acceptance of the change, gradual adoption of it, and finally, an internalization of it.[8]

Training professionals, who must work along with the organizational changes as they are occurring, need to anticipate and allow for supervisory reactions to the process. Until OD change agents have obtained a commitment from the supervisors involved, related training and development are likely to be ineffective.

SELF-DEVELOPMENT FOR SUPERVISORS

From a supervisor's point of view, training may be either active or passive. Unfortunately, in far too many cases, supervisory attitudes toward training and development are similarly passive. Supervisors take what is offered, reacting positively or negatively to it, or disregarding it, depending on their assessment of its practicality and relevance. Self-development, on the other hand, requires a decidedly proactive stance. Fortunately, self-development can be greatly enhanced by the support and guidance that training professionals can offer motivated supervisors.

Three Levels of Learning

Kur and Pedler believe that the greatest improvement in supervisory performance will occur through self-development, using selected organization development techniques. They agree that self-development "is the most complex, difficult form of learning," but they emphasize that it "results in more mature, more competent individuals." They advise that such learning takes place at three levels: (1) participants first acquire the learning specified by the organization of which they are a part; (2) they then identify their own needs and the resources available and how to evaluate, monitor, and control their own learning processes; and (3) they learn to manage through egalitarian, people-centered means.[9]

Approaches to Self-Development

Among the OD methods that Kur and Pedler discuss are such techniques as action learning, field study, joint development activities, and body-mind approaches. The most appropriate OD techniques for supervisory self-development, however, would appear to be far more pragmatic, as discussed in the following subsections.

Structured Experiences. The structured-experience approach places the supervisor in a learning situation involving accelerated experience, following a preprogrammed or structured set of activities requiring various levels of interaction. Emphasis is on discovery of information and new ways of behavior leading to problem solving rather than on expository learning. Structured experiences usually involve activity over relatively short intervals, seldom exceeding three hours.

Coaching. Coaching involves an informed helper's assisting the supervisor in problem solving or mastering new skills. In sales training, this is often called "curbstone coaching." One variant used in supervisory development has the trainer "shadowing" a supervisor for several days, after which the two "process," or discuss, each event, assessing the supervisor's handling of it and identifying alternative approaches that might be used in similar situations in the future.

Jack J. Phillips offers training professionals and line managers this cogent advise on coaching supervisors:

> Coaching presupposes that the vast majority of a supervisor's learning will occur on the job as a result of guided experience under the direction of effective managers. Middle managers should remember that coaching is not a one-time effort but a continuous process that involves discussions between manager and supervisor. The manager (coach) observes the supervisor, gives feedback, and plans specific actions to correct performance deficiencies. Because the process is repeated regularly, supervisors feel less anxiety toward coaching than toward typical performance appraisals. Realistic performance feedback is critical, but somehow managers confuse coaching with criticism and consequently avoid the process. Supervisors must have a thorough understanding of their duties and the standards by which they are evaluated. They must know and understand the goals, targets, and mission of their department, division, or organization. Performance feedback must be frank, open, and straightforward and supervisors must know when their performance is good and when it is unacceptable.
>
> There is a mistaken belief that only fast-track supervisors or marginal performers need coaching. In reality, all supervisors need coaching, including the large group of average performers. Coaching helps new supervisors become more productive in a short period of time. Coaching also helps marginal performers improve their performance to an acceptable standard. It helps average supervisors excel by identifying strengths and weaknesses and developing necessary skills. For the super performers, coaching helps maintain their outstanding performance records and [enables them to] advance to other jobs in the organization.[10]

Mentors. The value of the mentor approach may be greatly exaggerated, but it is an undeniably popular concept. A mentor is someone in a position of influence or authority who takes an interest in a particular supervisor and his or her career.

Supervisors should regard their mentors as sources of advice and guidance, rather than as individuals who can somehow open the doors to advancement. It helps to have someone who can function as a "friend in court" or who can lend a helping hand occasionally, of course. In general, however, mentors are most effective when they serve in coaching capacities or as sounding boards for supervisors' development plans.

Experiential Groups. Experiential groups include T-groups, sensitivity training, and encounter groups. Learning takes place as individuals discuss with group members the events that unfold during the life of the group. Although such groups were once very popular, results are often contradictory and nonproductive unless the learning sessions are conducted by professionally trained leaders under widely accepted professional guidelines. *Assertiveness training* might also fall into the experiential category. It has proved to be an effective way to raise the level of contribution and decisiveness of many supervisors who were overly passive or self-effacing in their managerial roles.

A Systems Approach

It is a truism worth repeating that supervisory training and development require the constructive interaction of many people in the organization if such

FIGURE 14-3 THE SUPERVISORY DEVELOPMENT NETWORK

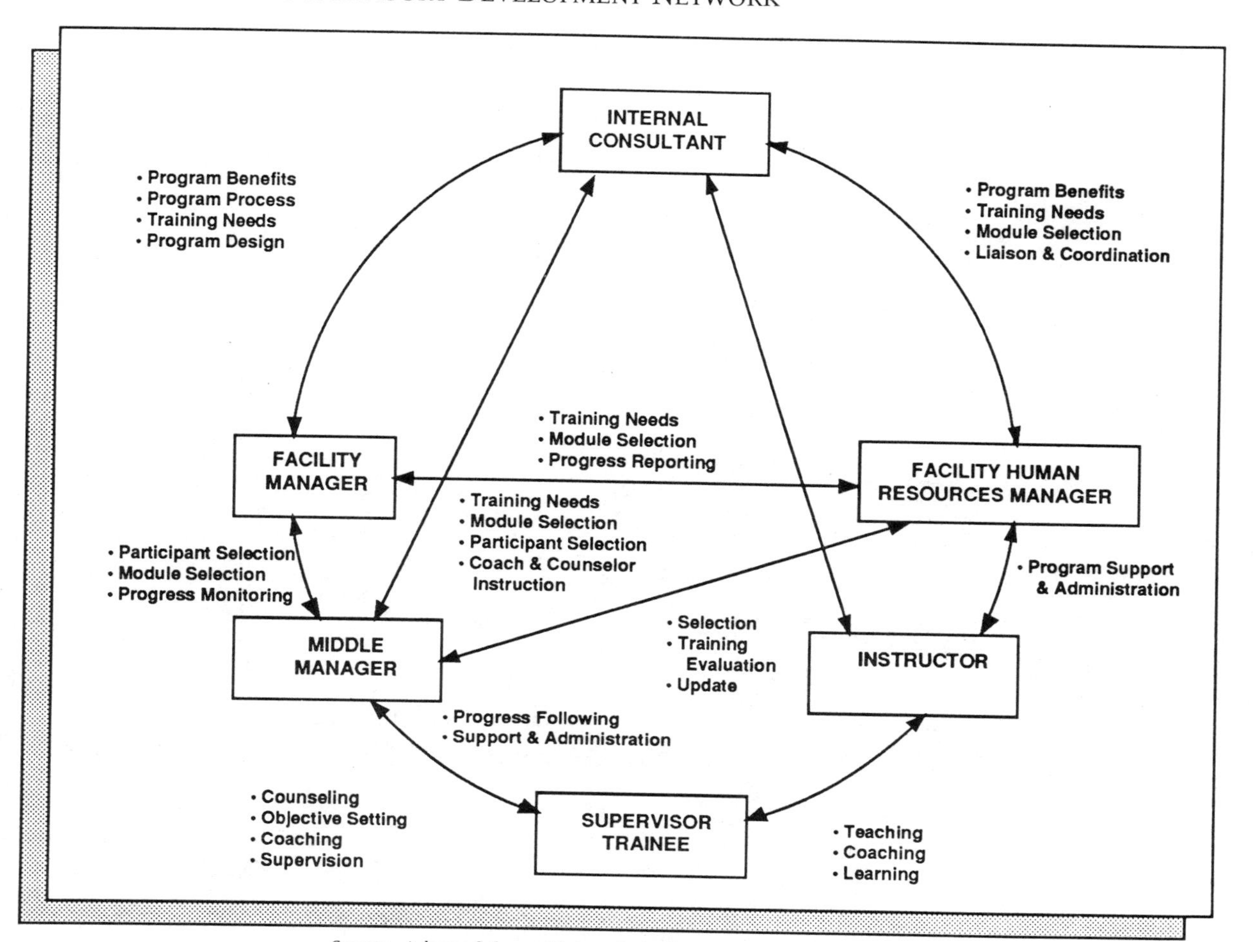

Source: Adapted from Walter S. Wikstrom, *Supervisory Training* (New York: The Conference Board, 1973), 122.

an effort is to be truly effective (as illustrated in figure 14-3). These include the middle manager, facility manager, internal consultant, facility human resources manager, and the instructor—all in addition to the individual supervisor.[11]

CAREER PLANNING FOR SUPERVISORS

Only a few organizations carry their career-path-planning programs into the supervisory ranks. Regardless of formal programs, however, supervisors will benefit from some sort of guidance from the human resources development professionals in their organization.

The Basis for a Career Plan

Supervisors should be alerted to the four essentials for developing a career path or plan:

FIGURE 14-4 SAMPLE CAREER PATH PLANNED FOR A SUPERVISOR

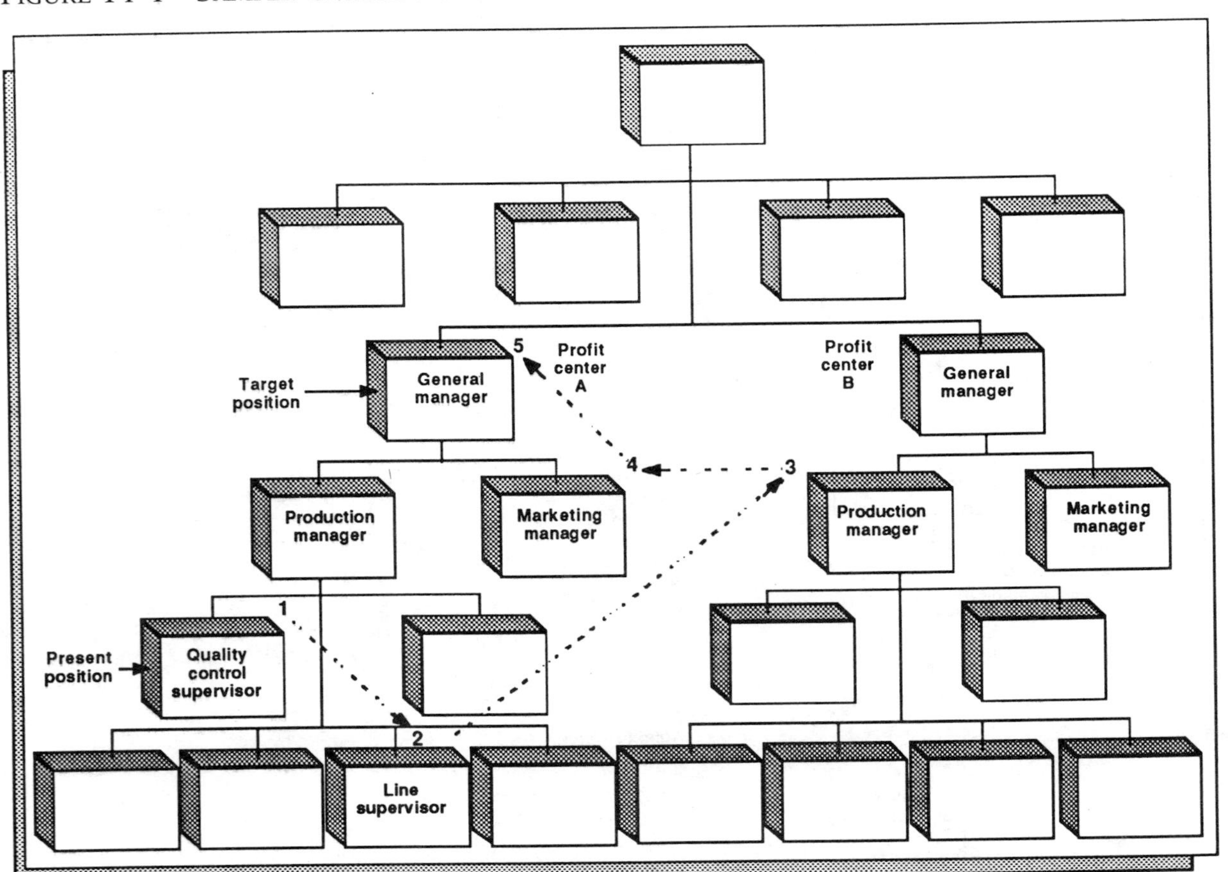

Source: Adapted with permission from Lester R. Bittel, *What Every Supervisor Should Know,* 5th ed. (New York: McGraw-Hill Book Company, 1984), 609.

1. *A candid self-assessment.* Many of the supervisory competency lists illustrated in chapter 3 or the needs-assessment lists in chapter 6 can serve as a basis for such an appraisal.
2. *Firm and realistic goals.* The goals presented earlier, in table 14-1, may serve as examples that a supervisor could follow to create his or her own set.
3. *A concrete program for development.* This has two elements:
   a. A *schedule* of self-improvement learning activities, with definite dates for starting and completing each activity.
   b. A *career path* (such as the one shown in figure 14-4) that plots a hypothetical but logical series of experiential assignments and advancements toward a specific goal.
4. *Motivation and commitment.* Supervisors should be apprised of the sacrifices that the road to advancement entails, the uncertainty of outcomes (no one can guarantee that effort and desire will bring about a promotion), and the need for persistence when disappointments occur or distractions arise.

Chapter 15

Program Evaluation and Follow-Up

INTRODUCTION

In evaluating the effectiveness of a training program, the program's results must be compared against its objectives. When the program or course has been completed, it is too late to set its goals. It also bears repeating that the goals for supervisory training, as for all training, should be related to pre-established training needs. *Needs analysis* (chapter 6) asks "What good *will* training do?" *Evaluation* asks "What good *did* the training do?" Accordingly, the needs analysis you perform will provide the criteria by which to measure your program's success.

EVALUATION: A FIVE-STEP PROCESS

The total process of program evaluation involves five basic activities. You must:

1. Identify the decision makers in the sponsoring organization who seek information about the program and validation of its effectiveness. These people influence the budgets that support the program, and it is essential to know their specific expectations in advance.
2. State the goals and objectives of the program and specifically define its content.
3. Translate these objectives into measurable standards that can be used for evaluation after the program is completed.
4. Define a specific method for obtaining these measurements.
5. Interpret the evaluation information provided by these measurements.

According to Del Gaizo, a supervisory-training program can be evaluated at four levels of impact:

- *Level 1.* The extent to which the participants "enjoyed" the program, in total and in each of its many variables—setting, leadership, practicality of methods used, and so on.
- *Level 2.* The extent to which participants assimilated the information or learned the skills during the training program.

- *Level 3.* The extent to which participants apply the acquired knowledge or skills back on the job.
- *Level 4.* The extent to which the program measurably affects the operations, productivity, or profits of the organization and the quality of the products or services offered by it.[1]

Del Gaizo acknowledges that measurements of level 4 accomplishments are difficult to obtain. Level 3 validation, he cautions, requires a rigorous methodology because it attempts to prove actual skill usage. To be sure on-the-job improvements derive from training rather than from other factors, he suggests that evaluators set up a control group (who have not had the training) from within the organization. In testing the results, he further recommends the following guidelines:

- To ensure consistency, use the same or a proven equivalent instrument (for example, a questionnaire) before and after training.
- To obtain objective opinions, interview the supervisors' managers and subordinates. However, because supervisors may choose subordinates with whom they are comfortable, pick a random cross section of all subordinates.
- Take measurements for the control and training groups simultaneously to minimize the chances of measuring changes that occur over time and in the work environment.
- Take pretraining measurements thirty to ninety days in advance. People sometimes behave in an unnatural manner if they know they are scheduled for a training program. Do posttraining measurements thirty to ninety days after the program.
- Maintain confidentiality. Subordinates may be justifiably worried about repercussions.
- Be sure that the instrument is reliable and delivers consistent results.
- Measure only what is actually taught and measure all the skills taught, not just a few.[2]

Traditional Evaluation Criteria

Validation criteria for supervisory training can be classified as (1) either subjective or objective and (2) either qualitative or quantitative. Objective, quantitative criteria are best, but such measures of results are often difficult to obtain. The Conference Board surveyed over three hundred companies offering supervisory training and found that subjective criteria were employed twice as frequently as objective ones, although almost all companies used two or more of the traditional criteria ranked in the box on the facing page.

EVALUATION TECHNIQUES

Swierczek and Carmichael have examined a great many traditional evaluation methods and suggest that the way in which each is used greatly affects

Evaluation Criteria for Supervisory-Training Programs Ranked According to Frequency of Usage

Subjective Criteria

156	Trainees' reactions, during or at close of program
90	Reactions of immediate superiors of trainees
42	Trainer's evaluation of program
41	Trainees' reactions, three to six months after training
33	Reactions of higher management
30	"Informal observation"
392	Total mentions

Objective Criteria

41	"Department's records"
38	Review of performance appraisals of trainees, following training
22	Records—of production, costs, quality, safety, or other factors
28	Records—of absences, turnover, tardiness, or grievances in trainees' unit, after training
19	Testing, at end of course
12	Testing, before and after course
10	Attitude surveys among employees being supervised by trainees, following training
9	Formal program-evaluation studies, conducted by company or by outside organization
8	Accomplishment of specific objectives
187	Total mentions

Source: Adapted from Walter S. Wikstrom, *Supervisory Training* (New York: The Conference Board, 1973), 39.

its effectiveness.[3] An understanding of the concept underlying each of the following methods also adds value to interpretation of the measures obtained.

Questionnaires and Instruments

The most commonly used evaluation measure is usually set up in checklist, forced-choice format asking program participants to make value judgments concerning various elements of the training just received. An example of this method is shown in the box on page 222. While this method has limited validity due to its subjective nature, it can be improved by adding some open-ended questions. Alternately, a completely open-ended questionnaire may be distributed at the end of a program segment. Two basic questions should be asked: "What skills did you learn as a result of this training?" and "How will you apply these skills back at work?" Swierczek and Carmichael advise that no instructions be provided the respondents in order to reduce the bias inherent in conventional evaluation checklists. The box on page 223 is a good example of an open-ended questionnaire.

Another common method of evaluating a program is to administer a standard "how-supervise" instrument both before and after the training. One such instrument that proved to be particularly effective uses a series of questions based on Likert's systems 1 through 4 (confidence in subordinates, feel

Sample Qualitative Evaluation Questionnaire

(Check one)

1. Generally, how helpful were the meetings to you?
   ____ Very helpful
   ____ Helped some
   ____ A complete waste of time

2. As a result of the program, did you obtain new insights into the subjects discussed?
   ____ Many
   ____ Some
   ____ Few

3. Did the program give you a better understanding of the subjects?
   ____ Much better
   ____ Somewhat better
   ____ No better
   ____ (No answer)

4. Was there enough group discussion in the meetings?
   ____ Too much
   ____ About right
   ____ Not enough

5. Did you feel free to ask questions or offer remarks in the meetings?
   ____ Felt entirely free
   ____ Felt hesitant about it
   ____ Never felt free

6. About how much did you learn that will help you on the job?
   ____ A great deal
   ____ Some
   ____ Very little

7. Did you find the meetings and the topics discussed interesting?
   ____ Almost always
   ____ Some of the time
   ____ Very uninteresting

8. Was the text interesting and worthwhile?
   ____ Very valuable
   ____ Somewhat valuable
   ____ Of limited value

9. Did the handout materials help you in study or review?
   ____ Very useful
   ____ Somewhat useful
   ____ Of limited use

10. For your purposes, do you evaluate this course as excellent, good, fair, or unsatisfactory? Please explain in the space provided below.

Open-Ended Questionnaire Used for Evaluation

SUPERVISORY WORKSHOP PROGRAM
Evaluation Sheet

Please be as specific as possible in answering the following:

1. As a result of taking the Basic Management Training Program, what are you able to do now that you were not able to do before you took the course?

2. What management methods and techniques are you aware of since completing the Basic Management Training Program that you were formerly not aware of?

3. Name one thing you are doing back on your job as a result of taking the Basic Management Training Program. This could include something new that you are trying or something you feel you are doing more effectively.

4. Which session or sessions of the Basic Management Training Program were most helpful to you? Why?

5. What would you like to be able to do more effectively in the future that the Basic Management Training Program did not provide for you?

6. On the scale below, rate the Basic Management Training Program in its entirety.

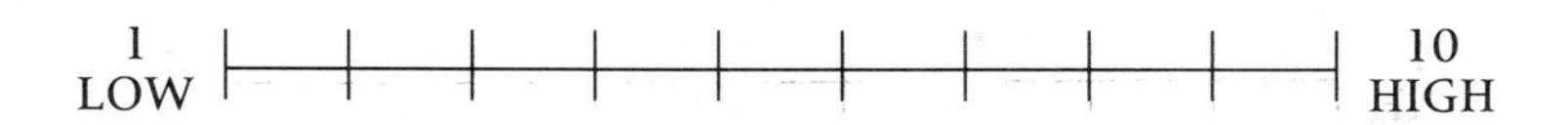

7. General comments:

free to talk, subordinates' ideas used, responsibility for goals, communication by goals, levels at which decisions are made, and so on).

As can be seen from the foregoing examples, evaluation checklists vary widely, ranging from "laundry lists" of detailed questions to a broad survey of general comments. When participants attend public, open-enrollment supervisory-training programs or courses, the evaluation variables are likely to be quite general. This is illustrated in table 15-1, a checklist developed by Inman, Olivas, and Robertson for use in evaluating supervisory training conducted at "institutes" serving participants from a variety of organizations.

The Influence of Environmental Conditions on Evaluation

Almost all evaluations, other than those dependent exclusively on performance documentation, are subject to uncontrollable influences in the supervisor's environment. Accordingly, Clement and Arand remind trainers of three contingency variables that should be considered when interpreting evaluations: (1) influence from the organizational setting (objectives, policies, practices, supervisor's authority to administer rewards and punishment, work-group expectations, and so on), (2) nature of the supervisor to be trained (education, experience, expectations, and so forth), and (3) problems to be solved by the training program (ranging from simple, tangible, and immediate to complex, ambiguous, and long-term). The authors observe, for example, that supervisory training is more effective with young, relatively new supervisors, responsible for a small number of subordinates and with a short period of total service.[4] In order to illustrate the interdependency of these three contingent influences, the authors have developed the matrix shown in table 15-2 on page 226.

METHODS FOR CONTINUING EVALUATION AND FOLLOW-UP

Training professionals must consider two questions regarding evaluations: (1) whether or not to conclude the evaluation at the end of the program and (2) what to do when evaluations are not satisfactory. Well-planned programs, following the techniques described in chapter 11, attempt to answer the first question by building in an action plan to assure that participants try out their new knowledge and skills on the job. That particular type of program also asks supervisors for feedback from their jobs, which provides a degree of indirect training evaluation. Some companies plan for (1) a periodic review by participants of the training's effectiveness or (2) a postcourse checklist to establish whether or not participants are using specific skills. One company employs a "course not completed until committed objectives are reached" approach. These latter two approaches provide a degree of program follow-up. Finally, two authorities suggest the use of a tool for diagnosing the causes of ineffective training (as revealed by evaluations), with a prescription for remedial action. All of these approaches are discussed in the balance of this section.

Periodic Review Sessions

The western computer-program developer whose planning manual was excerpted in chapter 10 (see the box titled "Leader's Guide for Planning and Operating a Supervisors' Workshop Program") suggests to its trainers that

TABLE 15-1
EVALUATION CHECKLIST

Management Institute Program: The program is designed to increase your level of personal and professional growth. Please rank the following according to what degree of value you perceive the Management Institute program has [had for] your personal and professional growth.

Variables: Please read the description of each variable carefully and *rate accordingly.*	High Value	Medium Value	Not Applicable	Low Value	No Value
Leadership Ability to take charge, to direct and coordinate the activities of others, to maintain control of situations and others, to achieve results through delegation and follow-up.					
Job Advancement The movement into higher management levels and responsibilities within your company as a result of promotions.					
Job Satisfaction and Fulfillment Those variables which make your job more challenging and satisfying, such as: achievement, recognition, responsibility, etc.					
Compensation The increased monetary value received for your contributions to the organization, which include increased salary, bonuses, insurance and other benefits.					
Human Relations The ability to work successfully and create a comfortable working environment with your fellow employees.					
Job Knowledge The ability to develop confidence and a thorough understanding of the job tasks needed to perform your job as a manager more effectively.					
Decision Making The ability to use logic and sound judgment in choosing a particular course of action; to generate and evaluate alternative courses of action.					

Source: Reprinted with permission from Thomas H. Inman, Louis Olivas, and Frank Robertson, "An Analysis of the Effectiveness of a Management Training Program," *Training and Development Journal* (June 1982): 85.

annual review sessions be held to follow up on its supervisory-training program. It describes the purpose of these refresher meetings like this:

> To review and reinforce the principles of leadership for continual awareness and development.
>
> a. Conduct refresher sessions as a reminder of subjects previously covered and as a stimulus to effective leadership practices.
>
> b. Recognize the significance and value of effective leaders by providing for their continual development.
>
> c. Encourage individual study for further personal development.

TABLE 15-2
CONTINGENCY FRAMEWORK FOR SUPERVISORY-TRAINING EVALUATION

Variable Dimension	The Manager	The Subordinate	The Organization
#1 Training Results	What is the person *doing* differently?	How has the subordinate's job improved?	What is the impact on overall job performance?
#2 Relative Effectiveness of Technique	Was new behavior thoroughly learned?	Is trainee able to translate information to subordinate needs?	Is trainee able to translate information to organization needs?
#3 Impact of Individual Differences	Was trainee willing/able to respond to the training?	Is trainee able to adjust new behavior to subordinate differences?	Is trainee able to adjust new behavior to organization norms?
#4 Impact of Environment	Can trainee apply new behavior to his or her job?	Does new behavior mesh with work group style?	Is there a reward for practicing new behavior?

Source: Reprinted from Ronald W. Clement and Eileen K. Arand, "Evaluating Management Training: A Contingency Approach," *Training and Development Journal* (August 1982): 42.

Follow-up Implementation Survey

One university institute administered a skills-knowledge/use survey before the program began and again six months afterward. Validated skill areas included: (1) identify and attempt to eliminate interruptions and time wasters, (2) assign tasks to subordinates, (3) provide subordinates with exact references to behavior in order to document performance problems, and (4) facilitate feedback from subordinates.[5] This technique also uncovers supervisory resistance to, or failure to adopt, theoretically sound practices such as "setting priority tasks on a regular basis" and "keeping daily logs."

The "Course Not Completed Until . . ." Approach

One particularly effective method that not only provides valid evaluations but also extends and reinforces supervisory training is reported by Morrisey and Wellstead. They take the position that "a participant in one of our supervisory training programs has not completed the program at the end of the scheduled class sessions. All participants must commit themselves to specific objectives on how they will apply some of what was learned. Then, they must send in a progress report 60 days later in order to earn their certificate of completion." The authors' procedure during the training period follows these five steps:

1. The trainer and participants discuss objectives, and their relation to what participants are learning, throughout the entire program.
2. The trainer conducts the first "objectives" workshop session (one to two hours, next-to-last day).
    a. Brainstorm for ideas on what to select.
    b. Establish means for measurement.
    c. Establish writing format.

3. Homework: the participants write a rough draft of objectives they wish to submit.
4. The trainer conducts a second "objectives" workshop session (one to two hours, last day).
   a. Critique rough drafts of objectives in small groups.
   b. Critique one "on the floor" from each small group.
   c. Participants rewrite objectives (if needed) and submit them to the instructor.
5. Instructor reviews objectives, comments in writing, and returns them to participants, keeping a copy of each for reference.

Follow-up procedures include these five additional steps:

1. Form letter sent to each participant after thirty days reminding him or her that a report form will be arriving in about three weeks and encouraging the participant to keep working at the agreed-upon objectives.
2. Report form sent to each participant one week before due date asking the following questions: (a) What results, both positive and negative, have you had so far in implementing your objectives? (Include any appropriate documentation you may have.) (b) What other specific changes have you made in the way you do your job as a result of the training program? Please describe the results of these changes, both positive and negative. (c) Based on your on-the-job experience since the end of the program, what two aspects would you change to make the program more meaningful for people in positions like yours?
3. Instructor receives completed report, reviews, and either approves it for a certificate or contacts the participant for additional action as needed.
4. Certificate sent with cover letter to participant's superior asking that it be awarded to him or her at an appropriate time.
5. Follow-up letter sent to all participants who have not returned their reports one week after deadline allowing them an extra week in which to report and opening the door for individual consultation if needed.[6]

These two training professionals use the "milestone chart" illustrated in figure 15-1 on page 228 to assure control over the evaluation process.

Diagnosis of Causes and Corrective Alternatives

Bakken and Bernstein observe that training may "fail" for a number of reasons, such as (1) poorly stated, ambiguous, or unmeasurable goals; (2) training content not fully relevant to the program's objectives; (3) use of inappropriate instructional techniques; (4) inadequate or improper delivery of the content—including such variables as instructor behavior, environmental constraints, and participant motivation and behavior; and (5) organizational factors that inhibit the transfer of training back to the job.[7] Bakken and Bernstein offer the matrix shown in table 15-3 as a guide to seeking possible solutions to the diagnosed causes of training failure.

FIGURE 15-1 MILESTONE CHART USED FOR EVALUATION FOLLOW-UP

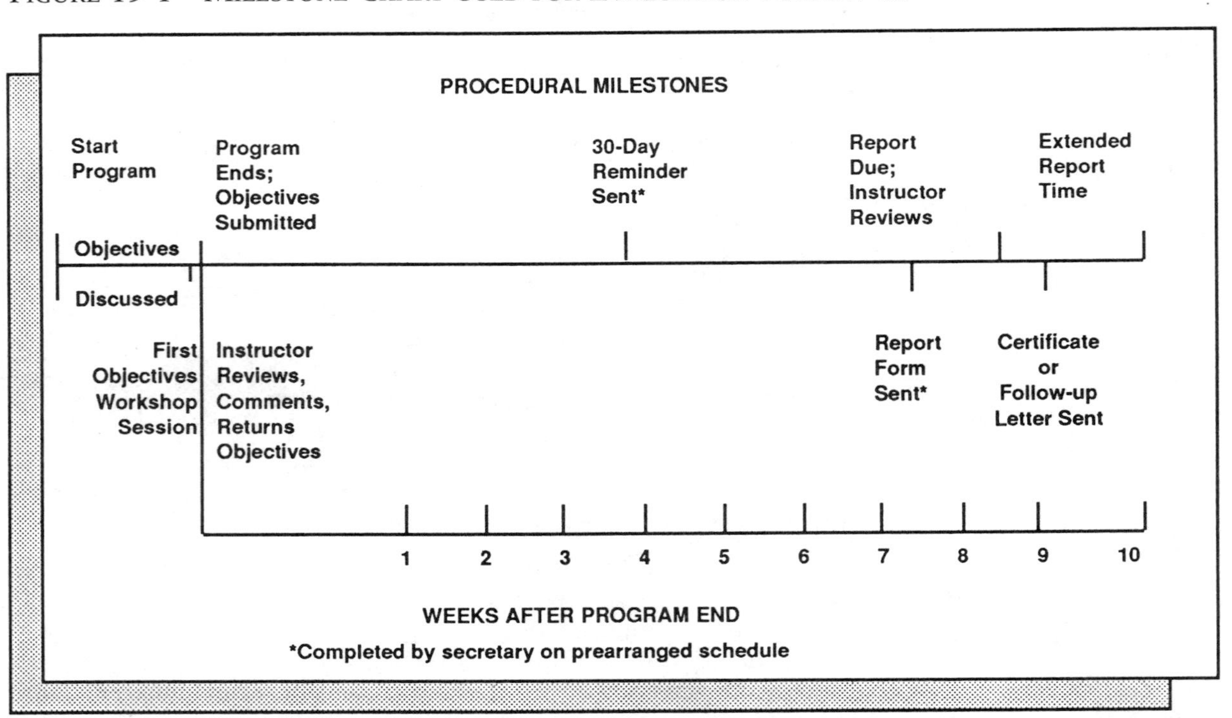

Source: Adapted with permission from George L. Morrisey and William R. Wellstead, "Supervisory Training Can Be Measured," *Training and Development Journal* (June 1980): 119.

EVALUATIONS, PROFIT CONTRIBUTION, AND BUDGET JUSTIFICATION

A hidden purpose of training evaluations is to provide justification for the training's cost. This is delicate ground to tread on, since so many variables can affect training outcomes. Training professionals often skirt the cost-justification issue and abide by the old adage: "If you have to prove the value of training, its sponsors are not ready for it." It is true, of course, that when an organization enjoys large revenues or profits, the pressure for justifying training costs (read "evaluating outcomes") is slight. When the economy takes a downturn, however, it's often quite a different story. Accordingly, there is merit in trying to translate training effort and outcomes into financial terms. Three approaches, with varying merit, are described below.

INCREASES IN RELATED SALES REVENUES

Western Federal Savings and Loan Association, with the headquarters in Marina del Rey, California, had ambitious goals for its 1983–84 supervisory-training program: to save the corporation money and time and to gain new customers. When the program was over, it had put four hundred supervisors in twenty-three branch offices through a behaviorally oriented, proprietary

TABLE 15-3
MATRIX FOR DIAGNOSING AND SOLVING TRAINING FAILURES

Possible Source of Failure	Possible Solution
Training objectives were not clearly defined.	Redefine objectives.
Course content was not relevant to training objectives.	Redesign content to reflect objectives.
Content was not based on appropriate assumptions or theories about how adults learn.	Redesign content using more appropriate models of learning.
Training was not delivered as desired.	
Instructors lack the required skills or expertise.	Train instructors.
Other factors (e.g., attendance) interfered with delivery.	Identify other factors. Alter those that are under the control of training department.
Organizational factors prevented transfer of training to the job.	Conduct a performance analysis to determine which factors hinder transfer.

Source: Reprinted from David Bakken and Alan L. Bernstein, "A Systematic Approach to Evaluation," *Training and Development Journal* (August 1982): 50.

program ("Xcellence," from Learning International). Specifically, the high-priority objectives of the program were to reduce employee overtime and turnover and increase new business through the savings and credit operations. Corporate operating improvements during the next fiscal year showed: overtime reduced by 58 percent, employee turnover cut by 16 percent, credit losses down by 67 percent, and new business development up by $4,319,673.[8] The definitive question, "To what extent can these improvements be attributed to improved supervision and, in turn, to the training program?" was not answered by a validated study. Nevertheless, the association was justifiably impressed by these figures.

Replacement-Cost Justification

Another way to calculate the financial effect of training is to place a dollar value on the retention of good supervisors who might leave or on poor supervisors whose performance, without participation in an effective training program, might remain unsatisfactory. This approach considers such replacement costs as (1) operating losses due to inefficiencies related to poor supervision, (2) training for an incumbent who still doesn't measure up, (3) training for the replacement, (4) operational downtime between when the incumbent leaves and when the replacement comes on board, (5) start-up time for the replacement, (6) relocation expenses for the replacement, and (7) legal and staff costs associated with removals and employment procedures.[9] Given a figure for the replacement cost of a single supervisor (pegged at $57,000 by one authority)[10] and a figure for supervisory training (estimated at $500 per supervisor per program), the economic benefit derived from the program can be calculated, as shown in the box on page 230. The training-cost variable in this method, is, of course, much easier to determine than the

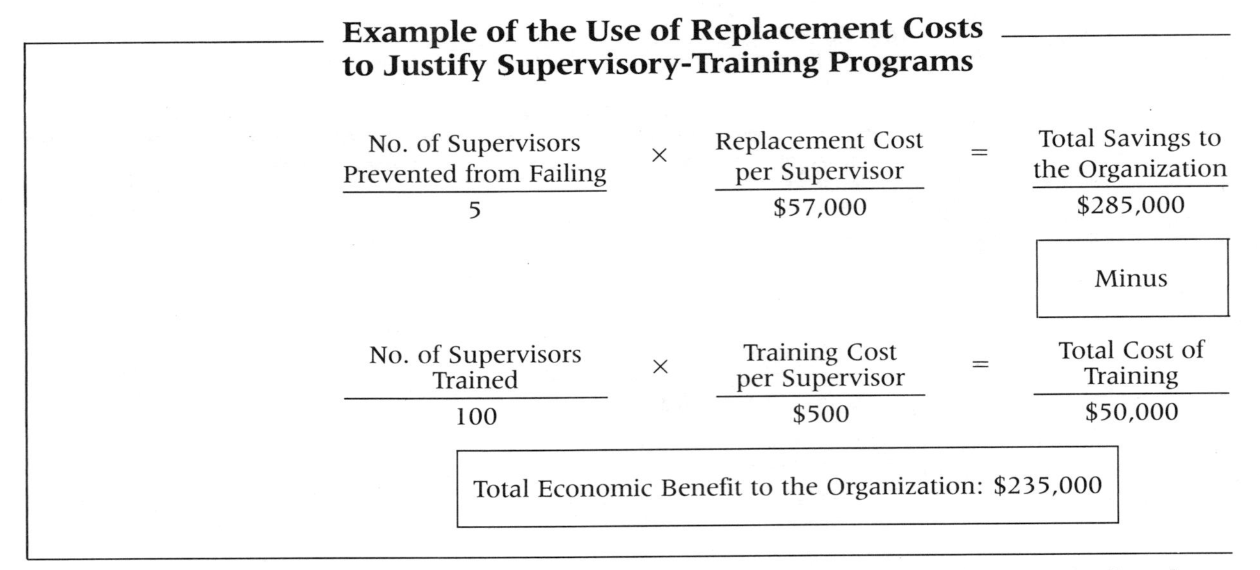

Source: Reprinted from Michael A. Sheppeck and Stephen L. Cohen, "Put a Dollar Value on Your Training Programs," *Training and Development Journal* (November 1985): 60.

Example of the Use of the Utility Approach to Justify Supervisory-Training Programs

Utility =

Years duration of effect on performance		Number trained		Performance difference between trained and untrained supervisors		Value		Number trained		Cost
2	×	20	×	.50	×	$18,000	–	(20	×	$1,000)

= $340,000 utility

Note: Value of supervisor's service is estimated at 60 percent of $30,000 annual salary.

Source: Adapted with permission from Michael A. Sheppeck and Stephen L. Cohen, "Put a Dollar Value on Your Training Program," *Training and Development Journal* (November 1985): 61.

replacement-cost variable, which has difficult-to-measure components. Such a weakness can lead to questions about the reliability of the savings claimed.

PERFORMANCE-IMPROVEMENT JUSTIFICATION

Justification can also be established based on an assessment of the performance improvement—or utility—resulting from the training received.[11] The key to this assessment is (or should be) a validated study of the difference in performance between a supervisor who has received training and one who has not. Schmidt, Hunter, and Pearlman, working with employees in the public sector, have shown that "the economic impact of [training] programs on work-force productivity" indicates a performance difference—or utility—of from 39 percent to 65 percent. They also estimate the "value" of a supervisor's service as between 40 percent and 70 percent of the supervisor's annual salary.[12] When Sheppeck and Cohen plug these utility percentages and service values into their formula (as shown in the box on the previous page), they are able to develop a figure indicating the long-term value of the training period.

A flaw similar to that associated with the replacement-cost method also weakens the utility approach: it is difficult to develop a validated utility figure for the difference in performance between trained and untrained supervisors. Nevertheless, the use of either or both of these budget-justification approaches adds substance at budget time and is better than no financial data at all.

APPENDIXES

Appendix 1

A Closer Look at the Use of Behavioral Modeling in Supervisory Training

Behavioral modeling is an instructional method whereby an individual is (1) shown a prescribed pattern of behavior reputed by theory, experience, and research to be effective in coping with a particular situation; (2) asked to imitate that behavior in the presence of an informed observer and a peer group; (3) given feedback by those witnesses concerning the fidelity of his or her performance and the skill with which each step is interpreted; (4) asked to transfer this modeled behavior to on-the-job applications; and (5) expected further to perfect this skill by repeated applications; which (6) are reinforced by (a) coaching and encouragement from the individual's peers and superiors and by the rewards of (b) improved personal relationships and (c) generally improved performance.

BACKGROUND ON BEHAVIORAL MODELING

The behavioral-modeling technique has been widely applied in business and industry, most notably at the General Electric Company, AT&T, Agway, Kaiser Aluminum and Chemical, Girard Bank, and Baltimore Gas & Electric Company. In turn, the effectiveness of behavioral modeling in improving supervisory performance has been widely tested in a number of research studies. The research confirms the claims that (1) effective behavioral patterns can be learned; (2) they can and will be applied by those who have been exposed to them; (3) subordinates perceive favorably the resultant changes in supervisory practices; and (4) as a result, measurable improvements may take place in employee attendance, turnover, and productivity.

The Theory behind Behavioral Modeling

Behavioral modeling has its roots in the work of B. F. Skinner, who showed that behavior can be changed by a system of punishment and rewards that provides benefits to those individuals who follow a prescribed behavior pattern and discourages them—either through punishment or by withholding rewards—from following a nonprescribed behavior pattern.

Material in this appendix has been adapted with permission from the author's *Course Management Guide,* which accompanies *What Every Supervisor Should Know,* 5th ed. (New York: McGraw-Hill Book Company, 1984), 5–10.

The behavior models themselves derive their validity from the various disciplines of psychology, sociology, and anthropology. The models represent behavior on the part of supervisors and managers that is most likely to produce favorable results in their interpersonal relationships. As such, the models are based on average behavior responses. If followed precisely, they will yield better-than-average results more than half the time. They will not always work, however, nor will they always get the best results. But they do represent the best of all beginnings for effective human relationships. The implication is that variations from, and changes in, the modeled behavior should take place only after the practitioner is certain that the model's prescribed sequence is not getting results.

Furthermore, much of the effectiveness of the model depends on the supervisor's sensitivity to nuances and timing in moving forward from one step to another or in moving backward to reinforce a previous step when it is discovered that an understanding or agreement has not been reached. As a consequence, continued practice with and application of the model are required for success.

An important aspect of behavioral modeling—emphasized by William Byham, of Development Dimensions—is that skills, and not theory, are taught. Behavioral modeling lays out a series of positive steps for handling each situation. These critical, or key, steps provide an organized, systematic procedure to be followed during the interaction between supervisor and subordinate. What is *not* specified is how much time must be spent on each step and exactly when to move ahead or retrace a step. Each supervisor must acquire these sensitivity skills by (1) practicing with the model with the aid of critiques from peers and an authoritative observer and (2) applying the model to real-life situations.

It should also be stressed that whereas each model differs from the others, there is a central focus among all models. For this reason, the models will often seem redundant to participants, and supervisors may criticize them on this account. Don't be distracted by this complaint. The basic idea of behavioral modeling is that the models should be pursued until they are internalized, becoming almost second nature to the individual. The central focus of most, if not all, behavioral models is illustrated in figure 9-1 (chapter 9). It presumes that in all superior-subordinate interactions, a successful exchange will occur only if three phases are completed:

- *Phase 1: Problem identification by the supervisor.* Essentially, the supervisor observes a behavior that is not appropriate. He or she carefully defines the inappropriate behavior and presents this view to the subordinate. The objective at this stage is to stimulate an awareness in the employee's mind of this behavior and the problem it causes. To do so, the supervisor must demonstrate how this behavior affects performance—not only that of the individual but also that of others—and the overall harmony or effectiveness of the work group.

- *Phase 2: Problem solving through the joint efforts of supervisor and subordinate.* The supervisor not only offers his or her knowledge of the problem-causing behavior but also extracts from the employee additional information that often only the employee knows. In addition, the supervisor encourages the employee to describe his or her feelings about the situation. Together, then, in participatory fashion, the two review the information and try to arrive at a solution that satisfies the employee as well as the supervisor. When an agreement is reached, it is important that the subordinate make a commitment to try out the action agreed on. In turn, the supervisor provides positive reinforcement by expressing a belief that the employee's action will solve the problem. Finally, to allow for difficulties in implementation, the supervisor establishes a date to follow up on the employee's progress toward the solution.

Phase 3: Implementation and progress review. The subordinate is given a reasonable amount of time to put the solution into effect. During that time, the supervisor stands ready to offer assistance if required. And at the agreed-on review date, the supervisor again meets with the employee to review progress toward the solution's goal. If the behavior has been improved as planned, the situation is closed out with positive reinforcement by the supervisor. If progress is unsatisfactory, the supervisor must repeat the model. The problem is restated, and the two again try to agree on a solution. At this point, however, the model may take a different turn. The supervisor explains what the consequences of unimproved performance will be—withholding of privileges or promotions, issuance of warnings or reprimands, and potential discharge (in short, negative reinforcement).

If performance is improving but is not yet up to expectations, the emphasis will be on positive reinforcement; the supervisor expresses confidence in the employee's ability to fully solve the problem. In all instances where performance is still less than what is required, commitment to action is again secured from the employee, and a new date is set for review.

ESSENTIAL ELEMENTS OF BEHAVIORAL-MODELING TRAINING

Practitioners of behavioral modeling don't always agree on exactly what should be included in behavioral modification programs. Nor do they always agree on the emphasis to be given to each element. Generally speaking, however, experts in the field do agree that the following elements are essential:

1. *A step-by-step demonstration of the key action a supervisor must take in handling a particular problem or situation.* Demonstrations are most commonly made on film or videotape, although they may be made on audiotape or with written dialogue. Sequence of steps is important; there is a disrupting tendency for individuals to skip a step or change the order of steps. This cannot be allowed. Participant attention to and involvement in the demonstration is vital. This is ensured by asking participants to observe the point in the dialogue where each action step takes place. For this to be an effective part of your program, it is recommended that you review the steps beforehand and make them available to students. Try to avoid debating beforehand (or even later) the validity of the steps and their sequence. Make the flat statement: "Experience shows that supervisors get better results when following these steps than when they don't. Our purpose is to observe how these steps are carried out by successful supervisors. Then you'll be given a chance to see if you can do the same. Later on, you'll be asked to try the steps out in real situations on your job. At that time, you can confirm or deny how well the steps work."

2. *A behavioral rehearsal in a supportive environment.* Participants are asked to practice the model in front of the seminar group exactly as it has been demonstrated. Note that this is not role-playing in the traditional sense. Trainees are instructed to limit their improvisation to statements and exchanges that support the model's steps and follow the prescribed sequence. Bernard Rosenbaum, a leader in the development and application of behavioral-modeling techniques, recommends that students also be given a number of complimentary written cases to analyze and practice on. Other practitioners recommend that participants provide the substance for model practices by writing up a situation based on their experience. In any event, practice is essential if the model behavior is to be internalized by the supervisors.
3. *Supportive feedback from peers and the instructor.* Other participants and the instructor must point out to the rehearsing supervisor omissions of steps and errors in sequence. Observers must also comment accurately and objectively on the execution of each step, the skill used in communicating its intent, the quality of listening exhibited, and the time allotted to the implementation of the step before moving forward. Observers' remarks, although specifically critical, should always reinforce good points and discourage imprecise modeling.
4. *Transfer of learning to actual job situations.* This is perhaps the most difficult phase, since it requires that the participants commit themselves to trying out the model in real situations. Many organizations extract a written "action contract" from each participant. Typically, the participants, while still in the seminar, are asked to describe one or more relevant situations in their own work. They then agree to apply the model to this situation (or to these situations) within a short period of time (a week or two) and report their experience back to the group. The box on the facing page illustrates the kind of data that might be required of participants in a transfer-tryout report.
5. *Follow-up by instructor and supervisor.* Application of the model almost always raises unanticipated difficulties. Rather than allow such problems to permanently discourage participants, behavioral-modeling programs usually incorporate a report-back session, wherein supervisors describe the results of their experiences. At that time, they are encouraged to assess their successes and failures and to seek ways to reinforce the former and avoid the latter. Their peers and the instructor can also help them find ways to (a) cope with unexpected developments in applying the model as well as (b) improve successes that were only marginal and change failures to successes.

VARIANTS IN BEHAVIORAL MODELING

There are differences of opinion about preparing and using behavior models, especially concerning the following approaches:

1. *Real or hypothetical situations?* Some organizations, in order to establish credibility and participant identification, will write their own, company-

Participant Evaluation and Feedback Report

Behavioral model: ______________________

Model step no.	Worked well?	Encountered a problem? Minor	Major	Describe the problem.	What will you do differently the next time to make this model work better for you so as to improve results?
1	_____	_____	_____	_____	_____
2	_____	_____	_____	_____	_____
3	_____	_____	_____	_____	_____
4	_____	_____	_____	_____	_____
5	_____	_____	_____	_____	_____

Instructions: If your trial of the model worked out well for a particular step, place a check mark in the first column. If you encountered a problem, check the appropriate major or minor column, describe the problem, and write out what you will do to improve your results the next time you apply this model.

specific cases and photograph them on company property. A majority of experts, however, believe that it is best to make the specifics and settings of the model demonstrations as neutral as possible. They believe that the greater the degree of specificity introduced, the greater the tendency of participants to quarrel with the details, thus allowing them to obscure or distract from the underlying thrust of the model.

2. *Negative or positive demonstrations?* Most behavioral-model builders believe that it is unwise to demonstrate negative, or nonproductive, behavior on the part of the supervisor. These advocates are concerned lest the negative and positive aspects become confused in the participant's mind. Other model builders believe that a demonstration of negative behavior on the part of the supervisor helps to underscore—or sell—the value of positive behavior.

3. *Rational or manipulative?* Many individuals, when first confronted with behavioral models, criticize them for their manipulative nature, claiming that the steps in the model can be used by supervisors unethically to trick subordinates into agreeing to do things they really don't want to do or that they don't believe in. The rebuttal offered by behavioral scientists to this argument is that the models are simply representations of rational—as opposed to irrational and emotional—interpersonal behavior. The models encourage supervisors to treat subordinates as responsible, thinking individuals who wish to have and are capable of having a hand in their own destiny. Most models presume that rational, fact-based approaches to interactive human problems generate longer-lasting, more productive results than do hit-and-miss, emotionally charged exchanges.

SOURCES OF MODELS

There are several notable suppliers of audiovisual film and/or videocassette models. Among these developers and publishers are:

Development Dimensions International (Pittsburgh, Pennsylvania)

Employee Development Systems (Kingwood, Texas)

McGraw-Hill Training Systems (Del Mar, California)

Mohr Development (Stanford, Connecticut)

Zenger-Miller (Cupertino, California)

The author participated with McGraw-Hill Training Systems in developing a series of fourteen modules in its "Supervision" modeling program.

BIBLIOGRAPHY

Instructors will find the following books and articles especially helpful in preparing and conducting behavioral-modeling training programs:

Byham, William, and James Robinson. "Interaction Modeling: A New Concept in Supervisory Training." *Training and Development Journal* (February 1976): 20.

Changing Human Behavior: Behavior Modification (a film). Pleasantville, N.Y.: Human Relations Media.

Donaldson, Les. *Behavioral Supervision: Practical Ways to Change Unsatisfactory Behavior and Increase Productivity.* Reading, Mass.: Addison-Wesley, 1980.

Gilbert, Thomas F. "The Behavior Engineering Model." In *Human Competence: Engineering Worthy Performance.* New York: McGraw-Hill Book Company, 1978.

Goldstein, Arnold P., and Melvin Sorcher. *Changing Supervisor Behavior.* New York: Pergamon Press, 1974.

Krackhardt, David, et al. "Supervisory Behavior and Employee Turnover: A Field Experiment." *Academy of Management Journal* 24, no. 2 (1981): 249–59.

Porras, Jerry I., and Brad Anderson. "Improving Managerial Effectiveness through modeling-based training." *Organizational Dynamics* (Spring 1981): 60.

The Power of Positive Reinforcement (a film). Del Mar, Calif.: CRM/McGraw-Hill Films.

Robinson, James C. *Developing Managers through Behavioral Modeling.* Austin, Tex.: Learning Concepts, 1983.

Robinson, James C. "Will Behavior Modeling Survive the '80s?" *Training and Development Journal* (January 1980): 22.

Rosenbaum, Bernard L. *How to Motivate Today's Workers: Motivational Models for Managers and Supervisors.* New York: McGraw-Hill Book Company, 1982.

Tosti, Donald T. "Behavior Modeling: A Process." *Training and Development Journal* (August 1980): 70.

Zemke, Ron. "Building Behavioral Models That Work—The Way You Want Them to Work." *Training/HRD* (January 1982): 22.

Appendix 2

Supervisory Films, Videotapes, and Packaged Programs

Literally thousands of audiovisual aids and programs are available for supervisory training. The lists that follow illustrate the sorts of materials and sources that are especially appropriate. These lists are by no means complete. Products and sources continue to change and grow. Furthermore, this appendix contains only audiovisual or computer-based references. The number of purely *audio* cassettes is simply too overwhelming to attempt to list and categorize here.

To keep abreast of what is on the market, training professionals are advised to regularly consult the journals and publications serving the human resources development field, their professional associations, and the many related directories.

FILMS AND VIDEOTAPES

The trend is for producers to provide their products in either 16 mm film or videotape in various standard formats. Most of these can be previewed (either free or for a fee), rented, or purchased outright—either directly from the producer or from a number of audiovisual distributors. There are also a great number of lending libraries from which audiovisuals can be borrowed free or for relatively low rental charges. A good listing of audiovisual producers, distributors, and libraries appears in the semiannual *Audio Visual Source Directory for Services and Products.* (The publisher is given in the final section of this appendix.) Readers might also consult the following sources: (1) *Educational Films Locator,* published annually by R. R. Bowker Company, New York; (2) *Books in Print* (at your library), which publishes listings of specialized film catalogs; and (3) the *Boston Public Library Film Catalog,* to which many public libraries have access.

The lists of films and tapes presented in the next subsections are grouped according to what appears to be their primary category of usage; however, many of these films may be employed to meet a fairly broad range of training objectives. Each film or tape listed is followed by an abbreviation indicating the source from which the item can be obtained. The key to these abbreviations is shown below:

AM American Media, West Des Moines, Iowa

AMA American Management Association, Watertown, Mass.

ASQC	American Society for Quality Control, Milwaukee, Wis.
BA	Barr Films, Pasadena, Calif.
BNA	BNA Communications, Rockville, Md.
CC	Calley Curtis Company, Hollywood, Calif.
CM	Creative Media, Div. of Betten, Baten, Hudson & Swab, Des Moines, Iowa
CRM	CRM/McGraw-Hill Films, Del Mar, Calif.
DA	Dartnell, Chicago, Ill.
GF	Gulf Publishing Company Video, Houston, Tex.
HRM	Human Relations Media, Pleasantville, N.Y.
ITC	International Training Consultants, Richmond, Va.
MI	Miller Video, Phoenix, Ariz.
NEM	National Educational Media, Encino, Calif.
NFL	NFL Films, Mt. Laurel, N.J.
PI	Producers International Company, Indianapolis, Ind.
RA	Ramic Productions, Newport Beach, Calif.
RT	Roundtable Films and Video, Beverly Hills, Calif.
WI	Wilson Learning, a John Wiley & Sons Company, Eden Prairie, Minn.
XI	Xicom, Toledo, N.Y.

SUPERVISOR'S ROLE AND FUNCTIONS

Do You Think You Can Manage?, XI

Everything You Always Wanted to Know about Supervision, AM

Eye of the Supervisor, NEM

The New Supervisor, BA

Profile of a Manager, NEM

What They Never Told You about Supervising, AMA

Who's in Charge?, XI

PLANNING, CONTROL, AND DECISION MAKING

The ABCs of Decision Making, CM

Creative Problem Solving: How to Get Better Ideas, CRM

Decision Making (series of three films), BA

Decisions, Decisions, XI

How to Manage by Results, AM

Managerial Control, NEM

The Practice of Supervising: Planning, Organizing, Controlling, BNA

Problem Solving—A Process for Managers, NEM

The Snarled Parking Lot, CRM

EMPLOYEE SELECTION AND TRAINING

Catching On, RT

A Good Start, DA

The Interview Film, BNA

The Interview: The Right Person, the Right Job, BA

I Told 'Em Exactly How to Do It, XI

More Than a Gut Feeling (interview), XI

The Most Likely to Succeed, MI

Pattern for Instruction, RT

Tell Me about Yourself, RT

The Training Memorandum, NEM

Who Wants to Play God?, AM

PERFORMANCE APPRAISAL

Feedback: Giving Constructive Criticism, AMA

How Am I Doing?, XI

The Human Touch in Performance Appraisal, AM

The Nuts and Bolts of Performance Appraisal, CM

Performance Appraisal, BA

Performance Appraisal: The Human Dynamics, CRM

MOTIVATION AND HUMAN RELATIONS

Climb to the Top, BA

Conflict, Conflict, BA

Conflict on the Line, CRM

Confronting Conflict, BNA

The Go-Gover, AM

The Joy of Involvement, RA

A New Look at Motivation, CRM

No Guts, No Glory, NFL

The Power of Positive Reinforcement, CRM

The Power of Purpose, WI

Productivity and the Self-Fulfilling Prophecy, CRM

Solving Employee Conflict, CM

The Supervisory Grid, BNA

Team Building, BNA
Why We Do What We Do, HRM
You Can Lead a Horse to Water, AM
You Pack Your Own Chute, AM

LEADERSHIP AND AUTHORITY

Delegate, Don't Abdicate, NEM
Delegation, CRM
The Effective Uses of Power and Authority, CRM
Leadership: Style or Circumstance?, CRM
No-Nonsense Delegation, CM
Put More Leadership into Your Style, BA

COMMUNICATIONS

Bottom Line Communications: Get to the Point, BA
Communicating Effectively, BA
Communications: The Nonverbal Media, CRM
The Effective Supervisor, AMA
Engineering an Agreement, RT
Listening Skills, HRM
The Power of Listening, CRM
Speaking Effectively, CRM
Verbal Reinforcement, CRM

PRODUCTIVITY AND QUALITY

Cost Management, NEM
Increasing Productivity, NEM
Quality Circles: Core Principles, AM
Supervisor's Role in Quality Control, ASQC

SPECIAL ASPECTS AND PROBLEMS OF SUPERVISION

The Administrative Woman, GF
Career Development, CRM
Discipline without Punishment, CRM
Dismissal: Controlling Employment Expense, PI
Do It Now, CC
Finding Time, CRM
The Manager and the Law, NEM
Managing Change, ITC
Managing Stress, CRM

Managing Stress, Anxiety, and Frustration, HRM

Negotiating: Strategy and Tactics, BA

Our Time Is a Very Shadow, ITC

Prescription for Absenteeism, DA

Sexual Harassment, AM

Stop Procrastinating: Act Now!, BA

The Stress Mess, BA

The Time Trap, AM

The Troubled Employee, DA

SUPERVISORY-TRAINING PROGRAMS AND PACKAGES

It is increasingly difficult to separate and categorize audiovisual aids and programs. There continue to be a great number of stand-alone audiovisual products dealing with single subjects and with little or no ancillary material. Nevertheless, a growing number of established as well as new producers are combining an assortment of audio and audiovisual aids—and computer software—into comprehensive, often integrated, packages. Some of these programs and packages provide an interactive medium by which the trainee can respond to, or conduct exchanges with, the medium. The trend seems to be toward the incorporation of computer-based simulations, since they can be designed for a great variety of interactions.

The following list of sources for such supervisory-training programs is, again, by no means all-inclusive:

Addison-Wesley Training Systems, Reading, Mass.
"The New-Supervisor Training Program"

AMA Film Video, Watertown, Mass.
"Professional Management for Manufacturing Supervisors"

Development Dimensions, International (DDI), Pittsburgh, Penn.
Various supervisory skills programs

Employee Development Systems, Kingwood, Tex.

Human Synergistics, Plymouth, Mich.

Industrial Training Corporation, Rockville, Md.

LDI Institute, Needham, Mass.
"Supervisory-Training Circles"

Longman Crown, Reston, Va.
"Management Performance" series

McGraw-Hill Training Systems, Del Mar, Calif.
"Supervision"

Mohr Development, Stamford, Conn.
Various supervisory programs

M. R. Communications Consultants, New York, N.Y.
"Management I for Supervisors"

Psychological Associates, St. Louis, Mo.
"Dimension Management Training—I"

Sterling Institute, Washington, D.C.

Wilson Learning Corporation, Eden Prairie, Minn.

Xerox Learning Systems, Stamford, Conn.
"Excellence" and others

Zenger-Miller, Cupertino, Calif.
"Supervision"

DIRECTORIES AND RELATED SOURCES OF INFORMATION

ASTD Buyer's Guide & Consultant Directory (annual)
American Society for Training and Development
P.O. Box 1443, Alexandria, Va. 22313

Audio Visual Source Directory of Services and Products (semiannual)
Motion Picture Enterprises Publications
Tarrytown, N.Y. 10591

Marketplace Directory
Training magazine
731 Hennapin Ave., Minneapolis, Minn. 55403

AMA Film/Video Catalog (proprietary producer)
85 Main St., Watertown, Mass. 02172

ROA Films (distributor)
914 North Fourth St., P.O. Box 661, Milwaukee, Wis. 53201

Video Training Centers (distributor)
1407 116th Ave., N.E. Bellevue, Washington, D.C. 98004

Appendix 3

Twenty-Five Model Course Outlines

The course outlines offered here serve mainly as models from which training professionals might more fully develop courses and outlines appropriate to their particular programs. Accordingly, these outlines tend to be generic and ought not to be used without modification. All outlines, however, have been seminar-tested with diverse supervisory populations and demonstrate sound pedagogical considerations in relating course content to objectives.

Each model is constructed in an identical modular format, consisting of four principal elements:

A. *Course synopsis,* which broadly describes the content indicated by the course title.

B. *Target audience,* which is classified according to extent of supervisory experience of the course participants:

- *Presupervisory trainees:* courses 1 and 2.
- *New or relatively inexperienced supervisors:* courses 3 through 13.
- *Experienced supervisors:* courses 14 through 20.
- *Second-level supervisors:* courses 21 through 25.

These classifications serve as indicators only and need not be rigidly observed in developing custom-designed courses or in selecting course participants.

C. *Course objectives,* which delineate both general and specific course outcomes as they affect course participants.

D. *Course outlines,* which illustrate major areas of subject coverage, with a rough indication of how content might be distributed over a schedule lasting two (or in some cases, three) days. Course length, especially, is subject to modification by the training professional, who must ultimately adjust the content to match the time allotted to it by the sponsoring organization.

COURSE 1: UNDERSTANDING THE NATURE OF SUPERVISORY WORK TWO DAYS

A. Course Synopsis

A course designed to promote employee awareness of the role and function of supervisors in an organization and to prepare nonsupervisory personnel for supervisory responsibilities.

B. Target Audience

For nonsupervisory, nonexempt employees who wish to explore the requirements of a supervisory position.

1. *Absolute requirements.* Individuals must be currently employed by the organization.
2. *Preferred requirements.* A record of higher-than-average performance evaluations.
3. *Precourse preparation.* Participants are to prepare beforehand a list of five factors that they find particularly attractive about their present job and three things about that job that they would avoid, improve, or eliminate if they were able to.

C. Course Objectives

Overall. To gain an understanding of how and why people come together in organizations, to recognize the nature and value of organizational goals and functions, and to become aware of the range and degree of responsibilities and activities entailed with a supervisory position.

Specific Course Outcomes. Participants who complete this course can be expected to:

1. Understand why people work and what causes them to be satisfied or dissatisfied with their jobs.
2. Distinguish between the goals and functions of private enterprise and public organizations or institutions.
3. Identify those factors and circumstances that encourage harmony or cause conflict between an individual's goals and those of the organization for which he or she works.
4. Recognize how management and supervision contribute to the harmony and effectiveness of an organization and attainment of its goals.
5. State the supervisor's functions and responsibilities within an organization.
6. Identify the sources, personal as well as organizational, from which supervisors draw their authority, power, and influence.
7. Appreciate the kinds and degrees of personal skills that supervisors must develop if they are to be effective in their job.

8. Be aware of the range of legal and organizational restrictions within which supervisors must function.
9. Make a more productive contribution as employees to the organization in which they work.

D. Course Outline

DAY 1

1. *Work in an organization.* Why people work; job and career expectations; satisfying work; dissatisfying work.
2. *Private and public organizations.* Organizations and their purpose; private enterprise; public and nonprofit organizations and institutions; similarities and differences between work in private and public organizations.
3. *Goals in conflict.* Typical oganizational goals of output, service, and resource conservation; impact on goal attainment of nonproductive and counterproductive employee performance and/or behavior; how individual and group goals can conflict; how individual and group goals can be harmonized.
4. *Management's role in organizations.* Managing, not doing; responsibility for the organization's resource-conversion process; overview of the planning, organizing, staffing, directing, evaluating, and controlling functions; relationship between management and employees.

DAY 2

5. *Supervisor's role in organizations.* Responsibility for resources, such as machinery and equipment, materials and supplies, funds, and people; responsibility for results, such as service output and quality, project completion; conformance to legislation, regulatory-agency rulings, and so forth; role as facilitators rather than doers.
6. *Sources of supervisory authority.* Organizational authority and status; personal sources of power and influence; equitability of authority and responsibility; accountability; gaining employees' acceptance of supervisory authority.
7. *Supervisory skills.* Technical skills; administrative skills; human relations skills; balancing a concern for output and results with a concern for people; emphasis on personal development.
8. *Legal and organizational constraints.* Federal and state laws regulating employment and equal opportunity; safety and health; wages and salaries; conformance to organizational policies and procedures; organizational channels.
9. *Toward more productive individuals.* Helping individuals to recognize their responsibilities to the organization; a fair day's work for a fair day's pay; encouraging self-discipline; individuals who manage themselves.

COURSE 2: UNDERSTANDING AND IMPROVING INTERPERSONAL RELATIONSHIPS AT WORK TWO DAYS

A. Course Synopsis

A course designed to promote an awareness and understanding of people's behavior at work, how individuals function in organizations, the kinds of behavior that promote cooperation and productivity and the kinds of behavior that cause conflict, and what supervisors and individuals can do to make work more satisfactory and productive.

B. Target Audience

For nonsupervisory, nonexempt employees who wish to explore the basis for effective working relationships so as to better comprehend a supervisor's responsibilities and also to make their own contributions to harmonious and productive workplace relationships.

1. *Absolute requirements.* Individuals must be currently employed by the organization and have completed course 1 or its equivalent.
2. *Preferred requirements.* A record of higher-than-average performance evaluations.
3. *Precourse preparation.* Participants are to prepare in writing beforehand a brief description of both of the following: (1) a work situation in which they observed a great deal of cooperation and (2) a work situation in which they observed a great deal of conflict.

C. Course Objectives

Overall. To provide a beginning knowledge of why people behave as they do at work and to use that knowledge to develop positive relationships among the people with whom participants work.

Specific Course Outcomes. Participants who complete this course can be expected to:

1. Understand how differences in personal attitudes and perceptions affect relationships.
2. Identify the needs that individuals hope to, and attempt to, fulfill at work.
3. Recognize the sources of on-the-job satisfaction and dissatisfaction and how these affect interpersonal relationships.
4. Initiate and receive clearer interpersonal communications.
5. Be sensitive to sources of interpersonal conflict.
6. Become aware of a number of alternative means of conflict resolution.

D. Course Outline

DAY 1

1. *Perceptions and attitudes.* How individuals perceive identical situations differently; persistence of attitudes in the face of contradictory data; Theory

X and Theory Y as illustrative of attitudes; how attitudes and perceptions determine relationships.

2. *Why people work.* Needs and motivation; work as a source of fulfillment; why people work even when they don't have to.
3. *Satisfaction and dissatisfaction.* Sources of both; how jobs can satisfy or dissatisfy an individual; characteristics of motivating jobs; interpersonal relationships as sources of satisfaction.

DAY 2

4. *Interpersonal communication.* Communications as a determining factor in relationships; barriers to communications; one-way and reciprocal communications; overcoming communications barriers.
5. *Conflict in work groups.* Sources of conflicts; differences in goals; differences in perceptions; scarcity of available resources; communications deficiencies; role conflicts.
6. *Resolving conflicts.* Avoiding; smoothing; compromising; forcing; confrontation; supervisor's role in resolution; individual's responsibility for developing productive interpersonal relationships.

COURSE 3: INTRODUCTION TO SUPERVISION TWO DAYS

A. Course Synopsis

An introductory course for recently appointed supervisors and all other supervisors who wish to acquire a basic understanding of the nature and scope of the supervisory management position and its responsibilities so as to better prepare themselves for developing the specific knowledge, attitudes, and skills needed to make their efforts productive.

B. Target Audience

For newly appointed or relatively inexperienced first-line supervisors.

1. *Absolute requirements.* Individuals must be currently employed as supervisors by the organization, with less than five years' experience at that management level.
2. *Preferred requirements.* None, except that individuals *not* currently employed as supervisors must have completed courses 1 and 2 or their equivalents.
3. *Precourse preparation.* Participants are to prepare beforehand a table of the resources they supervise, to include: (a) facilities, equipment, and machinery—together with an estimate of their replacement costs; (b) utilities and/or energy expenses in their department per year; (c) materials and supplies typically on hand, their amount and cost; (d) total monthly or

annual budget for their operation; (e) kinds of instruction or procedures manuals, directives, and so on they are guided by; and (f) number and titles of people working for them and total payroll cost for the department or section supervised.

C. Course Objectives

Specific Course Outcomes. Participants who complete this course can be expected to:

Overall. To comprehend the nature and scope of the supervisory position and the demands it places on those who hold that position, in order that course participants may prepare themselves to accept their responsibilities more knowledgeably and discharge them more effectively.

1. Accept and project a management viewpoint that entails a responsibility for results that are accomplished mainly through the efforts of others.
2. Sense the degree of personal empathy and interpersonal skills required of supervisors in order to attain productive results from a particular work situation.
3. Identify and evaluate the resources—equipment, materials and supplies, funds, and people—for which they are held responsible.
4. Determine the specific performance requirements for their jobs, especially with respect to output, quality of service, and control of expenses.
5. Understand the relationship among departmental goals, plans and schedules, and controls and the supervisors' involvement with all of these.
6. Understand the organization structure within which they work, the authority it grants, and the responsibility it assigns.
7. Grasp the concept of supervision as a problem-solving and decision-making activity, requiring initiative and decisiveness.
8. Make a judgment as to which knowledge, attitudes, and skills they must develop in the future in order to provide an effective balance between their various technical, administrative, and human relations functions.

D. Course Outline

DAY 1

1. *Management-mindedness.* Management's role in organizations; supervising versus doing; the supervisor as keystone or linking-pin; relationships with, and responsibilities to, others in the organization—higher-level managers, other supervisors, staff, and employees; legal restraints.
2. *Human relations awareness.* People as implementers; what employees expect from their jobs and their supervisors; self-awareness.
3. *Supervision of resources.* Resource identification and evaluation; equipment and machinery and tools; materials and supplies; energy, power, and utilities; information; facilities, buildings, and grounds; funds; human resources; resource conversion and conservation.
4. *Performance requirements.* Performance expectations and measurement; output, project completion, deadline conformance; service, quality, craftsmanship; expense controls.

DAY 2

5. *Planning and controlling.* Goals and objectives; plans, procedures, and schedules; controls; the supervisor's involvement in the planning process.
6. *Organizing and staffing.* Organization structures; responsibility, authority, and accountability; delegation; staffing responsibility; distribution and assignment of work.
7. *Problem solving and decision making.* Need for initiative and independent action; relationship to other phases of the management process.
8. *Self-development.* Technical skills; administrative skills; human relations skills; balancing personal skills; the supervisor's responsibility for self-development.

COURSE 4: UNDERSTANDING PEOPLE AT WORK TWO DAYS

A. Course Synopsis

A course designed to promote a responsible awareness of why people work and why they do or don't perform effectively, a knowledge of individual value systems, reasons for conflict in work situations, and methods supervisors can use to improve the effectiveness of their work groups.

B. Target Audience

For newly appointed or relatively inexperienced first-line supervisors.

1. *Absolute requirements.* Individuals must be currently employed as supervisors by the organization, with less than five years' experience at that management level, and have completed course 3 or its equivalent.
2. *Preferred requirements.* None, except that individuals *not* currently employed as supervisors must have completed courses 1, 2, and 3.
3. *Precourse requirements.* Participants are to prepare beforehand in writing, for seminar analysis and discussion, a brief description of (a) a situation in which an employee seemed to act unreasonably, (b) a situation in which a group of employees seemed to act unreasonably, and (c) a situation in which a group of employees were unexpectedly cooperative.

C. Course Objectives

Overall. To provide an introductory-level understanding of how people behave at work and why they behave in this manner, both as individuals and as members of work groups, and a supervisor's impact on, and ability to influence, that behavior.

Specific Course Outcomes. Participants who complete this course can be expected to:

1. Understand and recognize the personal needs that individuals hope to, and attempt to, fulfill by working.
2. Analyze and offer reasonable explanations for case examples and illustrations of individual behavior at work.

3. Utilize a knowledge of group interactions to more effectively supervise the work of small groups.
4. Identify differences in individual value systems and recognize the importance of a person's value system to that person.
5. Isolate the causes of conflict between individuals, between an individual and a work group, and between work groups.
6. Plan supervisory strategies for managing conflict in such a way as to further the goals of the supervisor's operation and the organization.

D. Course Outline

DAY 1

1. *Individual behavior.* Individual needs hierarchies; motivation at work; sources of satisfaction and dissatisfaction; impact on performance.
2. *Characteristics of motivating work.* Motivational factors; maintenance, or hygiene, factors; organizational constraints; process constraints; how supervisors can intervene to make work more attractive.
3. *Group processes.* Group norms; cohesion; status in groups; individual roles; methods for developing group cohesiveness.

DAY 2

4. *Values and attitudes.* Individual value systems; how values influence perceptions and attitudes; individual and group morale; impact on cooperation and effectiveness.
5. *Individual and group conflict.* Sources of on-the-job conflict; the inevitability and necessity of conflict; positive and negative effects of conflict.
6. *Conflict resolution.* Importance of superordinate goals; employee transfers; structural changes in the organization and in job design; strategies for improving interpersonal relationships within the work group.

COURSE 5: SUPERVISORS AS ACTIVATORS AND FACILITATORS TWO DAYS

A. Course Synopsis

A foundation course in leadership and communications, featuring development of leadership adaptability and effectiveness and use of delegation, plus skill building in organizational and interpersonal communications, with emphasis on listening and giving orders and instructions.

B. Target Audience

For newly appointed or relatively inexperienced first-line supervisors.

1. *Absolute requirements.* Individuals must be currently employed as supervisors by the organization, with less than five years' experience at that management level.

2. *Preferred requirements.* Completion of courses 3 and 4 or their equivalents.
3. *Precourse preparation.* Participants are to identify, and be able to report to the seminar group, three instances where communications represent (or have caused) problems in departmental operations: (a) between the supervisor and one or more employee(s), (b) between employees, and (c) between the supervisor and another supervisor or department representative.

C. Course Objectives

Overall. To acquire a basic understanding of the roles that leadership and communications play in activating a supervisor's department and to develop personal skills in effectively carrying out the leadership and communications functions at the departmental level.

Specific Course Outcomes. Participants who complete this course can be expected to:

1. Anticipate and fulfill the varying expectations that employees have for the leadership role to be played by their supervisor.
2. Modify their leadership style and employ it along a continuum ranging from autocratic to free-rein, depending on the situation and the individuals supervised.
3. Recognize and develop the sources of power, authority, and influence from which a supervisor can draw when exercising leadership.
4. Apply techniques of delegation to reduce excessive personal workloads and develop subordinates.
5. Understand the nature of the communication processes so as to maximize the impact of their communications efforts.
6. Apply interpersonal communication skills in such a way as to attain greater clarity and yield more productive employee responses.
7. Use active-listening techniques to improve understanding and rapport with employees.
8. Issue orders and instructions more effectively.

D. Course Outline

DAY 1

1. *Leadership expectations.* Characteristics of leaders; limitations of the trait approach; what employees expect from their supervisors; followership.
2. *Leadership styles.* Autocratic, democratic, free-rein, or participative; leadership continuum; results-centered leadership.
3. *Leadership sources.* Authority derived from the organization; sources of personal power and influence; acceptance theory of leadership; relationship between leadership and the supervisor's attitude toward employees, including Theory X and Theory Y.
4. *Delegation techniques.* Selecting tasks for delegation; granting authority commensurate with responsibility; accountability aspects; coaching, feedback, and control.

DAY 2

5. *Communications processes.* Communications as a process; organizational communications systems; open versus restricted systems; upward communications; three-dimensional communications; coping with the grapevine.
6. *Interpersonal communications.* What to communicate; how to communicate effectively—with individuals and with groups; spoken and written techniques; nonverbal communications; overcommunication.
7. *Listening skills.* Active versus passive listening; listening for content; listening for unspoken messages; use of questions.
8. *Giving orders and instructions.* Instructions, directions, commands, and requests; avoiding ambiguity; flexibility in allowing for employee initiative; dealing with misinterpretations and/or employee resistance.

COURSE 6: EFFECTIVE COMMUNICATION SKILLS TWO DAYS

A. Course Synopsis

An introductory course in the basic skills of face-to-face communications with individuals and small work groups, stressing the need for easy, effective, and ongoing exchanges and providing practice in oral communications and listening skills.

B. Target Audience

For newly appointed or relatively inexperienced first-line supervisors.

1. *Absolute requirements.* Individuals must be currently employed as supervisors by the organization, with less than five years' experience at that management level.
2. *Preferred requirements.* Completion of courses 3 and 4 or their equivalents.
3. *Precourse preparation.* Participants are to identify beforehand, and be prepared to discuss at the seminar, four specific examples of communications situations they have recently been involved in: (a) upward to a superior, (b) downward to an individual employee, (c) laterally to another supervisor or department, and (d) downward to a group of employees.

C. Course Objectives

Overall. To acquire a sensitivity to the need to communicate effectively with employees and others in the organization and to improve oral communication and listening skills.

Specific Course Outcomes. Participants who complete this course can be expected to:

1. Recognize operational situations that require communications and be able to apply the appropriate elements of the communications process to these situations.

2. Select information that is appropriate to a particular communications requirement.
3. Anticipate and overcome normal barriers to oral communications.
4. Present orders, instructions, and other relevant information to others effectively in face-to-face communications.
5. Listen actively and constructively to others in face-to-face interactions.
6. Exchange information effectively in a meeting of a small work group.

D. Course Outline

DAY 1

1. *Supervisors and the communications process.* The vital role of communications; how communications take place; getting attention; delivering the message; feedback for understanding; gaining acceptance for ideas; checking for resultant action.
2. *What to communicate.* Information typically needed in upward, downward, and lateral communications; orders and instructions; operating information; performance evaluations.
3. *Overcoming barriers to communications.* Organizational "noise"; differences in human perceptions; bias and prejudice; word problems and semantics; long and/or complex communications channels; overcommunication.

DAY 2

4. *Practice in face-to-face communications.* Identifying a communication goal; choosing the right language; importance of tone and manner; body language; value of repetition and feedback; developing good listening habits; sensitivity and empathy; closing the credibility gap.
5. *Practice in listening.* Listening for what people don't say; keeping alert to meanings; separating fact from opinion; active versus passive listening; avoiding interruptions; reading body language; developing empathy.
6. *Practice in communicating with small groups.* Beforehand preparation; sticking to your agenda; dealing with apathy; encouraging participation and feedback; pinning down responsibilities for future action.

COURSE 7: JOB AND WORK DESIGN AND CONTROL TWO DAYS

A. Course Synopsis

A rudimentary course in the basic principles and techniques for dividing up and balancing department work loads equitably and effectively, for arranging and simplifying work flow, and for planning and controlling work schedules and employee performance.

B. Target Audience

For newly appointed or relatively inexperienced first-line supervisors.

1. *Absolute requirements.* Individuals must be currently employed as supervisors by the organization, with less than five years' experience at that management level.
2. *Preferred requirements.* Completion of course 3 or its equivalent.
3. *Precourse preparation.* Participants are to determine beforehand, and bring with them, the following departmental information: (a) number and description of jobs normally completed in a standard time period—for example, one month or one year; (b) number of employees at each job level; (c) samples of a department budget and a department schedule, if available; and (d) sample of a work or job standard, if possible.

C. Course Objectives

Overall. To provide a working knowledge of the basic concepts of job and work design and control and an ability to apply these concepts to work distribution, work balancing, work flow, and schedule and performance control at the departmental level.

Specific Course Outcomes. Participants who complete this course can be expected to:

1. Make reasonable estimates of the number and types of employees needed to carry out a department's work so as to meet its stipulated goals.
2. Distribute work loads between departmental employees equitably and effectively.
3. Lay out, or arrange, the work to be done so that it moves smoothly from one position or workplace to another.
4. Schedule work so that interruptions are minimized and commitments are met on time.
5. Confirm existing, or traditional, work standards for output and quality and, where necessary, establish new ones.
6. Prepare and/or utilize information needed to maintain and control departmental operations and employee performance.

D. Course Outline

DAY 1

1. *Estimating the staff required.* Converting output goals and timetables into the required number of employee-days; converting employee-days into numbers of employees required; allowances for holidays, vacations, sicknesses, turnover, and start-up delays; dangers of overstaffing and understaffing.
2. *Balancing the work load.* Dividing up the work load according to required skills; matching work loads against personnel; routine work versus variable assignments and special projects; process-centered distribution; people-centered distribution; Work-Distribution Charts.
3. *Smoothing the work flow.* Process constraints versus people considerations;

work-flow principles; work-simplification principles; job enlargement, job enrichment, and the "work itself" concept.

4. *Scheduling the work.* Straight-line versus parallel scheduling techniques; allowing for start-up and put-away (or cleanup) delays; Gantt-type charts for planning and scheduling.

DAY 2

5. *Job and work standards.* Confirming existing work standards; establishing new work standards; sources of historical or traditional standards; work-measurement techniques; work-sampling techniques; gaining employee acceptance of work standards.

6. *Work-control methods.* Formal and informal departmental records for output, quality, attendance, promptness, and so forth; process- and project-control charts; Gantt-type charts for progress control; budgetary controls; the exception principle; handling employee resistance to controls.

COURSE 8: EMPLOYEE TRAINING AND DEVELOPMENT TWO DAYS

A. Course Synopsis

A practical course in supervisory skill building in the area of employee job training, stressing the four-step instruction process, trainee motivation, key-points identification, preparation of job breakdowns for training purposes, and preparation and use of employee-skills audits and training timetables.

B. Target Audience

For new or experienced supervisors.

1. *Absolute requirements.* Individuals must be currently employed as supervisors by the organization.
2. *Preferred requirements.* Completion of courses 3 and 4 or their equivalents.
3. *Precourse preparation.* Participants are to select, for discussion and practice purposes during the course, a specific job or operation performed under their supervision, preferably a relatively uncomplicated operation that is ordinarily repeated several times during the day—one that a comparatively inexperienced employee might be required to learn.

C. Course Objectives

Overall. To provide a fundamental knowledge of learning and training principles and practices so that participants may (1) more effectively prepare their subordinates for learning their jobs, (2) more accurately instruct them in proper work procedures, and (3) more productively plan and supervise the training and development of their employees.

Specific Course Outcomes. Participants who complete this course can be expected to:

1. Understand and apply the learning process in practical learning situations.
2. Use the four-step job instruction process to train employees.
3. Prepare employees for training so that they look forward to their instruction and self-development.
4. Demonstrate a job or operation by showing and telling exactly how it is to be done.
5. Identify and describe the key points that control whether or not a particular operation will be performed correctly.
6. Prepare an effective, written job breakdown for training purposes.
7. Develop a training plan for a particular job or operation.
8. Effectively supervise the employee training and development process.

D. Course Outline

DAY 1

1. *The learning process.* "Laws of learning"; knowledge, attitudes, and skills; learning readiness; senses and perceptions; learning plateaus; value of feedback; use of repetition; trainee involvement; differences among individuals.
2. *The four-step training process.* History and background; practical applications; overview of job instruction training and its four steps; cyclical nature of the process; examples.
3. *Preparing the trainee.* Importance of readiness; putting the trainee at ease; bridging from the familiar to the unfamiliar; establishing learning goals for a particular employee and job; explaining job importance; why a job must be done in the prescribed manner.
4. *Demonstrating a job.* Showing and telling in combination; demonstrating a complete job and its separate steps; alerting the trainee to critical (key) elements in the job; use of questions; letting the trainee try out the job; importance of follow-up; demonstrations and practice.
5. *Key-point identification.* How to recognize what can make or break a job; key-points checklist; examples and practice.
6. *Preparing a job-breakdown sheet.* Describing the knowledge required; specifying materials, tools or equipment, and training location; breaking the job down, together with key points; examples and practice.

DAY 2

7. *Developing a job-training plan.* Selecting a training sequence; training for accuracy; training for speed; variations from routine procedures; training in start-up and put-away activities; practice.
8. *Supervising the training process.* Induction and orientation training; the employee-skills audit; training timetables; performance evaluation and employee training and development.

COURSE 9: WORKSHOP IN EFFECTIVE TEAM BUILDING THREE DAYS

A. Course Synopsis

This course offers participants the opportunity to integrate the basic knowledge of supervisory principles gained in earlier courses and to practice application of this knowledge actively through hands-on experiences and simulations of on-job situations.

B. Target Audience

For newly appointed or relatively inexperienced first-line supervisors.

1. *Absolute requirements.* Individuals must be currently employed as supervisors by the organization, with less than five years' experience at that management level, and have completed courses 3, 4, 5, 6, and 7 or their equivalents.
2. *Preferred requirements.* None.
3. *Precourse preparation.* Participants are to prepare in writing beforehand, for analysis and discussion, (a) a list of five major unsolved or continuing problems observed in their operations, (b) a list of instances during which group discussions might be held in the participants' departments, and (c) a list of three specific sources of conflict in their work groups.

C. Course Objectives

Overall. To enhance supervisors' skills in unifying the operations for which they are responsible and in building an effective, cooperative work group.

Specific Course Outcomes. Participants who complete this course can be expected to:

1. Supervise their operations more effectively with respect to resource allocation, goal attainment, problem solving, and time management.
2. Make a more positive impact on group cohesiveness by increasing supervisory awareness of group processes, as affected by leadership power, communications, and various forms of participation.
3. Minimize counterproductive behavior and improve individual and group performance by focusing on issues of intragroup conflict, group problem solving, and positive approaches to discipline.

D. Course Outline

DAY 1: UNIFYING THE SUPERVISOR'S JOB

- *Suggested activities.* In-basket for identifying resource allocation range versus the supervisor's performance goals; exercises in time management and delegation; exercise in the use of formal problem-solving models.

DAY 2: DEVELOPING GROUP COHESIVENESS

- *Suggested activities.* Lead group discussions (exercises such as "The New-Truck Dilemma" and "Who Gets the Overtime?"); managing for group performance improvement (exercises that illustrate the management process, such as "Lego Man," "Enterprise," "Moon Tent," and "SWCC"); effects of power (exercises such as "Starpower" and "They Shoot Marbles").

DAY 3: CONTROLLING AND IMPROVING PERFORMANCE

- *Suggested activities.* Resolving intragroup conflict (exercises such as "Disarmament," "Negotiations," and "Ugli Orange"); integrated problem solving (exercises like "Camp Bigfoot" and "Parasol Assembly"); approaches to personal discipline, using case studies to analyze positive and negative aspects of discipline.

COURSE 10: TECHNIQUES FOR IMPROVING PLANS, SCHEDULES, AND RESULTS TWO DAYS

A. Course Synopsis

A course designed to improve basic skills in planning and scheduling work loads so that employees are used most effectively and work activities are completed on time and within budget limitations.

B. Target Audience

For newly appointed or relatively inexperienced supervisors.

1. *Absolute requirements.* Individuals must be currently employed as supervisors by the organization, with less than five years' experience at that management level.
2. *Preferred requirements.* Completion of courses 3, 4, and 7 or their equivalents.
3. *Precourse preparation.* Participants are to identify beforehand, and prepare in writing, a description of a scheduling problem in their operations, providing typical data about required output, equipment used during the process, number and types of employees involved, and duration of the operation, project, task, or activity.

C. Course Objectives

Overall. To provide a working knowledge of planning and scheduling fundamentals so that participants can develop effective work schedules in a way that utilizes equipment and human resources most productively.

Specific Course Outcomes. Participants who complete this course can be expected to:

1. Understand and apply the basic planning process to their operations.
2. Predict future work loads more accurately and use these predictions to more nearly level out peaks and valleys in work loads.
3. Determine the number of employees needed to fulfill the output requirements of a given master schedule.

4. Understand a number of basic planning techniques and select from them the most appropriate one for a particular planning and control problem.
5. Understand and apply a variety of departmental-level scheduling techniques, including loading and control charts.
6. Maintain control over the progress of plans and conformance to schedules, using standard monitoring and reporting procedures.
7. Develop for application a comprehensive plan and schedule for a planning problem at the participants' home site.

D. Course Outline

DAY 1

1. *The planning process.* Definition of plans; steps in the planning process; guidelines for developing a production plan; impact of master plans on a supervisor's operational plan.
2. *Anticipating the future.* Forecasting and look-ahead techniques; anticipating peaks and valleys in the work load; handling unscheduled tasks and projects; dependence on other departments; outside influences on departmental schedules.
3. *The master schedule.* The master schedule as the basis for departmental staffing estimates; how to justify a request for additional personnel; smoothing peaks and valleys in operational work loads.
4. *Planning techniques.* Short-range versus long-range plans; program evaluation and review technique (PERT); milestone planning and control; regular-time reporting.

DAY 2

5. *Scheduling techniques.* Long- versus short-term schedules; scheduling routine activities versus special activities; equipment-loading charts; personnel-loading charts; periodic-time reporting charts.
6. *Control methods.* Monitoring of planning and schedule progress; standard reporting systems; exception and variance reports; schedule-compliance reports; delay reports.
7. *Planning and scheduling project.* Analysis of a participant's specific planning and scheduling problem to develop a comprehensive plan and a schedule for its application at the participant's home site.

COURSE 11: INFORMATION MANAGEMENT FOR SUPERVISORS TWO DAYS

A. Course Synopsis

An introductory course in the concepts of electronic data processing providing basic knowledge about the operation of computers, data input and output technologies, and insights into computer programming and skill development in areas relating to the use of information, such as identifying various information sources, defining information needs, and managing information as a supervisory resource.

B. Target Audience

For newly appointed or relatively inexperienced first-line supervisors.

1. *Absolute requirements.* Individuals must be currently employed as supervisors by the organization, outside the data-processing function, and have less than five years' experience at that management level.
2. *Preferred requirements.* Completion of course 3 or its equivalent.
3. *Precourse preparation.* Participants are to prepare a written list beforehand of the information they believe is necessary to perform two aspects of their current job duties.

C. Course Objectives

Overall. To acquire an appreciation of the concept of information as an organizational resource and also basic skills in obtaining and managing information.

Specific Course Outcomes. Participants who complete this course can be expected to:

1. Understand the basic operations of a computer.
2. Recognize the advantages and limitations of computer input and output.
3. Appreciate the job requirements of a computer programmer.
4. Understand and use basic computer terminology.
5. Identify and select among various information sources.
6. Establish an efficient record-keeping system for an operation.
7. Work effectively with a systems analyst in developing an information-management system.
8. Perform elementary functions of managing an organization's information.

D. Course Outline

DAY 1

1. *Computer operations.* Computer construction and operation; hardware versus software.
2. *Computer input/output.* Available peripheral equipment for computer inputs and outputs; advantages and limitations of various devices; examples of appropriate use.
3. *Computer programming.* Popular computer languages; program development; program maintenance; flowcharting.
4. *Computer terminology.* Commonly used terms; the supervisor's relationship with computer operations.

DAY 2

5. *Selection of information sources.* Primary and secondary information sources; information attributes; cost-benefit analysis in information selection.

6. *Record-keeping systems.* Manual, mechanical, and computerized systems; working files and archival storage.
7. *Systems design and the supervisor.* The role of the systems analyst; nature and importance of user-supervisor involvement.
8. *Information management.* Elementary responsibilities of supervisors; legal considerations; protection of personal privacy.

COURSE 12: BUDGETING AND EXPENSE CONTROL FOR SUPERVISORS TWO DAYS

A. Course Synopsis

A basic course in the concepts of fixed and flexible budgeting, budget development and implementation, and cost or expense controls associated with purchases, materials and supplies, and labor payrolls.

B. Target Audience

For newly appointed or relatively inexperienced first-line supervisors.

1. *Absolute requirements.* Individuals must be currently employed as supervisors by the organization, with less than five years' experience at that management level.
2. *Preferred requirements.* Completion of course 3 or its equivalent.
3. *Precourse preparation.* Participants are to secure beforehand, if available, and bring with them to the seminar for analysis and discussion, the following forms and documents: blank departmental budget form, departmental budget, a budget report (monthly or annual), a purchase requisition and/or order, an inventory-control card, a time card, and a job cost sheet or card.

C. Course Objectives

Overall. To provide participants with a basic understanding of budget terminology and the budgeting process so that they may become more effective in controlling costs and expenses.

Specific Course Outcomes. Participants who complete this course can be expected to:

1. Understand the purpose of the budget, its essential terminology, and its application to expense control at the supervisory level.
2. Undertand how a budget is constructed from anticipated revenue and expense data.
3. Interpret a budget-variance report and take appropriate corrective action based on that report.
4. Comprehend the elements that contribute to a cost-accounting system and distinguish between variable and fixed expenses and between total and unit costs.

5. Apply rudimentary techniques of purchasing and inventory controls.
6. Contribute effectively to administrative processes for controlling labor and payroll times and costs.

D. COURSE OUTLINE

DAY 1: BUDGETING PROCESS

1. *Budgeting as a plan of action.* Types of budgets; fixed and flexible budgeting; master and departmental budgets; standard cost systems.
2. *The budgeting process.* Basis in historical costs; forecasting future expenses and revenues; budgeting as a continuous process; relationship between revenue and expense, or operating budgets; finding the optimum budget mix between too complex and too simple.
3. *Supervisors and the budget.* The budget report of variances; overbudget and underbudget; variances of material, labor, and overhead; rate variances; time variances; usage variances; volume variances; total versus unit cost variances.

DAY 2: COST CONTROLS

4. *Cost-accounting systems.* Components of product or service cost; unit and total costs; overhead costs; direct and indirect costs of labor and materials; cost behavior over time; prime cost and conversion costs.
5. *Purchasing and inventory controls.* The purchase requisition and the purchase order; inventory control—neither too little nor too much; ABC inventory control; the two-bin system.
6. *Labor-cost control.* Time cards and time sheets; the job-cost sheet; job-order costs; process cost; labor time and cost (wage) variances; techniques for controlling labor costs.

COURSE 13: IMPROVING THE QUALITY OF OFFICE, CLERICAL, AND SERVICE WORK TWO DAYS

A. COURSE SYNOPSIS

A practical course for supervisors who wish to improve the quality of work output in clerical, office, and service-type operations while still maintaining the required levels of output and/or productivity.

B. TARGET AUDIENCE

For inexperienced or experienced supervisors.

1. *Absolute requirements.* Individuals must be currently employed as first-line supervisors by the organization.
2. *Preferred requirements.* Completion of courses 3, 4, 7, and 8 or their equivalents.

3. *Precourse preparation.* Participants are to select beforehand, and bring with them to the seminar for analysis and discussion, two outputs from their operations. These could be letters, reports, mailings, completed forms, or examples of typical services performed.

C. Course Objectives

Overall. To provide a basic understanding of quality-control principles and practices so that participants can: (1) define standards of quality for their operations, (2) determine when quality is below standard, (3) take corrective action when needed, and (4) educate and motivate employees toward improved quality in their work.

Specific Course Outcomes. Participants who complete this course can be expected to:

1. Understand what contributes to or detracts from quality of workmanship in office, clerical, and service-type operations.
2. Establish practical, attainable standards for quality in their operations.
3. Measure quality of performance, including the use of basic statistical techniques.
4. Recognize quality problems as they arise.
5. Solve quality problems and take appropriate corrective action.
6. Cope with quality problems arising from purchased materials and supplies.
7. Improve employee attitudes toward quality and knowledge of how to attain better quality.

D. Course Outline

DAY 1

1. *Quality and quality-control concepts.* Concepts for supervising quality effectively; factors that contribute to quality; responsibility for quality; results of poor quality; the costs of quality.
2. *Setting quality standards.* Importance of standards; how to establish measurable standards; gaining employee acceptance of quality standards.
3. *Measuring the quality of performance.* Inspection; sampling; control charts; error detection; monitoring systems; variability; random versus meaningful defects; elementary statistical and probability concepts.

DAY 2

4. *Early-warning systems.* How to foresee quality problems before they become serious; problem detection; sampling, charts, complaints; quality audits; user feedback.
5. *Solving/correcting quality problems.* Tracing problems back to their origin; quality cause and effect; quality as part of the job; errors in new tasks and assignments; random errors versus true causes; actions to prevent further occurrences of errors.

6. *Monitoring supplier quality.* Specifying characteristics of purchased items; supplier selection; receiving inspection; vendor records and assessment; communications with suppliers; corrective action.
7. *Educating and motivating employees toward better quality.* Strengthening attitudes toward quality; educational approaches; improving capabilities for producing quality work; contests; communications; reward systems; penalties.

COURSE 14: NEW PERSPECTIVES IN SUPERVISION THREE DAYS

A. Course Synopsis

A review and update course for experienced supervisors who wish to improve their ability to adapt to the intensifying pace of change in their responsibilities by gaining fresh insights into the nature of the work environment, the underlying principles of the supervisory process, and the contemporary work force.

B. Target Audience

For experienced supervisors.

1. *Absolute requirements.* Individuals must be currently employed as supervisors by the organization, with five or more years' experience at that management level.
2. *Preferred requirements.* None.
3. *Precourse preparation.* Participants are to bring with them to the seminar, for analysis and discussion: (a) an example of a major change in either their job duties or their procedures; (b) a specific example of a communications breakdown within their departments; (c) a specific example of a difficult problem they face in employee motivation or discipline; and (d) a table listing the major physical resources of their departments (equipment, buildings and grounds, materials) and an estimate of their costs, the number of employees, their job titles and total payroll cost, and some measure of the expected monthly or yearly output of their departments.

C. Course Objectives

Overall. To enable participants to gain meaningful insight into changes taking place in the work environment, in order for them to become more adaptable and responsive to changing responsibilities and conditions and to maximize the effectiveness of their supervisory activities.

Specific Course Outcomes. Participants who complete this course can be expected to:

1. Respond more positively to changes in workplace conditions, the nature of their responsibilities, and the needs and expectations of their work force.
2. Develop a more constructive working climate for their employees.

3. Obtain the desired yield from the resources allocated to them.
4. Progress more directly toward the attainment of departmental goals.
5. Design and carry out plans and schedules for meeting assigned goals and deadlines.
6. Accept responsibility for organizing and developing the human resources under their supervision.
7. Accept responsibility for devising and/or implementing formal and informal controls over work progress and employee performance.
8. React more objectively to the individuality of employee behavior.
9. Comprehend how critical the leadership function is in the operation of a productive department.
10. Be alert to the vital role effective communication plays in their organizations.
11. Become aware of the need for sensitive, yet positive, monitoring and control of employee behavior and performance.
12. Commit themselves to the development of the personal skills needed to fulfill their supervisory responsibilities and maintain a productive and effective work force.

D. Course Outline

DAY 1

1. *A changing environment.* Environmental change; technological change; a changing public; organizational change; changing expectations of the work force; intensifying legal restrictions; self-assessment; techniques for coping with change.
2. *An assertive work force.* Higher levels of career and job expectations; desire for meaningful work; expectation of motivation rather than coercion; conflict between individual and organizational goals; techniques for making work meaningful.
3. *Intensifying responsibilities.* Responsibility for a conversion process; identifying departmental resource needs (equipment, materials, funds, and human resources); techniques for estimating and allocating resources.
4. *Emphasis on results.* Performance requirements for supervisors (service output and quality, expense and resource control and conservation); techniques for managing personal time and coping with stress.

DAY 2

5. *Developing workable plans.* Importance of goals; establishing incremental goals that lead to attainment of weekly, monthly, and annual goals; elements of successful plans; the role of policies and procedures; techniques for devising workable plans and schedules.
6. *Utilizing the organization.* The formal organization structure; responsibility, authority, and accountability; staffing specifications; employee selection, assignment, and training; techniques for distributing work equitably and efficiently.

7. *Controlling work performance.* Formal organizational controls; budgets and reports; performance evaluation; techniques for controlling processes and people.

DAY 3

8. *Sensitivity to employee motivations.* Contemporary views on motivation; individuals at work in organizations; individuality versus comformity; supervisors and Theory X and Theory Y.
9. *Understanding the leadership role.* Overview of leadership theories; employee views of leadership; followership; shared leadership; facilitating.
10. *Responding to communications needs.* Overview of communications in organizations; basic communicating systems; how to anticipate employee communications needs.
11. *Approaching discipline positively.* Need for evaluation and control of employee performance; distinguishing between productive and counterproductive behavior; developing constructive, positive attitudes and approaches toward discipline.
12. *Developing supervisory competence.* Specifying personal performance goals; planning for personal performance improvement; ways of developing technical, administrative, and human relations skills.

COURSE 15: TECHNIQUES FOR IMPROVING INTERPERSONAL RELATIONS: A WORKSHOP IN MOTIVATION AND COMMUNICATIONS TWO DAYS

A. Course Synopsis

A course designed to improve an experienced supervisor's skills as a communicator and to offer experiential opportunities to develop a deeper understanding of motivation and greater skill in motivating employees.

B. Target Audience

For experienced supervisors.

1. *Absolute requirements.* Individuals must be currently employed as supervisors by the organization, with five or more years' experience at that management level.
2. *Preferred requirements.* Completion of course 14 or its equivalent.
3. *Precourse preparation.* Participants are to (a) bring along a position description of a job they supervise and (b) be prepared to describe an incident involving an "unmotivated" employee.

C. Course Objectives

Overall. To provide supervisors with practical and/or hands-on experience in the use of job-related communications and motivation concepts and techniques.

Specific Course Outcomes. Participants who complete this course can be expected to:

1. Analyze behavioral incidents in terms of motivational concepts.
2. Design jobs so as to maximize their motivational content.
3. Establish behavioral performance objectives for a position under their supervision.
4. Provide positive and negative feedback to employees in a manner that enhances motivation.
5. Listen actively.
6. Develop beginning skills in a coaching relationship with employees.

D. Course Outline

DAY 1: MOTIVATION PRACTICE

1. *Motivation concepts.* Case analysis of employee behavior using Herzberg's satisfier and dissatisfier concepts and Maslow's hierarchy of human needs; expectancy/valence theory; path-goal theory.
2. *Designing motivating jobs.* Characteristics of motivating work; impact of job design on productivity and performance; practice in motivational job design.
3. *Behavior modification.* How to set behavioral objectives; how to discourage nonproductive behavior and reinforce productive performance.

DAY 2: COMMUNICATIONS PRACTICE

4. *Giving and receiving feedback.* Developing objectivity; reducing personal defensiveness; elements of good feedback and how to provide it.
5. *Active listening.* How to develop empathy; listening for feeling; listening for hidden agendas that undermine productive behavior.
6. *Counseling and coaching.* What the coaching role entails; what it can and cannot do; counseling techniques; potential and limitations of counseling and coaching.

COURSE 16: TECHNIQUES FOR MAKING LEADERSHIP MORE EFFECTIVE: A WORKSHOP IN SUPERVISORY LEADERSHIP TWO DAYS

A. Course Synopsis

An experiential course designed to allow mature supervisors to reexamine and practice various leader behaviors and styles in order to provide clearer direction and motivation for their work force.

B. Target Audience

For experienced supervisors.

1. *Absolute requirements.* Individuals must be currently employed as supervisors by the organization, with five or more years' experience at that management level.
2. *Preferred requirements.* Completion of courses 14 and 15 or their equivalents.
3. *Precourse preparation.* Participants are to think about beforehand, and be prepared to discuss at the workshop: (a) the kinds of supervisors they most like to work with and those they least like to work with and (b) which kind of superior they find allows them to be most effective as supervisors.

C. Course Objectives

Overall. To provide fresh insights into leadership effectiveness by encouraging participants to practice and evaluate the results of various leadership styles.

Specific Course Outcomes. Participants who complete this course can be expected to:

1. Recognize a variety of leadership styles.
2. Choose which leadership style is appropriate for a particular situation.
3. Identify their own habitual leadership style and understand its general advantages and disadvantages.
4. Become aware of the effect that a leader's actions can have on the quality of group discussions.
5. Adapt their own leadership style to the needs of a particular situation.
6. Improve interpersonal skills in group situations.

D. Course Outline

DAY 1: LEADERSHIP STYLES

1. *Leadership review.* Traditional concepts; autocratic, democratic, laissez-faire; Likert's four styles: leadership continuum; leadership and decision making using the Vroom-Yetton model.
2. *Choosing a leadership pattern.* Case analysis using various styles; Fiedler's three-factor leadership concept.
3. *Self-assessment.* Use of various analytical methods, such as LEAD and LBDQ.

DAY 2: LEADERSHIP TECHNIQUES

4. *Shared leadership.* The concept of participation; when and where it is most and least successful; group responses to the leader's behavior.
5. *Leading group discussions.* Participative goal setting; group method selection; when to yield control; how to retain control.
6. *Leadership practice.* Experiential exercises offering practice in various typical situations—and exercises like "The New-Truck Dilemma," "Who Gets the Overtime?" "Parasol Assembly," and "Camp Bigfoot."

COURSE 17: TECHNIQUES FOR APPRAISING AND IMPROVING EMPLOYEE PERFORMANCE: A WORKSHOP IN EMPLOYEE EVALUATION, DEVELOPMENT, AND DISCIPLINE THREE DAYS

A. Course Synopsis

A course designed for improving supervisory skills needed in the monitoring, maintenance, and development of human resources within an organization.

B. Target Audience

For experienced supervisors.

1. *Absolute requirements.* Individuals must be currently employed as supervisors by the organization, with five or more years' experience at that management level.
2. *Preferred requirements.* Completion of courses 14, 15, and 16 or their equivalents.
3. *Precourse preparation.* Participants are to prepare in writing beforehand, for analysis and discussion at the workshop: (a) one particularly difficult problem they have encountered in taking disciplinary action; (b) a brief description of any training and development activity they have supervised or participated in within the last six months; and (c) one copy each (if available) of a recently completed employee performance evaluation demonstrating outstanding, acceptable, and unacceptable performance.

C. Course Objectives

Overall. To enhance a supervisor's skills in dealing with immediate problems of employee behavior and in directing subordinates toward positive goal achievements that meet both individual and organizational objectives.

Specific Course Outcomes. Participants who complete this course can be expected to:

1. Understand the reason for and usefulness of appraising an employee's performance.
2. Gain a knowledge of several techniques commonly used for evaluating and reporting employee performance.
3. Recognize and anticipate the kinds of potential problems associated with performance appraisals.
4. Provide meaningful feedback to employees and develop plans with them for making positive changes in their performance.
5. Recognize specific needs for training, formulate clear development objectives, understand basic learning principles, and become aware of a variety of fundamental training techniques.
6. Evaluate the results of training and development programs in light of both individual and organizational objectives.

7. Demonstrate to employees the usefulness of organizational training and development programs.
8. Understand more clearly the dual objective of discipline as a technique for controlling employee behavior and as a means of assuring attainment of organizational goals.
9. Recognize the various characteristics that identify problem employees and select appropriate methods for dealing with them.
10. Apply discipline in such a way as to promote positive behavior modification.

D. Course Outline

DAY 1

1. *Performance appraisal.* The rationale for performance evaluation; performance defined; performance versus behavior; how to set performance goals.
2. *Appraisal methods.* Strengths and weaknesses of various methods, including straight ranking, forced distribution, and behavior scales; who should appraise; frequency and timing.
3. *Common errors in appraisal.* Overconsistency; differences among factors; lack of motivation; bias; unstated expectations; appraisal and discrimination.
4. *Performance feedback.* The appraisal interview; active listening; positive and negative criticism; defensive behavior; clarifying the "psychological contract"; counseling for improved performance.

DAY 2

5. Training as behavior change. Performance deficiency versus training deficiency; job analysis; establishing training objectives; principles of learning; motivation; law of effect; on-the-job instruction; operant conditioning; attitude development.
6. *Evaluation of change.* Internal validation (is there a measurable change in individual behavior?); external validation (has learning and behavior change contributed to attainment of organizational goals?); individual job fulfillment; public policy and training.
7. *Developmental feedback.* Planning for self-improvement; expectations and career development; motivation and personal growth.

DAY 3

8. *Discipline and control.* Fundamental purpose of discipline; positive and punitive approaches; impact of organizational performance.
9. *Diagnostic approaches.* Identifying and understanding "problem employees"; problems of intelligence and job knowledge; emotional problems; motivational problems; managers' assumptions about people and how these affect disciplinary approaches.

10. *Disciplinary actions.* Hot-stove rule; methods of maintaining discipline and order; appropriate discipline for various offenses; progressive discipline; methods of appeal; responsibility for taking disciplinary action.

COURSE 18: MANAGING CHANGE TWO DAYS

A. Course Synopsis

A course designed to help supervisors understand and anticipate the need for constructive change and improvements and to plan for their successful implementation.

B. Target Audience

For experienced supervisors.

1. *Absolute requirements.* Individuals must be currently employed as supervisors by the organization and have two or more years' service at that management level.
2. *Preferred requirements.* Completion of courses 3 and 4 or 14 and 15 or their equivalents.
3. *Precourse preparation.* Participants are to identify beforehand, and be prepared to discuss at the workshop: (a) an example of change that has recently taken place in their organization or operations and (b) an example of change that may (or will) take place in the near future.

C. Course Objectives

Overall. To gain an understanding of the nature of change and employees' reactions to it; to anticipate sources of, and reactions to, specific changes; and to develop skill in successfully introducing and implementing organizational changes and improvements.

Specific Course Outcomes. Participants who complete this course can be expected to:

1. Recognize general and specific sources of change in their organization or operations and distinguish between random change and planned change.
2. Anticipate the many ways in which employees are likely to react to change.
3. Analyze the driving and restraining forces affecting a specific change and distinguish between structural and people approaches to managing change.
4. Understand the three-phase sequence for implementing change, using the people-oriented approach.
5. Choose the most appropriate methods for implementing change from among the coercive, educational, and rational approaches.
6. Apply a number of techniques in carrying out a program for introducing and implementing change and improvement.

D. Course Outline

DAY 1

1. *Sources of change.* Changes in technology, social and economic conditions, legislative requirements, objectives and missions, organization and job relationships; random change versus planned change.
2. *Reactions to change.* Employee fears of increased job demands, economic loss, lowered status or influence, and so on; distorted perception of change's impact and effort needed to make the change; sense of being manipulated; inferred threat to group norms; slowdowns; overt and covert resistance; conflicts.
3. *Methods of dealing with change.* Analysis of driving and restraining forces; structured approach; people-oriented approach; supervisor's role as change agent; creating a climate for change.
4. *Three-phase sequence for inducing change.* Unfreezing—search, contact, diagnosis, and planning; implementing change; refreezing and stabilization.

DAY 2

5. *Implementing change.* Coercive approaches—pros and cons; prescriptive, educational approaches—pros and cons; rational or logical approaches—pros and cons; counseling and behavioral-modeling approaches—pros and cons.
6. *Techniques for assuring successful change.* Understanding employees' needs and perceptions; creating a desire for change; fostering employee participation; providing accurate communications; establishing specific goals for change; reducing employee anxieties; developing confidence; providing needed counseling, training, and support.

COURSE 19: TECHNIQUES FOR IMPROVING DEPARTMENTAL PRODUCTIVITY TWO DAYS

A. Course Synopsis

A course designed to improve supervisory skills in the techniques of productivity improvement, including defining productivity at the departmental level, identifying productivity problems, measuring productivity, and methods for improving it.

B. Target Audience

For experienced supervisors.

1. *Absolute requirements.* Individuals must be currently employed as supervisors by the organization, with at least two years' experience at that management level.
2. *Preferred requirements.* Completion of courses 3 and 4 or 14 and 15 or their equivalents.

3. *Precourse preparation.* Participants should identify beforehand, and bring with them for analysis, a particular area of their groups' output where they feel that productivity might be improved, along with available details such as yearly volume of output desired and attained, methods of measuring output and quality level (complaints, errors, callbacks, and so forth), and numbers of employees involved.

C. Course Objectives

Overall. To provide a fundamental knowledge of the factors that contribute to productivity, the techniques of productivity measurement, and methods for improving the quantity and quality of work output.

Specific Course Outcomes. Participants who complete this course can be expected to:

1. Understand and describe the elements of productivity, including quantity of work output, quality of work output, and meeting departmental objectives.
2. Comprehend why organizations in general have productivity problems and the reason for the decline in overall productivity.
3. Approach productivity improvement effectively by quantifying productivity expectations for their operations.
4. Select and apply appropriate measurement techniques for their operations.
5. Develop and apply plans for improving productivity through individual and group motivation, mutual goal setting, and intrinsic improvement in the structure of the work itself.
6. Improve productivity through the development of more effective plans and schedules for departmental operations.
7. Improve individual and group productivity through training and development programs.
8. Improve productivity by recommending the acquisition of machinery and equipment through capital expenditures.
9. Develop and apply a plan for improving the productivity of an operation under their supervision.

D. Course Outline

DAY 1

1. *Identification of productivity problems.* Defining and computing productivity measurements; productivity components—quantity and quality of work outputs, attainment of specified objectives.
2. *Productivity analysis.* Problems of productivity; changing work force; rising job expectations; shortages of resources; renewed emphasis on work quality as well as quantity.
3. *Quantifying work expectations.* Breaking a job down into tasks; work-flow analysis; establishing performance standards for quantity and quality of work.

4. *Work-measurement and work-improvement techniques.* Standard times and allowances; use of historical output data; time studies; work sampling; methods-improvement and work-simplification principles.
5. *Work improvement through better human relations.* Individual and group motivational approaches; participative goal setting and methods determination; concepts and application of job and work design, with emphasis on the work itself.

DAY 2

6. *Work improvement by planning and scheduling.* Work-distribution charts; daily job charting; milestone charts; work force balancing; planning ahead for peak loads.
7. *Work improvement by employee training.* Relating subpar performance to training needs; employee-skills inventories; matching training programs to productivity requirements.
8. *Work improvement through better use of equipment.* Recognizing opportunities for mechanization; justifying new equipment; capital-investment analysis; improving utilization of existing equipment.
9. *Productivity-improvement project.* Analysis of participants' productivity problems in order to integrate basic productivity-improvement approaches into a single, operable plan.

COURSE 20: PROBLEM-SOLVING AND DECISION-MAKING WORKSHOP TWO DAYS

A. Course Synopsis

A fundamental course for experienced supervisors aimed at structuring and formalizing problem solving and decision making through: (1) identification of types of problems and decisions, (2) analysis of quantitative methods of decision making, (3) practice in personal styles of decision making, and (4) consideration of group decision-making approaches.

B. Target Audience

For experienced supervisors.

1. *Absolute requirements.* Individuals must be currently employed as supervisors by the organization, with at least two years' experience at that management level.
2. *Preferred requirements.* Completion of courses 3 and 4 or 14 and 15 or their equivalents.
3. *Precourse preparation.* Participants should beforehand identify a specific problem in their operation that has resisted solution and write down for discussion in the seminar the key aspects of that problem.

C. Course Objectives

Overall. To provide a practical, working knowledge of a variety of approaches to problem solving and decision making so that participants may more effectively carry out those functions on their jobs.

Specific Course Outcomes. Participants who complete this course can be expected to:

1. Improve their ability to distinguish between the surface symptoms of a problem and its root causes.
2. Recognize various types of problems and select the most appropriate techniques for handling each type.
3. Understand a few basic numerical techniques for solving problems and making decisions and know how to apply each to their own operating situations.
4. Identify various personal decision-making styles and gain an understanding of their own styles.
5. Recognize situations that offer fact-based decision-making opportunities and learn about the use of group decision-making approaches in those situations.
6. Distinguish situations that require subjective decisions and learn about the use of group decision-making approaches in those situations.

D. Course Outline

DAY 1

1. *Systematic problem solving.* How to recognize and define a problem; problems versus symptoms; a systematic problem-solving framework; ways of identifying problems; problem solving as decision making.
2. *Types of problems and decisions.* Strategic, administrative, and operational problems; people-oriented operational problems (absenteeism, discipline, work output, turnover, and so on); other operational problems (scheduling, shortage of resources, lack of equipment, unclear objectives).
3. *Quantitative approaches.* Probability odds; payoff tables; decision trees; cost-benefit analysis; equipment-purchase decisions.
4. *Personal decision-making styles.* Exploitative autocratic; benevolent autocratic; participative democratic; use of a test instrument to measure each participant's style.

DAY 2

5. *Group decision making; factual issues.* Problems with right and wrong answers; quality of best individual solution versus compromise of the group; group decision-making exercise, with videotape option.
6. *Group decision making: subjective issues.* Problems without right and wrong answers; use of policies as guidelines in decision making; group exercise, with videotape option.

COURSE 21: MANAGING THE MANAGEMENT PROCESS TWO DAYS

A. Course Synopsis

An introduction to the management process, with emphasis on methods of planning and control, organizing concepts and organization structures, and the communications process in organizations.

B. Target Audience

For entry-level and middle-level managers to whom first-level supervisors report in production, clerical, staff, or service operations.

1. *Absolute requirements.* Individuals must be currently employed as managers (or second-level supervisors) and must manage the work of first-line supervisors.
2. *Preferred requirements.* Completion of the majority of courses 14 through 20 or their equivalents.
3. *Precourse preparation.* Participants are to prepare beforehand a list of (a) departments, sections, or functions supervised; (b) the amount of and/or annual cost of major resources used in their operations (supplies, power and fuel, people); and (c) ways in which their managerial performance is measured or evaluated.

C. Course Objectives

Overall. To comprehend the nature and significance of the management process and to acquire introductory skills in goal setting, planning, controlling, organizing, and communications.

Specific Course Outcomes. Participants who complete this course can be expected to:

1. Describe the management process, its purpose, and the manager's role in it.
2. Set long- and short-range goals for their operations and develop plans for attaining them.
3. Supervise the establishment of work standards, expense budgets, and progress- and procedures-reporting systems.
4. Recognize significant deviations from goals, standards, or plans and take appropriate action to correct these conditions.
5. Carry out the organizing process for the functions and activities for which they are responsible.
6. Recognize the variety and relative merits of organization structures available to managers.
7. Understand the communications process and recognize the potential barriers to it in their operations.
8. Choose and implement a communication system that is most appropriate for their operations.

D. Course Outline

DAY 1

1. *The management process.* Management defined; elements of the management process or cycle; management as problem solving and decision making; management and managers.
2. *The planning process.* Relationship between planning and control; planning premises; forecasting service needs and resource requirements; constructing long- and short-range plans.
3. *Goals and standards.* Setting primary and subsidiary objectives; supervising the establishment of work standards, key-area controls, and expense budgets; developing systems for monitoring and reporting.
4. *Exercise control.* Process and human controls; recognizing significant variances; measures for bringing variance conditions under control; when to modify plans or objectives.

DAY 2

5. *The organizing process.* Division of labor; job and function relationships; delegation; authority, responsibility, and accountability.
6. *Organization structure.* Principles of organization; formal and informal organizations; chain of command; line and staff organizations; functional and matrix organizations; span of control; centralization and decentralization.
7. *The communication process.* The management process and communications; the person-to-person communications process; barriers to communications; necessary communications skills for managers.
8. *Communications systems.* Formal versus informal systems; communications channels; communications systems—open versus restricted; communications media and their use.

COURSE 22: HUMAN RELATIONS IN ORGANIZATIONS TWO DAYS

A. Course Synopsis

A course designed to improve the understanding and skills of middle managers in dealing with the motivation and interrelationships of individuals in supervisory positions.

B. Target Audience

For entry-level and middle-level managers to whom first-level supervisors report in production, clerical, staff, or service organizations.

1. *Absolute requirements.* Individuals must be currently employed as managers

(or second-level supervisors) and must manage the work of first-line supervisors.

2. *Preferred requirements.* Completion of course 21 or its equivalent.
3. *Precourse preparation.* Participants are to bring with them to the seminar, for analysis and discussion: (a) a job description (if available) of one of their supervisors and (b) an incident involving an "unmotivated supervisor."

C. Course Objectives

Overall. To provide useful and practical information about the unique problems associated with managing supervisory personnel.

Specific Course Outcomes. Participants who complete this course can be expected to:

1. Understand and recognize the unique characteristics of supervisory personnel and "knowledge" workers.
2. Understand and identify individual behavioral manifestations reflecting various contemporary concepts of motivation.
3. Create organizational conditions that encourage greater motivation among their supervisory personnel.
4. Understand and evaluate various aspects of group interrelationships, especially the dynamics between supervisors.
5. Plan effective programs for managing conflict in their organizations and promoting cooperation between supervisors.

D. Course Outline

DAY 1

1. *How supervisors are different.* Unique characteristics of supervisory personnel; self-selection; social activity; proclivity for leadership; reliance on knowledge rather than skills.
2. *What motivates supervisors.* Basic motivational theory; Herzberg's satisfiers and dissatisfiers; McClelland's achievement, power, and affiliation studies; other contemporary insights into supervisory motivation.
3. *Designing motivating organizations.* Case-study analysis of motivating and nonmotivating conditions; analysis of participants' experience in nonmotivating situations; design of motivating organizational conditions.

DAY 2

4. *Group dynamics among supervisors.* Basic dynamics; impact of roles; agenda analysis; group norms and their influence; power in groups; status and its impact on conflict and cooperation.
5. *Conflict management.* Positive and negative aspects of conflict; techniques for resolving conflict; case-study analysis; design of programs for conflict resolution.

COURSE 23: MANAGING OTHER MANAGERS TWO DAYS

A. Course Synopsis

A course designed to equip managers of first-line supervisors with a fuller understanding of the interactions and interdependencies of unit supervisors and enable these managers to acquire skills for obtaining greater coordination and cooperation from unit supervisors in implementing organizational plans and attaining organizational goals.

B. Target Audience

For entry-level and middle-level managers to whom first-level supervisors report in production, clerical, staff, or service organizations.

1. *Absolute requirements.* Individuals must be currently employed as managers (or second-level supervisors) and must manage the work of first-line supervisors.
2. *Preferred requirements.* Completion of course 21 or its equivalent.
3. *Precourse preparation.* Participants are to prepare in writing beforehand, for analysis and discussion at the seminar: (a) a list of the activities they manage, with the kinds and numbers of employees in each unit; and (b) an example of a particularly difficult problem in securing cooperation between operating units of their organization.

C. Course Objectives

Overall. To develop skills in setting objectives and maintaining control over a variety of activities managed by first-line supervisors and learn about different approaches for improving the effectiveness of these supervisors' job performance.

Specific Course Outcomes. After completing this course, participants can be expected to:

1. Become aware of the need for superordinate goals that lead to internal cooperation.
2. Allocate resources more rationally between the units of the organization.
3. Focus the attention of their subordinates on performance expectations and measurable results.
4. Review supervisory performance more objectively and effectively.
5. Comprehend the nature of, and cope with, the power structure within the organization they manage.
6. Improve intraorganizational cooperation and minimize conflict.
7. Delegate, coach, and counsel more effectively.
8. Encourage and assist in the planning of training and development for their supervisors.

D. Course Outline

Day 1

1. *Superordinate goals.* The role of goals for organizations; hierarchy of objectives; goals at the supervisory level; interdependency of goals; planning for the attainment of superordinate goals.
2. *Resources allocation.* Analyzing goals and plans from a resources point of view; matching resources to unit needs; evaluating requests for resources; when to say yes, when to say no.
3. *A results orientation.* Mutual goal setting with supervisors; emphasis on performance results; extent of leeway in choosing operating methods; coping with various management styles.
4. *Supervisory performance appraisal.* Objective and subjective factors; criticism and reinforcement; securing commitments for performance improvement.

Day 2

5. *Power in organizations.* Managers and achievement; managers and affiliation; managers and power; analysis of individual management styles.
6. *Maximizing cooperation.* Competition from a positive and negative point of view; refocusing a subordinate's attention on superordinate goals; a win/win approach to intraorganizational problem solving.
7. *Delegation and coaching.* What to delegate and when to delegate; delegating appropriate authority as well as responsibility; what and when not to delegate; coaching to improve delegated activities; the role of counseling; distinguishing between coaching and counseling situations.
8. *Supervisory development.* Analysis of needs to improve knowledge, attitudes, and skills; relating training to performance evaluation; on-job and off-job training; emphasis on self-development; planning a supervisory training and development program.

COURSE 24: ORGANIZATION DESIGN AND STAFFING TWO DAYS

A. Course Synopsis

A course designed for managers who will build on to an existing operation or begin a new department, agency, or function—emphasizing basic guidelines for designing organization structures and techniques for staffing them effectively.

B. Target Audience

For entry-level and middle-level managers to whom first-level supervisors report in production, clerical, staff, and service organizations.

1. *Absolute requirements.* Individuals must be currently employed as managers (or second-level supervisors) and must manage the work of first-line supervisors.

2. *Preferred requirements.* Completion of course 21 or its equivalent.
3. *Precourse preparation.* Participants are to bring with them to the seminar, for analysis and discussion, enough data about their operations so as to fully describe: (a) overall mission or purpose, (b) functions performed, (c) number and titles of supervisory personnel, and (d) numbers and titles of all other employees.

C. Course Objectives

Overall. To introduce the middle-level manager to the basic principles of organization analysis and design and to provide practice in the development of organizing and staffing skills.

Specific Course Outcomes. Participants who complete this course can be expected to:

1. Generate clear and practical statements of an organization's goals and purpose.
2. Understand and apply the principles of departmentalization.
3. Recognize the need for, and prescribe, different organization forms or structures in different situations.
4. Understand and contribute effectively to the job-analysis, design, and specification process.
5. Convert forecasts of organization service demand to departmental work loads and quantitative employment requirements.
6. Understand and contribute effectively to the staffing, recruitment, selection, and training processes.

D. Course Outline

DAY 1: STRUCTURING THE ORGANIZATION

1. *Organization analysis and objectives.* Identifying the underlying purpose of an organization; preparing a written statement of purpose; developing goals and objectives to clarify and support the basic purpose.
2. *Principles of departmentalization.* Optimum division of tasks; rationales for grouping tasks; task relationships; functional groupings; service groupings; matrix groupings.
3. *Basic organization structures.* Organization charting to illustrate structure; mechanistic models of organization structure; line, line and staff and divisional organizations; centralized and decentralized organizations; matching organization purpose with organization structure.

DAY 2: STAFFING THE ORGANIZATION

4. *Assessing staffing needs.* Identifying the essential characteristics of the people needed to staff a particular organization; job analysis and specification; prescribing job activities, decisions, and relationships.
5. *Human resources planning.* Quantitative aspects of staffing; forecasting service requirements; matching anticipated organizational work loads with employment requirements; influence of turnover, absences, transfers, and retirements.

6. *Human resources implementation.* Staffing and recruitment sources and procedures; selection techniques; limitations set by compensation scales and length of service; employee training and development programs.

COURSE 25: ORGANIZATIONAL CHANGE AND DEVELOPMENT TWO DAYS

A. Course Synopsis

A course designed to help managers analyze and improve the effectiveness of their organizations in light of anticipated change and increasingly restricted resources. Emphasis will be on application of behavioral sciences techniques to the organization analysis, design, and staffing processes.

B. Target Audience

For entry-level and middle-level managers to whom first-level supervisors report in production, clerical, staff, and service organizations.

1. *Absolute requirements.* Individuals must be currently employed as managers (or second-level supervisors) and must manage the work of first-line supervisors.
2. *Preferred requirements.* Completion of courses 21 and 24 or their equivalents.
3. *Precourse preparation.* Participants are to bring with them to the seminar, for analysis and discussion, a chart of their organization structure and sufficient data to fully describe its overall mission or purpose, functions performed, and numbers and titles of supervisory and nonsupervisory personnel.

C. Course Objectives

Overall. To enable managers to plan for and implement organizational change and improvements (1) by acquiring an understanding of the related behavioral technology and (2) by practicing skills in applying organization development (OD) techniques to gain employee acceptance of change.

Specific Course Outcomes. Participants who complete this course can be expected to:

1. Accept the inevitability of organizational change and the need to plan for its implementation.
2. Comprehend the nature and scope of the organization development process, its application, and its limitations.
3. Gather appropriate data for organization diagnosis; identify factors that will aid or interfere with changes in the existing structure; and design a new set of functions, new relationships, and a new organization chart.
4. Become aware of, and make choices among, a variety of problem-solving methods associated with the OD process.
5. Communicate the facts about change to employees and give and receive feedback from them in a constructive manner.

6. Plan and carry out a number of "intervention" techniques in order to build a more effective team under the redesigned organization structure and staffing conditions.

7. Reduce conflict and enhance acceptance of the organizational changes through planned confrontation encounters with individuals and groups.

D. Course Outline

DAY 1

1. *Reasons for organizational change.* Changes in technology, social and economic conditions, organizational objectives and missions; regulatory directives; restricted or reduced resources; desire for improved effectiveness; random change versus planned change.

2. *The organization development process.* Unfreezing the present organization structure; initiating change and developing an action plan; refreezing and stabilizing the new structure.

3. *Organization diagnosis and planning.* Using surveys, interviews, and participative techniques; problem identification; matching OD alternatives to driving and restraining forces in the situation; designing a new structure of functions, new relationships, and a new organization chart.

DAY 2

4. *Implementing organizational change.* Evaluation of various OD strategies; coercive approaches; reeducational approaches, rational approaches; case studies.

5. *Communicating change.* Separating fact from rumor—techniques for reducing fear and anxiety; establishing a climate for constructive information exchange; giving and receiving feedback from supervisors and employees.

6. *Role-development activities.* Building the new team by role analysis and role negotiation; participative exercises.

7. *Confrontation activities.* Problem and conflict resolution through confrontation; confrontation meetings with individuals and groups; participative exercises.

Appendix 4

Instructional Materials, Forms, and Worksheets from a Model Productivity-Improvement Program

The following material is taken from a model productivity-improvement course such as outlined on pages 198–200 of chapter 13 and Course 19 in appendix 3. It will provide more detailed background for instructors with limited experience in the subject. The material may be distributed in its entirety to supervisors prior to their participation in such a course, or parts of it may be extracted for incorporation in handouts. Included is an array of forms and worksheets commonly used to systemize the work-improvement techniques presented in the course.

HOW TO SEARCH FOR AND SELECT A WORK-IMPROVEMENT PROJECT

At the conclusion of your supervisory workshop, you will be asked to demonstrate your managerial proficiency by successfully completing a work-improvement project. This discussion is designed to get you off on the right foot by showing you how to look for, and choose, a project that stands the best chance of being successful.

What Work Improvement Is

Work improvement is any planned activity that increases productivity or reduces waste. Work improvement is a tried and proven technique. It is known by many names, such as *methods improvement, operations analysis, waste reduction, cost improvement, quality improvement, systems and procedures improvement,* and *work simplification.* Work-improvement projects include such ordinary, but valued, accomplishments as (1) finding a way to serve just one more client a day without adding to staff and (2) devising a method for making an obsolete form usable rather than printing a new one.

Work improvement can also cover major overhauls of a department's paperwork system so as to shorten the time needed to process a request or a report. It can call for a radical change in the layout of an office or shop. Or it can include the introduction of simple conservation measures like a plan for saving heat, light, water, or fuel. It can also involve successful efforts to improve the quality of what is presently being done, such as reducing the number of typing or filing errors or even the number of callbacks of maintenance crews or complaints from customers.

In most instances, work improvement is accomplished by finding ways for people to work smarter rather than harder. That's because the more efficient way of doing things is usually the easier way, as well.

What Your Responsibility Is

The responsibility for initiating and carrying out work-improvement projects is an essential part of the supervisory and management job function. Supervisors who are rated high for performance routinely search for areas where they might increase productivity or cut down on waste. But that's only the beginning of today's story. Productivity in the United States—in both the private and public sector—has fallen dangerously low. This is especially true when our productivity is compared with the nations that compete with us for the world's markets or the world's attention. As a result, there is a heated demand almost everywhere in the United States for increased output and quality of workmanship in relation to costs. Chances are that your own voice is among the hue and cry.

It is only natural, of course, to be concerned about the possible impact that work improvement can have on jobs and employment. Almost certainly, some jobs will be eliminated or modified. Some disruptions in traditional employment will take place. But in general, work-improvement activities protect, rather than endanger, jobs. Work improvement demonstrates to stockholders, customers, taxpayers, and the community a responsiveness to their requests for greater efficiency and conservation. Accordingly, when a department or agency has a record of increased productivity, lessened waste, and improved client services, it goes a long way toward justifying adequate budgets and staffs.

The Main Idea: Improve Output and Cut Waste

Work improvement is aimed at increasing productivity—of facilities and equipment; of materials; of monies spent; and especially, of people. At its core, work improvement is concerned with just one main idea: getting at least as much out of an effort as is put into it (hopefully, even more than is put into it, but always at least as much). Let's look at this idea more closely:

1. Whenever an organization sets out to accomplish something, it must take into account:

   a. What goes into the effort. This is called the *input,* or *resources.*

   b. What the effort consists of. This is called the *conversion process.*

   c. What comes out of the effort. This is called the *output,* or results.

   This idea can be drawn as a "system," or "model," which looks like figure A-1.

2. The main idea of work improvement is to increase the productivity ratio—that is, the ratio of output to input. This ratio can be drawn as in figure A-2.

FIGURE A-1 MODEL OF WORK ACCOMPLISHMENT

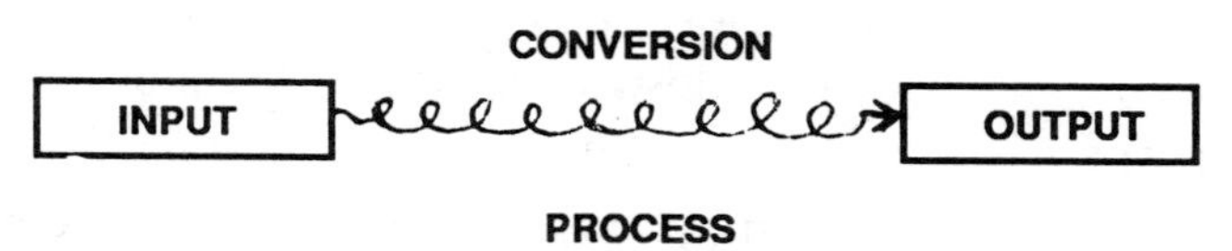

FIGURE A-2 THE RATIO OF INPUT TO OUTPUT

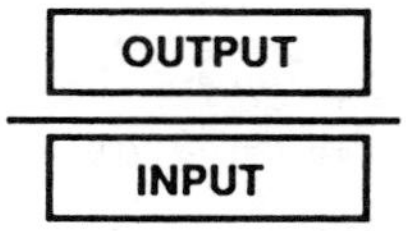

OUTPUT

INPUT

FIGURE A-3 THE RELATIONSHIP BETWEEN INPUT AND OUTPUT

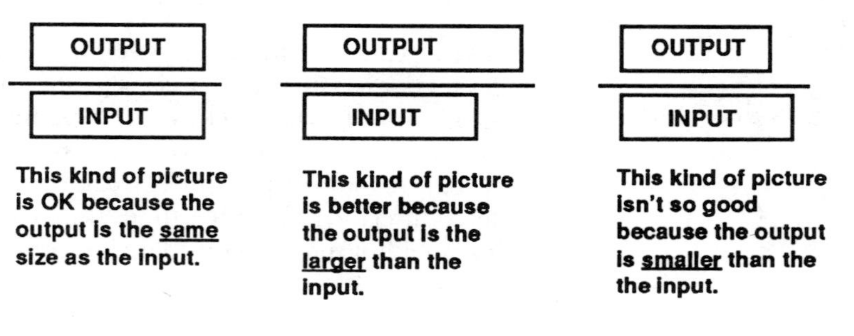

FIGURE A-4 THE GOALS OF WORK IMPROVEMENT

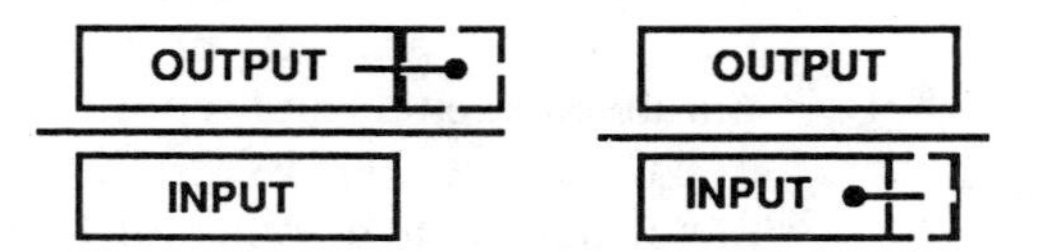

3. Specifically, work improvement seeks ways to make certain that outputs are always equal to or greater than inputs. Graphically, it looks like figure A-3.
4. In other words, work improvement is the art and science of making outputs larger or inputs smaller, as shown in figure A-4.
5. This can be accomplished in two ways:
   a. By changing the amount and/or nature of the inputs so as to make them smaller in relation to the outputs.
   b. By improving the methods used during the conversion process so as to require fewer inputs or to increase or extend the outputs.

A Closer Look at the Three Vital Elements of Productivity

Now that we've seen how work improvement hinges on the three basic productivity elements of input, conversion process, and output, let's go back and take a closer look at them. We'll first examine inputs and outputs.

Inputs. These are the resources used by an organization to attain its results or objectives (sometimes called goals, sometimes missions). Inputs typically include:

- A *facility* (really a place to work), which has space, heat, light, power, parking lots, lunchrooms, rest rooms, and so on.
- *Equipment* (like desks and blackboards) and *machinery* (like copying machines, lawn mowers, and telephones) needed to carry on the process.
- *Materials* and *supplies* used either (1) to make a product (like metal for automobiles and chlorine for treated water) or (2) to help, or be used up, in the processing (like paper, ink, chemicals, and floor wax).
- *Information,* such as operating manuals, procedures, blueprints, and directives needed to guide the conversion process.
- *People* to carry on the process, either *directly* (like machinists, typists, file clerks, tax assessors, or road crews—or anyone assigned to your particular operation) or *indirectly.* (This can include helpers and advisers, but also just about anyone not considered in the mainstream of your operation. Sometimes these indirect personnel work for your department and may be considered direct to you; other times they work in other departments as direct personnel but may be considered indirect to your operation.)
- *Money* needed to acquire, operate, and maintain all of the above.

Outputs. These are the end products or services produced by the conversion process from the inputs. Outputs are most commonly thought of in terms of *quantities.* They can include just about any kind of thing you can think of. For example: products produced, machines maintained, programs designed, numbers of letters and reports typed, inches of correspondence filed, numbers of passenger tickets issued or customers served or machines repaired, gallons of sewage treated, miles of highway center strip painted, numbers of bills mailed or telephone calls answered or ledger columns totaled or engineering reports prepared.

Output is also judged by its *quality*—by how good the quantity produced really was. If your department were making a product, it would be judged by the number of its imperfections or by how poorly the item performed. But when your "product" is a service, it is more likely to be judged by the number of errors made (in typing or filing or in calculating customer invoices, for example). Quality of output can also be judged by how often a job must be done over again, by the number of callbacks (received by a maintenance repairperson, for example), and by how many complaints are registered by your clients.

Output is also affected by *time.* It is one thing, for instance, to complete an assignment with no errors in one week. It is quite another thing if it takes two weeks. So it does make a rather big difference if work takes longer to do than normal, if a project deadline is not met, or if overtime is needed to get the job done on time. Thus, the quantity and quality of output become really meaningful only after you know how long it took to attain the result.

Finally, output is also measured by its *cost*, which, in turn, is related back to the inputs and the cost of operating the conversion process. Here again, it is one thing to get the job done not only properly and on time but within its prescribed budget. It's quite another thing to do all that but at an expense that exceeds the budgeted amount.

Conversion Process. This is the activity that supervisors and managers are paid to oversee. They must make sure (1) that it is carried out according to established practices and procedures and (2) to look continually for ways of improving on these practices and procedures. Conversion processes, by their nature, are highly specialized and differ widely from operation to operation. Even in office and clerical work, conversion processes cover the spectrum from general clerical and information processing to typing, filing, copying, tabulating, keypunching, analyzing, preparing, accounting, administering, verifying, auditing, issuing, and so on. In many service-type operations, the processing includes such activities as housekeeping, repairing, sanitizing, water treating, maintaining, brush cutting, road clearing, stores keeping, distributing, transporting, and power generating. Your operation may include some of these activities and many more.

Work improvement is concerned with the way in which the processing activities are arranged physically, in what sequence they are pursued, with what kinds of equipment and supplies, under what kind of environmental conditions, and by what kinds and number of people.

Pinning Down the "Work Output Unit"

Selection of a good work-improvement project to attack is made easier when you are able to clearly identify the "work output unit" associated with it. Almost every kind of activity that accomplishes something can be counted—at the end of the hour, day, week, or whatever period is appropriate. A departmental output that can be counted is called a "work output unit." We can count such things as tons produced, orders filled, tickets issued, windows washed, or telephone calls placed. Some organizations have several work output units. A purchasing department, for example, may measure the number of purchase requisitions received and processed, number of bids received, number of purchase orders issued, number of vendor visits, total dollars of capital goods purchased, total dollars of operating supplies purchased, aggregate number of days that materials received from vendors are late, and number and percentage of shipments rejected by inspectors.

The work output unit can be expressed in absolute numbers, in dollars, in percentages so as to show ratios or relationships, in pounds (of materials weighed), in gallons (of waste water pumped), in linear feet (of fence rail painted), in square feet (of flooring relaid), in acres (of lawns mowed), or in numbers of applicants interviewed, criminals apprehended, or cases reviewed and settled.

In sizing up possible work-improvement projects, it is essential that you be able to identify one or more measurements that can serve as work output units for your department. Without the ability to make such measurements, it will be difficult to compare output with input in the first place and to judge how much of an improvement you have made after your project is completed.

HOW TO FIND WORK-IMPROVEMENT OPPORTUNITIES

Your first assignment for the work improvement course will be to find something in your department or organization that you believe could stand improvement. As you may have suspected from the discussion about the key elements of productivity, there are three basic areas for your project search: inputs, outputs, and the conversion process. But you must, of course, know what to look for in these places.

Three Key Words

The key words in your search for work-improvement opportunities are these: problems, complaints, and dissatisfaction. What *problems,* for example, are you encountering in the input areas—with facilities, equipment, materials, information, people, or budget allocations? What kinds of *complaints* are you hearing about output—about missed deadlines, imprecise workmanship or mistakes, discourteous or delayed service, or budget overruns? What kinds of *dissatisfaction* do you, your boss, or staff people have about the way your operations and processes are conducted—about interruptions, delays, lost time, wasted materials, idle equipment, or unassigned personnel? It is from these problems, complaints, or dissatisfactions—resulting from inputs, outputs, or the conversion process—that you will uncover a prime work-improvement target.

Critical Questions to Ask

In many instances, these problem-complaint-dissatisfaction signals will alert you to more work-improvement projects than you can handle. In that case, your biggest decision will be which one to attack first. If this should not be the case, however, there are a number of probing questions that may uncover vulnerable work-improvement targets. For example:

- Has the trend in your department's usage of a particular input been upward over the past months or year? If so, can it be justified by a parallel increase in output? If such an increase in output is not apparent, what accounts for the rise in usage?
- Have you accepted as "fixed" a particular input cost (such as a basic supply, like copy paper) that might be associated with a variable cost (like storage space for the paper) that can be reduced even if the "fixed" item cannot?
- Are you accepting as "normal" a bottleneck or delay that might be reduced or eliminated if other factors were changed?
- Have you been using and reusing the same work or production schedules for a long period of time? If so, they may be "standardizing" assignments in a way that is no longer appropriate or efficient.
- Do you accept or require the same standards of performance from equipment and/or employees today that you did a year ago? If so, you should check to see whether these standards are still operative or whether they

have been obsoleted by changes in equipment speeds and capacities, for example, or in specified output requirements for the operation.

- Is the "yield"—the extent of usage you get from a given material or supply—the same as or greater than it was a year ago? For example, does a gallon of detergent cover the same square footage of wall or floor space as it did previously? If not, is this due to a less effective substitute product or to waste in product application?
- Has the trend in a particular output measure been downward over the past months or year? If so, can this be attributed to a demand for greater service per unit of work output (such as an agency requirement that a welfare recipient be visited three times per period instead of twice) or to a reduction in available inputs (such as a cut in staff assigned to that operation)? If no increased demands for service or reduction in inputs is apparent, what accounts for the decline in output?
- Have you observed equipment that is unusually idle recently? Are you accepting too high a degree of unused machine or space capacity anywhere? If so, this represents an input source that might be employed more effectively somewhere else.
- Are you satisfied with how busy your employees presently are? If there are not enough assignments to keep a particular employee fully occupied, are there other places or assignments where this human resource could be used more effectively?
- Are there instances where the process flow of work from one desk to another, for instance, backtracks instead of moving smoothly from station to station? Retracing steps and movements is wasteful.
- Are there instances where the same work is done twice (such as having a verification take place at two different work stations) without good reason? Duplication of effort is a major source of work-improvement projects.
- Has there been an increase in errors, mistakes, or service complaints in any of your operating areas? To what can this be attributed? Does it represent a condition that should be treated by work improvement?
- How much time and effort does it take to set up a new job in your department (such as changing over from processing one kind of form to another) compared with the length of time that the job will be worked on? If it takes a half a day to get ready to run a one-day job, that would suggest a need for improvement. Slow start-ups or setups, even on routine assignments, are good targets of opportunity.
- How much time and effort does it take to put away materials and shut down equipment at the end of a shift or run compared with the time spent productively on that particular assignment? Overlong shutdown, wash-up, and put-away periods are susceptible to work improvement.

Picking a Winning Project

"Dig where the diamonds are," says the old adage. So it should be with your choice of a work-improvement project. Select one, especially the first one, that has the best chance of succeeding, even if only in a small way. Don't be too ambitious at the outset. You can attack the projects with the bigger potential payoffs later on.

Experts in work improvement suggest that after you have identified a number of possible projects, you should select the project that has as many of the following characteristics as you can find:

1. The work output unit is already defined.
2. Work output is easy to measure or count.
3. Good records of output and expense are available.
4. Input resources can be identified and readily measured or counted.
5. The process or operation under surveillance is fairly repetitive, as opposed to a one-of-a-kind job.
6. Process conditions and methods are under your direct supervision and control.
7. The project area selected is broken out as a line item in your budget.
8. The project area is not currently a subject of employee grievances or dispute.
9. Employees who work in the project area believe that the work methods could and should be improved.
10. Your superior agrees that the project is a desirable one.

It can be added that if you are looking ahead to how the improvement might be carried out, these two considerations are also important:

11. The cost to implement anticipated changes is relatively small.
12. Anticipated changes can be made over a short period of time so that results can be demonstrated as quickly as possible.

A Preview of How Work Improvement Is Achieved

This discussion has focused on what work improvement is, why it is important, what your role in work-improvement projects should be, and how to pick a potentially successful work-improvement project. This is all prologue. It provides the foundation on which you can build your knowledge of work-improvement techniques so that you can create and implement your own improvements. The work-improvement course is designed to provide you with (1) a general understanding of several basic work-improvement approaches and techniques and (2) practice in applying them—especially to the work-improvement project you have chosen. Among the techniques you will learn about during the work-improvement course are the following:

- *Work sampling,* to determine quickly where time is wasted.
- *Job or operation breakdown,* to identify the many segments of every job.
- *Process symbols,* the shorthand of work-improvement analysis.
- *Flow-process chart,* to represent an operation or a job in graphic form, suitable for analysis.
- *Flow diagram,* to show how work progresses through a department.
- *Process analysis,* to find the weak spots that can be improved.

- *The 80/20 rule,* to pinpoint where major work-improvement efforts should be undertaken.
- *Work simplification,* to locate places where unnecessary work can be eliminated, job segments can be combined, flow sequence can be unsnarled, and the total operation can be simplified.
- *Value analysis,* to help you clarify process and output objectives so as to concentrate on only the vital functions of the operation.

WHAT NEXT?

Your next assignment is to think about, investigate, and identify at least three possible work-improvement opportunities in your department. Record the data you gather on the worksheet shown in the box on page 298.

Now, using the checklist of winning-project characteristics in the box on page 299, compare the three projects you identified. *Review your evaluation* of these projects with your associates and with your superior. *Choose the one* you have the most confidence in. *Have your superior initial the project you have selected* on your worksheet. *Bring the worksheet* with you to the workshop.

FORMS AND WORKSHEETS

There are a number of different forms and charts that are commonly used to systematize each of the various work-improvement techniques identified in the course and discussed in the instructional materials. Here is a sampling of what they look like and how they may be applied to a variety of jobs for which supervisors are responsible in the private and public sectors.

WORK-SAMPLING STUDY TALLY SHEET

Most people do not, and cannot, work 100 percent of the time each day on the most productive part of their work assignments. They encounter delays of all kinds, such as waiting for assignments, instructions, and supplies. Many jobs entail travel to and from the work site. And there are always personal needs to attend to. Accordingly, work sampling is a rough way to get some idea, over a relatively short period of time, of how much time employees spend productively. It requires that the supervisor set up categories for the principal work activities, as shown in figure A-5 (p. 300). Just a few categories will do, especially those that help to distinguish between actually working on the main part of the job and those other activities that may or may not be necessary. The supervisor then makes a series of random (different times, different hours) observations of employees at work over, say, a five-day period. Each time an observation is made, a tally mark is placed in the appropriate box of the Work-Sampling Study form. After about fifty to one hundred observations have been made, the tally marks are totaled. From this count, the supervisor can get a rough idea of where the employees' nonproductive time occurs. The next task, of course, is to try to find ways to reduce the percentage of nonproductive time. In the example in figure A-6 (p. 300), it might be possible to make job assignments at the job site at the end of one day so that crews can go directly to the next job the following day. This would reduce time lost getting assignments and also cut down on travel time.

Worksheet for Identifying Winning Projects

Project A

1. Describe the problem, complaint, dissatisfaction, or condition that needs improvement:

2. Identify the location of the possible project.
   a. Your department or organization: ______
   b. The specific location of the process or condition: ______

3. Relevant data for this project.
   a. Job classifications of employees directly involved: ______
   b. Number of employees involved: ______
   c. Pay scale of employees involved: ______
   d. Materials and/or supplies involved; describe: ______
   e. Monthly usage of supplies involved: $ ______
   ______ Other units, such as lbs. or gallons
   f. Machinery or equipment involved; describe, including capacity: ______
   g. Work output unit; define: ______
   h. Total number of work output units involved: ______
   i. Other relevant data, such as power or fuel consumption: ______

Project B

as above

Project C

as above

Worksheet for Comparing Project Potential

Winning Characteristics	Project A	Project B	Project C
1. Work output unit already defined	________	________	________
2. Work output unit easy to measure or count	________	________	________
3. Good records of output and expense	________	________	________
4. Input resources easy to measure or count	________	________	________
5. Ongoing, repetitive project	________	________	________
6. Process under your supervision and control	________	________	________
7. Budget data available for this project	________	________	________
8. Project area not subject of grievance	________	________	________
9. Employees believe methods can be improved	________	________	________
10. Your superior likes this project	________	________	________
11. Implementation cost will be small	________	________	________
12. Changes can be made and results attained quickly	________	________	________

An important aspect of work sampling should be stressed: employees should *always* be informed in advance that such a study is being made. They do not ordinarily object to work sampling because, in the great majority of cases, the delays observed are due not to employee choice but to poor planning and scheduling or other conditions beyond their control.

Figure A-7 on page 301 presents a comprehensive work-sampling study of clerical employees, using eight different categories of activities. The observation sheet shows how a code number for each category observed for each employee is entered in the table at "random" times for one day, beginning at 9:09 A.M. and finishing at 4:39 P.M. In this example, a total of 990 observations were made of the five employees in the study. Then averages for the group of employees as a whole were computed. With the data reported this way, no one employee is singled out for analysis.

Work-Distribution Chart

When faced with assigning work to a number of people who must perform a variety of jobs, the Work-Distribution Chart (figure A-8 on page 302) is a convenient way of balancing the workload among them. The starting point

FIGURE A-5 WORK-SAMPLING STUDY TALLY SHEET

Work-Sampling Study			
Department: ______		Subject: ______	
Operator(s): ______		Date: ______	
Work activity	Observations	Totals	Percent of all observations
1.			
2.			
3.			
4.			
5.			
Totals			

Source: Reprinted with permission from Lester R. Bittel, *Improving Supervisory Performance* (New York: McGraw-Hill Book Company, 1976), 246.

FIGURE A-6 SAMPLE COMPLETED WORK-SAMPLING STUDY TALLY SHEET

Work-Sampling Study			
Department: ROAD MAINTENANCE		Subject: CUTTING CREW	
Operator(s): JAKE, TONY, LINDA		Date: July 21-25	
Work activity	Observations	Totals	Percent of all observations
1. GETTING ASSIGNMENTS AT YARD	𝍸 𝍸 II	12	15
2. TRAVEL TO SITE	𝍸 𝍸 𝍸 I	16	20
3. WORKING	𝍸 𝍸 𝍸 𝍸 𝍸 𝍸 𝍸 𝍸	40	50
4. IDLE, PERSONAL TIME	𝍸 𝍸 II	12	15
5.			
Totals		80	100

Source: Reprinted with permission from Lester R. Bittel, *Improving Supervisory Performance* (New York: McGraw-Hill Book Company, 1976), 246.

FIGURE A-7 SAMPLE WORK-SAMPLING STUDY TALLY SHEET AND ANALYSIS FOR A STUDY OF CLERICAL EMPLOYEES

Work-Sampling Study of Clerical Employees
Observation Sheet

Name of Typist	Random Observation Times								
	9:09	9:57	11:18	1:15	2:43	3:11	3:52	4:21	4:39
Chavez	7	8	1	1	3	5	6	3	1
Yost	2	1	6	4	1	3	7	6	2
Albers	7	4	5	1	8	1	1	3	8
Dowdy	7	8	7	4	1	1	2	1	8
Calabrese	4	1	2	5	7	5	1	4	1

Date: 7/21 Supervisor (Observer): F. Diehl

Activity Category Code Numbers
1. Typing
2. Taking dictation
3. Transcribing from machine
4. Clerical activity at desk
5. Away from desk, but in office
6. Talking, telephoning
7. Personal
8. Not in office

Summary of 990 Observations

Category	**Number of observations**	**Percentage of observations**
1. Typing	487	49.2
2. Taking dictation	23	2.3
3. Transcribing from machine	86	8.7
4. Clerical activity at desk	71	7.2
5. Away from desk, but in office	36	3.6
6. Talking, telephoning	68	6.9
7. Personal	113	11.4
8. Not in office	106	10.7

Source: Reprinted with permission from Lester R. Bittel, *Improving Supervisory Performance* (New York: McGraw-Hill Book Company, 1976), 429.

is to make some rough estimate of the number of hours each week that are usually required to complete each activity. The hours required are placed in the first column of figure A-8 for each of six activities—in this case, beginning with ledger posting and finishing with internal cost reports. The total number of hours required is 160. If employees work a 40-hour week, this tells the supervisor that four employees will be needed to do the work. The next step is to establish—by trial and error—the weekly time distribution for each employee. Skills and grade levels must be taken into account, of course. The objective is to come up with an equitable distribution of the total workload

FIGURE A-8 WORK-DISTRIBUTION CHART

Work Distribution Chart

Department Consolidated Accounting and Data Processing

Tasks or activities to be done each week	Total time (in hours) for each task each week	Weekly time distribution in hours per employee			
		Kay	Lil	Dale	Candy
Ledger posting	30				
Accounts receivable	30				
Accounts payable	30				
Payroll	40				
Monthly statements	10				
Internal cost reports	20				
Total hours	160	40	40	40	40

Source: Reprinted with permission from Lester R. Bittel, *Improving Supervisory Performance* (New York: McGraw-Hill Book Company, 1976), 414.

FIGURE A-9 SAMPLE COMPLETED WORK-DISTRIBUTION CHART

Work-Distribution Chart

Department Consolidated Accounting and Data Processing

Tasks or activities to be done each week	Total time (in hours) for each task each week	Weekly time distribution in hours per employee			
		Kay	Lil	Dale	Candy
Ledger posting	30	10		10	10
Accounts receivable	30				30
Accounts payable	30			30	
Payroll	40		40		
Monthly statements	10	10			
Internal cost reports	20	20			
Total hours	160	40	40	40	40

Source: Reprinted with permission from Lester R. Bittel, *Improving Supervisory Performance* (New York: McGraw-Hill Book Company, 1976), 414.

FIGURE A-10 PROCESS SYMBOLS AND THEIR USE

Symbol	Example	Example	Example
Operation  ○	**Wrapping Part**	**Drill Hole**	**Typing Letter**
	An operation represents the main steps in the process. Something is created, changed, or added to. Usually transportations, inspections, delays, and storages are more or less auxiliary elements. Operations involve activites such as forming, shaping, assembling, and disassembling.		
Transportation  ⇨	**Move material by truck**	**Persons moving between locations**	**Move material by carrying (messenger)**
	Transportation is the movement of the material or worker being studied from one position or location to another. When materials are stored beside or within two or three feet of a bench or machine on which the operation is to be performed, the movement used in obtaining the material preceding the operation and putting it down after the operation is considered part of the operation.		
Inspection □	**Examine for quality and quantity**	**Review for accuracy**	**Checking for information**
	Inspection occurs when an item or items are checked, verified, reviewed, or examined for quality and not changed.		
Delay  D	**Material waiting "in" basket**	**Person waiting in line**	**Waiting for a signature**
	A delay occurs when conditions do not permit or require immediate performance of the next planned action.		
Storage  △	**Suspense copy in file**	**Material in warehouse**	**Filed for permanent record**
	Storage occurs when something remains in one place, not being worked on in a regular process, awaiting further action at a later date, permanent storage or disposal.		

Source: Reprinted with permission from Lester R. Bittel, *Improving Supervisory Performance* (New York: McGraw-Hill Book Company, 1976), 501.

that will assure its being completed at the end of the week. Figure A-9 on page 302 shows how such a distribution might look.

PROCESS SYMBOLS

When trying to find ways to simplify work, it has been found extremely helpful to break up a job (which may take only a few minutes or as long as a day, perhaps) into a number of smaller segments. It has further been observed that for almost any process, regardless of its specific nature, its segments will fall into one of five classifications. Figure A-10 above illustrates these classes and how each might apply to a number of different kinds of processes. Each classification is identified by an appropriate symbol. These symbols become a convenient kind of "shorthand" that helps in breaking up (or down) a job for analysis. Note that the round symbol indicates an "operation," the designation for the most important segment of a job. This symbol tells the analysts

FIGURE A-11 FLOW-PROCESS CHART

Flow-Process Chart

Summary

	Present		Proposed		Difference	
	No.	Time	No.	Time	No.	Time
Operations						
Transportations						
Inspections						
Delays						
Storages						
Distance Traveled		ft		ft		ft

Job ______________________

☐ Person or ☐ Material ______________________

Chart begins ______________________

Chart ends ______________________

Charted by ______________________ Date ____________

	Details of (Present / Proposed) Method	Operation	Transport	Inspection	Delay	Storage	Distance in feet	Quantity	Time	Notes
1										
2										
3										
4										
5										
6										
7										
8										
9										
10										
11										
12										
13										
14										
15										
16										
17										
18										
19										
20										
21										
22										
23										
24										
25										
26										
27										
28										
29										
30										

Source: Reprinted with permission from Lester R. Bittel, *Improving Supervisory Performance* (New York: McGraw-Hill Book Company, 1976), 321.

FIGURE A-12 SAMPLE FLOW-PROCESS WORKSHEET SHOWING STEPS IN PRESENT METHOD

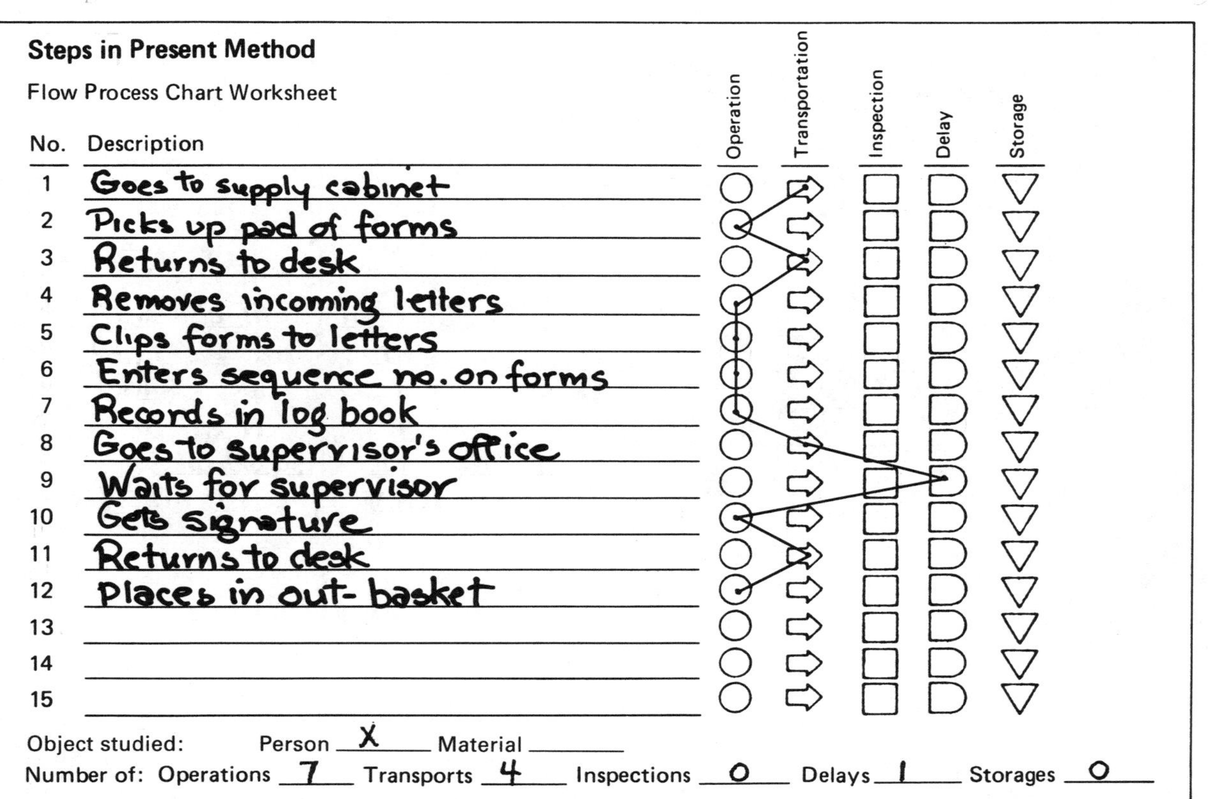

Steps in Present Method

Flow Process Chart Worksheet

No.	Description	Operation	Transportation	Inspection	Delay	Storage
1	Goes to supply cabinet					
2	Picks up pad of forms					
3	Returns to desk					
4	Removes incoming letters					
5	Clips forms to letters					
6	Enters sequence no. on forms					
7	Records in log book					
8	Goes to supervisor's office					
9	Waits for supervisor					
10	Gets signature					
11	Returns to desk					
12	Places in out-basket					
13						
14						
15						

Object studied: Person X Material ____

Number of: Operations 7 Transports 4 Inspections 0 Delays 1 Storages 0

Source: Reprinted with permission from Lester R. Bittel, *Improving Supervisory Performance* (New York: McGraw-Hill Book Company, 1976), 322.

that something vital is being accomplished. All the other symbols represent segments of a job that may be necessary to support the operation but that might possibly be eliminated.

FLOW-PROCESS CHART

The Flow-Process Chart is a form that analysts employ to record their breakdown analysis. The basic form is shown in figure A-11. It can be used to trace the present job flow or to illustrate a proposed improvement in it. It can be used to follow the activities of a *person* performing the work or of a *material* being worked on, like an insurance form, purchase requisition, or payment voucher.

Using the Flow-Process Chart, the analyst simply records the present flow of activity from segment to segment by drawing a connecting line between the symbols for each step of the process. Figure A-12 shows how this is done for a study of a clerk who is processing an insurance claim. Note that steps 2, 4, 5, 6, 7, 10, and 12 involve an operation that advances the work. All others represent transportations (of the clerk) or delay. Figure A-13 shows a proposed method for simplifying the job. The proposed method (1) calls for the forms to be stored initially at the clerk's desk so that no travel is required at that stage, (2) provides sequentially numbered forms so that the clerk need

FIGURE A-13 SAMPLE FLOW-PROCESS WORKSHEET SHOWING STEPS IN A PROPOSED METHOD

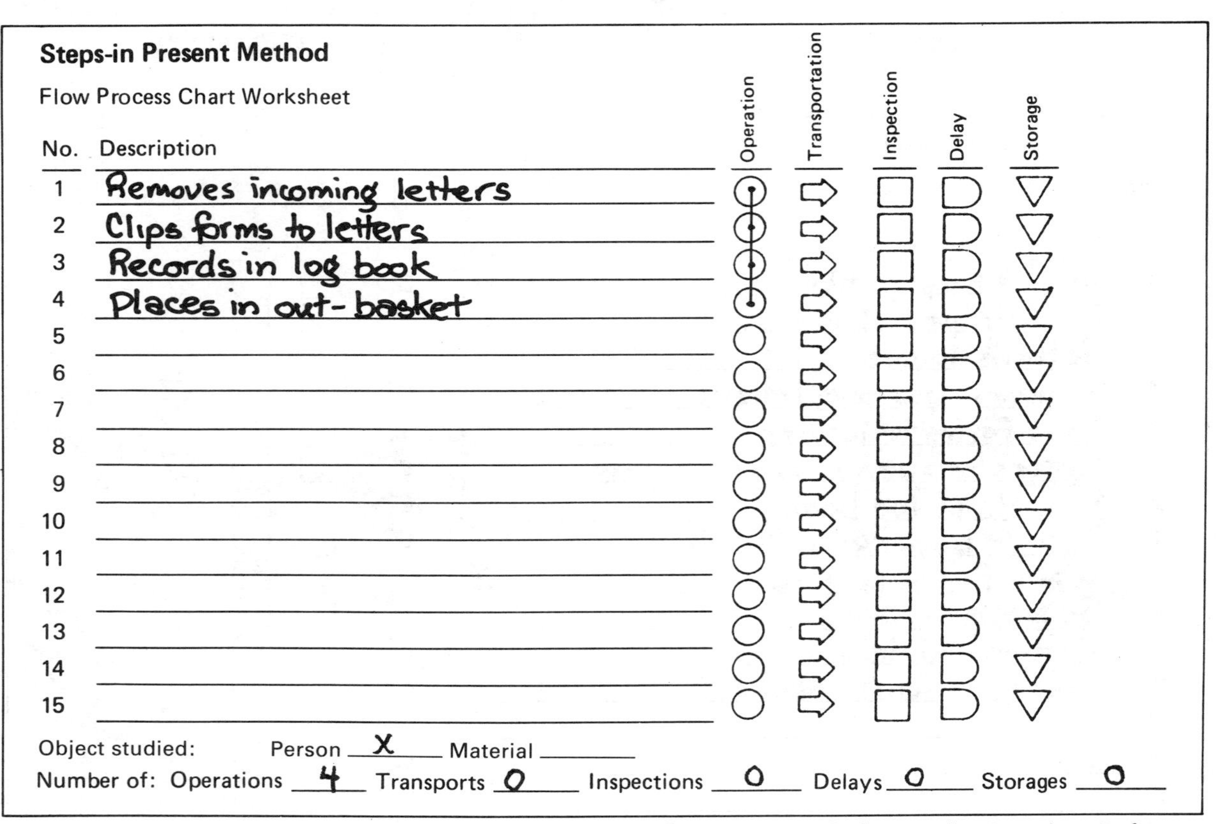

Steps-in Present Method

Flow Process Chart Worksheet

No.	Description	Operation	Transportation	Inspection	Delay	Storage
1	Removes incoming letters	●				
2	Clips forms to letters	●				
3	Records in log book	●				
4	Places in out-basket	●				
5						
6						
7						
8						
9						
10						
11						
12						
13						
14						
15						

Object studied: Person X Material ______

Number of: Operations 4 Transports 0 Inspections 0 Delays 0 Storages 0

Source: Reprinted with permission from Lester R. Bittel, *Improving Supervisory Performance* (New York: McGraw-Hill Book Company, 1976), 322.

FIGURE A-14 FLOW DIAGRAM SHOWING PRESENT METHOD FOR PROCESSING A PARTS REQUISITION FROM A SUBCONTRACTOR

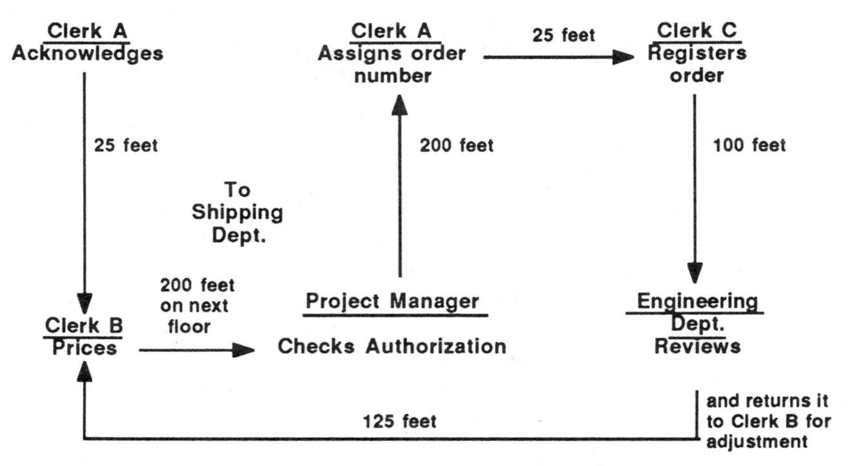

Source: Reprinted with permission from Lester R. Bittel, *Improving Supervisory Performance* (New York: McGraw-Hill Book Company, 1976), 505.

FIGURE A-15 SAMPLE FLOW DIAGRAM SHOWING A PROPOSED METHOD FOR PROCESSING A PARTS REQUISITION FROM A SUBCONTRACTOR

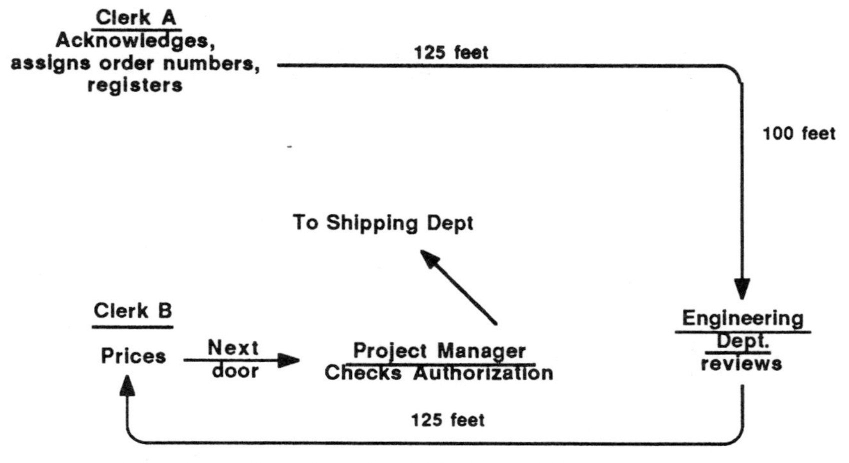

Source: Reprinted with permission from Lester R. Bittel, *Improving Supervisory Performance* (New York: McGraw-Hill Book Company, 1976), 505.

not perform the numbering activity, and (3) eliminates present steps 8, 9, 10, and 11 by having the completed form routed from the clerk's out-basket by office mail to the supervisor and, after signature, directly to the next stage rather than back to the clerk. Thus, the proposed method eliminates from the clerk's job three operations, four transportations, and one delay.

FLOW DIAGRAM

Many job processes are affected not only by the sequence in which they are performed but also by the physical layout of the workplace. For this reason, many analysts use a Flow Diagram in conjunction with the Flow-Process Chart. The Flow Diagram, like the one shown in figure A-14, provides a bird's-eye view of the work as it moves from person to person and place to place. This particular diagram was used to analyze the work flow in processing a parts requisition from a subcontractor. As you can see, there is a lot of backtracking as the order moves from clerk A to clerks B and C for pricing and registry, to the engineering department for review, and to the project manager for checking the authorizations before finally being released to the shipping depot. Figure A-15 shows how the entire process can be simplified and shortened by (1) combining clerk A and clerk C's work under clerk A; (2) routing the order directly to the engineering department, which forwards it after review to clerk B for pricing; (3) and moving the project manager's office to the same floor as, and next door to, clerk B.

NOTES

Notes

NOTES FOR CHAPTER 1

1. "*Training* Magazine's Industry Report: 1984," *Training* (October 1984): 39–40.
2. Anthony Patrick Carnale, "The Learning Enterprise," *Training and Development Journal* (January 1986): 18–26.
3. Lester R. Bittel and Jackson E. Ramsey, "The Limited, Traditional World of Supervisors," *Harvard Business Review* (July–August 1982): 26–36; and *Report of the National Survey of Supervisory Management Practices* (Harrisonburg, Va.: Center for Supervisory Research, James Madison University, April 1982, 17–23.
4. *Foremen Thinking: A Survey for the Foremanship Foundation* (Princeton, N.J.: Opinion Research Corporation, 1970, R–3.
5. Lester R. Bittel, *What Every Supervisor Should Know,* 5th ed. (New York: McGraw-Hill Book Company, 1984), 13.

NOTES FOR CHAPTER 2

1. Stuart M. Klein, and R. Richard Ritti, *Understanding Organizational Behavior* (Boston: Kent Publishing Company, 1980), 60–63.
2. Keith Davis, "The Supervisory Role," in *Supervisory Management: Tools and Techniques,* ed. M. Gene Newport (St. Paul, Minn.: West Publishing Company, 1976), 5.
3. Rensis Likert, *New Patterns of Management* (New York: McGraw-Hill Book Company, 1970).
4. M. Scott Myers, *Every Employee a Manager* (New York: McGraw-Hill Book Company, 1970), 99.
5. "Guide to Supervisory Development," *Supervisory Development Program.: Basic Course* (Washington, D.C.: Department of the Army, August 1962), 15.

6. Joseph Prokopenko and Lester R. Bittel, "A Modular Course-Format for Supervisory Development," *Training and Development Journal* (February 1981): 142.

7. Opinion Research Corporation, *Foremen Thinking: A Survey for the Foremanship Foundation* (Princeton, N.J.: Opinion Research Corporation, 1970), i.

8. Jackson E. Ramsey and Lester R. Bittel, "Men and Women Who Turn the Key on American Productivity," *National Forum* (Winter 1984): 43–46.

9. Opinion Research Corporation, *Supervision in the 80s: Trends in Corporate America* (Princeton, N.J.: Opinion Research Corporation, 1984), 6.

10. Lester R. Bittel and Jackson E. Ramsey, "New Dimensions for Supervisory Development," *Training and Development Journal* (March 1983): 12–20.

11. *Foremen Thinking,* x.

12. Vernon L. Seguin, "Are Purchasing Supervisors Different?" *Journal of Purchasing and Materials Management* 20, no. 3 (Fall 1985): 27–31.

13. R. L. LaForge, Mary C. LaForge, and L. R. Bittel, "A Survey of Supervisory-Level Marketing Managers," *Akron Business and Economic Review* 15, no. 2 (Summer 1984): 47–52.

14. R. L. LaForge, J. E. Ramsey, and L. R. Bittel, "A Survey Profile of the Problems, Practices, and Attitudes of Engineering Supervisors," paper no. 84-WA/Mgt.-1 (New York: American Society of Mechanical Engineers, December 1984).

NOTES FOR CHAPTER 3

1. Archie B. Carroll and Ted F. Anthony, "An Overview of the Supervisor's Job," *Personnel Journal* (May 1986): 228–49.

2. William C. Byham, "Assessment Center Method," in *Handbook for Professional Managers,* ed. L. R. Bittel and J. E. Ramsey (New York: McGraw-Hill Book Company, 1985), 40–43.

3. James L. Hayes, "Management Measurement," *Printing Impressions* (October 1980): 81.

4. Corporate Human Resources Department, Honeywell, "Honeywell Selection System Performance Standards Statements for First-Line Factory Supervisors," in Herbert Northrup, Lawrence Vanden Plas, Ronald Cowin, and William E. Fulmer, *The Objective Selection of Supervisors* (Philadelphia: The Wharton School, University of Pennsylvania, 1978), 230–31.

5. "What's Ahead in Personnel?" *Industrial Relations News* (March 1978): 3.

6. Pamela R. Jones, Beverly Kaye, and Hugh R. Taylor, "You Want Me to Do What?" *Training and Development Journal* (July 1981): 56–62.

7. M. Pedler, J. Burgoyne, and T. Boydell, *A Manager's Guide to Self-Development* (New York: McGraw-Hill Book Company, 1978).
8. Katherine Culbertson and Mark Thompson, "An Analysis of Supervisory Training Needs," *Training and Development Journal* (February 1980): 58–62.
9. Saul W. Gellerman, "Supervision: Substance and Style," *Harvard Business Review* (March 1976): 89–87. See also W. Earl Sasser, Jr., and Frank S. Leonard, "Let First-Level Supervisors Do Their Job," *Harvard Business Review* (March/April 1980): 50–60.
10. William H. Cover, "Stepping Back to Basics," *Training and Development Journal* (November 1975): 3–6.
11. Quoted in Ron Zemke, "Should Supervisors Be Counselors?" *Training/HRD* (March 1983): 53.
12. Charles R. Macdonald, *Performance Based Supervisory Development: Adapted from a Major AT&T Study* (Amherst, Mass.: Human Resources Development Press, 1982), 24.
13. H. Kent Baker and Steven H. Holmberg, "Stepping Up to Supervision: Making the Transition," *Supervisory Management* (September 1981): 10–18.
14. This research is extensively reported in Macdonald, *Performance Based Supervisory Development,* 190–210.
15. Douglas W. Bray, "The Assessment Center Method," in *Training & Development Handbook,* 2d ed., ed. Robert L. Craig (New York: McGraw-Hill Book Company, 1976), 14–16.

NOTES FOR CHAPTER 4

1. Lester R. Bittel and Jackson E. Ramsey, "Misfit Supervisors—Bad Apples in the Managerial Barrel," *Management Review* 72, no. 2 (February 1983): 8–13.
2. H. W. Northrup, R. M. Cowin, L. G. Vanden Plas, and W. E. Fulmer, *The Objective Selection of Supervisors: A Study of the Informal Practices and Two Models of Supervisory Selection* (Philadelphia: The Wharton School, University of Pennsylvania, 1978).
3. Carl A. Benson, "New Supervisors: From the Top of the Heap to the Bottom of the Heap," *Personnel Journal* (April 1976): 176–78.
4. William E. Fulmer, "The Making of a Supervisor," *Personnel Journal* (March 1977): 140–41.
5. William T. Wolz, "How to Interview Supervisory Candidates from the Ranks," *Personnel* (September–October 1980): 31–39.
6. William C. Byham, "Assessment Center Method," in *The Handbook for Professional Managers,* edited by Lester R. Bittel and Jackson E. Ramsey, McGraw-Hill, New York, 1985, pp. 40–43.

NOTES FOR CHAPTER 6

1. Lester R. Bittel and Jackson E. Ramsey, "New Dimensions for Supervisory Development," *Training and Development Journal* (March 1983): 12–20.

2. Elmer H. Burack, "Self-Assessment: A Strategy of Growing Importance," *Training and Development Journal* (April 1979): 48–52.

3. Scott B. Parry and Edward J. Robinson, "Management Development: Training or Education?" *Training and Development Journal* (July 1979): 8–13.

4. Charles R. Macdonald, *Performance Based Supervisory Development: Adapted from a Major AT&T Study* (Amherst, Mass.: Human Resources Development Press, 1982), 22–23.

NOTES FOR CHAPTER 7

1. Stan Carnarius, "So You're Going to Handle Supervisory Training," in *Supervisory Training: Approaches & Methods,* ed. Bradford L. Boyd (Alexandria, Va.: American Society for Training and Development, 1976), 3–10.

2. Gordon L. Lippitt, *A Handbook for Visual Problem Solving* (Bethesda, Md.: Development Publications, 1973), 107.

3. Ibid., 107–10.

4. Ivor K. Davies, *Instructional Techniques* (New York: McGraw-Hill Book Company, 1981), 258–60.

5. Ibid., 267–69; and P. M. Fitts and M. I. Posner, *Human Performance* (Monterey, Calif.: Brooks/Cole Publishing Company, 1967).

6. Department of the Army, "The Role of the Supervisor," *Supervisor Development Program: Basic Course,* Civilian Personnel Pamphlet 41-B-1 (Washington, D.C.: Department of the Army, August 1962), 152–53.

7. Jeanie Marshall, "Get a Good Group Response," *Training and Development Journal* (April 1985): 75–76.

NOTES FOR CHAPTER 8

1. J. Prokopenko and Lester R. Bittel, "A Modular Course Format for Supervisory Development," *Training and Development Journal* (February 1981), 20–21.

2. Walter S. Wikstrom, *Supervisory Training,* Conference Board Report no. 612 (New York: The Conference Board, 1973), 11.

NOTES FOR CHAPTER 9

1. Ronald J. Bula, "Survey of Management Training Needs in Wisconsin," *Training and Development Journal* (January 1985): 64–65.
2. Walter S. Wikstrom, *Supervisory Training,* Conference Board Report no. 612 (New York: The Conference Board, 1973), 21.
3. William J. McKeon, "How to Determine Off-Site Meeting Costs," *Training and Development Journal* (May 1981): 116–22.
4. Wallace Wohlking and Hannah Weiner, "Structured and Spontaneous Role-Playing," *Training and Development Journal* (June 1981): 111–21.
5. Bernard L. Rosenbaum, "Common Misconceptions about Behavioral Modeling and Supervisory Skill Training (SST)," *Training and Development Journal* (August 1979): 40–44.
6. Geneva Waddell, "Simulations: Balancing the Pros and Cons," *Training and Development Journal* (January 1982): 80–83.
7. Paul E. Torgerson and R. D. Foley, "Business and Management Simulations," in *Handbook for Professional Managers,* ed. L. R. Bittel and J. E. Ramsey (New York: McGraw-Hill Book Company, 1985), 838–41.
8. Inez Ramsey, "Computer-Aided Instruction," in *Handbook for Professional Managers,* ed. L. R. Bittel and J. E. Ramsey (New York: McGraw-Hill Book Company, 1985), 132–33.
9. Jack J. Phillips, "Training Supervisors outside the Classroom," *Training and Development Journal* (February 1986): 46–49.
10. Ibid., 46.

NOTES FOR CHAPTER 10

1. Laurence M. Weinstein and Elizabeth Swain Kasl, "How the Training Dollar Is Spent," *Training and Development Journal* (October 1982): 90–96.
2. William J. McKeon, "How to Determine Off-Site Meeting Costs," *Training and Development Journal* (May 1981): 116–22.
3. "Who, What and Where" (organizational survey), *Training* (October 1984): 39.
4. Paul Chaddock, "When Managers Do the Training," *Training and Development Journal* (January 1986): 47–48.

5. Carl A Benson, "New Supervisors: From the Top of the Heap to the Bottom of the Heap," *Personnel Journal* (April 1976): 176–78.

6. Lester R. Bittel and Jackson E. Ramsey, *Report of the National Survey of Supervisory Management Practices* (Harrisonburg, Va.: Center for Supervisory Research, James Madison University, April 1982).

7. Scott B. Parry and Edward J. Robinson, "Management Development: Training or Education?" *Training and Development Journal* (July 1979): 8–13.

8. Martin M. Broadwell, "Supervisory Training in the 80s," *Training and Development Journal* (February 1980): 44.

9. William E. Fulmer, "The Making of a Supervisor," *Personnel Journal* (March 1977): 140–41.

10. Ronald R. Short, "Managing Unlearning," *Training and Development Journal* (July 1981): 37–44.

11. William C. Byham, "Changing Supervisory and Managerial Behavior," *Training and Development Journal,* Part I (April 1977): 3–8; Part II (May 1977): 10–16.

NOTES FOR CHAPTER 11

1. Edward O. Malott, Jr., "Planning for Meetings and Conferences," in *Handbook for Professional Managers,* ed. L. R. Bittel and J. E. Ramsey (New York: McGraw-Hill Book Company, 1985), 160.

2. Malott, "Planning for Meetings and Conferences," 161.

3. Frank O. Hoffman, "Getting Line Managers into the Act," *Training and Development Journal* (March 1981): 68–73.

4. Steven M. Rosenthal and Bob Mezoff, "Improving the Cost/Benefit of Management Training," *Training and Development Journal* (December 1980): 102–6.

5. R. H. Pelfrey, "Supervisory Management Development Program with Impact!" in *Supervisory Training: Approaches & Methods,* ed. Bradford B. Boyd (Alexandria, Va.: American Society for Training and Development, 1976), 57–62.

6. Hoffman, "Getting Line Managers into the Act."

NOTES FOR CHAPTER 12

1. Danny G. Langdon, "The Individual Management Development Program," *Training and Development Journal* (March 1982): 78–82.

2. Ernest A. Doud, Jr., and Edward J. Miller, "First-Line Supervisors: Key to Improved Performance," *Management Review* (December 1980): 18–24.

3. Nancy Kelley, "Zale Corporation's Career Development Program," *Training and Development Journal* (June 1982): 71.

4. Ibid., 73–75.

5. Reba Davis and Jack Balderson, *Word-Processing Supervision* (Indianapolis, Bobbs-Merrill Educational Publishing, 1984).

6. Jackson E. Ramsey, "Supervisory Development," in *Human Resources Management and Development Handbook,* ed., William R. Tracey (New York: AMACOM, 1985), 979–80.

NOTES FOR CHAPTER 13

1. "What Kind of Management Development Improves Productivity?" an interview by *Training and Development Journal* (January 1984): 17–19.

2. Ibid.

3. Ibid.

4. Ibid.

5. Lester R. Bittel and Jackson E. Ramsey, "The Limited, Traditional World of Supervisors," *Harvard Business Review* (July–August 1982): 26–36.

6. Lester R. Bittel and Jackson E. Ramsey, *Report of the National Survey of Supervisory Management Practices* (Harrisonburg, Va.: Center for Supervisory Research, James Madison University, April 1982).

7. Ibid., 199.

8. Frank M. Gryna, *Quality Circles: A Team Approach to Problem Solving* (New York: AMACOM, 1981), 34, 41, 48.

9. Wayne S. Rieker, "Management's Role in Quality Circles," in *Transactions of the Second Annual Conference, International Association of Quality Circles* (1980), 45.

10. Ralph Barra, *Putting Quality Circles to Work: A Practical Strategy for Boosting Productivity and Profits* (New York: McGraw-Hill Book Company, 1983), 76–77.

11. Ibid.

12. Ibid.

13. Gryna, *Quality Circles,* 56.

14. David W. Ewing, *Do It My Way or You're Fired: Employee Rights and the Changing Role of Management Prerogatives* (New York: John Wiley & Sons, 1983), 219–20.

15. Daniel R. Levinson, *Personal Liability of Managers and Supervisors for Cor-*

porate EEO Policies and Decisions, Equal Employment Advisory Council Monograph Series No. 1 (Washington, D.C.: Equal Employment Advisory Council, 1982), 25.

16. *The Supervisor's EEO Handbook,* rev. ed. (New York: Executive Publications, 1977), 4–6.

NOTES FOR CHAPTER 14

1. Edward H. Wolfe, "Supervisory Development: The Need for an Integrated Strategy," *Training and Development Journal* (March 1983): 28–31.
2. Paul W. Cummings, "Supervisory Expectations versus Organizational Reality," *Training and Development Journal* (September 1976): 37–41.
3. Lester R. Bittel and Jackson E. Ramsey, *Report of the National Survey of Supervisory Management Practices* (Harrisonburg, Va.: Center for Supervisory Research, James Madison University, April 1982), 64–65.
4. Michael W. Millican, "Absence of Overtime Pay Is Upsetting to Supervisors," *The Washington Post,* December 4, 1977, K13.
5. Wolfe, "Supervisory Development," 30.
6. Lester R. Bittel and Jackson E. Ramsey, "What to Do about Misfit Supervisors: Part II," *Management Review* (March 1983): 37–43.
7. Guvenc G. Alpander, "The Synergism of OD and Supervisory Development," *Training and Development Journal* (March 1984): 26.
8. Daryl R. Conner and Robert W. Patterson, "Building Commitment to Organizational Change," *Training and Development Journal* (April 1982): 18–30.
9. C. Edward Kur and Mike Pedler, "Innovative Twists in Management Development," *Training and Development Journal* (June 1983): 37–43.
10. Jack J. Phillips, "Training Supervisors outside the Classroom" *Training and Development Journal* (April 1982): 48.
11. Opinion Research Corporation, *Supervision in the 80s: Trends in Corporate America* (Princeton, N.J.: Opinion Research Corporation, 1984), 122.

NOTES FOR CHAPTER 15

1. Edward Del Gaizo, "Proof That Supervisory Training Works," *Training and Development Journal* (March 1984): 30–31.
2. Ibid.
3. Frederic William Swierczek and Lynne Carmichael, "The Quantity and

Quality of Evaluating Training," *Training and Development Journal* (January 1985): 95–99.

4. Ronald W. Clement and Eileen K. Arand, "Evaluating Management Training: A Contingency Approach," *Training and Development Journal* (August 1982): 39–43.
5. Swierczek and Carmichael, "The Quantity and Quality of Evaluating Training."
6. George L. Morrisey and William R. Wellstead, "Supervisory Training Can Be Measured," *Training and Development Journal* (June 1980): 118–21.
7. Bakken, David and Alan L. Bernstein, "A Systematic Approach to Evaluation."
8. Linda Daly, "Supervisory Training an ROI Plus," *Training and Development Journal* (November 1985): 20.
9. Michael A. Sheppeck and Stephen L. Cohen, "Put a Dollar Value on Your Training Programs," *Training and Development Journal* (November 1985): 59–62.
10. S. L. Cohen, "The Bottom Line on Assessment Center Technology," *Personnel Administration* (1980).
11. Sheppeck and Cohen, "Put a Dollar Value on Your Training Programs."
12. F. L. Schmidt, J. E. Hunter, and K. Pearlman, "Assessing the Economic Impact of Personnel Programs on Work-Force Productivity," *Personnel Psychology* (1982).

BIBLIOGRAPHY

Bibliography

Bittel, Lester R. *Essentials of Supervisory Management.* New York: McGraw-Hill Book Company, 1981.

———. *What Every Supervisor Should Know.* 5th ed. New York: McGraw-Hill Book Company, 1984.

Bittel, Lester R., and Jackson E. Ramsey. *The National Survey of Supervisory Management Practices.* Harrisonburg, Va.: Center for Supervisory Research, James Madison University, 1982.

Blake, Robert R., and Jane Srygley Mouton. *The Grid for Supervisory Effectiveness.* Austin, Tex.: Scientific Methods, 1975.

Boyd, Bradford B. *Management-Minded Supervision.* 3rd ed. New York: McGraw-Hill Book Company, 1984.

Boyd, Bradford, B., ed. *Supervisory Training: Approaches and Methods.* Alexandria, Va.: American Society for Training and Development.

Broadwell, Martin M. *The New Supervisor.* 3d ed. Reading, Mass.: Addison-Wesley Publishing Company, 1984.

———. *The Practice of Supervision: Making Experience Pay.* 2d ed. Reading, Mass.: Addison-Wesley Publishing Company, 1984.

———. *The Supervisor as an Instructor.* 4th ed. Reading, Mass.: Addison-Wesley Publishing Company, 1984.

———. *The Supervisor and On-the-Job Training.* Reading, Mass.: Addison-Wesley Publishing Company, 1986.

Broadwell, Martin M., ed. *Supervisory Handbook: A Management Guide to Principles and Applications.* New York: John Wiley & Sons, 1985.

Broadwell, Martin M., and William F. Simpson. *The New Insurance Supervisor.* Reading, Mass.: Addison-Wesley Publishing Company, 1981.

Catt, Stephen E., and Donald S. Miller. *Supervisory Management and Communication.* Homewood, Ill.: Richard D. Irwin, 1985.

Christenson, C., T. W. Johnson, and J. E. Stinson. *Supervising.* Addison-Wesley Publishing Company, Reading, Mass.: 1982.

Davis, Reba, and Jack Balderston. *Word-Processing Supervision.* Indianapolis, Ind.: Bobbs-Merrill Educational Publishing, 1984.

Donaldson, Les. *Behavioral Supervision: Practical Ways to Change Unsatisfactory Behavior and Increase Productivity.* Reading, Mass.: Addison-Wesley Publishing Company, 1980.

Dubrin, Andrew J. *The Practice of Supervision: Achieving Results through People.* Dallas, Tex.: Business Publications, 1980.

Eckles, R., R. Carmichael, and B. Sarchet. *Supervisory Management: A Short Course in Supervision.* 2d ed. New York: John Wiley & Sons, 1981.

Elbert, Norbert F., and Richard Discenza. *Contemporary Supervision.* New York: Random House, 1985.

Feldman, Edwin P., and George B. Wright, Sr. *The Supervisor's Handbook.* New York: Frederick Fell Publishers, 1982.

Fulmer, Robert M., and S. G. Franklin. *Supervision.* 2d ed. New York: Macmillan Publishing Company, 1982.

Gardner, James E. *Training the New Supervisor.* New York: AMACOM, 1983.

Gray, Jerry R. *Supervision: An Applied Behavioral Science Approach to Managing People.* Boston: Kent Publishing Company, 1984.

Haimann, Theo, and Raymond Hilgert. *Supervision: Concepts and Practices of Management.* 3d ed. Cincinnati, Ohio: South-Western, 1982.

Halloran, J. *Supervision: The Art of Management.* Englewood Cliffs, N.J.: Prentice-Hall, 1981.

Imundo, Louis V. *Effective Supervisor's Handbook.* New York: AMACOM, 1980.

Jackson, J. H., and T. V. Keaveny. *Successful Supervision.* Englewood Cliffs, N.J.: Prentice-Hall, 1980.

Keys, Bernard, and Joy Henshall. *Supervision.* New York: John Wiley & Sons, 1984.

Kirkpatrick, Donald L. *A Practical Guide for Supervisory Training and Development.* 2d ed. Reading, Mass.: Addison-Wesley Publishing Company, 1983.

Lambert, Clark. *The Complete Book of Supervisory Training.* New York: John Wiley & Sons, 1984.

Lowery, Robert C. *Supervisory Management: Guidelines for Application.* Englewood Cliffs, N.J.: Prentice-Hall, 1985.

Luthans, F., and M. J. Martinko. *The Practice of Supervision and Management.* New York: McGraw-Hill Book Company, 1979.

Macdonald, Charles R. *Performance-Based Supervisory Development: Adapted from a Major AT&T Study.* Amherst, Mass.: Human Resources Development Press, 1982.

Morgan, B. S., and W. A. Schiemann. *Supervision in the 80s: Trends in Corporate America.* Princeton, N.J.: Opinion Research Corporation, 1984.

Mosley, Donald C., Paul H. Pietri, Jr., and Leon C. Megginson. *Supervisory Management: The Art of Working with and through People.* Cincinnati, Ohio: South-Western, 1985.

Muczyk, Jan, Eleanor Brantley Schwartz, and Ephraim Smith. *Principles of Supervision: First- and Second-Level Management.* Columbus, Ohio: Charles E. Merrill Publishing Company, 1984.

Newport, M. G., ed. *Supervisory Management: Tools and Techniques.* St. Paul, Minn.: West Publishing Company, 1976.

Northrup, H. R., L. G. Vanden Plas, R. M. Cowin, and W. B. Fulmer. *The Objective Selection of Supervisors.* Philadelphia: The Wharton School, University of Pennsylvania, 1978.

Philips, Jack J. *Improving Supervisors' Effectiveness.* New York: AMACOM, 1979.

Preston, P., and T. W. Zimmerer. *Management for Supervisors.* 2d ed. Englewood Cliffs, N.J.: Prentice-Hall, 1983.

Radde, Paul O. *Supervising: A Guide for All Levels.* San Diego, Calif.: Learning Concepts, University Associates, 1981.

Riggs, James L. *Productive Supervision.* Englewood Cliffs, N.J.: Prentice-Hall, 1985.

Rosenbaum, Bernard L. *How to Motivate Today's Workers: Motivation Models for Managers and Supervisors.* New York: McGraw-Hill Book Company, 1982.

Rue, Leslie W., and Lloyd L. Byars. *Supervision: Key Link to Productivity.* 2d ed. Homewood, Ill.: Richard D. Irwin, 1986.

Schoen, S. H., and D. E. Durand. *Supervision: The Management of Organizational Resources.* Englewood Cliffs, N.J.: Prentice-Hall, 1979.

Shapiro, S. L. *Supervision: An Introduction to Business Management.* New York: Fairchild, 1978.

Steinmetz, L. L., and H. R. Todd, Jr. *First-Line Management: Approaching Supervision Effectively.* 3d ed. Plano, Tex.: Business Publications, 1983.

Tagliaferri, Louis E. *Successful Supervision.* New York: John Wiley & Sons, 1979.

Van Dersal, William B. *The Successful Supervisor: In Government and Business.* 4th ed. New York: Harper & Row, 1985.

Wasmuth, W. J., and L. Greenhalgh. *Effective Supervision: Developing Your Skills through Critical Incidents.* Englewood Cliffs, N.J.: Prentice-Hall, 1979.

Index